THE MAKING OF MODERN THEOLOGY
NINETEENTH- AND TWENTIETH-CENTURY TEXTS

This major series of theological texts is designed to introduce a new generation of readers—theological students, students of religion, professionals in ministry, and the interested general reader—to the writings of those Christian theologians who, since the beginning of the nineteenth century, have had a formative influence on the development of Christian theology.

Each volume in the series is intended to introduce the theologian, to trace the emergence of key or seminal ideas and insights, particularly within their social and historical context, and to show how they have contributed to the making of modern theology. The primary way in which this is done is by allowing the theologians chosen to address us in their own words.

There are three sections to each volume. The Introduction includes a short biography of the theologian, and an overview of his or her theology in relation to the texts which have been selected for study. The Selected Texts, the bulk of each volume, consist largely of substantial edited selections from the theologian's writings. Each text is also introduced with information about its origin and its significance. The guiding rule in making the selection of texts has been the question: In what way has this particular theologian contributed to the shaping of contemporary theology? A Select Bibliography provides guidance for those who wish to read further both in the primary literature and in secondary sources.

Series editor John W. de Gruchy is Professor of Christian Studies at the University of Cape Town, South Africa. He is the author of many works, including *Church Struggle in South Africa,* and *Theology and Ministry in Context and Crisis.*

Volumes in this series
1. Friedrich Schleiermacher: Pioneer of Modern Theology
2. Rudolf Bultmann: Interpreting Faith for the Modern Era
3. Paul Tillich: Theologian of the Boundaries
4. Dietrich Bonhoeffer: Witness to Jesus Christ
5. Karl Barth: Theologian of Freedom
6. Reinhold Niebuhr: Theologian of Public Life
7. Karl Rahner: Theologian of the Graced Search for Meaning
8. Gustavo Gutiérrez: Essential Writings
9. G. W. F. Hegel: Theologian of the Spirit

G. W. F. Hegel (1770–1831)

THE MAKING OF MODERN THEOLOGY

Nineteenth- and Twentieth-Century Texts
General Editor: John W. de Gruchy

G. W. F. HEGEL
Theologian of the Spirit

PETER C. HODGSON
Editor

FORTRESS PRESS
MINNEAPOLIS

G. W. F. HEGEL
Theologian of the Spirit
The Making of Modern Theology

Cover graphic: Engraved by Friedrich Wilhelm Bollinger, from the painting by Christian
Xeller (with permission of Schiller-Nationalmuseum, Marbach-am-Neckar)
Cover design: Neil Churcher
Editor's photo: Fabry Studios

LIbrary of Congress Cataloging-in-Publication Data

Hegel, Georg Wilhelm Friedrich, 1770–1831.
    [Selections. English. 1997]
    G. W. F. Hegel : theologian of the the spirit / Peter C. Hodgson, ed.
       p.   cm. — (The making of modern theology)
    Includes bibliographical references and index.
    ISBN 0-8006-3408-X (alk. paper)
    1. Hegel, Georg Wilhelm Friedrich, 1770–1831—Contributions in
philosophy of religion. 2. Religion—Philosophy—History—19th
century. I. Hodgson, Peter Crafts, 1934– . II. Title.
III. Series.
B2949.R3H38213 1997
200'.1—dc21

                                                                    96-40257
                                                                     CIP

Manufactured in the U. S. A.   AF 1-3408

01   00   99   98   97   1   2   3   4   5   6   7   8   9   10

In memoriam

J. Michael Stewart

1920–1994

CONTENTS

ACKNOWLEDGMENTS

The editor and publisher acknowledge with thanks permission to reprint the following translations of works by G. W. F. Hegel:

From *Three Essays, 1793–95,* edited and translated by Peter Fuss and John Dobbin, pp. 30–58. Copyright © 1984 by University of Notre Dame Press. Used by permission of the publisher.

From *Early Theological Writings,* translated by T. M. Knox with an introduction and fragments translated by Richard Kroner, pp. 253–81. Copyright © 1971 by University of Pennsylvania Press. Used by permission of the publisher.

From *Faith and Knowledge,* translated by Walter Cerf and H. S. Harris, pp. 55–66, 189–91. Copyright © 1977 by State University of New York Press. Used by permission of the publisher.

From *System of Ethical Life and First Philosophy of Spirit,* edited and translated by H. S. Harris and T. M. Knox, pp. 178–86. Copyright © 1979 by State University of New York Press. Used by permission of the publisher.

From *Lectures on the Philosophy of Religion,* edited by Peter C. Hodgson, translated by R. F. Brown, P. C. Hodgson, and J. M. Stewart with the assistance of H. S. Harris: Vol. 1:113–47, 310–28; Vol. 2:233–38; Vol. 3:163–247. Copyright © 1984, 1985, 1987 by University of California Press. Used by permission of the publisher.

EDITOR'S NOTE

When Fortress Press suggested including a volume on G. W. F. Hegel in the Making of Modern Theology series, I responded with interest. Hegel's writings on theological and religious themes are, with the exception of the lectures on the philosophy of religion, rather dispersed and inaccessible. T. M. Knox published an excellent translation of Hegel's *Early Theological Writings* in 1948, and for a number of years Hegel's religious thought was best known in the English-speaking world on the basis of this text. However, Knox omitted several of the most important early writings, and this deficit was not corrected until 1984. In the same year, the first of three volumes of a new critical edition and translation of Hegel's *Lectures on the Philosophy of Religion* appeared. This large work has not generally been accessible to students, although the lectures of 1827 were extracted and published in a one-volume paperback edition in 1988. For critically important but very difficult texts on religion in the *Phenomenology of Spirit* and the *Encyclopedia of the Philosophical Sciences,* English readers have had to rely on inadequate and uninterpreted translations.

Thus the present volume attempts to fill an acknowledged void. I could not have completed it without the help of J. Michael Stewart of Farnham, England, who prepared new translations of selections from the *Phenomenology,* of the section on Absolute Spirit from the *Encyclopedia,* and of Hegel's Foreword to Hinrichs's *Religion.* He died on December 27, 1994, before he could complete his work on the *Phenomenology;* consequently I translated the final two texts on religion. I am indebted to Robert R. Williams for checking my work and suggesting revisions.

My collaboration with Michael Stewart goes back to 1981, when he joined the translation team for the *Lectures on the Philosophy of Religion* and soon became its most indispensable member and a good friend. The text of the 1824 lectures, an extended excerpt of which is included in this volume, is largely his work. Stewart was formerly acting chief of the English translation section of UNESCO in Paris, and an interested student of Hegel since his studies in German and philosophy at Cambridge and London. Subsequently he and Robert F. Brown collaborated on a new translation of Hegel's *Lectures on the History of Philosophy,* and he and I worked together on translations of Walter Jaeschke's *Reason in Religion* and Hegel's Heidelberg lectures on *Natural Right and Political Science.* His contribution to Hegel studies in English has been substantial, and this volume is dedicated to his memory.

PETER C. HODGSON
Divinity School, Vanderbilt University

INTRODUCTION
G. W. F. HEGEL:
THEOLOGIAN OF THE SPIRIT

HEGEL'S LIFE AND CAREER IN BRIEF[1]

The year 1770 was auspicious for art and thought. The spring of that year brought the birth of Friedrich Hölderlin and William Wordsworth, and the winter, Ludwig van Beethoven. Between the two poets and the composer there was born, on August 27, one who achieved in philosophy a greatness comparable to theirs in poetry and music, Georg Wilhelm Friedrich Hegel. His father was a civil servant of Württemberg Lutheran stock; his mother was devoutly named Maria Magdalena Fromm. The son must have inherited something of his father's worldliness and his mother's *Frömmigkeit*, for his accomplishment as a philosopher of religion was to create a philosophical theology that transformed the metaphorical language of religion into a conceptuality that spoke to the modern world, while at the same time it provided that world with spiritual depth and meaning. Perhaps among the birth-year mates there was a mystical linkage. Is it too fanciful to suggest that Hegel became the Beethoven of philosophy, and Beethoven the Hegel of music? For they both sought pattern, harmony, and redemption in—and only in—a world of conflict, disharmony, and suffering. As for Hegel and Hölderlin, there is sad irony in the fact that the latter's youthful genius came to a tragic end in madness the same year that the former's greatest work of genius was published, 1807.

The young Hegel attended the Stuttgart *Gymnasium* from 1777 to 1788, where he proved to be an exemplary student and read the classical authors along with Shakespeare, Rousseau, Lessing, Goethe, and Schiller. There never seemed to be any question that he would study theology and take up a career in ministry, so he entered the theological seminary of Tübingen in 1788, where he formed a close friendship with Friedrich Hölderlin and Friedrich Schelling. Schelling was five years younger than Hegel and Hölderlin but entered the seminary as an exceptionally precocious student only two years after them. These three, finding the theological orthodoxy of their professors stultifying, educated themselves in the political, literary, and philosophical literature of the Enlightenment, and they embraced the ideals of the French Revolution with enthusiasm. They also imbibed deeply of the German and Swabian mystics. During this period Hegel began writing fragmentary essays for his own edification, in which among other

1

things he explored the possibility of creating a new folk religion that would integrate all aspects of life (see below, selection 1.1).

Hegel completed his studies in 1793, but he did not take up a career in ministry. Instead he accepted a position as house tutor for a wealthy family in Berne, Switzerland, where he had considerable free time and access to a rich library. Here he broadened his knowledge of modern philosophy and studied Immanuel Kant seriously for the first time. He produced more exploratory essays in which he was severely critical of the "positivity" of Christianity while extolling a Kantian religion of morality. In the fall of 1796, with the assistance of Hölderlin, he obtained a similar tutorial position in Frankfurt, which brought him into closer proximity with his friends. Here he began to explore the possibility of combining the beauty of Greek folk religion with the moral law of Kantianism in the shape of spiritual beauty or love, which he now saw to constitute the heart of Christianity as a religion of spirit. Spirit unifies opposites in a pantheism of love. Several of the fragments written during this period were given the title "The Spirit of Christianity and Its Fate" (see selection 1.2) when they were published, along with Hegel's other early writings, in 1907 by Herman Nohl.

Upon his father's death in 1799, Hegel received a modest inheritance that allowed him to accept a position as an unsalaried lecturer (*Privatdozent*) at the University of Jena, where he joined Schelling in 1801. Students paid small fees to attend his lectures on logic and metaphysics, the philosophies of nature and spirit, ethics and natural right, and the history of philosophy. These lectures not only provided additional income but also gave Hegel the opportunity to experiment with various elements that gradually evolved into his philosophical system (see selection 2.2). It was a period of remarkable intellectual fertility for him. His first publications were two book-length essays, "The Difference between Fichte's and Schelling's System of Philosophy," and a comparative study of Kant, Friedrich Heinrich Jacobi, and Johann Gottlieb Fichte entitled "Faith and Knowledge" (selection 2.1). In 1805 he completed his doctoral dissertation and was appointed to an assistant professorship. A year later, as Napoleon defeated the Prussian troops at the Battle of Jena, Hegel finished under considerable duress his most famous work, the *Phenomenology of Spirit* (selection 3), a few hundred copies of which were printed early in 1807.

For financial and personal reasons, Hegel found it necessary to leave Jena. He moved to Bamberg to become editor of a newspaper; but a year later, in 1808, he was fortunate to be offered a position as rector of a *Gymnasium* in Nuremberg, where among other things he taught religion and speculative logic to his pupils. In 1811, the 41-year-old philosopher married a woman half his age, Marie von Tucher; it proved to be a union that endured in mutual love until his death. During the next three years Hegel fathered three children (the first died shortly after birth)[2] and published three volumes of his *Science of Logic*. The latter work sufficiently established his reputation that in 1816 he was offered university professorships in Heidelberg, Erlangen, and Berlin. The Erlangen and Berlin offers were couched in qualifications (it was wondered whether after so many years of high school instruction Hegel still had the ability to teach at the university level, or, given the difficulty of his logic, to lecture with any clarity at all), so he accepted the offer from Heidelberg. His lectures there, covering a full range of philosophical topics with the exception of religion, proved to be a great success, and he published in 1817 the *Encyclopedia of the Philosophical Sciences* (see selection 4), a compendium of the entire system of philosophy intended as a textbook to accompany his lectures.

In the next year, 1818, Hegel was recruited by the Prussian Minister of Education, von Altenstein, to become professor of philosophy at the University of Berlin, filling a chair left vacant by Fichte's death in 1814, and there he remained until his death. Through the impact of his books and lectures Hegel's fame spread throughout Europe, and Hegelianism began to form as a philosophical school. In 1820 he completed a textbook on political philosophy, *Elements of the Philosophy of Right;* it was to be the last work he himself published. The *Philosophy of Right* generated considerable controversy because in it as well as in his public activity Hegel attempted to steer a middle course between revolutionary and restoration politics. There was considerable political turmoil in Prussia at the time, and Hegel found himself in the delicate situation of being supported in his office by the aristocratic establishment while sympathizing with liberal reform movements. Consequently he had numerous enemies on the right and the left, and his position in Berlin was never completely secure.

In the summer of 1821 Hegel lectured for the first time on philosophy of religion, which was the final major element of his system to be elaborated in detail. When these lectures were repeated in subsequent years—1824 .(selection 6), 1827, and 1831—they varied greatly in structure and content, indicating the fluidity and openness with which Hegel approached this and other topics. He was constantly appropriating new material and responding to specific issues and challenges (see selection 5).

In a strict sense the Hegelian system came into existence as a fixed entity only after Hegel's death, which occurred suddenly on November 14, 1831, during an epidemic of cholera. In little over a month following his death, his wife, students, and friends had arranged to publish his collected works, including lecture manuscripts and auditors' notebooks on the major topics covered in Berlin—history of philosophy, logic and metaphysics, and the philosophies of history, art, right, and religion. With

3

Hegel's voice silenced, his former students and disciples within a few years fell into warring factions; and the controversy over Hegel's thought continues to this day.

PHILOSOPHY OF RELIGION AS THEOLOGY

Religion was at the center of the controversy from the beginning. Hegel's intention in addressing religious themes was not clearly understood in his time, and many suspected that he set out to convert the subject matter of theology into a purely immanent, human phenomenon. Or, if that was not the case, then the way in which he reinterpreted Christian doctrines in a strange philosophical conceptuality effectively undercut traditional theism. Hegel, it was believed, was either an atheist or a pantheist.

By contrast with these gross misrepresentations, Hegel insisted that the proper topic of philosophy of religion is precisely the nature and reality of God. Philosophy of religion cannot properly limit its concern to the phenomenon of religion; rather it must recognize that religion itself encompasses the relationship of human beings to God. Religion intends an actuality that lies beyond it—but this transcendent referent had been rendered problematic by Enlightenment philosophy, history, psychology, and natural science. Traditionally, the question of the reality-status of God had been addressed within philosophy by metaphysics or natural theology. But the claims of these disciplines were severely questioned by Kant's critique of pure reason. Moreover, the authority of scripture and the historical basis for Christianity had been challenged by critics such as Lessing, and the alternative of a purely rational or natural religion favored by the Enlightenment was undercut by David Hume.

Philosophy of religion came on the scene as an alternative to the discredited metaphysics of natural theology, and according to Walter Jaeschke[3] it faced two options. It could, on the one hand, develop a new philosophical theology within itself, or perhaps borrow one from another source, in order to have a foundation for cognitive knowledge of God and thus provide an adequate account of how religion conceives itself. Or, on the other hand, it could conclude that no such foundation is available and thus "confine itself to regarding religion as a specifically human expression of life. It has then no right to take what appears as divine to be anything other than human." The latter option is the one that has prevailed since Ludwig Feuerbach: the divine is nothing other than the essence of the human projected on a screen of transcendence. Anthropological, sociological, psychological, and historical interpretations of religion have come to the fore, and for them the problematic character of God-talk could be regarded as a matter of scientific indifference.

Hegel, however, took the first option; and he regarded the intimations of the latter course that were already discernible in his time to spell disaster not only for religious faith but also for human culture. Since neither classical metaphysics, nor the Enlightenment rational theologies, nor the Kantian doctrine of moral postulates, nor Friedrich Schleiermacher's orientation of theology to religious feeling were in his judgment satisfactory accounts of faith in God, Hegel set out to recover the conceptual foundations of religion by creating a postcritical speculative theology of his own. That was the true agenda of his lectures on the philosophy of religion.

Jaeschke points out that Hegel became aware of this agenda only gradually and through sustained reflection.[4] By the end of the Frankfurt period he was clear about the need for a philosophical renewal of the doctrine of God and religion, but not about how to accomplish it. God could not be the extraworldly, omnipotent superperson of classical theism, or the abstract supreme being of the Enlightenment, or the preceptor and executor of the Kantian moral law. In Frankfurt Hegel began to develop a theory of the divine as the unification of nature and freedom, finite and infinite, but he had not yet arrived at the decisive category of *Geist* (spirit) to describe it. However, basic conceptual decisions were made during Hegel's tenure in Jena and completed by the time of writing the *Phenomenology of Spirit*. On the one hand, philosophy of religion is placed in the context of a reconstructed system of thought. On the other hand, it does not dissolve into logic or purely philosophical knowledge, nor is it a patchwork of ethical and aesthetic considerations. Rather philosophy of religion is a distinctive sort of philosophical or speculative theology, which claims that a postmetaphysical way of thinking about God is possible and that religion is a unique shape of consciousness alongside psychological, ethical, and aesthetic experience. The place of philosophy of religion in relation to the other human sciences was established in the *Phenomenology*, but not its internal form and content. That was achieved only with the Berlin lectures.

At the very beginning of these lectures, Hegel told his hearers:

God is the beginning of all things and the end of all things; [everything] starts from God and returns to God. God is the one and only object of philosophy. [Its concern is] to occupy itself with God, to apprehend everything in God, to lead everything back to God, as well as to derive everything particular from God and to justify everything only insofar as it stems from God, is sustained through its relationship with God, lives by God's radiance and has [within itself] the mind of God. Thus philosophy *is* theology, and [one's] occupation with philosophy—or rather *in* philosophy—is of itself the service of God.[5]

Such a linkage between theology and philosophy was once found in the Middle Ages; and the time had come to reestablish it, Hegel argued, since modern theologians have abandoned their vocation of knowing *God,* as opposed to knowing only human subjectivity or investigating only what was *once* believed. Indeed, it is now philosophy rather than theology that preserves and interprets the central Christian doctrines.[6]

Hegel returned to this theme at the end of the lectures. "The goal of philosophy is the cognition of the truth—the cognition of God because God is the absolute truth. . . . Philosophy knows God essentially as concrete, as the spiritual, realized universality that is not jealous but communicates itself." The Enlightenment is not pleased when philosophy defends the rationality of the Christian religion or shows that the truth is deposited in religion. The task of philosophy—or of "the [branch of] philosophy that is theology"—is "to show forth the rational content of religion [*die Vernunft der Religion*]."[7] Or, expressed slightly differently: "Philosophy is to this extent theology," that it presents the reconciliation of God with the world, this reconciliation being the peace that does not "surpass all reason" but is itself precisely reason.[8]

Theology, then, is a branch of philosophy that concerns itself with the knowledge of God and exhibits the rational content of religion. It does this by raising the symbolic, metaphorical, representational language of religion into a conceptual, scientific terminology—and precisely this is the agenda of Hegel's lectures on the philosophy of religion. Theology, in brief, is a "science of religion" and "the intellectual science of God." Without cognition of God, theology is but "a noisy gong and a clanging cymbal."[9]

In the controversies following his death, Hegel would have aligned himself with the theologians of the Hegelian middle who sought to carry forward the agenda of a scientific theology (Karl Daub, Philipp Marheineke, Karl Rosenkranz, Ferdinand Christian Baur),[10] as opposed to the radicals of the Hegelian left who rejected all religion as mythological and illusory (Bruno Bauer, David Friedrich Strauss, Ludwig Feuerbach, among others), and the conservatives of the Hegelian right who sought to restore orthodoxy or establish a speculative theism or a "positive" philosophy of mythology (such as I. H. Fichte, C. H. Weisse, and Friedrich Schelling in his later writings).[11] In the subsequent history of philosophy and theology, however, right down to our own time, the deconstructive critics of the left and the neoconservatives of the right have prevailed against the Hegelian middle. The speculative theology of the middle has been derided as "ontotheology" by the left and as "heterodoxy" by the right.

THEOLOGIAN OF THE SPIRIT

We can with some justification, then, speak of Hegel as a "theologian"— but why a "theologian of the spirit"? The answer is that "spirit" identifies for Hegel the distinctive ontological quality of God. The charge of "ontotheology" leveled against Hegelianism is correct so long as the term is defined in accord with Hegel's innovative, indeed "heterodox" approach: these terms of derision can be turned to good effect. According to Cyril O'Regan, Hegelian ontotheology contends that the shared content of theology and philosophy is truth or God, and that this content can be known, but also that the dominant form of knowledge encapsulated in the Christian metanarrative is seriously deficient. Thus Hegel undertook a speculative redescription of the narrative, oriented to the trinitarian self-manifestation of God in "moments" or "epochs" that can also be grasped in logical or conceptual form as the foundational structure of reality itself. The being of God (the *ontos* of *theos*) discloses itself to be not pure immediacy or abstract substance or "supreme being" (*das höchste Wesen*) but rather "spirit" (*Geist*) in the sense of energy, movement, life, revelation, differentiation and reconciliation.[12] Spirit designates a God who is intrinsically self-revelatory, self-manifesting; God is not locked up within godself but is knowable and related to the world. Spirit is not an aspect or person of the divine Trinity but the Trinity as such and as a whole, considered as an encompassing act or process of creating, communicating, consummating—an act by which God's own being is engendered and accomplished as well as that of the world.[13] Such a position represents a sharp break with traditional metaphysical theology, the Kantian critique of which Hegel shares, but he insists that God is the most actual of subjects—absolute intersubjectivity—rather than being merely a human projection or an ethical postulate. Any theology worthy of the name is in this sense an ontotheology.

Hegel's decisive breakthrough to this insight came in the *Phenomenology of Spirit,* which assumed the dramatic pattern of a *Bildungsroman,* a novel of formation and development. When the parentheses are removed from the *Phenomenology,* it is clear, says O'Regan, that the ultimate subject of becoming is neither the human individual nor society but God, the transcendental signified—or, in Hegelian terms, neither subjective spirit nor objective spirit but absolute spirit. Thus Hegel gives an ontotheological as opposed to a merely anthropological reading of the metanarrative. The emergent subjectivity of both individual human beings and the human community are elements in the becoming of the divine (inter)subjectivity. This whole process is what Hegel means by *Geist.*[14]

The evolution of Hegel's theology of spirit can be traced through the documents contained in this volume. Already in one of the early writings, "The Spirit of Christianity and Its Fate" (1799), there are hints that spirit is the condition of possibility for a nonextrinsic relationship between the divine and the human, which is a relationship of spirit to spirit, a unity that embraces difference. "The hill and the eye which sees it are object and subject, but between humanity and God, between spirit and spirit, there is no such cleft of objectivity and subjectivity; one is to the other an other only in that one recognizes the other." In reflecting on John 4:24 ("God is spirit, and they that worship him must worship him in spirit and in truth"), Hegel writes: "How could anything but a spirit know a spirit? . . . Faith in the divine is only possible if in believers themselves there is a divine element which rediscovers itself." Believers are not illumined by an exterior light; "on the contrary, their own inflammability takes fire and burns with a flame that is their own" (see below, p. 65). Hegel is employing here characteristically mystical language and spiritual images. The christology contained in this essay is also pneumatological: Jesus is one who is filled by the Spirit, who proclaims the inbreaking kingdom of God as a communion of the Spirit (consisting in harmonious love and renewing life), and who must depart so that the Spirit may come and dwell within the community (below, pp. 67–69).

In *Faith and Knowledge* (1802), the concept of absolute spirit is present—it is the true infinite that includes finitude within itself and overcomes it—but the category "spirit" itself is lacking. At the beginning of the Jena lecture fragment, "The Resumption of the Whole into One" (1802–1803), Hegel remarks that "in religion the ideal shape of spirit is real, while its real side is ideal." This means that the ideality of the divine takes on an empirical reality that reflects spirit back to itself. The goal of religion is "to let spirit appear in spiritual shape," as opposed to the sensuous shapes of nature and art (see below, p. 86).

Spirit is the highest of the stages of consciousness whose odyssey is traced in the *Phenomenology of Spirit* (1807); it appears when reason, which mediates the difference between consciousness and self-consciousness, assumes the shapes of ethical life, art, religion, and philosophy. In the preface to this work a definition of spirit begins to be fashioned (see below, pp. 93–101). "That substance is essentially subject is expressed in the notion that represents the absolute as *spirit*—the most sublime concept, one appertaining to the modern age and its religion." The spiritual on the one hand is what is essential, substantial, or has being *in itself* (consciousness); on the other hand, it relates itself to itself, it knows itself as subject in relation to an object recognized to be other than itself, it has being *for itself* (self-consciousness). Yet in its being outside itself it remains within itself, that is, it has being *in and for itself*, and as such it is reason or *spiritual substance*. *Absolute* spirit is that spiritual substance whose recognitive relationships are all internal to itself: it is the whole that embraces all otherness, everything finite and determinate, within itself. *Finite* spirit, by contrast, recognizes otherness to subsist outside it, and it finds itself involved in relationships that limit and restrict it; just this is the meaning of its finitude. Common to absolute spirit and finite spirit is that both entail relationships

8

of consciousness. Spirit is free, pure, rational relationality, which presupposes sense as the soil of objectification and difference but is itself metasensual.

The etymological and biblical association of spirit with fluid natural forces (wind, breath, light, fire, water) is present but remains below the surface for Hegel. Spirit *is* the vitality or energy that gives and sustains life, but for human life it is the energy and relationality of consciousness that is distinctive. Consciousness is of necessity embodied, just as God is embodied by the world; without the world God is absolute idea but not yet absolute *spirit*. Thus spirit presupposes the sensuous but transfigures it, raises it to pure thought, which is the most concentrated form of energy. The German term *Geist* has at its root the idea of being moved powerfully, as in fear or amazement, a movement associated with the sudden drawing in or expelling of breath. In this way it is linked to the Hebrew, Greek, and Latin words for "spirit," all of which carry the base meaning of "breath" or "wind." *Geist* also means, in a more restrictive sense, "mind," and thus it supports the cognitive twist Hegel applies to the concept of spirit. Strictly speaking, one should say "recognitive," since it is relationships of *recognition* that constitute spirit.[15]

The interpretation of spirit in the *Phenomenology* is further specified when the Christian or revelatory religion is examined (see below, pp. 116–36). Here absolute spirit is known to be "knowledge of itself in its divestment: spirit is the being that is the process of retaining identity with itself in its otherness. . . . Consequently in this religion the divine being is revealed. Its revelatoriness consists manifestly in this, that what it is, is known." It is known as *spirit,* "as essence that is essentially self-consciousness." Something is hidden from consciousness if its object is only an alien other and if consciousness does not know its object as itself. The true shape of spirit is to be revelatory self-consciousness; and God is manifest as the universal self or self-knowing subject, which encompasses within itself all finite subjects.

Another striking formulation is found when Hegel turns in the *Phenomenology* to the third of the trinitarian figures (see below, pp. 130–36). The truth is neither identity (sameness) nor difference but the movement between them, the process by which they turn into each other. With respect to God and the natural world, we can say that the divine is natural and human to the extent that God is *not*, or does not *remain*, merely essential being (*Wesen*); while nature and humanity are divine precisely *in* their essential being, as distinct from their determinate and finite being (*Dasein*). But in *spirit* "the two abstract sides are posited as they are in truth, namely as sublated," both annulled and preserved (*aufgehoben*). Thus spirit designates the relationship of the divine to the human and the human to the divine, and in this way it acquires a religious as well as an epistemological and ontological connotation. With respect to the divine Trinity, the "Holy Spirit" is the third moment or element, in which the first two elements, the abstract being of the "Father" and the concrete, crucified being of the "Son," are annulled and preserved. Reconciliation occurs in the third moment as spiritual unity in which distinctions are present as sublated moments; reconciliation is the substance of spiritual community, the community constituted by the indwelling of the Spirit.

Hegel's later writings do not advance beyond the *Phenomenology* as far as a theoretical conception of spirit is concerned, but the language in which this conception is formulated is often simpler and clearer. At the beginning of the treatment of "Absolute Spirit" in the *Encyclopedia of the Philosophical Sciences* (§ 554), there occurs the following concise statement: "Absolute spirit, while an identity that is eternally self-contained, is likewise an identity that is returning and has returned into itself [from difference]." It is this return that evokes religion, which "is to be seen as proceeding from and located in the subject no less than as proceeding from absolute spirit." The religious relationship is not merely a human product but the doing of absolute spirit itself, "which is present as spirit in its community."

Spirit is obviously a central theme of the *Lectures on the Philosophy of Religion,* so pervasive in fact that it is best considered in connection with the commentary on the 1824 texts provided below. There is, however, one significant passage that seems to gather up much that Hegel strives to say about spirit, and says it with striking imagery: "Spirit is an eternal process of self-cognition in self-consciousness, streaming out to the finite focus of finite consciousness, and then returning to what spirit actually is, a return in which divine self-consciousness breaks forth" (see p. 250). The image of "streaming out" captures the fluid quality that spirit quintessentially is. A variant to this passage from Hegel's miscellaneous papers (n. 49) contains even more vivid imagery:

> Spirit is an eternal process of self-cognition, dividing itself into the finite flashes of light of individual consciousness, and then re-collecting and gathering itself up out of this finitude—inasmuch as it is in the finite consciousness that the process of knowing spirit's essence takes place and that the divine self-consciousness thus arises. Out of the foaming ferment of finitude, spirit rises up fragrantly.

These passages are notable both for the clarity with which eternal spirit is understood to be the energy suffusing the whole process while remaining dependent upon the process for its self-actualization, and for the use of sensuous mystical images—"streaming out," "finite flashes of light," "the foaming ferment of finitude," the "fragrance" of spirit—that are indebted to Meister Eckhart and Jacob Boehme.

In what follows a brief commentary is provided on each of the texts contained in this volume, following the order in which they are printed and using the same headings. The commentary consists primarily of a synopsis and clarification of the argument in an attempt to make these difficult writings more accessible. More detailed information about the texts and their sources is found at the beginning of each selection.

EARLY THEOLOGICAL WRITINGS

Religion Is One of Our Greatest Concerns in Life

This early essay (below, pp. 39–57), written as Hegel completed his theological studies at Tübingen in 1793, has more the character of a series of musings about loosely connected themes than of a focused essay. First, Hegel is interested to explore the interplay of sensuality, subjectivity (heart, feelings), and reason (notably practical reason) in religion. Religion is a matter of heart, not of dogma or teaching, yet some form of positive religion and religious instruction is necessary. In this connection, a distinction is necessary between authentic reason or wisdom (*Vernunft*), and Enlightenment understanding or intellect (*Verstand*)—a distinction that remains fundamental for Hegel thereafter.

The author waxes eloquent in his critique of objective, institutional religion, yet at the same time he wants to makes religion a public force, not a merely private piety. His ideal of a public religion is the folk religion (*Volksreligion*) of the ancient Greeks: it imbues the soul with power, enthusiasm, spirit, and it forms a universal community of the spirit free of idolatrous, fetishistic beliefs. At the same time he sees the need for the continuance of private religion, which is concerned with the training of individuals, inducements to virtue, and the provision of comfort and care. Just how the tension between public and private religion might be adjudicated is not further explored.

In the final part of the essay, which is the most connected, Hegel lays out three elements in the constitution of a folk religion: (*a*) its teachings must be founded on universal reason, which affirms the all-transcending love of God; (*b*) it must engage both the heart and the imagination, and thus it is made up of concepts (doctrines), essential customs (myths), and ceremonies (sacrifices as expressions of gratitude);[16] (*c*) all of life's needs are bound up with it, so it is essential that religious doctrines and practices not be cut off from the rest of life. The cultivation or education of a people as a whole requires both folk religion and political institutions. It is evident that the young Hegel and his friends were exploring the possibility of becoming enlightened religious educators, of creating a new folk religion that might accomplish in their own time what the Greeks accomplished in theirs. But Hegel also recognized this to be nothing but a wistful dream, appropriately embodied in a mythological figure ("the genie of nations"), and the essay ends with the sober remark that this "fair youth . . . has fled from the earth."

The Divine in a Particular Shape

This selection (pp. 58–71) is taken from one of the essays comprising what is now called "The Spirit of Christianity and Its Fate" (composed in 1798–1799). It is the earliest version perhaps, and one of the clearest, of Hegel's speculative theology of incarnation. From romantic devotee of Greek folk religion and enlightened critic of positive religion, Hegel evolved in a few years into a passionate defender of Christian mystery. The unity of divine and human nature is "pure life" from which all determinacy and opposition are removed, and thus it cannot be grasped by reflection but only by intuition and inspiration. The activity of the divine is a unification of spirits, and only spirit can grasp and embrace spirit. Hegel thinks that the Jewish culture of the time was unsuited to spiritual comprehension, yet Jesus and the Johannine evangelist, both obviously Jewish, succeeded in expressing deep spiritual insight despite conceptual and linguistic limitations.

Thus Hegel is attracted to the *logos* doctrine of the Gospel of John, but he also draws attention to the "son of God" and "son of humanity" language common to all the gospels and presumed to derive from Jesus himself. The relation of a son to a father "is a living relation of living beings, a likeness of life." "Father and son are simply modifications of the same life, not opposite essences." Each individual is a part and at the same time the whole, the living relatedness. In a living thing, "the part of the whole is one and the same as the whole": there is one tree, yet every branch is a tree if planted. Thus "son of God" expresses a "modification" of the divine, and likewise "son of humanity" is a modification of the human, an individual subsumed under the universal, "humanity." Now these two sons are conjoined in Jesus of Nazareth. "The son of God is also son of humanity; the divine in a particular shape [*Gestalt*] appears as a human being." The particular gestalt in which the divine appears is simply a human shape, the shape of one who lived, taught, and died in a particular way, and in whom is represented the whole of humanity.

This connection is a "holy mystery" because it is life itself, and thus it can be grasped only mystically or by faith, not by the objectifying categories of the two-natures doctrine. God is the existential counterpart (*Gegenstand*), not the epistemological object (*Objekt*), of faith. Faith is a relationship of spirit to spirit, a feeling of harmony, or unification. "Faith in the divine is only possible if in believers themselves there is a divine element which rediscovers itself . . . in that on which it believes." Here Hegel imbibes of mystical images (light, fire) and is pointing toward a mystical gnosis, both of which locate him in a heterodox trajectory of Christian tradition. "Only a modification of the Godhead can know the Godhead."

Faith is, however, only the beginning of a relationship that culminates in friendship. As long as Jesus remained physically present, his followers remained believers only. Even this objectivity must be removed to enter into a purely spiritual relationship with God, animation by the Holy Spirit. Thus Hegel makes much of the Johannine saying that Jesus must depart in order for the Spirit to come (John 14:16, 16:7). With the transition from Jesus to the Spirit there occurs a transition from faith in a counterpart to an actual living in and with Christ. The divine is now present in the disciples as in Jesus; the purely inward unity of love and friendship is accomplished. The culmination of faith is "the return to the Godhead whence humanity is born," and this return "closes the circle of human development."

Jesus himself articulated this idea with the image of the kingdom of God. The word "kingdom" is inadequate to express the "divine unification of humanity" if, as its political usage suggests, it means a union through domination and subjugation as opposed to "the beauty of the divine life of a pure human fellowship," which is utterly free. Yet properly construed, the kingdom of God "comprises the whole of religion as Jesus founded it," a communion of life in God—a beautiful idea, to be sure, but one flawed by an "incompleteness" that would give fate power over it. This incompleteness, Hegel hints, was its attempt to overleap nature, its flight from the division and struggles of real life, and its failure to achieve practical implementation other than on the smallest scale. The "fate" of Jesus and the church—the fate of the spirit of Christianity—is an unresolved tension between the inner truth of the gospel and the exigencies of the external world.

JENA WRITINGS

Faith and Knowledge

Our selection (pp. 72–84) provides only the introduction and conclusion to this work, which Hegel published in 1802. The introduction argues that the Enlightenment and its aftermath, which Hegel calls "the culture of reflection," has succeeded in destroying both faith and knowledge. Reason has dismissed religion as merely positive, and itself has become mere intellect or understanding, knowing nothing except that it knows nothing. The void of knowing is filled with the subjectivity of longing and divining; the latter is called "faith," but it is not true faith in the sense of having a counterpart or a relationship other than to itself.

The turn to subjectivity, which is the principle of the "North" or of Protestantism, is in itself an authentic turn, for beauty and truth do present themselves as feelings, persuasions, love, which establish contact with the subjectivity of the believer, and the latter must be constructively engaged in the act of knowing. Objectively speaking, the "sacred grove" of the ancients has been reduced to "mere timber" for moderns. There is no gainsaying this, but it is still possible to attain sublimity in the form of feeling, eternal longing, perfect vision, blissful enjoyment.

Religion ought to resist the empirical doctrine of happiness (eudaemonism), which orients values solely to this world, but in fact it succumbs to it. The fixed principle of this culture is that the finite is absolute, the sole reality. Opposed to it is another fixed principle, namely that the absolute is the eternal, the incalculable, the inconceivable, the empty—an incognizable God beyond the boundary of reason. But a God who is utterly opposed to the finite is limited by the finite and in this respect is finite as well. Thus piety readily passes over into self-help: "the poetry of Protestant grief . . . is transformed into the prose of satisfaction." John Locke and the eudaemonists, argues Hegel, have transformed philosophy into empirical psychology; theirs is a subjectivity whose reason is solely immersed in finitude, renouncing any intuition or cognition of the eternal. The philosophies of Kant, Fichte, and Jacobi, despite their intentions to the contrary, are the "completion and idealization" of this empirical psychology. By setting up infinity as the antithesis of the finite, they make it finite too; they achieve only an idealism of the finite, of a subjectivity that reflects itself back to itself. So these philosophies are "nothing but the culture of reflection raised to a system." Human beings "are not a glowing spark of eternal beauty, or a spiritual focus of the universe, but an absolute sensibility." Humans may have faith in a realm beyond the barrier that cannot be crossed, but this merely adds a touch of "alien supersensuousness" to their underlying sensibility. It is rather as though a painting were permitted to depict only the melancholy longing of human faces but not the gods themselves. Or, to vary the artistic metaphor, it is ironic to complain, as these philosophers do, of being deprived of one's deprivation when after seeing only the feet of a figure the whole work of art is revealed. The fact is that they want to hold on to their precious finitude, whereas the true infinite "consumes and consummates" finitude.

In the conclusion, following detailed analyses and critiques of Kant, Jacobi, and Fichte, Hegel sums all of this up in the pithy statement that these modern philosophies have "recast the dogmatism of being into the dogmatism of thinking, the metaphysic of objectivity into the metaphysic of subjectivity." Dogmatism remains, taking on "the hue of inwardness, of the latest cultural fashion." Hegel cleverly turns the two dogmatisms against each other. By negating false objectivism (the metaphysic of objectivity), reflective philosophy (the metaphysic of subjectivity) plays a necessary though transitional role in the birth of speculative philosophy. It represents the moment of nothingness, the pure night of infinity, of infinite grief, the feeling that "God godself is dead." But this "speculative Good Friday" is recognized by speculative philosophy to be only a moment of the supreme idea, of the absolute, through which it must necessarily pass in order to achieve its resurrection to the serene freedom of its shape, which is the shape of spirit. This is because the true absolute, the true infinite, includes finitude within itself and overcomes it. Only when finitude has come into its own through reflective philosophy—the speculative Good Friday—is the absolute able to rise into its true and infinite subjectivity, to come into its own as absolute *spirit*.

The Resumption of the Whole into One

In this fascinating fragment (pp. 85–92) dating from 1802–1803, Hegel is beginning to locate the philosophy of religion in the whole system of philosophy. Religion is closely related to other cultural manifestations of spirit, such as ethical life, art, and philosophical science, but it is not reducible to any of them. It differs not only in form but also has a distinctive content in the sense that it is tied to the cultic life of a people and its experience of reconciliation, its intuition of the absolute. Religion brings about "the resumption of the whole into one," and in this sense it functions as the culmination of the philosophical system. Yet the religion that functions this way is really identical with philosophy; it is a philosophical religion.

Hegel also hints in this fragment at the internal structure of philosophy of religion. He identifies three forms of religion as it appears in world history, corresponding to the logical moments of identity, difference, and mediation. The problematic running through all the forms is how spirit takes shape in the world, i.e., how the ideality of spirit becomes real and how its real side is ideal: for religion there is no *Geist* without *Gestalt*, no spirit without sensible or intellectual configuration. The first form of religion, that of identity, typifies nature religion and the religion of art, both of which are seen to be historically embodied by Greek religion; here the shape of spirit is that of nature (the old Greek mythologies) and of the beautiful human figure (the Greek dramatists and philosophers).

The second form, that of difference, seems to encompass a disparate totality made up of Jewish, Roman, and Christian religions. For all of these religions, the gods are dispelled from nature (the womb of identity), but with differing results. Judaism is left with the anguish of infinite separation between the divine and the human; Roman religion substitutes for its dismembered gods an abstract, dead universality; while Christianity reestab-

15

lishes a oneness with the absolute in a single human being. The Christian idea of reconciliation is elaborated in the form of a Trinity, which reenacts the moments of the dialectic: absolute thought (the Father), creation (the eternal and incarnate Son), the realized identity of objective world and eternal thought (the Holy Spirit). Hegel adds this notable remark: "The divinity in which [reconciled] love finds its own felicity must come to be the *Mother of God* herself." Is this a reference to a fourth person of the Godhead, the holy Mary, forming a divine quaternity? Or is the Mother of God another name for the figure of comfort and regeneration, the Holy Spirit? There is precedent for the latter in certain strands of Gnostic and Syrian Christianity, which subsequently influenced German pietism (Gottfried Arnold, Hermann Francke, Count Zinzendorf).[17] In any event, this is a thought experiment to which Hegel did not return (although in the *Phenomenology of Spirit* he does say that the love of the spiritual community is symbolized by the figure of the mother).

The third form of religion in world history is envisioned to be a philosophical religion of the spirit. Hegel imagines that through the mediation of philosophy a new form of world religion will emerge out of Christianity. Catholic beauty and holiness have been destroyed by Protestant worldliness and cannot be brought back; yet nature and world have not truly been reconciled in Protestantism, and there remains only a secular form of infinite grief. What is called for is a new religion of a free people, a religion in which reason "has found once more its reality as an ethical spirit, a spirit which is bold enough to assume its pure shape on its own soil and in its own majesty." Hegel seems to be playing once again with the ideal of a folk religion, but this too is a thought experiment that is not repeated in later writings. Perhaps its place is taken by the portrayal in the Berlin philosophy of religion lectures of the kingdom of the Spirit; however, the latter represents the fullest realization of the Christian ideal, not the establishment of a post-Christian religion. These various explorations bear testimony to the fertility of Hegel's mind during the years in Jena.

PHENOMENOLOGY OF SPIRIT

The Absolute as Spirit

Our first selection (pp. 93–101) from the *Phenomenology of Spirit* (1807) is a portion of the Preface, which was written after the main body of the text was composed. In it Hegel's ontotheological intention, veiled in much of the work, becomes evident. Everything depends, he says, on comprehending that "the true"—essential being or being itself, the absolute, the divine—is "subject" no less than "substance." This means that the true is not simple essence or immediate identity but rather an action that negates, ruptures, and reinstates itself, reflects itself back to itself in otherness. The life of God may indeed be expressed as "the play of love with itself"; but this is merely an insipid idea "if the seriousness, the anguish, the patience, and the labor of the negative are lacking in it." Subjectivity entails negation and its labor; it is a *result,* a process, a becoming, not a given. The divine subjectivity is the truth that is the whole (*das Ganze*). "But the whole is nothing other than the essence consummating itself through its development." The divine whole is absolute in the sense that all relations are internal to it. Negation, rupture, and differentiation occur within it; it is not limited by another essence outside it. It is, to use a term coined by Raimon Panikkar,[18] a "cosmotheandric" whole, not merely a divine whole; it encompasses and constitutes all that is, *cosmos* and *anthropos* as well as *theos*—and as such it is "spirit." Hegel expresses this by saying that the true is actual only as a "system," a structured and interrelated wholeness. This is what is meant, he says, when one refers to "the absolute as *spirit,*" which is the "most sublime" of modern concepts. It means that the absolute is relational and processual. Spirit is what is actual in a triple mediation: it is essence or has being *in itself* (abstract, ideal divinity); it relates itself to itself or is being *for itself* in other-being (determinate, real worldliness); and in this being outside itself it remains within itself and is thus *in and for itself* (the interplay of ideality and reality, divinity and world).

Spirit that knows itself as spirit is knowledge or science, *Wissenschaft.* Such knowledge is the actuality of spirit; it is the fluid or medium in which spirit spiritualizes, the realm spirit builds for itself, the very element that is the stuff of spirit. This "ethereal element" is "pure self-recognition in absolute otherness." Knowledge presupposes otherness and difference, but recognizes itself in the other. Spirit comes to self-recognition through the long and laborious journey of history; the phenomenology of spirit traces the stages along this path. The subject or agent of this historical action is not merely individual human subjects but absolute spirit itself, the whole, the true, the system. Humans as thinkers and doers play a necessary role in this process, but it encompasses and consumes them.

The excerpted portion of the Preface concludes with a meditation on the "tremendous power of the negative," which is the "energy of thought," the power that drives the dialectic. The negative appears above all as death, the nonactual that deactualizes—that of which all living things have an instinctive dread. Yet "the life of spirit is not the life that is afraid of death and keeps itself untouched by devastation, but the life that endures death and maintains itself in it. It attains its truth only when, in utter dismemberment, it finds itself." Spirit gains its power "only by looking the negative in the face and lingering over it. This lingering over it is the magic power that converts the negative into being." *Geist* is what goes on, brings new life out of death; the life thus brought forth is deeper, richer, stronger than the youthful innocence on which death has not yet cast its shadow.

The Science of the Experience of Consciousness

The primary task of Hegel's Introduction to the *Phenomenology*, translated here in full (pp. 101–10), is to establish a strong link, indeed a dialectical identity, between cognition and its content, between concept and object, knowing and being. Cognition is not merely an instrument by which to grasp absolute being; it is the absolute itself. It is a common fallacy to think of the absolute as standing on one side and cognition (or consciousness) on the other. Contra Kant, we must recognize that by investigating knowing we are in fact investigating the thing itself. Thus the science of the experience of consciousness, of the path taken by the soul as it journeys through its successive configurations, is not merely an epistemological and anthropological investigation. It is also an ontological and theological one: it is an account of absolute spirit's return to itself through finite spirit's rise to consciousness of the absolute.

The goal is attained when knowing no longer needs to go beyond itself, when it finds its own self, when concept corresponds to object, and object to concept. Hegel does not regard this as an empirical state of affairs attained once and for all—and certainly not in his own time and his own philosophy. Our historical state is rather one of unending quest through countless determinate negations. There is no shortcut that avoids the wealth and detail of determinacy and difference. Every time consciousness thinks it has finally glimpsed itself as its own object, it is driven on to a new shape. This is the very nature of "absolute knowledge" itself. It is not a blank whole, not a barren identity, but all the endless and inexhaustible details of life that we are tempted to pass over. It is "absolving" knowledge, releasing itself into the life-and-death struggle of history. It is the determinacy that encompasses all determinacies.

Religion

At the beginning of chapter 7 on religion (pp. 110–16), Hegel offers a famous recapitulation of the preceding chapters of the *Phenomenology* (see n. 2). Religion has appeared in the shapes of consciousness hitherto considered, but only from the point of view of consciousness that is conscious *of* absolute being; absolute being in and for itself, the *self*-consciousness of spirit, has not appeared in those forms. This signals a transition from an anthropological to an ontotheological perspective, and it hints that the self-manifestation or self-revelation of the absolute will be a central theme in the discussion of religion proper.

The shapes of spirit appear in a temporal sequence, a history of religions. The religions constitute the determinately existing actuality of the whole of spirit, which *is* only as the differentiating and self-returning movement of these its aspects. The whole of spirit, the spirit of religion as such, is a movement away from immediacy toward the knowledge of what spirit is in and for itself, toward a shape that is perfectly identical with its essence. Hegel believes that this movement attains its consummation in a particular historical religion, Christianity, which consequently is the absolute or revelatory religion. The phenomenological arrangement of this progression, however, differs from the historical sequence in which the religions have appeared. There seems to be no single line of advance since each religiocultural trajectory at some point retrogresses, a "knot" forms, and spirit moves to another trajectory, so that there are in fact many lines in history, which can be "bundled" but not amalgamated.

Hegel then outlines his phenomenological arrangement of religions, which identifies three major moments or bundles: (1) Immediate religion, or natural religion, in which the distinction between consciousness and self-consciousness has not yet emerged. Spirit remains in immediate unity with itself, or knows itself as its object in natural or immediate shape alone.[19] (2) The religion of art, or Greek religion, where spirit knows itself in a *sublated* natural shape, which is a product of conscious activity, a work of art. (3) The revelatory or Christian religion, where spirit attains its true shape in a self-consciousness that is both divine and human; but the representational form in which this is expressed must still pass over into absolute knowing. This is Hegel's first sustained effort to establish the internal arrangement of philosophy of religion. While the basic knots remain in place, the bundled contents will vary drastically as the treatment is refined in the Berlin lectures two decades later.

The Revelatory Religion

Our next selection (pp. 116–36) omits the brief discussion of natural religion and the lengthy discussion of the religion of art found in chapter 7 of the *Phenomenology*. At the beginning of the third part of the chapter, revelatory religion, Hegel is concerned to show how and why the transition occurred from Greek and Roman to Christian religion. The transitions, "knots," or breaks in history are of critical importance. Hegel's attention to them shows that he did not subscribe to a naively progressivist view of history; rather his vision was deeply tragic, though encompassed within a tragicomic metanarrative for which both alienation and reconciliation are ongoing realities. What happened, on Hegel's version, was that the ethical spirit and beauty of Greek religion was lost in the Roman world, leaving only the finite self with its abstract legal status and its pretentious claim,

"The self is absolute being." This "levity" inevitably somersaulted into an "unhappy consciousness," the recognition that finitude cannot satisfy the human soul. Such was the tragic fate of the certainty of self that aims to be in and for itself alone and is conscious of the loss of all essentiality; it was the anguish that pronounces God to be dead, that knows Greek religion and art now merely to be "beautiful fruit plucked from the tree." The Romans, amazingly, celebrated this death of the gods by collecting them in their pantheon; but in so doing they unwittingly brought on the birth pangs of spirit's new emergence. (Hegel's discussion of Roman religion is only a slightly veiled critique of the religious situation of his own time.)

Turning specifically to the revelatory religion, Hegel articulates its core insight in terms of a speculative theory of incarnation. Such a theory has two sides: the first side is the divine becoming human (substance divests or empties itself of itself and becomes self-consciousness); the second is the human becoming divine (self-consciousness divests itself of itself and makes itself into a universal self). There is a divestment of the divine and an exaltation of the human such that the two become one: here Hegel has adopted the classic Lutheran doctrine of the two states of Christ (humiliation and exaltation), but he probes its meaning with astonishing insight. If we had only the latter side, the self-exaltation of the human, then spirit would only be imagined into existence; this is the visionary dreaming (*Schwärmerei*) that conjures divinity out of itself. No, the first side, the divestment of the divine, must also be there as an objective reality in the shape of an actual human being. That spirit is present for the immediate certainty of faith is not merely imagined; rather "it is actual in the believer." Consciousness does not set out from its own inner life and connect the idea of God with it; "rather it starts from an existence that is immediately present and recognizes God in it." Hegel's position in brief seems to be this: faith *does* have an objective historical referent and point of departure, but it cannot be proved from history that this point of departure has the *significance* attributed to it by faith; the only proof in this instance is the proof of the Spirit.

By descending from its eternal simplicity, the absolute being (the "Father") attains for the first time its "highest being" (see n. 7)—which is not the remote and inaccessible deity of rationalism but a divesting, absolving, relational being that comes down into history and makes itself manifest (the "Son"). Essential being (*Wesen*) becomes existent, determinate being (*Sein, Dasein*)—and this is to say that it becomes spirit (*Geist*), "the being that is the process of retaining identity with itself in its otherness." Spirit in the immediacy of self-consciousness is the particular individual Jesus of Nazareth, as contrasted with the universal self-consciousness of the religious community. But this individual human being, "as whom absolute being is manifest," is subject to the conditions of time, space, and mortality: his being passes into having been and his sensible presence into spiritual presence. This is the passage from the Son to the Spirit.

These temporal and spatial categories, endemic to the representational form of religion, are not adequate to the truth of absolute spirit. Consequently, Hegel moves on (see n. 11) to provide a speculative redescription of the central Christian theologoumenon, the Trinity, which contains the true content but in less than adequate form. The three constitutive moments, conceptually expressed, are pure thought, representation, and self-consciousness. *Pure thought* designates the immanent or intradivine Trinity, which is not an empty essence but already the *implicit* fullness of absolute spirit (see n. 12). *Representation (Vorstellung)* designates the second moment, that of creation, fall, incarnation, life and death, symbolically encapsulated in the figure of the Son. Representation is not merely an epistemological category but an ontological one (see n. 14). It designates a divine doing, not merely a human knowing. *God* sets godself forth (*vorstellen*) in and as world; this is an essential element in the process of God's becoming spirit. The referent of representation is real history, not fanciful myth, although what happens in history is often recounted in mythical form.

The third moment is that of *self-consciousness* or infinite intersubjectivity, which is associated by Christian faith with the Holy Spirit, resurrection, reconciliation, and the community of faith (see n. 19). Hegel observes that "absolute being" would be an empty name if in truth there were an absolute other to it or an irreparable fall from it. "Absolute" must mean then that all of God's relations are internal rather than external. *Within* the divine whole there is genuine otherness and radical difference, but it is only when essential being is reflected back into itself that it is spirit. Hegel launches at this point into a complex discussion of the ontological status of good and evil. Evil seems to take two forms: on the one hand, it is a withdrawal into self, a becoming self-centered, in other words a failure to make the move from the first moment to the second; but on the other hand, it is a matter of getting stuck in the second moment, revelling in separation and estrangement, failing to come back into self. In both cases, it is a stopping short of spirit, a failure in spiritualization.

Hegel's discussion of spiritual community and spiritual resurrection is incredibly rich and dense. He is describing here a process by which the divine being's individual self-consciousness (as Christ) becomes universal, becomes the religious community. Death is transfigured from the nonbeing of the historical individual Jesus into the universality of the spirit, which lives, dies, and rises daily in the community. Particularity dies away in universality, representation in concept. What dies in the death of the mediator is not only "the already dead husk stripped of its essential being," but also the abstraction of the divine being. The abstract supreme being must die, along with the historical mediator, in order for the concrete universal, world-encompassing spirit, to be born (see n. 26). Spirit is the movement in which absolutely opposed things recognize themselves as the same and are reconciled. This reconciliation or atonement is a process intrinsic to the divine life, not a satisfaction attained by paying a penalty. It is a present reality, not something that happened once in the distant past or that will come only in the distant future (see n. 27).

The community is filled by eternal love, symbolized by the figure of the mother, but this is a love that is only felt, not yet grasped in consciousness. Reconciliation occurs for the community in the heart, but its consciousness is still ruptured. Reconciliation appears to it to lie in the beyond, while the present world is not yet transfigured, does not yet have a spiritual shape. This inward and incomplete character of reconciliation indicates for Hegel the necessity of making one more transition—from revelatory religion to absolute knowing. But does philosophy really accomplish the transfiguration of the world any more successfully than religion does?

ENCYCLOPEDIA OF THE PHILOSOPHICAL SCIENCES: ABSOLUTE SPIRIT

Hegel did not address the topic of religion in its own right again until the first edition (1817) of the *Encyclopedia of the Philosophical Sciences,* although ontotheological passages are found in the *Science of Logic* (1812–1816), and Hegel gave instruction in religion to his pupils in the Stuttgart Gymnasium. The treatment of religion in the *Encyclopedia* is highly compressed and formal, and it is limited to only one part of the subject, whose place in the whole of the philosophy of religion remained unclear until the Berlin lectures of 1821.[20] But the *Encyclopedia* text (below, pp. 137–54) contains some very important passages and offers an interesting variation on the internal arrangement of what is here called "revealed religion" as opposed to "revelatory religion" (see n. 8).

The section on Absolute Spirit opens with this definition: "Absolute spirit, while an identity that is eternally self-contained, is likewise an identity that is returning and has returned into itself" (§ 554). Religion, as one of the shapes constituting this return, "is to be seen as proceeding from and located in the subject no less than as proceeding from absolute spirit, which is [present] as spirit in its community." Thus the science of religion must be both anthropological and theological. The two aspects, subjective consciousness and absolute spirit, come together as an inward process in the form of *faith,* which, in worship, sublates the antithesis "into a spiritual liberation."

Art, as the first of the shapes of absolute spirit, is "the concrete intuition and representation of implicitly absolute spirit as the ideal" (§§ 556–63). Art needs not only sensuous material but also the given forms of nature, of which the human is the highest because only in it can "spirit have its corporeality and thus its intuitable expression." Art is a transfiguration, not an imitation, of nature, but absolute spirit cannot be made truly explicit in its shapes; spirit remains hidden beneath or within the shape of beauty, which can achieve only an "imbuing" of its forms by the spirit. Art is a human work, a product of individual genius; the artist is the master of the god, and no divine *self*-manifestation takes place here.

Art and religion are of course closely associated since art is one of the forms by which religious content is expressed. The advent of fine or beautiful art (*schöne Kunst*) portends the decline of the nature religions, which are still bound to sensuous externality. The religion of fine art (Greek religion) and the religion of symbolic art or sublimity (Jewish religion) must have concrete spirituality as their principle. But even these are "only a stage in liberation, not the supreme liberation itself." Intuition must pass over into revelation.

Revealed religion (§§ 554–71) is thus the second of the shapes of absolute spirit. Authentic religion is revealed by God, who is not jealous, who does not withhold what God is. As spirit, God is intrinsically revelatory, for "spirit is only spirit insofar as it is *for* spirit." If God is to be taken seriously in religion, then it is from *God* that the definition of religion must begin. But to grasp what God is as spirit calls for "profound speculation." It embraces the following propositions, which Hegel elaborates from a work by the jurist-theologian Göschel (who had become his disciple, see n. 10): "God is only God to the extent that God knows godself; God's self-knowing is, further, a self-consciousness in humanity and humanity's knowledge *of* God, which proceeds to humanity's self-knowing *in* God." The medium of divine revelation and self-knowing is not a directly given oracle from God or a body of sacred teachings but the very process of human consciousness and knowing.

The form of religious knowledge is representational, which means that the constitutive elements of the divine content are understood as phenomena following one another, a web of happenings in temporal succession and spatial dispersion. These finite reflective categories are sublated in faith and worship but not yet translated into speculative concepts.

Combining both conceptual and representational forms, we can say that the spheres or elements in which the absolute content presents itself are as follows: universality (immanent Trinity), particularity (creation and governance of the world, the work of the eternal Son), and individuality (the history of redemption, reconciliation, and restoration, the work of the temporal

Son who passes into the Spirit). This arrangement (see n. 11) goes back to the first edition of the *Encyclopedia* (1817) and is similar to the 1821 philosophy of religion lecture manuscript. It differs from the *Phenomenology* and the later philosophy of religion lectures (1824, 1827, 1831), for which the second moment encompasses both creation and incarnation and is associated with the figure of Christ, while the third moment is that of the community of faith and the Spirit. Hegel experimented with both arrangements. The *Encyclopedia* arrangement is more christological in the sense that the Son is associated with both the second and third moments, sharing the latter with the Spirit (of course it is the indwelling Spirit that makes Jesus to be the Christ, so that what is involved is really a pneumatological christology); while the *Phenomenology* and later philosophy of religion arrangement is more traditionally trinitarian and at the same time more radically pneumatological in the sense that the third moment is exclusively that of the Spirit and is also the consummation of the first two moments.[21] It was typical of Hegel to engage in such thought-experiments: each approach contains insight and truth, but only the totality of approaches is *the* truth.

Philosophy (§§ 572–77) is the unity of art and religion. Artistic intuition is not merely held together to form a whole as in religion; it is also combined into a simple spiritual intuition and then raised to self-conscious thought. Philosophy grasps the *necessity* of the shared content of art and religion as well as of their distinct forms, and thus it is liberated from the one-sidedness of all forms.

This consideration led Hegel to add a lengthy remark to § 573 in the 1827 and 1830 editions on the relationship of philosophy and religion. Both their difference of forms and their identity of content must be recognized. Religion itself, he points out, criticizes its own forms as it approximates speculative thinking or becomes scientific theology. If it does not do so, it will fall prey to rationalistic critiques of the contradictions in faith, by which rationalism advances its own principle of formal identity and finitization of content. Speculative philosophy/theology is reproached for having too little of God in it for positive religion, too much for rationalism and piety. The charge of atheism, that philosophy has too little of God, has grown rare; more common is the charge of pantheism, that it has too much of God. The latter charge arises from modern piety and theology, which eschew any specific knowledge of God and hold only to a God in general, while occupying themselves with merely historical matters (what was *once* believed). But no serious philosophy, claims Hegel in a lengthy excursus (see n. 16), has ever held to pantheism in the strict sense that everything simply *is* God: this is an absurdity.

What is at issue here is the relationship between God and the world, and Hegel offers one of his most lucid discussions of the matter. Reflective

24

understanding separates God as essence from finite, worldly appearance, and then establishes an external, "incomprehensible" link between them. Speculative philosophy, by contrast, is concerned not with abstract unity or mere identity, the empty absolute, but with concrete unity, which entails at every stage distinctive determinations of which there are a great number and diversity, the last and deepest of which is absolute spirit itself—the determinacy that encompasses all determinations. The critics who bring the charge of pantheism and barren identity "lose sight of the chief point of interest, namely the manner in which unity is determinate." Instead of recognizing unity in the diverse ways it is determinate, they grasp only the most external and worst sort of unity, namely composition, which they falsely attribute to philosophy. On their own compositional view, God would have to dwell in the interspace of things (the "God of the gaps," n. 19), and there would be an infinite splintering of the divine actuality in materiality.

The manner in which unity is determinate: this is a leitmotiv of Hegel's philosophy. It is present in the following summary of the *Encyclopedia* (§ 574): "the concept of philosophy . . . is the logical idea [*das Logische*] with the signification that it is universality attested in concrete content as in its actuality. In this manner science has returned to its beginning: its result is the logical idea but as a spiritual principle [*das Geistige*]." The movement is from abstract to concrete, determinate unity. Spirit is the most intense and also the most diverse sort of unity. The return to the beginning but with difference inscribes the figure of a spiral, a figure that is articulated conceptually by the three figures of the philosophical syllogism (see n. 20). Each of the terms of the syllogism (the logical idea, nature, spirit) in turn assumes middle position and couples the other two. In this way concrete, determinate unity is established. Hegel concludes with a phrase reminiscent of Aristotle (n. 21): "The eternal idea that exists in and for itself is eternally active, engendering and enjoying itself as absolute spirit."

FOREWORD TO HINRICHS'S *RELIGION:* THE RECONCILIATION OF FAITH AND REASON

Hegel took the occasion of writing this Foreword (below, pp. 155–71) to return to a topic with which he had long been concerned and also to address a challenge that newly confronted him in 1822. It is one of his most accessible writings on religion. The reconciliation of faith and reason is not genuine, he argues, if faith has become devoid of content and reason has renounced the cognition of truth. There is no longer any discord between them because there is no longer any object of dispute.

Faith is properly defined as both the subjective fact of being convinced *and* the church's objective creed, its credo. Education is a process of internalizing the truth, which first impinges externally in words and letters. The church is properly engaged in education in both senses—in mediating the doctrinal tradition and in bringing about inner conviction. Conviction comprises the subjective aspect of faith: a "taking-as-true" (*Fürwahrhalten*) with reasons, in this case the reasons provided by and for representational thinking.

Reason is properly understood as cognition of truth. The Enlightenment critique of reason was necessary because in the doctrinal and metaphysical tradition finite objects of understanding were confused with and represented as eternal truth. But the Enlightenment left thought with *only* finite material and eschewed any possibility of knowing truth in and for itself. Enlightenment theology was left without any known truth or objective content, and thus without any possibility of a *doctrine* of faith (a *Glaubenslehre,* see n. 1).

The mention of *Glaubenslehre* leads Hegel into a discussion of the work recently published by his theological colleague in Berlin, Friedrich Schleiermacher. One suspects that this was a primary occasion for his writing the Foreword, since the second volume of Schleiermacher's *Der christliche Glaube* was not published until 1822, and Hegel had been able to take only brief account of the first volume in his philosophy of religion lectures of the previous summer. Schleiermacher and others were claiming that only in the region of *feeling* can spirit still find a place to encounter the eternal; only here can the impulse to truth take refuge. Hegel had no objection to feeling as such, only to the claim that it is the sole or predominant form of cognition. However, Hegel understood "feeling" (*Gefühl*) as "sensibility" (*Empfindung*), thus as an indeterminate, sense-based mode of knowledge that can be filled with any content, whereas Schleiermacher intended something quite different by "feeling," namely a prereflective awareness of the whence and whither of existence (see nn. 4, 6). Hegel never seemed to appreciate this distinction, and thus he insisted that, while there may be a natural feeling of the divine, the divine is properly present only in and for spirit, and that spirit consists not in natural life but in being reborn. Animals live according to natural feeling, and if religion is the feeling of dependence, then a dog would be the best Christian. The heart of religion is not a feeling of dependence but a feeling of freedom. Only free spirit can have religion.

The need of our time, as Hegel sees it, is for a substantial, objective content of truth, and this can be provided only by thinking, not feeling. The conviction of faith needs the testimony of the indwelling spirit of truth. Religion requires a science of religion—a theology, whose proper content is not history but present rational cognition. The cognition of God is what raises humans above animals, makes them happy or blessed. Yet at the pinnacle of modern culture is a reversion to the ancient notion that God is uncommunicative—a turn against the revelatory heart of Christianity and spirit. What is theology without cognition of God? Hegel answers with the words of the Apostle: a noisy gong and a clanging cymbal.

LECTURES ON THE PHILOSOPHY OF RELIGION (1824)

The culmination of Hegel's life-long engagement with religion was attained in his Berlin lectures on the philosophy of religion, which were delivered on four occasions between 1821 and 1831, each lecture course differing significantly from the others. For the reasons indicated in our editorial remarks at the beginning of chapter 6 (p. 172), the selections contained in the present volume are from the lectures of 1824, including the complete texts of the "Introduction" and Part 3 ("The Consummate Religion"), a substantial selection from Part 1 ("The Concept of Religion"), and a brief introduction to Part 2 ("Determinate Religion").

Introduction: On the Philosophy of Religion

Hegel's opens his "Introduction" (below, pp. 173–89) with a meditation (taken from the lecture manuscript of 1821 without much alteration) on the object of religion. This object is the supreme or absolute object, God, in whom all things human find their beginning, center, end, and truth. The divine object exists strictly for its own sake and has no relation to anything external and totally alien to itself; this is why it is called "absolute." It surely does have relations, but these are all internal, being constituted by God's creation of the world as the dimension of otherness within the divine plenitude. Religion's occupation with this object is an utterly free and liberating occupation—as opposed to Schleiermacher's feeling of utter dependence—because in it human beings find their own essential being and fulfillment.

Philosophy too, like religion, has God as its only proper object. The object of philosophy *of religion*, however, is not simply God but religion itself as the *relationship* of God and consciousness. And this is a clue to the real nature of God. For God is not an abstract being of the understanding but is rather grasped as spirit, and spirit includes the subjective side within it, the side of religion. "God can only be genuinely understood in the mode of God's being as *spirit*, by means of which God makes godself into the counterpart of a community and brings about the activity of a community in relation to God." God is spirit, not finite but absolute spirit, and this means "that God is not only the being that maintains itself in thought but also the being that appears, the being that endows itself with revelation and objectivity."

Hegel moves on to a positioning of the speculative philosophy of religion in relation to alternative theologies of the time: rational theology, theology of feeling, historical theology. Much of this discussion is anticipated in the Hinrichs Foreword. Noteworthy are his remarks about biblical interpretation. It should be clear, he says, that interpretation introduces our own thoughts and interests, which always go beyond (or against) the words of the text. Biblical commentaries disclose more about the prejudices of their own time than about the content of scripture, which through the ages has been twisted like a "wax nose" to every prevailing agenda. Noteworthy too is his comment that historically-minded theologians are like "counting-house clerks" who keep the accounts of other people's wealth but have no assets of their own. This is not to say that theology ought to renounce its positive doctrinal content, but rather that it is the theologian's responsibility to articulate the meaning of this content afresh as opposed to relying on fixed formulations of the past.

These and other preliminary questions must finally be set aside, however, because they cannot be settled in advance of actually *doing* philosophy of religion. Just as the only way to learn to swim is to go into the water, so also the only way to investigate the capacity of cognition is to engage in cognitive acts. Reason can only be investigated rationally, by reason itself. And once reason is brought on the scene, we are engaged with the object of religion. "God is essentially rational, is rationality that is alive and, as spirit, is in and for itself." Reason is both method and content; God is both the way and the truth—and the life. The methodological questions raised by the "Introduction" thus seem to dissolve, and we are led on immediately into the subject matter, which unfolds itself in three stages: the concept of religion, the objectification of the concept in the determinate religions, and the return of the concept to itself in the revelatory or consummate religion.

The Speculative Concept of Religion

Our selection (below, pp. 190–201) omits the first part of "The Concept of Religion," which is called "Empirical Observation," summarized in the editorial remarks preceding the text. The problem that emerges from an empirical approach to religion is how a relationship between finite and infinite is actually possible. For it appears from an empirical perspective either that God remains totally other and beyond, cut off from finite relationships and cognition, or that finitude itself is alone what is real and good, projecting images of itself on the screen of transcendence. In either case we are locked into finitude. This impasse can be broken, Hegel claims, only if the *infinite overreaches* the finite, both encompassing and transcending it, thus itself constituting the passage from finite to infinite. Thereby is established an *affirmative* relationship of finitude, not to itself, but to God—affirmative in the sense of negating the negativity of finitude. This is the speculative insight: negation of the negative entails a reversal in the sense of a reflection thrown back by a mirror (Latin, *speculum*). What is reflected in our relationship to God is God's own self-relatedness. The speculative insight is articulated through the category of *spirit*. Spirit is not simply on *one* side, finite or infinite; rather it constitutes both sides and is the "inner connectedness" between them:

> Absolute spirit is itself that which connects itself with what we have put on the other side [namely, consciousness] to distinguish it. Thus, on a higher plane, religion is this idea, the idea of spirit that relates itself to itself, *the self-consciousness of absolute spirit*. Within this its *self-consciousness*, there falls also its consciousness, which was previously defined as relationship. Thus in the highest idea, religion is not the affair of the single human being; rather it is essentially the highest determination of the absolute idea itself.

From this definition of the concept of religion Hegel moves on to a consideration of the "necessity" of the religious standpoint. Philosophy must demonstrate the necessity of all its concepts, but to demonstrate the necessity of something entails starting from something else. In the case of religion, this means everything preceding the philosophy of religion in the philosophical encyclopedia—the logical idea, which "unlocks itself in the resolve" (see n. 7) to become nature; the natural world, which has the implicit destination of becoming spirit through the breaking open of its "rind" of externality; the stages of the consciousness of spirit as it rises to the absolute. But there is something misleading here if we think of absolute spirit as a "result." "*Absolute truth cannot be a result; it is what is purely and simply first, unique*. It is what takes up simply everything into itself—the absolute plenitude in which everything is but a moment." The relations it has are self-constituted and internal: the extraordinary thing about the absolute is that it can create and contain *real differences* within this plenitude, and that it can move in and through these differences without obliterating them as they rise to consciousness of it. The rise of finite spirit to the absolute is at the same time the return of absolute spirit to itself. Thus "the result casts off its position as result and develops a *counterthrust*, so to speak, against this movement." The counterthrust is the speculative reversal, imaged in the 1821 lectures as a stream flowing in opposite directions (see n. 8).

The concept of religion thus established corresponds to the self-consciousness of absolute spirit. Absolute spirit is conscious of being *for itself* as spirit, that is, there is a distinction in its being, which is natural life and consciousness. God is the unity of the natural and the spiritual; spirit overreaches this difference, is the unity of itself and its other. Thus it is to be expected that the exposition or realization of the concept of religion is

29

nothing other than the development of the idea of God, which has the following moments (see n. 9): (1) the substantial, absolute, purely subjective unity of nature and spirit, or the logical idea at rest within itself (see n. 10); (2) the differentiation of nature and spirit from the idea and from each other; and (3) the self-positing of what is differentiated in absolute affirmation. The first moment is the "abstract concept" of God found variously in all religions; the second is the "theoretical" religious relationship, which presupposes the difference within which divine appearing and human knowing can transpire (and both transpire in the mode of "representation" or "setting forth," *Vorstellung*); and the third is the "practical" religious relationship, namely the cultic practices by which difference is sublated and reconciliation accomplished. In the remainder of "The Concept of Religion," omitted from our selection, Hegel analyzes the latter two relationships.

Determinate Religion: Introduction

As noted in the editorial remarks preceding the text, "Determinate Religion" is by far the largest of the three parts of the lectures, and it is impossible to do justice to its rich contents in the present volume. Only the text of the brief "Introduction" to Part 2 is included (pp. 201–4), but even this is misleading because the threefold organizational structure it outlines actually corresponds to that provided in the previous lectures (1821), not to the twofold pattern that emerged in the course of lecturing in 1824.

A brief summary of "Determinate Religion" is also provided in the "Survey of the Stages of Our Discussion" found in the general "Introduction" to the lectures (below, pp. 187–89). The concept, Hegel says, resolves to determine itself; absolute spirit resolves to be in a determinate mode. Spirit's being is not immediate but is a self-producing that involves distinctions and directions, paths toward a goal that is spirit's ultimate or final self-recognition. Spirit does not attain the goal without having traversed the path. The distinct stages of consciousness by which spirit produces itself yield the determinate religions.

There are three ways to consider these religions. First, each religion is viewed as a pure determination of thought. This yields its abstract or metaphysical concept of God, which also assumes the form of a proof of the existence of God. Second, the representational forms in which the distinctive God-consciousness of a religion expresses itself are examined. Finally attention is addressed to the cultic activity of each religion, which is the unification of that religion's thought-determination and representational form. Cultic activity indicates the historical side of the religions. Viewed from the perspective of the concept, we can grasp the necessity of the historical progression of religions. The religions have not arisen in a contingent manner; it is spirit that governs what is inward and brings it forth. What *is*, is also *rational*. Hegel explains that by "what is" he means not the merely phenomenal or merely existing, but what *actually* is, the *Wirklichkeit* constituting the God-world nexus. A similar assertion occurs in the published *Philosophy of Right*, but a more cautious formulation is found in Hegel's earliest lectures on the philosophy of right, where he says the rational *must happen* or *come into being*.[22] Hegel's intent is not to legitimate whatever exists as rational, but to discern the coming into being of rationality, which is a dynamic and unfinished process.

As to the merely phenomenal, there can be many different historical constructions. Hegel's almost playful experimentation with the systematic arrangement of "Determinate Religion" is proof of this. At the beginning of the treatment in 1824, he envisions a fourfold division: (1) immediate religion or nature religion, where God is recognized in natural images (African, North American, Asian religions); (2) the religion of spiritual individuality, in which either natural life no longer has any substantiality over against the divine subject (Jewish religion), or the natural and spiritual are united in individual human subjects (Greek religion); (3) the religion of external, finite purposiveness (Roman religion); and (4) the absolute religion, where spirit comes into being fully for itself in accord with an inward and infinite purposiveness. These four stages, Hegel suggests, can be compared to those of human life: childhood, youth, maturity, old age. In the actual delivery of the 1824 lectures, however, despite the assertion that this is a "necessary classification that follows objectively from the nature of spirit," Roman religion becomes a brief appendage to the religion of spiritual individuality, and absolute religion is treated separately in the third main part. The order remains the same, but the fourfold division (or threefold division, since absolute religion was never intended to be treated under the category of "determinate religion") becomes a twofold one. Further experimentation is found in the 1827 and 1831 lectures.

Christianity: The Consummate Religion

The full text of Part 3 of the 1824 lectures is provided in this edition (pp. 204–59). For a discussion of the several names employed by Hegel to designate the Christian religion, see the editorial remarks at the beginning of the selection.

INTRODUCTION

Authentic spirituality knows that both sides of the religious relationship—consciousness and God—are incorporated into a whole that comprises God's own self-consciousness. The absolute is religion—the relation of infinite spirit to finite spirit—not a majestic isolated supreme being. Theology at first seems to be about the cognition of God as something solely objective and absolute, separate from subjective consciousness; but in fact the proper object of theology is religion itself, the relationship. The great advance of our age, Hegel acknowledges, is that subjectivity has been recognized as an essential moment; but subjectivity can become one-sided and self-enclosed, cut off from any content other than itself. Our age bears a striking similarity with that of the Roman emperors to the extent that we limit ourselves to merely contingent and finite contents and exercise a finite, formal, spiritless, and ultimately decadent subjectivity. The absolute religion, by contrast, is the religion of *infinite*, *substantial*, and *spiritual* subjectivity. In this way Hegel at once marks the historical passage from Roman to Christian religion and restates his central critique of modernity.[23]

The absolute or consummate religion is also the revelatory religion. "Revealing" means determining oneself to be for an other, hence revealing is the essence of spirit. "A spirit that is not revelatory is not spirit." God's self-revelation is not something that happened once or a few times in the past; rather it is an eternal and ongoing act. "This *actus* is what God is." *What* God reveals is not descriptive information about God but simply that "God *is* manifestation, i.e., the process of constituting these distinctions within godself."

Finally, this is the religion of truth and freedom. "Truth" means that in what is objective and different spirit is related not to something that is utterly alien but to another form of spirit itself. "Freedom" expresses the same thing but with the emphasis on the overcoming of the estrangement in difference; hence freedom appears as reconciliation (recognition of self in other), and reconciliation appears as freedom (an activity or movement that makes estrangement disappear).

I. THE METAPHYSICAL CONCEPT OF GOD

A religion's abstract or metaphysical concept designates the fundamental way in which it knows God and affirms the existence of God (see n. 5). For the so-called proofs, the central question is always how the concept of God relates to the reality or being of God. The cosmological and teleological proofs (found in various determinate religions) start from finite being and conclude to the infinite concept. The ontological proof, on the other hand, starts from the concept of God and shows how God's being necessarily follows from it. This is the proof that is characteristic of Christianity, and it was Anselm of Canterbury who first formulated it in convincing fashion: God is conceived as the most perfect and thus as the most real of all beings. The assumption is that perfection includes reality as one of its predicates.

Kant attempted to refute this proof by appealing to the common-sense knowledge that we can indeed build intellectual castles in the air. But Kant, according to Hegel, did not demonstrate the difference between concept and reality; he merely assumed it in popular fashion. Anselm, on the other hand, merely assumed the unity of concept and reality. The task of speculative philosophy is to *demonstrate* the unity while also explaining the difference. It does this by showing that the concept or logical idea simply *is* the movement by which it determines it to be; that is, it is the dialectical movement of self-determination into being. This is the result of the science of logic, and Hegel believes that it supplies the demonstrative force lacking in the original form of the ontological proof. In the 1824 lectures Hegel does not actually run through the demonstration, nor does he go on to make the point found in the 1827 and 1831 lectures that the Christian idea of the incarnation of God is a representational form of the proof: God becomes the sort of God that God is only by self-realization in world-process, by appearing in a concrete historical figure. At this point we can speak properly of God's determinate being or *existence (Dasein)*, not merely of God's abstract being or reality. In virtue of incarnation, *Dasein* becomes a predicate of God.[24]

II. THE DEVELOPMENT OF THE IDEA OF GOD

This "development" serves as the "concrete representation" of God in the Christian religion (see n. 14). Its constitutive elements are trinitarian. Expressed representationally, they are (1) the idea of God in and for itself (the "Father," the immanent Trinity); (2) worldly representation and appearance (the "Son"); (3) community and cultus (the "Spirit"). Expressed conceptually, the elements are (1) eternal being within and present to itself, universality (*Allgemeinheit*); (2) appearance, particularity (*Besonderheit*), being for others; (3) return from appearance into self, absolute singularity, individuality (*Einzelheit*), or subjectivity (see n. 16). These representational and logical forms can be supplemented by forms based on consciousness (thought, representation, subjectivity), space (outside the world, world, inner world or community), and time (eternity, past, present/future).[25]

A. THE FIRST ELEMENT: THE IDEA OF GOD IN AND FOR ITSELF

This is the element of pure thought or intuition in which the distinction between subject and object is not yet strictly present. Universality does have a distinction or differentiation within itself, but the latter is contained in such a way that the harmony of the whole is not disturbed.

Christian theology has expressed this as the idea of the immanent Trinity: God is defined as universal spirit that particularizes itself but remains identical with itself in the process. This is a mystery whose truth can be grasped only by speculative thought, by reason (*Vernunft*). For sense-based thought and the understanding (*Verstand*), the Trinity is a matter of counting, of numbers, which results in a mathematical conundrum (how can three equal one?). Hegel notes that "reason can employ all the *relationships* of the understanding, but only insofar as it destroys the *forms* of the understanding." The latter cannot grasp the dialectic of living things, of spiritual unity, of friendship, love, and family. To speak of God as subsisting in three "persons" seems to take being-for-self to the extreme. Yet in love and friendship persons maintain themselves and achieve subjectivity or personality. God is not three personalities but one personality that constitutes itself in the dialectic of love and friendship, of self-relatedness and other-relatedness, of "fatherhood" and "sonship" coming together in spiritual communion, in the third that is also first. This life-process transpires within the godhead as well as outside it. Inwardly it is "nothing but a play of self-maintenance, a play of self-confirmation." Outwardly, however, it becomes deadly serious.

Before moving on from the immanent or intradivine to the outer or inclusive Trinity,[26] Hegel surveys traces of the Trinity found in other religio-philosophical traditions, notably Gnosticism and Neoplatonism, which are powerful forces shaping his own interpretation.

B. THE SECOND ELEMENT: REPRESENTATION, APPEARANCE

The representational knowledge of Christianity focuses on two aspects of God's relationship with the world: differentiation and reconciliation.

1. *Differentiation.* As we have seen, there is already a differentiation-and-reunion within the divine life, which makes God logically if not existentially complete. Representation posits the distinction within the divine life as also taking place in time and space, leading to a creation and fall. God goes forth and appears in the realm of finitude. Hegel's discussion of this matter in the 1824 lectures is rather obscure and could give the impression that it is only from the point of view of representation that creation actually occurs. But the reality of the finite world is not in doubt. This is clear from the 1827 lectures, where Hegel says that the divine idea, "in its act of determining and dividing, . . . *releases* the other to exist as a free and independent being. The other, released as something free and independent, is *the world* as such." Because otherness is already a moment within the divine idea, the idea is free to allow this its own *other* also to obtain "the determinacy of other-*being*, of an actual entity," without losing itself or giving itself up. This is Hegel's theology of creation, expressed in the emanationist language of Neoplatonism and mysticism.[27]

In the condition of natural immediacy, human beings are neither good nor evil but innocent. Their proper destiny is to obtain the knowledge of good and evil, thus actualizing their implicit rationality and assuming moral responsibility. Knowledge necessarily posits distinction and separation, which in turn lead to negation, rupture, estrangement, and finally evil. This is tragic in the sense that a necessary condition for goodness, namely knowledge, also entails the estrangement that leads to evil. In the state of separation, I choose to exist for myself alone, turned in upon myself, cut off from the universal: this is where evil resides. The self-knowledge thus engendered "is what produces the disease and is at the same time the source of health." The process of healing begins with our recognition that nothing finite can satisfy us. Out of the infinite anguish of the world emerges an infinite longing for reconciliation.

2. *Reconciliation.* How is this longing satisfied? Only by establishing the possibility, necessity, and actuality of the appearance of the idea of reconciliation in a concrete historical individual. The appearance is *possible* because divine and human natures are not in themselves incompatible; the truth is their concrete unity instead. The appearance is *necessary* because the human subject cannot bring about this unity on its own account; it is withdrawn into itself in a flight from reality. Because it is a sensible consciousness, the unity must appear for it in an immediate and sensible form. Faith's claim is that the unity does *actually* appear—in the only sensuous shape appropriate to God as spirit, that of a human being. "This is the monstrous reality whose necessity we have seen."

How can such an appearance be verified? As to the content of the appearance, the unity of finite and infinite spirit, it is a purely inner verification, a witness of the Spirit to our spirits. Philosophy brings this inner witness into the light of thinking and shows that God "*has* to generate the Son, has to distinguish godself from godself, in such a way that what is distinguished is wholly God godself." As to the location of the appearance at a particular time and place, it is a matter of showing, from the point of view of world-historical dynamics, that "the time had come." But the claim that a particular historical individual, Jesus of Nazareth, is the Christ, the one who unites divine and human nature within himself—this requires an interpretation of the details of his life and death.

Hegel's examination of these details is interesting. First he notes that this is the history of a single, immediate human being in all his contingency and temporal relations; hence to say that God is present here entails a veritable divine divestment. Second, he calls attention to Jesus' teaching, which speaks to the intuitive side of human consciousness, evoking vivid images such as that of the "kingdom of God," which designates "real divinity," "God's *Dasein*" or "spiritual actuality," and which also represents a negation of everything worldly, a revolutionary affirmation of the universal that ignores and overthrows all institutions such as property relations. Perfect independence of worldly relationships is the primal soil of spirituality;

mutual love is the principal commandment. Finally, Hegel attends to the death of Jesus, which is viewed by faith not simply as the death of a human martyr but as the veritable death of God godself. Thereby negation is posited as an essential moment in the nature of the divine spirit. God is satisfied—but only by godself, not by human sacrifice. The satisfaction consists in the fact that both the first and the second moments of God's life are negated: neither does God remain closed up within godself, nor does death finally separate us from God. Rather in the third moment death itself is negated, it becomes what reconciles, becomes love itself. This is the moment of resurrection, of the communal, spiritual presence of God in Christ.

Hegel's point seems to be that faith does require a historical point of departure; without historical details such as these, there would be no objective content to which faith is oriented. But the conviction that it is indeed God who is active in this history is based on the witness of the Spirit, not on outward attestations or sensory verifications such as miracles. The true miracle is the Spirit itself: it is God's power over minds rather than nature, and this power leaves the freedom of human spirits intact. This power is manifested in the formation of the great community of the Christian church. The community forms with the passing of the sensible figure into a spiritual shape, a Comforter.

C. THE THIRD ELEMENT: COMMUNITY, SPIRIT

1. *The Origin of the Community.* The community originates with the reorientation of faith from a sensible appearance of the past to a spiritual nexus of the present in which reconciliation is actualized. This transition is termed the "outpouring of the Holy Spirit," which could only occur after the historical Christ had passed away. Now it is love itself, rather than a historical figure, that is objective. Hegel believes that Catholicism advances no further than the objectifying representation of the Son, along with other figures such as the Mother of God and the saints, while Protestantism "brings forth spirit in itself, begetting itself in its self-consciousness." He goes on to make the well-known remark that "only by philosophy can this simply present content be justified, not by history. What spirit does is no history [*Historie*]." This certainly does not mean that at a deeper level spirit is not historical; rather it is precisely spirit that constitutes divine and human historicality, the ever-present future-oriented process of self-realization through differentiation and reunification. But the "happening" of spirit is not empirically demonstrable from past events; in this sense it is no *Historie*. This point is especially emphasized in the 1824 lectures: there is no proof of faith from history, even though faith does have a historical point of departure—not as a sheer "that" (Søren Kierkegaard) but as a "what" (see n. 48).

2. *The Subsistence of the Community.* The spiritual community is sustained by institutional practices that can also threaten its spirituality. These include the rite of baptism, personal rebirth through authoritative teaching and the witness of the Spirit, and the partaking of communion. Differences within the Christian religion stem from different ways of understanding how Christ is present in the eucharist: in sensuous externality (the Catholic version), in spirit (the Lutheran), or in memory (the Reformed). It is notable that Hegel makes no mention of preaching, of which he apparently had a low opinion from painful personal experience. His emphasis on rebirth or regeneration in place of the proclamation of the Word, together with his sacramental understanding of divine presence, give his ecclesiology an ecumenical cast that, despite its stereotyped picture of Catholicism, has made it more available to a modern Catholic sensibility than might otherwise have been expected from this avowed Lutheran. Hegel seems to envision a form of Christianity that will transcend confessional splits.

3. *The Realization of Faith.* The realization of faith involves a transformation or recasting of the community, a move from pure devotion into the objective world. Hegel identifies three phases in the process, but his choice of examples seems rather arbitrary and artificial. First, there is a realization of faith in the natural heart, filled with its inclinations, passions, egoism. The community of faith both struggles against the world and falls into worldliness, taking its corruption into itself. This seems to describe the condition of the early and medieval church.

Second, as a byproduct of the Protestant turn to the subject, there emerges the reflective philosophy of subjectivity, which posits an autonomous self over against the authoritative tradition. Its abstract thinking and principle of identity assail the inner content of the church, the Trinity. Hegel identifies two antithetical instances of this identity: Enlightenment rationalism, which issues in an apotheosis of the finite self (see n. 55); and Islamic religion, which submerges the self in the abstract oneness of God (n. 56). Both pose deadly threats to authentic spirituality because in different ways they sever the religious relationship between God and self. This odd pairing of Enlightenment and Islam is not found in any of the other lectures.

The reflective thinking of the Enlightenment has carried the day, emptying both heart and heaven. Religion and its content could seek refuge in feeling, but the better option is to "take refuge in the concept," that is, turn to speculative philosophy in place of a failed theology. The goal of philosophy, after all, is the cognition of truth, and God is the absolute truth. "Philosophy knows God essentially as concrete, as the spiritual, realized universality that is not jealous but communicates itself." The task of philosophy—or of the branch of philosophy that is theology (n. 58)—"is to show forth the rational content of religion." Likewise, Hegel concludes, the purpose of these lectures has been "to reconcile reason with religion in its manifold forms."

TRANSLATIONS AND NOTES

Existing translations are utilized for the selections from the early theological writings, the Jena writings, and the *Lectures on the Philosophy of Religion* (selections 1, 2, 6). These translations have been checked for accuracy and slightly revised to bring them into conformity with certain stylistic parameters of the present volume, namely the use of a "down" style for all common nouns and adjectives, the use of non-gendered language for deity, and the use of inclusive language for humans. The alteration of a few specific terms in translation is discussed in the notes to the individual selections. Terms for "being" are perennially troublesome in Hegel translations: *Sein* (being), *Dasein* (determinate being, existence), *Seiende(s)* (a being or entity, subsisting or actual being), and *Wesen* (being, essence, essential being).

The translation of selections from the *Phenomenology of Spirit*, the *Encyclopedia of the Philosophical Sciences*, and the Foreword to Hinrichs's *Religion* (selections 3, 4, 5) have been made especially for this volume by J. Michael Stewart and revised by Peter C. Hodgson (except for the final selection from the *Phenomenology*, which is translated by Hodgson). We have followed the translation principles and glossary established for our earlier work (with Robert F. Brown) on the *Lectures on the Philosophy of Religion*.[28]

Notes for the selections from the early theological writings and the Jena writings derive principally from the original translators (Fuss and Dobbins, Knox, Cerf and Harris, Harris and Knox). They have been supplemented or modified where appropriate by the present editor, but without specific indication to this effect. Notes for the selections from the *Phenomenology of Spirit* and the *Encyclopedia* are by Hodgson, drawing to some degree on the annotations to the new critical German editions of these works. Notes to the Hinrichs Foreword are also by Hodgson, incorporating some information provided by Eric von der Luft in his edition of Hinrichs's *Religion*. Notes for the *Lectures on the Philosophy of Religion* are adapted from the English edition; these in turn were originally prepared by Hodgson, with the assistance of Brown and Stewart, on the basis of the German critical edition by Walter Jaeschke.

SELECTED TEXTS
1

EARLY THEOLOGICAL WRITINGS
(1793–1800)

RELIGION IS ONE OF OUR GREATEST CONCERNS IN LIFE

This is one of Hegel's earliest essays, written at the age of 23 in 1793 while he was a student in the theological seminary at Tübingen. It was first published by Herman Nohl in Hegels theologische Jugendschriften *(Tübingen, 1907) as the first of several fragments to which Nohl gave the collective title "Volksreligion und Christentum." The remaining fragments were written while Hegel was a private tutor in Berne from 1793 to 1794. In these essays Hegel was concerned with how religion might become a vital, integrative, ethically transformative force in not only the personal life of individuals but also the cultural, social, and political life of a people (*Volk*), a concern that remained within him until his last days. The youthful Hegel was convinced that Christianity, in either dogmatic-supernaturalist or enlightened-rationalist dress, was no longer such a force, and for this reason he was attracted to the ancient Greek public or folk religion (*Volksreligion*). But he knew already in 1793–1794 that the Greek ethos could not be restored in the modern world (this "fair youth . . . has fled from the earth"), and this was just the dilemma that at the time seemed irresolvable. Gradually he became aware that one must come to terms with actuality as it presents itself to one's own time and place, and that the rational is always already present in it—"the rose in the cross of the present" demanding of us "hard labor," as he expressed it in the Preface to the* Philosophy of Right. *The later Hegel's hard labor was in part that of releasing the transformative power of Christianity from its dogmatic and rationalist encrustations. We see already in this early essay the extent to which Hegel was sensitive to the sensuous and cultic aspects of religion, and this helps to explain why later he insisted on the validity of sensible intuition (*Anschauung*) and imaginative representation (*Vorstellung*) as modes of apprehending truth, alongside that of the philosophical concept (*Begriff*).*

The title of our selection is from the first line of the essay, in accord with the practice of current Hegel scholarship for identifying untitled writings. The translation and notes (slightly revised and edited) are by Peter Fuss and John Dobbins in their volume Three Essays, 1793–1795: The Tübingen

Essay, Berne Fragments, The Life of Jesus *(Notre Dame: University of Notre Dame Press, 1984), pp. 30–58. These essays were omitted from T. M. Knox's partial translation of Nohl's edition. A more literal translation of the Tübingen essay is provided by H. S. Harris in* Hegel's Development: Toward the Sunlight, 1770–1801 *(Oxford: Clarendon Press, 1972), pp. 481–507; it has been consulted by Fuss and Dobbins. The translation has been modified for this volume to render it gender-inclusive, and Hegel's additions and deletions (footnoted by the translators) have generally been omitted.*

Religion is one of our greatest concerns in life. Even as children we were taught to stammer prayers to the deity, with our little hands folded for us so as to point up toward the supreme being. Our memories were laden with a mass of doctrines, incomprehensible at the time, designed for our future use and comfort in life. As we grow older, religious matters still fill up a good deal of our lives; indeed for some the whole circuit of their thoughts and aspirations is unified by religion in the way that a wheel's outer rim is linked to the hub. And we dedicate to our religion, in addition to other feast days, the first day of each week, which from earliest youth appears to us in a fairer and more festive light than all the other days. Moreover, we see in our midst a special class of people chosen exclusively for religious service; and all the more important events and undertakings in the lives of people, those on which their private happiness depends—birth, marriage, death and burial—have something religious mixed in with them.

But do people reflect as they become older on the nature and attributes of the being toward whom their sentiments are directed—or in particular on the relation of the world to that being? Human nature is so constituted that the practical element in sacred teaching, that in it which can motivate us to act and which becomes a source of consolation for us as well as the source of our knowledge of duty, is readily manifest to the uncorrupted human sensibility. On the other hand, the instruction (i.e., the concepts as well as everything only externally connected with [the practical]) that we receive from childhood on, and which accordingly makes such an impression on us, is something that is, as it were, grafted onto the natural need of the human spirit. Although this relation is frequently immediate enough, it is, alas, all too often capricious, grounded neither in bonds indigenous to the nature of the soul nor in truths created and developed out of the concepts . . . .[1]

We should not be so enthralled by the sublime demand of reason on humankind (the legitimacy of which we wholeheartedly acknowledge whenever our hearts happen to be filled with reason), or by alluring descriptions (the products of pure and lovely fantasy) of wise or innocent persons, as to ever hope to find very many such people in the real world, or to imagine that we might possess or behold this ethereal apparition here or anywhere else. [Were we not in fact so easily enthralled,] our sensibility would be less often clouded by a peevish disposition, by dissatisfaction with what we in fact encounter; nor would we be so terrified when we believe ourselves obliged to conclude that sensuality is the predominating element in all human action and striving. It is no easy matter to tell whether mere prudence or actual morality is the will's determining ground. Granted that the satisfaction of the instinct for happiness is the highest goal of life, if we but know how to calculate well enough, the results will outwardly appear the same as when the law of reason determines our will. However scrupulously a system of morality may require us to separate *in abstracto* pure morality from sensuality and make the latter more subservient to the former, when we consider the life of human beings as a whole we must make equally full allowance for their sensuality, for their dependence on external and internal nature (i.e., both on the surroundings in which they live and on their sensual inclinations and blind instinct).

But human nature is quickened, so to speak, solely by virtue of its rational ideas. Just as a dish well prepared is permeated by salt, which must impart its flavor to the whole without showing up in lumps—or even as light, which cannot be exhibited as a substance, nonetheless suffuses everything, showing its influence throughout all nature (e.g., breaking upon objects in various ways, thus giving them their shape, and generating wholesome air via plants, etc.)—so likewise do the ideas of reason animate the entire fabric of our sensual life and by their influence show forth our activity in its distinctive light. Indeed reason as such seldom reveals itself in its essence; and in its effect pervades everything like fine sand, giving each and every inclination and drive a coloring of its own.

By its very nature, religion is not merely a systematic investigation of God, God's attributes, the relation of the world and ourselves to God, and the permanence of our souls; we could learn all this by reason alone, or be aware of it by other means. Nor is religious knowledge merely a matter of history or argumentation. Rather, religion engages the heart. It influences our feelings and the determination of our will; and this is so in part because our duties and our laws obtain powerful reinforcement by being represented to us as laws of God, and in part because our notion of the exaltedness and goodness of God fills our hearts with admiration as well as with feelings of humility and gratitude. And so religion provides morality and the well-springs of its activity with a new and nobler impetus—it sets up a new and stronger dam against the pressure of sensual impulses. But if religious motives are to have an effect on sensuality, they too must be sensual; hence among sensual people religion itself is sensual. Of course such

41

motives, insofar as they are at all moral, lose a bit of their majesty. But they have thereby acquired such a human aspect, and have so perfectly adapted themselves to our feelings that, led by our hearts and lured on by the beauteous images of our fancy, we readily forget that cool reason disapproves of such images or indeed even forbids so much as comment on this sort of thing.

When we go on to speak of religion as public, we still of course take it to include the concepts of God and immortality as well as everything connected with them, but specifically insofar as these constitute the conviction of a whole people, influencing their actions and way of thinking. Moreover, we include the means whereby these ideas are both taught to the people and made to penetrate their hearts—a means concerned not only with the immediate (e.g., I refrain from stealing because God has forbidden it), but directed more especially to ends that, while removed from the immediate, must by and large be reckoned as more important. Among these we include the uplifting and ennobling of the spirit of a nation so as to awaken in its soul the so often dormant sense of its true worth, and to encourage a self-image colored with the gentler hues of goodness and humanity; for not only should it resist debasing itself or allowing itself to be degraded, but it should refuse to settle for being "merely" human.

Now although the main doctrines of the Christian religion have remained essentially the same since their inception, one doctrine or another has been, depending on the times and circumstances, left altogether in the dark, while some other doctrine has been given the limelight and, unduly emphasized at the expense of the one obscured, stretched much too far or interpreted much too narrowly. Yet it is the entire body of religious principles and the feelings flowing from them—above all the degree of strength with which these are able to influence modes of action—that is decisive in a folk religion. Upon an oppressed spirit, one which, under the burden of its chains, has lost its youthful vigor and begun to age, such religious ideas can have little impact. At the beginning of maturation the youthful spirit of a people feels its power and exults in its strength; it seizes hungrily upon any novelty (albeit never upon anything that would put fetters on its proud and free neck), and then typically tosses it aside in favor of something else. By contrast, an aging spirit is characterized by its firm attachment to tradition in every respect. It bears its fetters as an old man endures the gout, grumbling but unable to do more. It lets itself be pushed and shoved at its master's whim, and it is only half conscious when it enjoys itself—not free, open, and bright with the appealing gaiety that invites camaraderie. Moreover, its festivals are but occasions for chatter, since old folk prefer gossip to everything else. Here there is no boisterousness, no full-blooded enjoyment.

Exposition of the Difference between Objective and Subjective Religion;
The Importance of This Exposition in View of the Entire Question

Objective religion is *fides quae creditur* [the faith that is believed]; under-standing and memory are the powers that do the work, investigating facts, thinking them through, retaining and even believing them. Objective religion can also possess practical knowledge, but only as a sort of frozen capital. It is susceptible to organizational schemes; it can be systematized, set forth in books, and expounded discursively. Subjective religion on the other hand expresses itself only in feelings and actions. If I say of someone that he has religion, this does not mean that he is well schooled in it, but rather that his heart feels the active presence, the wonder, the closeness of the deity, that his heart knows or sees God in nature and in the destinies of humans, that he prostrates himself before God, thanking God and glorifying God in all that God does. The actions of such an individual are not per-formed merely with an eye to whether they are good or prudent, but are motivated also by the thought: *This is pleasing to God*—which is often the strongest motive. When something pleases him or when he has good for-tune he directs a glance at God, thanking God for it. Subjective religion is thus alive, having an efficacy that, while abiding within one's being, is actively directed outward. Subjective religion is something individual, objective religion a matter of abstraction. The former is the living book of nature, of plants, insects, birds and beasts living with and surviving off each other—each responsive to the joys of living, all of them intermingled, their various species everywhere together. The latter is the cabinet of the natural-ist, full of insects he has killed, plants that are desiccated, animals stuffed or preserved in alcohol; what nature had kept totally apart is here lined up side by side; and whereas nature had joined an infinite variety of purposes in a convivial bond, here everything is ordered to but a single purpose.

The entire body of religious knowledge belonging to objective religion, then, can be the same for a large mass of people, and in principle could be so across the face of the earth. But having been woven into the fabric of sub-jective religion, it comprises only a small and relatively ineffectual part of it, and in fact varies within each individual. For subjective religion the chief question is whether and to what extent our sensibility is inclined to let itself be determined by religious impulses, i.e., how susceptible are we to religion sensually; then further, what makes an especially strong impression upon the heart, what kinds of feelings are most cultivated in the soul and hence most readily elicited. Some people have no feeling whatever for the more tender representations of love, so that impulses derived from the love of God sim-ply do not affect their hearts; the organs with which they feel are rather more blunt, being roused only by the stimulus of fear (thunder, lightning, etc.). The chords of their hearts simply do not resonate to the gentle stroke of love.

Other people are deaf to the voice of duty; it is quite useless to try to call their attention to the inner judge of actions which supposedly presides in humanity's own heart, i.e., to conscience itself. In them no such voice is ever heard; rather, self-interest is the pendulum whose swinging keeps their machine running. It is this disposition, this receptivity that determines how in each individual subjective religion is to be constituted.

We are schooled in objective religion from childhood, and our memory is laden with it all too soon, so that the as yet supple understanding, the fine and delicate plant of an open and free sensibility, is often crushed by the burden. As the roots of the plant work their way through loose soil, they absorb what they can, sucking nourishment as they go; but when diverted by a stone they seek another path. So here, too, when the burden heaped on memory cannot be dissolved, the now sturdier powers of the soul either shake loose of it altogether or simply bypass it without drinking in any nourishment.

Yet in each person nature has planted at least the seed of finer sentiments, whose source is morality itself; she has implanted in everyone a feeling for what is moral, for ends beyond those attaching to mere sensuality. It is the task of education, of culture, to see to it that this precious seed is not choked out and is allowed to sprout into a genuine receptivity for moral ideas and feelings. And religion, precisely because it cannot be the first to take root in our sensibility, needs to find this already cultivated soil before it can flourish.

Everything depends on subjective religion; this is what has inherent and true worth. Let the theologians squabble all they like over what belongs to objective religion, over its dogmas and their precise determination: the fact is that every religion is based on a few fundamental principles which, although set forth in the different religions in varying degrees of purity, however modified or adulterated, are nonetheless the basis of all the faith and hope that religion is capable of offering us. When I speak of religion here, I am abstracting completely from all scientific (or rather metaphysical) knowledge of God, as well as from the relationship of the world and ourselves to God, etc; such knowledge, the province of discursive understanding, is theology and no longer religion. And I classify as religious only such knowledge of God and immortality as is responsive to the demands of practical reason and connected with it in a readily discernible way. (This does not preclude more detailed disclosures of special divine arrangements on humanity's behalf.) Further, I here discuss objective religion only insofar as it is a component of subjective religion. But I do not intend to investigate which religious teachings are of the greatest interest to the heart or can give the soul the most comfort and encouragement; nor how the doctrines of any particular religion must be constituted if they are to make a

44

people better and happier. Rather my concern is with what needs to be done so that religion with all the force of its teaching might be blended into the fabric of human feelings, bonded with what moves us to act, and shown to be efficacious, thus enabling religion to become entirely subjective.

When it actually is so, it reveals its presence not merely by hands clasped together, knees bent, and heart humbled before the holy, but by the way it suffuses the entire scope of human inclination (without the soul being directly conscious of it) and makes its presence felt everywhere—although only mediately or, if I may so express it, negatively, in and through the cheerful enjoyment of human satisfactions. Subjective religion's role in the performance of the nobler deeds and the exercise of the finer, philanthropic virtues is not, to be sure, a direct one; its influence is discreet, it lets the soul carry on these tasks freely and openly without inhibiting the spontaneity of its actions. Any expression of human powers, whether of courage or considerateness, cheerfulness or delight in life itself, requires freedom from an ill-natured tendency toward envy along with a conscience that is clear and not guilt-ridden; and religion helps foster both of these qualities. Furthermore, its influence is also felt insofar as innocence, when combined with it, is able to find the exact point at which delight in extravagance, high-spiritedness, and firmness of resolve would degenerate into assaults upon the rights of others.

Subjective Religion

Inasmuch as theology (whatever its source, even if in religion) is a matter of understanding and memory, while religion is a concern of the heart stemming from a need of practical reason, it is clear that the powers of the soul activated in each of them differ considerably, and that our sensibility has to be made receptive in a different way for each. For our hope to be vindicated that the highest good—one dimension of which we are duty-bound to actualize—will become actual in its totality, our practical reason demands belief in a divinity, in immortality.

This, at any rate, is the seed from which religion springs. But when religion is thus derived, it is in fact conscience (the inner sense of right and wrong, as well as the feeling that wrong-doing must incur punishment and welldoing merit happiness) whose elements are being analyzed and articulated in clear concepts. Now, it may well be that the idea of a mighty and invisible being first took root in the human soul on the occasion of some fearful natural phenomenon; God may first have revealed godself through weather that made everyone feel God's presence more closely—if only in the gentle rustling of the evening breeze. Be that as it may, the human soul eventually experienced a moral feeling such that it found in the idea of religion something that answered to its need.

Religion is sheer superstition whenever I seek to derive from it specific grounds for action in situations where mere prudence is sufficient, or when fear of divinity makes me perform certain actions by means of which I imagine that it might be placated. No doubt this is how religion is constituted among many a sensual people. Their representation of God and how God deals with human beings is bound to the idea that God acts in accordance with the laws of human sensibility and acts upon their sensuality. There is little of the truly moral in this notion. However, the concept of God and my recourse to God (worship) is already more moral—hinting at consciousness of a higher order, determined by nonsensual ends (even though superstitions like the above may still be involved)—when my feeling that everything depends on God's decision leads me to beseech God's support concerning the eventual outcome of an undertaking, when my belief in God's dispensing good fortune only to the just and inflicting misfortune on the unjust and presumptuous becomes at least as pervasive as belief in fate or in natural necessity, and when religion at last gives rise to principles of moral conduct.

While objective religion can take on most any color, subjective religion among good people is basically the same: what makes me a Christian in your eyes makes you a Jew in mine, Nathan says.[2] For religion is a matter of the heart, which often deals inconsistently with the dogmas congenial to understanding and memory. Surely the worthiest people are not always those who have done the most speculating about religion, who are given to transforming their religion into theology, and who are in the habit of replacing the fullness and warmth of faith with cold cognitions and deft displays of verbal dexterity.

Religion in fact acquires very little through the understanding, whose operations and skeptical tendencies are more likely to chill than warm the heart. And whoever finds that other peoples' modes of representation—heathens, as they are called—contain so much absurdity that they cause him to delight in his own higher insights, his own understanding, which convinces him that he sees further than the greatest of humans saw, does not comprehend the essence of religion. Someone who calls his Jehovah Jupiter or Brahma and is truly pious offers his gratitude or his sacrifice in just as childlike a manner as does the true Christian. Who is not moved by the splendid simplicity and guilelessness of someone who, when nature has bestowed its goods on him, thinks at once of his greatest benefactor and offers him the best, the most flawless, the first-born of his grain and sheep? Who does not admire Coriolanus who, at the apex of his good fortune, was mindful of Nemesis, and asked the gods (much as Gustavus Adolphus humbled himself before God during the battle of Luetzen) not to glorify the spirit of Roman greatness but rather to make him more humble?

Such dispositions are for the heart and are meant to be enjoyed by it with simplicity of spirit and feeling, rather than be criticized by the cold understanding. Only an arrogant sectarian, fancying himself wiser than all persons of other parties, could fail to appreciate the guileless last wish of Socrates to have a rooster delivered to the god of health, could remain unmoved by the beauty of his feeling in thanking the gods for death, which he regarded as a kind of convalescence, or could bring himself to make the malicious remark offered by Tertullian.[3]

A heart that does not speak louder than the understanding (unlike that of the friar in the scene from *Nathan* above), or that just keeps silent, allowing the understanding all the time it needs to rationalize some course of action—a heart like that isn't worth much to begin with: there is no love in it. Nowhere do we find a finer contrast between the voice of uncorrupted feeling, i.e., a pure heart, and the obstinacy of the understanding than in the Gospels. With what warmth and affection Jesus allows a woman of former ill-repute to anoint his body, accepting this spontaneous outpouring of a beautiful soul which, filled with remorse, trust, and love, refuses to be inhibited by the rabble around her. And this even as several apostles who are too cold of heart to empathize with her deepest feeling, her beautiful gift of trust, belie their pretensions to charitableness by indulging in cutting side-remarks.

What a sterile and unnatural observation it is that good old Gellert makes someplace (much like Tertullian, *Apologia*, ch. 46: *deum quilibet opifex*)[4] to the effect that a small child nowadays knows more about God than the wisest heathen. This is as if the treatise on morality I have sitting in my closet—which I can use to wrap up a stinking cheese if I see fit—were of greater value than the perhaps at times unjust heart of a Frederick the Second. For in this respect the difference between Tertullian's *opifex*, or Gellert's child who has had the theological leaven beaten into him along with the catechism, and the paper containing moral pronouncements is on the whole not very great. A genuine consciousness acquired through experience is lacking in them to nearly the same degree. . . .[5]

The difference between a pure religion of reason, which worships God in spirit and in truth, affirming that God is served through virtue alone, and an idolatrous faith, which imagines it can curry God's favor by some means other than a will that is in itself good, is so great that in comparison the latter is utterly worthless. In fact the two are completely different in kind. It is nonetheless of the utmost importance for us to discourage any fetishistic mode of belief, to make it more and more like a rational religion. Yet a universal church of the spirit remains a mere ideal of reason; and it is hardly possible to establish a public religion that would really do everything it could to rid itself of fetishistic belief. So the question naturally arises: How would a folk religion have to be constituted so that (*a*) negatively, the opportunity for people to become fixated on the letter and the conventions of religion would be minimized, and (*b*) positively, the people would be guided toward a religion of reason and become receptive to it?

Whenever moral philosophy posits the idea of saintliness as consisting of moral conduct at its highest, of moral exertion to the fullest, the objection will be raised that such an idea is beyond human attainment (which the moral philosophers themselves concede) because human beings need motives other than pure respect for the moral law, motives more closely bound up with their sensuality. Such an objection does not prove that humans ought not to strive, for all eternity if need be, to approximate to this idea, but merely that, given our crudeness and our powerful propensity toward the sensual, one ought to be content to elicit from most people a mere legality that does not demand the kind of purely moral motives (cf. Matt. 19:16) for which they feel little or no affinity. Nor does such an objection deny that much has already been gained if crude sensuality is at least in some way refined and *some* interest in higher things is aroused—if propensities are awakened other than sheer animal drives, ones more amenable to the influence of reason and approximating to morality a little more closely. For in this way it is at least possible that, whenever the clamor of the senses dies down a little, moral dispositions might begin to make their presence known. In fact it is generally conceded that cultivation of *any* kind would already be a gain. Hence what this objection really comes down to is that it is altogether unlikely that humankind, or even a single individual, will ever in this world be able to dispense entirely with nonmoral promptings.

Now we do in fact have a number of feelings, woven into our very nature, which do not arise out of respect for the law and hence are not moral, which are inconstant and unstable and do not deserve respect because of any inherent worth, but which are nevertheless to be cherished because they serve to inhibit evil dispositions and even help bring out the best in us. All the benign inclinations (sympathy, benevolence, friendliness, etc.) are of this sort. But this empirical aspect of our character, confined as it is to the arena of the inclinations, does contain a moral sentiment bent on weaving its delicate thread throughout the entire fabric. Indeed the fundamental principle of our empirical character is love, which is somewhat analogous to reason in that it finds itself in other people. Forgetting about itself, love is able to step outside of a given individual's existence and live, feel, and act no less fully in others—just as reason, the principle of universally valid laws, recognizes its own self in the shared citizenship each rational being has in an intelligible world. The empirical character of human beings is still of course affected by desire and aversion; but love, even though as a principle of action it is subrational,[6] is not self-serving. It does not do the right thing merely because it has calculated that the satisfactions resulting from its course of action are purer and longer lasting than those resulting from sensuality or the gratification of some passion. This principle, then, is not refined self-love, in which the ego is in the end always the highest goal.

Empiricism is of course absolutely useless in the establishment of foundational principles. But when it comes to having an effect on people, we must take them as they are, seeking out every decent drive and sentiment through which, albeit without directly enhancing their freedom, their nature can be ennobled. In a folk religion in particular it is of the utmost importance that the imagination and the heart not be left unsatisfied: the imagination must be filled with large and pure images, and the heart roused to feelings of benevolence. Setting these on a sound course is all the more crucial in the context of religion, whose object is so great and sublime; for both the heart and the imagination all too easily strike out on paths of their own or let themselves be led astray. The heart is seduced by false notions and by its own indolence; it becomes attached to externals, or finds sustenance in feelings of false modesty, thinking that with these it serves God. And the imagination, taking to be cause and effect what is merely accidental, comes to expect the most extraordinary and unnatural results. Human beings are such many-sided creatures that anything can be made of them; the intricately woven fabric of their feelings has so many strands that there is nothing that cannot be attached to it at some point. This is why they have been capable of the silliest superstitions, and of the greatest ecclesiastical[7] and political slavery. Folk religion's primary task is to weave these fine strands into a noble union suitable to their nature.

The main difference between folk religion and private religion is one of aim. Through the mighty influence it exerts on the imagination and the heart, folk religion imbues the soul with power and enthusiasm, with a spirit indispensable for the noble exercise of virtue. On the other hand, the training of individuals in keeping with their character, counsel in situations where duties conflict, special inducements to virtue, comfort and care in the face of personal suffering and misfortune—all such things must be left to private religion. That this is not the concern of a public folk religion is evident from the following considerations:

(*a*) Situations that involve a conflict of duties are so complex that I can satisfy my conscience only by falling back on the counsel of upright and experienced persons or by recourse to the conviction that [come what may] duty and virtue constitute the highest principle of conduct—assuming of course that this conviction has been in some way established by public religion and so become available to me as a maxim of action. But public instruction, like the moral training mentioned above, is too tedious; and not even this conviction is in the least capable of making us amenable in the moment of action to hair-splitting casuistical rules. If it were, the result would be a perpetual scrupulosity quite contrary to the resoluteness and strength requisite for virtuous action.

(b) If virtue is not the product of indoctrination and empty rhetoric but is rather a plant which, albeit with proper tending, grows out of one's own driving force and power, then the various arts invented allegedly to produce virtue as though in a hothouse (where it would be incapable of failure) actually do more damage to people than just letting them grow wild. By its very nature public religious instruction involves not only an attempt to enlighten the understanding concerning the idea of God and our relation to God, but also an effort to make our obligations to God the ground of all other duties, whereby the latter become at once more urgent and more binding. But there is something strained and farfetched about this derivation. It involves a relationship whose connection only the understanding comprehends, one that tends to be rather forced and is not at all evident, at least to common sense. Ordinarily, the more inducements we are offered for doing our duty, the cooler we become toward it.

(c) The only true comfort in suffering (for pain [*Schmerzen*][8] there is no comfort; strength of soul is all that can be pitted against it) is trust in divine providence. Everything else is idle talk which the heart does not heed.

How is a folk religion to be constituted? (Here folk religion is understood in an objective sense.)

(a) With respect to objective religion.

(b) With respect to ceremonies.

A.   I.   Its teachings must be founded on universal reason.

     II.   Imagination, the heart, and the senses must not go away empty-handed in the process.

    III.   It must be so constituted that all of life's needs, including public and official transactions, are bound up with it.

B.   What must it avoid?

Fetishistic beliefs, including one that is especially common in our prolix age, namely the belief that the demands of reason are satisfied by means of tirades against enlightenment and the like. As a result, people are endlessly at loggerheads over points of dogma without doing anything constructive either for themselves or for anyone else.

I

The doctrines [of a folk religion], even if resting on the authority of some divine revelation, must of necessity be constituted so that they are actually authorized by the universal reason of humanity, whereby one is no sooner made aware of them than one perceives and recognizes their binding force. For even if such doctrines either claim to furnish special means of obtaining God's favor or promise all sorts of privileged insights and detailed information concerning otherwise inaccessible matters, the disclosures they provide are intended to serve one's rational intellect, not just one's fantasy. Moreover, since doctrines such as these sooner or later come under fire from thinking persons and end up as objects of controversy, our practical interest in them invariably gets misdirected as the endless bickering of various factions issues in rigid symbols expressive of little but their own intolerance. And since these doctrines remain unnatural in their link to the true needs and demands of rationality, they lend themselves to abuses, especially as they become ingrained and hardened through habit. Surely they could never of themselves gain sufficient weight in human feeling to be a pure and genuine force in direct alignment with morality.

But the doctrines must also be simple; and indeed they are simple, if only they be truths of reason, because as such they require neither the machinery of erudition nor a display of laborious demonstrations. By virtue of such simplicity, they would exert all the more power and impact on our sensibility, on the determination of our will to act; thus concentrated, they would have a far greater influence and play a much bigger part in cultivating a people's spirit than is the case when commandments are piled up and ordered artificially so as always to be in need of many exceptions.

At the same time, these universal doctrines must be designed for humans, i.e., must be in keeping with the level of morality and spiritual cultivation attainable by a given people—which is no easy task to determine. Some of the noblest—and for humankind most interesting—ideas are scarcely suitable for adoption as universal maxims. They appear to be appropriate only for a handful of ripened individuals who, having endured many trials, have already succeeded in attaining wisdom. In such individuals they have become sure beliefs, and in situations where such beliefs are truly supportive they have become matters of unshakable conviction. Thus, for instance, the belief in a wise and benevolent providence: when it is alive and of the right sort, it goes hand in hand with the complete acceptance of God's will.

Now this tenet and everything connected with it is also undeniably the main doctrine of the whole Christian community, whose teachings in general reduce to the all-transcending love of God toward which everything moves. Day in and day out God is represented to us as being ever present and close by, as bringing about everything that goes on around us. And this is not just represented as being somehow necessarily linked with our morality and everything we hold sacred, it is even given out as a matter of complete certainty on the basis of the abundant assurances God provides us and through all the deeds God performs to convince us of it incontrovertibly. And yet as experience teaches, a mere thunderclap or a cold night can cause the masses to become very faint-hearted in their trust in divine providence and in their patient submission to God's will, it evidently being only within the capability of the wise man to quell impatience and anger over frustrated hopes, and to overcome despair over misfortunes. Such abrupt abandonment of trust in God, this sudden changeover to dissatisfaction with God, is facilitated not only by accustoming the Christian populace from childhood on to pray incessantly, but even more by forever seeking to persuade it of the most urgent necessity for doing so through promises that such prayers will surely to some degree be answered.

Moreover, suffering humanity has been furnished with such a motley assortment of reasons for proffering solace in misfortunes that in the end one might well come to regret not having a father or mother to lose once a week, or not being struck blind. With incredible acuity, this way of thinking has taken to pursuing and pondering over the wildest range of physical and moral effects. And since these were alleged to be the designs of providence, it was supposed that one had herewith attained keener insight into its plans for humankind, both in the broad perspective and in detail. But no sooner do we lose patience with this, unwilling to merely lay our finger across our lips and lapse into awe-stricken silence, than we tend to find ourselves prey to an arrogant inquisitiveness that presumes to nothing short of mastery of the ways of providence—a propensity reinforced (though not among the common people) by the many idealistic notions currently in vogue. All of which contributes little indeed to the furthering of contentment with life in general and acquiescence in God's will.

It might be interesting to compare all of this with what the Greeks believed. On the one hand, their faith—that the gods favor those who are good, and leave evildoers to the tender mercies of a frightful Nemesis—was based on a profoundly moral demand of reason and lovingly animated by the warm breath of their feelings, rather than on the cold conviction, deduced from single instances, that everything turns out for the best (a conviction that can never truly come alive). On the other hand, among them misfortune was misfortune, pain was pain. What had happened could not be altered. There was no point in brooding over whatever such things might mean, since their *moira*, their *anangkaia tychē*,[9] was blind. But then they submitted to this necessity willingly and with all possible resignation. And at least this much can be said in their favor: one endures more easily what one has been accustomed from childhood on to regard as necessary, and that the pain and suffering to which misfortune naturally gives birth did not occasion in them the much more burdensome and unbearable anger, the despondency and discontent we feel. This faith, since it embraced not only respect for the course of natural necessity but also the conviction that humans are governed by the gods in accordance with moral laws, seems humanly in keeping with the exaltedness of the divine and the frailty of humans in their limited perspective and dependence on nature.

Doctrines that are simple and founded upon universal reason are compatible with every stage of popular education. And the latter comes gradually to modify the former in accordance with its own transformations, albeit more with respect to its external effects, i.e., those having to do with what the sensuous imagination depicts.

In keeping with how they are constituted, these doctrines, if they are founded on universal human reason, can have no other purpose than to influence the spirit of a people in but a general way—and to do so partly in and of themselves and partly through the closely connected magic of powerfully impressive ceremonies. They have no business interfering in the execution of civil justice or usurping the role of one's private conscience. Nor, since the way in which they are formulated is simple as well, will they easily give rise to squabbles over their meaning. And, since they demand and stipulate very little that is positive (reason's legislation being in any event merely formal), the lust for power on the part of the priests of such a religion remains circumscribed.

II

Any religion purporting to be a folk religion must be so constituted that it engages the heart and imagination. Even the purest religion of reason must become incarnate in the souls of individuals, and all the more so in the people as a whole. In order that our fantasy be given a proper outlet, one orienting it onto a path it can decorate with its beautiful flowers without drifting off into romantic extravagances, it would be best to tie myths to the religion itself from the very outset. Now the doctrines of the Christian religion are for the most part tied to history and represented historically. The stage, even if other than mere humans acted on it, is set here in this mundane realm. Thus our imagination is provided with a readily discernible goal. To be sure, our imagination is still given some room to rove: if colored with black bile it can paint a frightful world for itself, or—since the spirit of our religion has banished all the beautiful colorations of sense as well as everything that has charm, even while we have become far too much people of words and reason to take much delight in beautiful images—it may well lapse into childishness.

With regard to ceremonies, on the one hand no folk religion is conceivable without them; on the other, nothing is harder to prevent than their being taken by the populace at large for the essence of religion itself. Now religion consists of three things: (*a*) concepts, (*b*) essential customs, and (*c*) ceremonies. Thus if we regard baptism and the eucharist as rites involving certain extraordinary benefits and indulgences which we as Christians are duty-bound to perform so as to become more perfect, more moral, then they belong to the third class. Sacrifices belong here too; but they cannot properly be called ceremonies, for they are essential to the religion with which they are connected. They are part of its structure, whereas ceremonies are mere embellishments, the formal aspect of this structure.

Sacrifices themselves can be looked at from two perspectives:

(*a*) In part they were brought to the altars of the gods as propitiation, as atonement, as an attempt either to commute a much-feared physical or moral punishment into a fine or to ingratiate oneself into the lost favor of the supreme lord, the dispenser of rewards and punishments. Such practices are of course deemed unworthy and rightly censured on grounds of their irrationality and their adulteration of the whole concept of morality. But we have to keep in mind that an idea of sacrifice as crass as this has never really gained ascendancy anywhere (except perhaps in the Christian church),[10] and we have to appreciate the value of the feelings activated in the process, even if they were not pure: a solemn awe of the holy being, a contrite heart humbly prostrated before him, and the deep trust that drove a troubled soul crying out for peace to this anchor. Think of a pilgrim burdened by the weight of his sins. He has left behind the comforts of home, his wife and children, his native soil, to wander through the world barefoot and clad in a hair-shirt. He hunts for impassable tracts to torment his feet. He sprinkles the holy places with his tears. Seeking repose for his ravaged spirit, he finds relief in every tear shed, in every mortification. He is urged on by the thought "Here Christ walked, here he was crucified for me," a thought from which he gains renewed strength, renewed self-confidence. But is it really for us, incapable of such a state of mind merely because of other notions prevalent in our time, to react to such a pilgrim and such simplicity of heart with the Pharisaic sentiment "Well, I am more sensible than people like that"? Is it for us to heap ridicule upon his pious sentiments? Then again, expiatory pilgrimages like this do form a subspecies of precisely the sort of sacrifice I was speaking of above, being offered up in the very same spirit as those penances.

(*b*) But there is another, milder spirit of sacrifice, one germinating in a gentler latitude, that was probably the more original and universal. It was based on gratitude and benevolence. Filled with the sense of a being[11] higher than the human, and aware of its indebtedness to this being for every-

thing, it was confident that it would not scorn what was offered it in all innocence. It was disposed to implore the help of this being at the outset of every
undertaking, and to sense its presence in every joyous experience, every
good fortune attained. Thinking of Nemesis before partaking of any pleasure, it offered to its god the first fruits, the flower of every possession, invit-
ing him into its home confident that he would abide there willingly. The
frame of mind that offered such a sacrifice was far removed from any notion
of having hereby atoned for its sins or expiated some portion of their justly
deserved punishment. Nor did its conscience persuade it that in this manner
Nemesis might be appeased and induced to give up not only her claims on it
but her laws governing the restoration of moral equilibrium as well.

Essential practices like these need not be bound more closely to religion
than to the spirit of the people; it is preferable that they actually spring from
the latter. Otherwise their exercise is without life, cold and powerless, and
the attendant feelings artificial and forced. On the other hand it may be that
these are practices that are not essential to folk religion anyway, although
they may be to private religion. Thus for instance we have the eucharist as
it exists in its present form throughout Christendom, although originally it
was intended as a meal for communal enjoyment.

The indispensable characteristics of ceremonies designed for a folk religion are:

(*a*)[12] First and foremost, that they contain little or no inducement to
fetishistic worship—that they not consist of a mere mechanical operation
devoid of spirit. Their sole aim must be to intensify devotion and pious sentiments. Perhaps the only pure means for eliciting such an effect, the one
least susceptible to misuse, is sacred music and the song of an entire people—perhaps also folk festivals, in which religion is inevitably involved.

III

As soon as any sort of wall is put between doctrine and life—as soon as
they become in any way separated or lose touch with each other—we begin
suspecting that there is something wrong with the very form of this religion. Perhaps it is too preoccupied with empty verbiage. Perhaps excessive
and hypocritical demands are being made on the people, demands repug-
nant to their natural needs, to the impulses of a well-ordered sensibility (*tēs
sophrosynēs*).[13] Or possibly both at once. If a religion makes people feel
shame over their moments of joy and merriment, if someone has to slink
into the temple because he has made a spectacle of himself at a public festival, then its outer form is too forbidding for it to expect anyone to give up
life's pleasures in favor of its demands.

A folk religion must be a friend to all life's feelings; it should never
intrude, but should seek to be a welcome guest everywhere. And if it is to

have real effect on a people, it must also be their companion—supportive of their undertakings and the more serious concerns of their lives as well as of their festivals and times of fun. It must not appear obtrusive, must not become a nagging schoolmarm, but rather initiate and encourage. The folk festivals of the Greeks were all religious festivals, and were held either in honor of a god or of a man deified because of his exemplary service to his country. They consecrated everything, even their bacchantic excesses, to some deity; and the dramas they staged in the public theater had a religious origin which they never disavowed, even as they became more cultivated. Thus, for instance, Agathon did not forget the gods when he carried off a prize for his tragedy; the very next day he arranged a feast for them (*Sympos.*, p. 168).[14]

A folk religion—engendering and nurturing, as it does, great and noble sentiments—goes hand in hand with freedom. But our religion would train people to be citizens of heaven, gazing ever upward, making our most human feelings seem alien. Indeed at the greatest of our public feasts we proceed to the enjoyment of the holy eucharist dressed in colors of mourning and with eyes downcast; even here, at what is supposed to be a celebration of human brotherhood, we fear we might contract venereal disease from the brother who drank out of the communal chalice before. And lest any of us remain attentive to the ceremony, filled with a sense of the sacred, we are nudged to fetch a donation from our pocket and plop it on a tray. How different were the Greeks! They approached the altars of their friendly gods clad in the colors of joy, their faces, open invitations to friendship and love, beaming with good cheer.

The spirit of a nation is reflected in its history, its religion, and the degree of its political freedom; and these cannot be taken in isolation when considering either the individual character or their influence on each other. They are bound together as one, like three companions none of whom can do anything without the others even as each benefits from all. The improvement of individual morality is a matter involving one's private religion, one's parents, one's personal efforts, and one's individual situation. The cultivation of the spirit of the people as a whole requires in addition the respective contributions of folk religion and political institutions.[15]

Ah, to the soul that retains a feeling for human splendor, for greatness in great things, there radiates from distant bygone days an unforgettable image. It is the picture of the genie [*Genius*] of nations, son of fortune and freedom, pupil of a fine imagination. He too was tied to mother earth by the brazen fetters of basic need. But by means of his sensibility and imagination he cultivated, refined, and beautified them to such an extent that, garlanded with roses given by the Graces, he was able in the midst of these chains to take delight in them as his own handiwork, as part of his own self.

His servants were joy, gaiety, and poise, and his soul was suffused with the consciousness of its power and freedom. But his more intimate playmates were friendship and love—not the wood faun but sensitive, soulful Amor, adorned with all the allurements of the heart and of sweet dreams.

Thanks to his father, himself a favorite of Fortune and a son of Force, he had ample trust in his own destiny and took pride in his deeds. His warm-hearted mother, never harsh or reproachful, left her son to nature's nurturing; good mother that she was, she refused to cramp his delicate limbs in tight swaddling. She would rather play along with the moods and inspirations of her darling than think to curb them; in harmony with these, his nurse [i.e. religion] reared this child without fear of the rod or ghosts in the dark, without the bittersweet honey bread of mysticism or the fetters of words which would keep him perpetually immature. Instead she had him drink the clear and healthful milk of pure sensations. With the flowers of her fine and free imagination she adorned the impenetrable veil that removes the deity from our gaze, conjuring up behind it a realm inhabited by living images onto which he projected the great ideas his heart brings forth in all the fullness of its noble and beautiful sentiments. Just as the nanny in ancient Greece was a friend of the family and remained a friend of her charge the rest of her life, so his nurse [again, religion] remains his friend even while he, unspoiled as he is, freely expresses his gratitude and returns her love. A good companion, she shares in his pleasures and takes part in his games; and he in turn never finds her a bother. Yet she always maintains her dignity; and his conscience rebels whenever he slights it. Her dominion holds sway forever, for it is based on the love, the gratitude, the noblest feelings of her ward. She has coaxed their refinement along, she has obeyed his imagination's every whim—yet she has taught him to respect iron necessity, she has taught him to conform to this unalterable destiny without murmur.

We know this genie [*Genius*] only by hearsay. We have only a few traces on a handful of surviving reproductions that enable us to contemplate and lovingly admire his likeness; and these can but awaken a painful longing for the original. He—the fair youth we love even in his more light-hearted moments, when among the whole retinue of the Graces he inhales from every flower the balsam breath of nature, the soul that they had breathed into it—has fled from the earth.[16]

THE DIVINE IN A PARTICULAR SHAPE

In his early writings, Hegel explored and tested several religious options. During the Tübingen years (1788–1793), it was primarily the ideal of a folk religion, as seen from our first selection. While in Berne (1793–1796), Kant's religion of morality had a major impact and served as the basis of Hegel's critique of the "positivity" (the historical, institutional, and dogmatic forms) of the Christian religion. After moving to Frankfurt in 1796, however, Hegel sought a "spiritual" enrichment of both folk religion and the Enlightenment. Richard Kroner suggests[1] that if the soul of Greek religion was beauty, and if the reason of Kantian philosophy was morality, then Hegel concluded that the ultimate truth was moral or spiritual beauty, and this truth he discovered in the Christian Gospel in the form of love—a love that assumed concrete shape in the figure of Jesus. This is the thesis of the essays collected by Nohl under the title "The Spirit of Christianity and Its Fate" (written over a period of several months in 1798–1799). Judaism now replaced institutional Christianity as the epitome of a positive religion based on moral obedience and the utter transcendence of the absolute. Later Hegel came to a more affirmative assessment of Judaism, but in these early essays it was portrayed in almost entirely negative terms, even if it served as the spiritual home for the birth of Christianity. Jesus was a Jew who penetrated to the inner truth of Judaism and transformed it into a religion of spiritual love.

Our selection is from the fourth essay in this group. Knox calls it "The Religious Teaching of Jesus," but for a title we have adopted a suggestive phrase that occurs within the essay, "The divine in a particular shape [Gestalt] appears as a human being." In this section Hegel is preoccupied with the relationship of the divine and the human (a relationship that is "life itself") as it comes to expression in the teaching and person of Jesus. Drawing especially on the Gospel of John, he offers both a critique and a reconstruction of the doctrine of the incarnation—a doctrine that, he remarks later (in the philosophy of religion lectures), is the "speculative midpoint" of philosophy.

In the first essay comprising "The Spirit of Christianity and Its Fate," Hegel summarizes the spirit of Judaism as epitomized in the radical "servitude" of Abraham. In the second and third, he examines two aspects of the moral teaching of Jesus: the Sermon on the Mount is contrasted with the Mosaic law and Kant's ethic, and love is proclaimed as the transcendence of penal justice and the reconciliation of opposites. In the final essay, following our selection, he addresses the fate of Jesus and the church, that fate being an unresolved contradiction between the inner truth of the Gospel and the exigencies of the external world. The dilemma from Hegel's point of view was that the spiritual freedom envisioned by the Gospel could not be actualized in ethical and political reality.

Source: Early Theological Writings, *translated by T. M. Knox, with an introduction and fragments translated by Richard Kroner (Chicago: University of Chicago Press, 1948; r.p.: University of Pennsylvania Press, 1971), selections from pp. 253–81. The translation has been checked against the German text,* Hegels theologische Jugendschriften, *ed. Herman Nohl (Tübingen, 1907), pp. 302–24, and at a few places modified. The italicization that Knox introduced into the text is not retained. For this edition the translation has been rendered gender-inclusive, and biblical passages are given in modern English (following the NRSV) with references added in brackets when necessary. Hegel's biblical quotations and allusions are sometimes imprecise; they are translated here as he gives them.*

. . . To the Jewish idea of God as their lord and governor, Jesus opposes a relationship of God to human beings like that of a father to his children.

Morality cancels domination within the sphere of consciousness; love cancels the barriers in the sphere of morality; but love itself is still incomplete in nature. In the moments of happy love there is no room for objectivity; yet every reflection annuls love, restores objectivity again, and with objectivity we are once more on the territory of restrictions. What is religious, then, is the *plērōma* [fulfillment] of love; it is reflection and love united, bound together in thought. Love's intuition seems to fulfil the demand for completeness; but there is a contradiction. Intuition, representative thinking, is something restrictive, something receptive only of something restricted; but here the object intuited [God] would be something infinite. The infinite cannot be carried in this vessel.

To conceive of pure life means trying to abstract from every deed, from everything which the human being was or will be. Character is an abstraction from activity alone; it means the universal behind specific actions. Consciousness of pure life would be consciousness of what humanity is, and in it there is no differentiation and no developed or actualized multiplicity. This simplicity is not a negative simplicity, a unity produced by abstraction (since in such a unity either we have simply the positing of one determinate thing in abstraction from all other determinacies, or else its pure unity is only the negatively indeterminate, i.e., the posited demand for abstraction from everything determinate. Pure life is being). Plurality is nothing absolute. This pure life is the source of all separate lives, impulses, and deeds. But if it comes into consciousness as a belief in life, it is then living in believers and yet is to some extent posited outside them. Since, in thus becoming conscious of it, they are restricted, their consciousness and the infinite cannot be completely in one. Humanity can believe in a God only by being able to abstract from every deed, from everything determinate, while at the same time simply clinging fast to the soul of every deed and everything determinate. In anything soulless and spiritless there can be nothing divine. If persons always feels themselves determined, always doing or suffering this or that, acting in this way or that, then what has thus been abstracted and delimited has not been cut off from the spirit; on the contrary, what remains permanent for them behind these passing details is only the opposite of life, namely, the dominant universal. The whole field of determinacy falls away, and beyond this consciousness of determinacies there is only the empty unity of the totality of objects as the essence dominating determinacies. To this infinite field of lordship and bondage there can be opposed only the pure sensing of life which has in itself its justification and its authority. But by appearing as an opposite, it appears as something determinate in a determinate human being [Jesus] who cannot give an intuition of purity to profane eyes bound to mundane realities. In the determinate situation in which he appears, this human being can appeal only to his origin, to the source from which every shape of restricted life flows to him; he cannot appeal to the whole, which he now is, as to an absolute. He must call on something higher, on the father who lives immutable in all mutability.

Since the divine is pure life, anything and everything said of it must be free from any [implication of] opposition. And all reflection's expressions about the relations of the objective being [*das Objektive*] or about that being's activity in objective action must be avoided, since the activity of the divine is only a unification of spirits. Only spirit grasps and embraces spirit in itself. Expressions such as "command, teach, learn, see, recognize, make, will, come (into the kingdom of heaven), go," express the relations of an objective being to us only if spirit is receiving something objective to it. Hence it is only in inspired terms that the divine can [properly] be spoken of. Jewish culture reveals a consciousness of only one group of living relationships, and even these in the form of concepts rather than of virtues and qualities of character. This is all the more natural in that the Jews had to express, in the main, only relations between strangers, beings different in essence, e.g., compassion, bounty, etc. John is the Evangelist who has the most to say about God and the bond between God and Jesus. But the Jewish culture, which was so poor in spiritual relationships, forced him to avail himself of objective ties and matter-of-fact phraseology for expressing the highest spiritual realities, and this language thus often sounds harsher than when feelings are supposed to be expressed in the parallelistic style [*Wechsel-Stil*]. "The kingdom of heaven; entry into the kingdom; I am the door; I am the true bread, who eats my flesh," etc.—into such matter-of-fact and everyday ties is the spiritual forced. . . .

The beginning of John's Gospel contains a series of propositional sentences which speak of God and the divine in more appropriate phraseology. It is to use the simplest form of reflective phraseology to say: "In the beginning *was* the Logos; the Logos *was* with God, and God *was* the Logos; in him *was* life" [John 1:1, 4]. But these sentences have only the deceptive semblance of judgments, for the predicates are not concepts, not universals like those necessarily contained in judgments expressing reflection. On the contrary, the predicates are themselves once more something being and living. Even this simple form of reflection is not adapted to the spiritual expression of spirit. Nowhere more than in the communication of the divine is it necessary for recipients to grasp the communication with the depths of their own spirit. Nowhere is it less possible to learn, to assimilate passively, because everything expressed about the divine in the language of reflection is *eo ipso* contradictory; and the passive spiritless assimilation of such an expression not only leaves the deeper spirit empty but also distracts the intellect which assimilates it and for which it is a contradiction. This always objective language hence attains sense and weight only in the spirit of readers and to an extent which differs with the degree to which the relationships of life and the opposition of life and death have come into their consciousness.

Of the two extreme methods of interpreting John's exordium, the most objective is to take the Logos as something actual, an individual; the most subjective is to take it as reason; in the former case as a particular, in the latter as universality; in the former, as the most single and exclusive reality, in the latter as a mere *ens rationis*. God and the Logos become distinct because actual being [*das Seiende*] must be taken from a double point of view [by reflection], since reflection supposes that that to which it gives a reflected form is at the same time not reflected; i.e., it takes actual being (i) to be the single [*das Einzige*] in which there is no partition or opposition, and (ii) at the same time to be the single which is potentially separable and infinitely divisible into parts. God and the Logos are only different in that God is matter in the form of the Logos: the Logos itself is with God; both are one. The multiplicity, the infinity, of the actual [*das Wirkliche*][2] is the infinite divisibility actualized: by the Logos all things are made; the world is not an emanation of the Deity, or otherwise the actual would be through and through divine. Yet, as actual, it is an emanation, a part of the infinite partitioning, though in the part (*en autō* is better taken with the immediately preceding *oude hen ho gegonen*), or in the one who partitions ad infinitum (if *en autō* is taken as referring to *logos*), there is life. The single entity [*das Einzige*], the restricted entity, as something opposed [to life], something dead, is yet a branch of the infinite tree of life. Each part, to which the whole is external, is yet a whole, a life. And this life, once again as something reflected upon, as divided by reflection into the relation of subject and predicate, is life (*zōē*) and life understood (*phōs* [light], truth). These finite entities have opposites; the opposite of light is darkness. . . .

The most commonly cited and the most striking expression of Jesus' relation to God is his calling himself the "son of God" [*huios tou theou*] and contrasting himself as son of God with himself as the "son of humanity" [*huios tou anthrōpou*]. The designation of this relation is one of the few natural expressions left by accident in the Jewish speech of that time, and therefore it is to be counted among their happy expressions. The relation of a son to his father is not a conceptual unity (as, for instance, unity or harmony of disposition, similarity of principles, etc.), a unity which is only a unity in thought and is abstracted from life. On the contrary, it is a living relation of living beings, a likeness of life. Father and son are simply modifications of the same life, not opposite essences, not a plurality of absolute substantialities. Thus the son of God is the same essence as the father, and yet for every act of reflective thinking, though only for such thinking, he is a separate essence. Even in the expression "A son of the stem of Koresh," for example, which the Arabs use to denote the individual, a single member of the clan, there is the implication that this individual is not simply a part of the whole; the whole does not lie outside him; he himself is just the whole which the entire clan is.[3] This is clear too from the sequel to the manner of waging war peculiar to such a natural, undivided people: every single individual is put to the sword in the most cruel fashion. In modern Europe, on the other hand, where each individual does not carry the whole state in himself, but where the bond is only the conceptual one of the same rights for all, war is waged not against the individual, but against the whole which lies outside him. As with any genuinely free people, so among the Arabs, the individual is a part and at the same time the whole. It is true only of objects, of things lifeless, that the whole is other than the parts; in the living thing, on the other hand, the part of the whole is one and the same as the whole. If particular objects, as substances, are linked together while each of them yet retains its character as an individual (as numerically one), then their common characteristic, their unity, is only a concept [*Begriff*], not an essence [*Wesen*], not an actual being [*ein Seiendes*]. Living things, however, are essences, even if they are separate, and their unity is still a unity of essence. What is a contradiction in the realm of the dead is not one in the realm of life.

A tree which has three branches makes up with them one tree; but every "son" of the tree, every branch (and also its other "children," leaves and blossoms) is itself a tree. The fibers bringing sap to the branch from the stem are of the same nature as the roots. If a [cutting from certain types of] tree is set in the ground upside down it will put forth leaves out of the roots in the air, and the boughs will root themselves in the ground. And it is just as true to say that there is only one tree here as to say that there are three.

This unity of essence between father and son in the Godhead was discovered even by the Jews in the relation to God which Jesus ascribed to himself (John 5:18): "He makes himself equal with God in that he calls God his father." To the Jewish principle of God's domination Jesus could oppose the needs of humans (just as he had set the need to satisfy hunger over against the festival of the Sabbath), but even this he could do only in general terms. The deeper development of this contrast, e.g., [the discovery of] a primacy of the practical reason, was absent from the culture of those times. In his opposition [to Judaism] he stood before their eyes only as an individual. In order to remove the thought of this individuality, Jesus continually appealed, especially in John, to his oneness with God, who has granted to the son to have life in himself, just as the father has life in himself. He and the father are one; he is bread come down from heaven, and so forth. These are hard words (*sklēroi logoi*), and they are not softened by being interpreted as imagery or misinterpreted as the uniting of concepts instead of being taken spiritually as life. Of course, as soon as intellectual concepts are opposed to imagery and taken as dominant, every image must be set aside as only play, as a by-product of the imagination and without truth; and, instead of the life of the image, nothing remains but objects.

But Jesus calls himself not only son of God but also son of humanity. If "son of God" expressed a modification of the divine, so "son of humanity" would be a modification of the human. But humanity is not one nature, one being [*Wesen*], like the Godhead; it is a concept, an *ens rationis*. And "son of humanity" means here "something subsumed under the concept of humanity." "Jesus is human" is a judgment proper; the predicate is not a being but a universal (*anthrōpos*, humanity [*der Mensch*]; *huios anthrōpou*, a human being [*ein Mensch*]). The son of God is also son of humanity; the divine in a particular shape appears as a human being. The connection of infinite and finite is of course a "holy mystery,"[4] because this connection is life itself. Reflective thinking, which partitions life, can distinguish it into infinite and finite, and then it is only the restriction, the finite regarded by itself, which affords the concept of humanity as opposed to the divine. But outside reflective thinking, and in truth, there is no such restriction. This meaning of the "son of humanity" comes out most clearly when the "son of humanity" is set over against the "son of God," e.g. (John 5:26-27), "For just as the father has life in himself, so he has granted the son also to have life in himself, and he has given him authority to execute judgment, because he is the son of humanity." Again (vs. 22), "The father judges no one but has given all judgment to the son." On the other hand, we read (John 3:17; Matthew 18:11), "God did not send the son into the world to condemn the world, but in order that the world might be saved through him." Judgment is not an act of the divine, for the law, which is in the judge, is the universal opposed to the person who is to be judged, and judgment (in law) is a judgment (in logic), an assertion of likeness or unlikeness, the recognition of a conceptual unity or an irreconcilable opposition. The son of God does not judge, sunder, or divide, does not hold to an opposite in its opposition. An utterance, or the stirring, of the divine is no lawgiving or legislation, no upholding of the mastery of the law. On the contrary, the world is to be saved by the divine, and even "save" is a word improperly used of the spirit, for it denotes the absolute impotence, in face of danger, of the person on its brink, and to that extent salvation is the action of a stranger to a stranger. And the operation of the divine may be called "salvation" only insofar as the person saved was a stranger, not to his essence, but only to his previous plight. . . .

The relation of Jesus to God, as the relation of a son to his father, could be apprehended as a piece of knowledge or alternatively by faith, according as one puts the divine wholly outside oneself or not. Knowledge posits, for its way of taking this relation, two natures of different kinds, a human nature and a divine one, a human essence and a divine one, each with personality and substantiality, and, whatever their relation, both remaining two because they are posited as absolutely different. Those who posit this absolute difference and yet still require us to think of these absolutes as one in their inmost relationship do not dismiss the intellect [*Verstand*] on the ground that they are asserting a truth outside its scope. On the contrary, it is the intellect which they expect to grasp absolutely different substances which at the same time are an absolute unity. Thus they destroy the intellect in positing it. Those who (i) accept the given difference of the substantialities but (ii) deny their unity are more logical. They are justified in (i), since it is required to think God and humanity, and therefore in (ii), since to cancel the cleavage between God and humanity would be contrary to the first admission they were required to make. In this way they save the intellect; but when they refuse to move beyond this absolute difference of essences, then they elevate the intellect, absolute division, destruction of life, to the pinnacle of spirit. It was from this intellectualistic point of view that the Jews took what Jesus said.

When Jesus said, "The father is in me and I in the father; who has seen me has seen the father; who knows the father knows that what I say is true; I and the father are one,"[5] the Jews accused him of blasphemy[6] because though born a man he made himself God. How were they, the poor, to recognize divinity in a human being, possessing only a consciousness of their misery, of the depth of their servitude, of their opposition to the divine, of an impassable gulf between the being of God and the being of humans?

Spirit alone recognizes spirit. They saw in Jesus only the human being, the Nazarene, the carpenter's son whose brothers and kinsfolk lived among them; so much he was, and more he could not be, for he was only one like themselves, and they felt themselves to be nothing. The Jewish multitude was bound to shatter his attempt to give them the consciousness of something divine, for faith in something divine, something great, cannot make its home in a hut.[7] The lion has no room in a nut[shell], the infinite spirit none in the prison of a Jewish soul, the whole of life none in a withering leaf. The hill and the eye which sees it are object and subject, but between humanity and God, between spirit and spirit, there is no such cleft of objectivity and subjectivity; one is to the other an other only in that one recognizes the other; both are one. . . .

The essence of Jesus, i.e., his relationship to God as son to father, can be truly grasped only by faith; and faith in himself is what Jesus demanded of his people. This faith is characterized by its object [*Gegenstand*], the divine. Faith in a mundane reality is an acquaintance with some kind of object [*Objekt*], of something restricted. And just as an object [*Objekt*] is other than God, so this acquaintance is different from faith in the divine.[8] "God is spirit, and they that worship him must worship him in spirit and in truth" [John 4:24]. How could anything but a spirit know a spirit? The relation of spirit to spirit is a feeling of harmony, is their unification; how could heterogeneity be unified? Faith in the divine is only possible if in believers themselves there is a divine element which rediscovers itself, its own nature, in that on which it believes, even if it be unconscious that what it has found is its own nature. In all human beings there is light and life; they are the property of the light. They are not illumined by a light in the way in which a dark body is when it borrows a brightness not its own; on the contrary, their own inflammability takes fire and they burn with a flame that is their own. The middle state between darkness (remoteness from the divine, imprisonment in the mundane) and a wholly divine life of one's own, a trust in one's self, is faith in the divine. It is the inkling, the knowledge, of the divine, the longing for union with God, the desire for a divine life. But it lacks the strength of [that state of mind which results when] divinity has pervaded all the threads of one's consciousness, directed all one's relations with the world, and now breathes throughout one's being. Hence faith in the divine grows out of the divinity of the believer's own nature; only a modification of the Godhead can know the Godhead. . . .

This faith, however, is only the first stage in the relationship with Jesus. In its culmination this relationship is conceived so intimately that his friends are one with him. See John 12:36: "Until[9] you yourselves have light, believe in the light, so that you may become the children of light." Between those who only have faith in the light and those who are the children of light, there is a difference similar to that between John the Baptist, who only bore witness of the light, and Jesus, the light individualized in a human being. Just as Jesus has eternal life in himself, so too those who believe in him shall attain everlasting life (John 6:40). The living association with Jesus is most clearly expounded in John's account of his final discourse: They in him and he in them; they together one; he the vine, they the branches; in the parts the same nature, a life like the life in the whole [cf. John 14:20; 15:1ff.]. It is this culminating relationship which Jesus prays his father to grant to his friends and which he promises them when he shall be removed from them. So long as he lived among them, they remained believers only, for they were not self-dependent. Jesus was their teacher and master, an individual center on which they depended. They had not yet attained an independent life of their own. The spirit of Jesus ruled them, but after his removal even this objectivity, this partition between them and God, fell away, and the spirit of God could then animate their whole being. When Jesus says (John 7:38-39): "He who believes in me, out of his belly *shall* flow rivers of life," John remarks that this was spoken of the thorough animation by the Holy Spirit which was still to come; they had not yet received the spirit because Jesus was not yet glorified.

All thought of a difference in essence between Jesus and those in whom faith in him has become life, in whom the divine is present, must be eliminated. When Jesus speaks of himself so often as of a preeminent nature, this is to contrast himself with the Jews. From them he separates himself and thereby his divinity also acquires an individual form [a uniqueness peculiar to himself]. "I am the truth and the life; he who believes in me"—this uniform and constant emphasis on the "I" in John's Gospel is a separation of his personality from the Jewish character; but however vigorously he makes himself an individual in contrast with the Jewish spirit, he equally vigorously annuls all divine personality, divine individuality, in talking to his friends [about himself]; with them he will simply be one, and they in him are to be one. John says (2:25) of Jesus that he knew what was in everyone; and the truest mirror of his beautiful faith in nature is his discourse at the sight of uncorrupted beings (Matthew 18:1 ff.): If you do not become like children, you shall not enter the kingdom of God; whoever is the most childlike is the greatest in heaven. Whoever welcomes one such child in my name welcomes me. Whoever is capable of sensing in the child the child's pure life, of recognizing the holiness of the child's nature, has sensed my essence. If any of you sully this holy purity, it would be better for you if a millstone were fastened round your neck and you were drowned in the depth of the sea. Oh! the grievous necessity of such violations of the holy! The deepest, holiest sorrow of a beautiful soul, its most incomprehensible riddle, is that its nature has to be disrupted, its holiness sullied. Just as for the intellect the most incomprehensible thing is the divine and unity with God, so for the noble heart is alienation from God. Take care that you do not despise one of these little ones, for I tell you that in heaven their angels continually see the face of my father in heaven. . . .[10]

Jesus explains this unity in another way (Matthew 18:19): "If two or three of you agree about anything you ask, it will be done for you by my father." The expressions "ask" and "vouchsafe" are relative strictly to a unification in respect of objects (*pragmata* [things]); it was only for a unification of this kind that the matter-of-fact language of the Jews had words. But here the object in question can be nothing but the reflected unity (the *symphōnia tōn duoin ē triōn* [agreement of two or three]); regarded as an object, this is a beautiful relationship, but subjectively it is unification; spirits cannot be one in objects proper. The beautiful relationship, a unity of two or three of you, is repeated in the harmony of the whole, is a sound, a concord with the same harmony and is produced thereby. It *is* because it is in the harmony, because it is something divine. In this association with the divine, those who are at one are also in association with Jesus. Where two or three are united in my spirit (*eis to onoma mou* [into my name], cf. Matthew 10:41), in that respect in which being and eternal life fall to my lot, in which I am, then I am in the midst of them, and so is my spirit.

Thus specifically does Jesus declare himself against personality, against the view that his essence possessed an individuality opposed to that of those who had attained the culmination of friendship with him (against the thought of a personal God[11]), for the ground of such an individuality would be an absolute particularity of his being in opposition to theirs. A remark about the unity of lovers is also relevant here (Matthew 19:5-6): Man and wife, these two, become one, so that they are no longer two. Therefore what God has joined together, let no one separate. If this "joining" were supposed to have reference solely to the original designation of the man and the woman for one another, this reason would not suffice against divorce, since divorce would not cancel that designation, that conceptual unification; it would remain even if a living link were disrupted. It is a living link that is said to be something divine, effected by God's agency.

Since Jesus gave battle to the entire genius of his people and had altogether broken with his world, the completion of his fate could be nothing save suppression by the hostile genius of his people. The glorification of the son of humanity in this downfall is not negative (does not consist in a renunciation of all his relations with the world) but positive (his nature has foregone the unnatural world, has preferred to save it in battle and defeat rather than consciously submit to its corruption or else unconsciously and increasingly succumb to corruption's stealthy advance). Jesus was conscious that it was necessary for his individual self to perish, and he tried to convince his disciples also of this necessity. But they could not separate his essence from his person; they were still only believers. When Peter recognized the divine in the son of humanity, Jesus expected his friends to be able to realize and bear the thought of their parting from him. Hence he speaks of it to them immediately after he had heard Peter utter his faith. But Peter's terror of it showed how far his faith was from the culmination of faith. Only after the departure of Jesus' individual self could their dependence on him cease; only then could a spirit of their own or the divine spirit subsist in them. "It is to your advantage that I go away," Jesus says (John 16:7), "for if I do not go away, the Comforter will not come to you"—the Comforter (John 14:16ff.), "the spirit of truth, whom the world cannot receive because it does not know him; I will not leave you orphaned; I am coming to you and you shall see me; because I live, you also will live." When you cease merely to see the divine in me and outside yourselves, when you have life in yourselves, then will the divine come to consciousness in you also, because you have been with me from the beginning (John 15:27), because our natures are one in love and in God. "The spirit will guide you into all truth" (John 16:13), and will remind you of all the things that I have said to you. The spirit is a Comforter. To give comfort means to give the expectation of a good like the one lost or greater than the one lost; so you shall not be left behind as orphans, since as much as you believe you are losing me, so much will you receive in yourselves.

Jesus also contrasts individuality with the spirit of the whole. Whoever (Matthew 12:31ff.) blasphemes a human being (blasphemes me as the son of humanity), will be forgiven, but whoever blasphemes the spirit itself, the divine, will not be forgiven, either in this age or in the age to come. Out of the abundance of the heart (verse 34) the mouth speaks; the good person brings good things out of a good treasure, and the evil person brings evil things out of an evil treasure [verse 35]. Those who blaspheme the individual (i.e., blaspheme me as an individual self) shut themselves out only from me, not from love; but they who sunder themselves from God blaspheme nature itself, blaspheme the spirit in nature; their spirit has destroyed its own holiness, and they are therefore incapable of annulling their separation and reuniting themselves with love, with holiness. By a sign you could be shaken, but that would not restore in you the nature you have lost. The Eumenides[12] of your being could be terrified, but the void left in you by the demons thus chased away would not be filled by love. It will only draw your furies back again, and, now strengthened by your very consciousness that they are furies of hell, they complete your destruction.

The culmination of faith, the return to the Godhead whence humanity is born, closes the circle of human development. Everything lives in the Godhead, every living thing is its child, but the child carries the unity, the connection, the concord with the entire harmony, undisturbed though undeveloped, in itself. It begins with faith in gods outside itself, with fear, until through its actions it has [isolated and] separated itself more and more; but then it returns through associations to the original unity which now is developed, self-produced, and sensed as a unity. The child now knows God, i.e., the spirit of God is present in the child, issues from its restrictions, annuls the modification, and restores the whole. God, the Son, the Holy Spirit! . . .

What Jesus calls the "kingdom of God" is the living harmony of human beings, their fellowship in God; it is the development of the divine among human beings, the relationship with God which they enter through being filled with the Holy Spirit, i.e., that of becoming God's sons and living in the harmony of their developed many-sidedness and their entire being and character. In this harmony their many-sided consciousness chimes in with one spirit and their many different lives with one life, but, more than this, by its means the partitions against other godlike beings are abolished, and the same living spirit animates the different beings, who therefore are no longer merely similar but one; they make up not a collection but a communion, since they are unified not in a universal, a concept (e.g., as believers), but through life and through love.

The Jewish language gave Jesus the word "kingdom," which imports something heterogeneous into the expression of the divine unification of humanity, for it means only a union through domination, through the power of a stranger over a stranger, a union to be totally distinguished from the beauty of the divine life of a pure human fellowship, because such a life is of all things the freest possible. This idea of a kingdom of God completes and comprises the whole of religion as Jesus founded it, and we have still to consider whether it completely satisfies nature or whether his disciples were impelled by any need to something beyond, and, if so, what that need was.

In the kingdom of God what is common to all is life in God. This is not the common character which a concept expresses, but is love, a living bond which unites the believers; it is this feeling of unity of life, a feeling in which all oppositions, as pure enmities, and also rights, as unifications of still subsisting oppositions, are annulled. "I give you a new command," says Jesus [John 13:34-35], "that you love one another; by this everyone will know that you are my disciples." This friendship of soul, described in the language of reflection as a being [Wesen], as spirit, is the divine spirit, is God who rules the communion. Is there an idea more beautiful than that of a nation [Volk] of human beings related to one another by love? Is there one more uplifting than that of belonging to a whole which as a whole, as one, is the spirit of God whose sons the individual members are? Was there still to be an incompleteness in this idea, an incompleteness which would give a fate power over it? Or would this fate be the nemesis raging against a too beautiful endeavor, against an overleaping of nature?

In love a human being has found him- or herself again in another. Since love is a unification of life, it presupposes division, a development of life, a developed many-sidedness of life. The more variegated the manifold in which life is alive, the more the places in which it can be reunified, the more the places in which it can sense itself, the deeper does love become. The more extended the multiplicity of the relations and feelings of the lovers and the more deeply love is concentrated, the more exclusive it is and the more indifferent to the life of other persons. Its joy communes with every other life and recognizes it [as life], yet it recoils if it senses an [exclusive] individuality in the other. The more isolated human beings stand in respect of their culture and interest, in their relation to the world, and the more idiosyncracies they have, the more does their love become restricted to itself [i.e., to their own group, instead of spreading throughout the world]. If it is to be conscious of its happiness, if it is to give happiness to itself as it is fond of doing, it must isolate itself, must even create enmities for itself. Therefore the love which a large group of people can feel for one another[13] admits of only a certain degree of strength or depth and demands both a similarity in mind, in interest, in numerous relationships of life, and also a diminution of individualities. But since this community of life, this similarity of mind, is not love, it can be brought home to consciousness only through its definite and strongly marked expressions. There is no question of a correspondence in knowledge, in similar opinions; the linking of many persons depends on similarity of need, and it reveals itself in objects which can be common, in relationships arising from such objects, and then in a common striving for them and a common activity and enterprise. It can attach itself to a thousand objects of common use and enjoyment, objects belonging to a similar culture, and can know itself in them. A group of similar aims, the whole range of physical need, may be an object of united enterprise, and in such enterprise a like spirit reveals itself; and then this common spirit delights to make itself recognized in the peace [of the group], to be gay in unifying the group, since it enjoys itself in gladness and play.

The friends of Jesus kept together after his death; they ate and drank in common. Some of their brotherhoods wholly abolished property rights against one another; others did so partly by their profuse almsgiving and contributions to the common stock. They conversed about their departed friend and master, prayed together, strengthened one another in faith and courage. Their enemies accused some of their societies of even having wives in common, an accusation which they lacked purity and courage enough to deserve, or of which they had no need to feel shame. In common many withdrew to make other people sharers in their faith and their hopes; and because this is the sole activity of the Christian community, proselytizing is that community's essential property. Beyond this common pleasure, enjoying, praying, eating, believing and hoping, beyond the single activity of spreading the faith, of enlarging the community of worship, there still lies a prodigious field of objectivity which claims activity of many kinds and sets up a fate whose scope extends in all directions and whose power is mighty. In love's task the community scorns any unification save the deepest, any spirit save the highest. The grand idea of a universal philanthropy,[14] a shallow idea and an unnatural one, I pass over, since it was not this which was the aspiration of the community. But the community cannot go beyond love itself. Apart from the relationship of the common faith and the revelations of this common possession in the appropriate religious actions, every other tie in other objective activities is alien to the community, whether the purpose of such a tie be the achievement of some end or the development of another side of life or a common activity. Equally alien is every spirit of cooperation for something other than the dissemination of the faith, every spirit which reveals and enjoys itself in play in other modes and restricted forms of life. In such a spirit the community would not recognize itself; to have done so would have been to renounce love, its own spirit, and be untrue to its God. Not only would it have forsaken love, it would have destroyed it, since its members would have put themselves in jeopardy of clashing against one another's individuality, and must have done this all the more as their education was different; and they would thereby have surrendered themselves to the province of their different characters, to the power of their different fates. For the sake of a petty interest, a difference of character in some detail, love would have been changed into hatred, and a severance from God would have followed. This danger is warded off only by an inactive and undeveloped love, i.e., by a love which, though love is the highest life, remains unliving. Hence the contranatural expansion of love's scope becomes entangled in a contradiction, in a false effort which was bound to become the father of the most appalling fanaticism, whether of an active or a passive life.[15] This restriction of love to itself, its flight from all determinate modes of living even if its spirit breathed in them, or even if they sprang from its spirit, this removal of itself from all fate, is just its greatest fate; and here is the point where Jesus is linked with fate, linked indeed in the most sublime way, but where he suffers under it.

2

JENA WRITINGS
(1802–1803)

FAITH AND KNOWLEDGE

In 1801 Hegel moved from Frankfurt to Jena, where he began his university career as a lecturer, and where his relationship with Friedrich Schelling was renewed (they had been classmates in the Tübingen seminary). Together Hegel and Schelling edited The Critical Journal of Philosophy, *and in the first issue of the second volume (July 1802) Hegel published a lengthy essay,* Faith and Knowledge (Glaube und Wissen), *which followed by less than a year his first acknowledged publication,* The Difference between Fichte's and Schelling's System of Philosophy. *According to its title page, the topic of* Faith and Knowledge *was to be "the reflective philosophy of subjectivity in the complete range of its forms as Kantian, Jacobian, and Fichtean philosophy." Whereas in the earlier work Fichte had been contrasted with Kant, now he was seen as the logical culmination of Kant's critical philosophy. Critical philosophy is "reflective philosophy" in the sense that what the mind knows is only a "reflection" of its own subjective categories. Against Kant's epistemological skepticism, Jacobi asserted the immediate certainty of religious knowledge or faith, while Fichte completed the reconciliation of finite reason with religious faith already implicit in Kant. For both Kant and Fichte, in Hegel's view, faith is subjected to the criteria of autonomous reason and loses its grounding in the self-manifestation of the absolute, upon which is based what Schelling and Hegel called "speculative" intuition, which mirrors the truth of the whole rather than simply its own limited subjectivity. In opposition to the rationalistic reduction of faith, which Hegel regarded as characteristic of Enlightenment culture, true philosophical knowledge depends on the religious consciousness and experience of the absolute—not an alien, transcendent, other-worldly absolute but an immanent absolute that subjects itself to negation in the historical Good Fridays of this world.*

The bulk of Faith and Knowledge *consists of detailed expositions and critiques of Kant, Jacobi, and Fichte. Our selection is limited to the Introduction (which we have titled "The Culture of Reflection") and the Conclusion (titled "The Speculative Good Friday"). It contains some of Hegel's most compelling images and many of the seeds of his later thought about religion. The source is G. W. F. Hegel,* Faith and Knowledge, *trans. Walter Cerf and H. S. Harris (Albany: State University of New York Press, 1977), pp. 55–66, 189–91. The translation has been edited to conform to our gen-der-inclusive, down style, and it has been compared with the German text in* Gesammelte Werke, *vol. 4 (ed. Hartmut Buchner and Otto Pöggeler; Hamburg, 1968), pp. 315–24, 412–14, on the basis of which a few revisions are made. The translators' notes are slightly abbreviated.*

The Culture of Reflection

Civilization has raised this latest era so far above the ancient antithesis of reason and faith, of philosophy and positive religion, that this opposition of faith and knowledge has acquired quite a different sense and has now been transferred into the field of philosophy itself. In earlier times philosophy was said to be the handmaid of faith. Ideas and expressions of this sort have vanished and philosophy has irresistibly affirmed its absolute autonomy. Reason, if it is in fact reason that appropriates this name, has made itself into such an authority within positive religion that a philosophical struggle against the positive, against miracles and suchlike, is now regarded as obsolete and unenlightened. Kant tried to put new life into the positive form of religion with a meaning derived from his philosophy, but his attempt was received poorly, not because it would have changed the meaning peculiar to these forms, but because they no longer appeared to be worth the bother.[1] The question arises, however, whether victorious reason has not suffered the same fate that the barbarous nations in their victorious strength have usually suffered at the hands of civilized nations that weakly succumbed to them. As rulers the barbarians may have held the upper hand outwardly, but they surrendered to the defeated spiritually. Enlightened reason won a glorious victory over what it believed, in its limited conception of religion, to be faith as opposed to reason. Yet seen in a clear light the victory comes to no more than this: the positive element with which reason busied itself to do battle, is no longer religion, and victorious reason is no longer reason. The new-born peace that hovers triumphantly over the corpse of reason and faith, uniting them as the child of both, has as little of reason in it as it has of authentic faith.

Reason had already gone to seed in and for itself[2] when it envisaged religion merely as something positive and not idealistically. And after its battle with religion the best that reason could manage was to take a look at itself and come to self-awareness. Reason [*Vernunft*], having in this way become mere intellect [*Verstand*], acknowledges its own nothingness by placing that which is better than it in a *faith outside and above* itself, as a *beyond* [to be believed in]. This is what has happened in the *philosophies of Kant, Jacobi, and Fichte.* Philosophy has made itself the handmaid of a faith once more.

According to *Kant,* the supersensuous is incapable of being known by reason; the highest idea does not at the same time have reality. According to *Jacobi,* "Reason is ashamed to beg and has no hands and feet for digging."³ Only the feeling and consciousness of its ignorance of the true is given to humanity, only an inkling, a divination of the true in religion, reason being something subjective, though universal—an instinct. According to *Fichte,* God is something incomprehensible and unthinkable. Knowledge knows nothing save that it knows nothing; it must take refuge in faith.⁴ All of them agree that, as the old distinction put it, the absolute is no more against reason than it is for it; it is beyond reason.⁵

The Enlightenment, in its positive aspect, was a hubbub of vanity without a firm core. It obtained a core in its negative procedure by grasping its own negativity. Through the purity and infinity of the negative it freed itself from its insipidity but precisely for this reason it could admit positive knowledge only of the finite and empirical. The eternal remained in a realm beyond, a beyond too vacuous for cognition so that this infinite void of knowledge could only be filled with the subjectivity of longing and divining. Thus what used to be regarded as the death of philosophy, that reason should renounce its existence in the absolute, excluding itself totally from it and relating itself to it only negatively, became now the zenith of philosophy. By coming to consciousness of its own nothingness, the Enlightenment turns this nothingness into a system.

In general, imperfect philosophies immediately pertain to [i.e., arise from] an empirical necessity just because they are imperfect. So it is through and in this empirical necessity that their imperfect aspect is to be comprehended. The empirical is what is there in the world as ordinary existence [*Wirklichkeit*]. In empirical philosophies it is present in conceptual form, as one with consciousness, and therefore justified. [But] on the one hand, the subjective principle shared by the philosophies of Kant, Jacobi, and Fichte [does not pertain to empirical necessity because it] is by no means a restricted expression of the spirit of a brief epoch or a small group. [And] on the other hand, [these philosophies taken together are not empirical or imperfect because] the mighty spiritual form that is their principle achieved in them perfect self-consciousness, perfect philosophical formation and definitive self-expression as cognition.

The great form of the world spirit that has come to cognizance of itself in these philosophies is the principle of the North, and from the religious point of view, of Protestantism. This principle is subjectivity for which beauty and truth present themselves in feelings and persuasions, in love and intellect. Religion builds its temples and altars in the heart of the individual. In sighs and prayers the individual seeks for the God whom he denies to himself in intuition, because of the risk that the intellect will cognize what is intuited as a mere thing, reducing the sacred grove to mere timber.[6] Of course, the inner must be externalized; intention must become effective in action; immediate religious sentiment must be expressed in external gesture; and faith, though it flees from the objectivity of cognition, must become objective to itself in thought, concepts, and words. But the intellect scrupulously distinguishes the objective from the subjective, and the objective is what is accounted worthless and null. The struggle of subjective beauty must be directed precisely to this end; to defend itself properly against the necessity through which the subjective becomes objective. That beauty should become real in objective form, and fall captive to objectivity, that consciousness should seek to be directed at exposition and objectivity themselves, that it should want to shape appearance or, shaped in it, to be at home there—all this should cease; for it would be a dangerous superfluity, and an evil, as the intellect could turn it into a thing [zu einem Etwas]. Equally, if the beautiful feeling passed over into an intuition that was without grief, it would be superstition.

That it is subjective beauty which grants this might to the intellect seems at first glance to contradict its yearning which flies beyond the finite and to which the finite is nothing. But the grant is as much a necessary aspect [of its relation to the intellect] as is its striving against the intellect. This will be brought out more fully in our exposition of the philosophies of this subjectivity. It is precisely through its flight from the finite and through its rigidity that subjectivity turns the beautiful into things—the grove into timber, the images into things that have eyes and do not see, ears and do not hear.[7] And if the ideals cannot be reduced to the black and stones of a wholly explicable [verständig] reality, they are made into fictions. Any connection with the ideals will than appear as a play without substance, or as dependence upon objects and as superstition.

Yet alongside of this intellect which everywhere sees nothing but finitude in the truth of being, religion has its sublime aspect as feeling [Empfindung], the love filled with eternal longing; for it does not get hung up on any transitory sight [Anschauung] or enjoyment, it yearns for eternal beauty and bliss. Religion, as this longing, is subjective; but what it seeks and what is not given to it in sighting [Schauen],[8] is the absolute and the eternal. For if the longing were to find its object, then the temporal beauty of a subject in its singularity would be its happiness, it would be the perfection of a being belonging to the world; but to the extent that religion as longing actually singularized beauty it would be nothing beautiful [as far as the longing itself is concerned].[9] But [what the longing does not recognize is that] when empirical existence is the pure body of inward beauty, it ceases to be something temporal and on its own. The intention abides unpolluted by its objective existence as an action; and neither the deed nor the enjoyment will be built up by the intellect into something that is opposed to the true identity of the inner and the outer. The highest cognition would be the cognition of what that body is wherein the individual would not be single [and separate], and wherein longing reaches perfect vision [*Anschauung*] and blissful enjoyment.

When the time had come, the infinite longing that yearns beyond body and world reconciled itself with existence.[10] But the reality with which it became reconciled, the objective sphere acknowledged by subjectivity, was in fact merely empirical existence, the ordinary world and ordinary matters of fact [*Wirklichkeit*]. Hence, this reconciliation did not itself lose the character of absolute opposition implicit in beautiful longing. Rather, it flung itself upon the other pole of the antithesis, the empirical world. Although the reconciliation was sure of itself and firm in its inner ground because of the absolute and blind natural necessity [of empirical existence], it was still in need of an objective form for this [inner] ground. Being immersed in the reality of empirical existence, this reconciliation has an unconscious certainty which must, by the same necessity of nature, seek to secure justification and a good conscience. At the conscious level it was the doctrine of happiness that brought about this reconciliation. The fixed point of departure here is the empirical subject, just as what it becomes reconciled with is ordinary life [*Wirklichkeit*]: the empirical subject is allowed to confide in ordinary life and surrender to it without sin. The utter crudity and vulgarity that are at the bottom of this doctrine of eudaemonism are redeemed only by its striving toward justification and good conscience. But reason cannot achieve this justification and good conscience through the idea, since the empirical is [here] absolute. Only the objectivity of the intellect can attain the concept, which has presented itself in its most highly abstract form as so-called pure reason.

So the dogmatism of the Enlightenment-flurry [*Aufklärerei*] and of eudaemonism did not consist in declaring virtuous happiness and enjoyment to be the highest good; for when happiness is conceived as idea, it ceases to be something empirical and contingent, and it ceases to be something sensuous. In the highest being [*höchstes Dasein*] rational action and highest enjoyment are one. Only if we isolate the ideal aspect of the highest being, can we then call it rational action. And only if we isolate the real aspect can we call it enjoyment and feeling. It does not matter whether we wish to apprehend the highest being from the side of its ideality or from the side of its reality; [for] if highest bliss is highest idea, then rational action and highest enjoyment, ideality and reality, are equally contained in it and are identical. Every philosophy sets forth nothing else but the construction of highest bliss as idea. In reason's cognition of the highest enjoyment, the possibility of distinguishing them [rational action and enjoyment] vanishes immediately; concept and infinity which dominate action, and reality and finitude which dominate enjoyment, are absorbed into one another. Polemics against happiness will be dismissed as empty chatter when this happiness is recognized to be the blissful enjoyment of eternal intuition. But of course what is nowadays called eudaemonism refers to a happiness that is empirical, a sensual enjoyment, not the bliss of eternal vision.[11]

Infinity or the concept is so directly opposed to this absoluteness of the empirical and finite being that they condition one another and they are one with each other.[12] Since the one is absolute in its being-for-itself, so is the other; and the third, which is the true first, the eternal, is beyond this antithesis. The infinite, the concept, being in itself empty, the nothing, receives its content from what it is connected with as its opposite, that is, the empirical happiness of the individual. What is called wisdom and science consists in positing everything under the unity of the concept whose content is absolute singularity, and in calculating [the worth of] each and every form of beauty and expression of an idea, wisdom and virtue, art and science from this point of view. That is to say, all this has to be treated as something that does not exist in itself, for the only thing that is in itself is the abstract concept of something that is not idea but absolute singularity.

The fixed principle of this system of culture is that the finite is in and for itself, that it is absolute, and is the sole reality. According to this principle, the finite and singular stands on one side, in the form of manifoldness; and anything religious, ethical and beautiful is thrown onto this side because it can be conceived as singular by the intellect. On the other side there is this very same absolute finite but in the form of the infinite as concept of happiness. The infinite and the finite are here not to be posited as identical in the idea; for each of them is for itself absolute. So they stand opposed to each other in the connection of domination; for in the absolute antithesis of infinite and finite the concept is what does the determining. However, above this absolute antithesis and above the relative identities of domination and empirical conceivability, there is the eternal. Because the antithesis [between the infinite and the finite] is absolute, the sphere of the eternal is the incalculable, the inconceivable, the empty—an incognizable God beyond the boundary stakes of reason. It is a sphere that is nothing for intuition since intuition is only allowed to be sensuous and limited. Equally, it is nothing for enjoyment since only empirical happiness exists, and nothing for cognition since what is here called reason consists solely in calculating the worth of each and every thing with respect to the singularity, and in positing [i.e., subsuming] every idea under finitude.

This is the basic character of eudaemonism and the Enlightenment. The beautiful subjectivity of Protestantism is transformed into empirical subjectivity; the poetry of Protestant grief that scorns all reconciliation with empirical existence is transformed into the prose of satisfaction with the finite and of good conscience about it. What is the relation of this basic character to the philosophies of Kant, Jacobi, and Fichte? So little do these philosophies step out of this basic character that, on the contrary, they have merely perfected it to the highest degree. Their conscious direction is flatly opposed to the principle of eudaemonism. However, because they are nothing but this direction, their positive character is just this principle itself; so that the way these philosophies modify eudaemonism merely gives it a perfection of formation, which has no importance in principle, no significance for reason and philosophy. The absoluteness of the finite and of empirical reality is still maintained in these philosophies. The infinite and the finite remain absolutely opposed. Ideality [*das Idealische*] is conceived only as the concept. And in particular, when this concept is posited affirmatively, the only identity of the finite and infinite that remains possible is a relative identity, the domination of the concept over what appears as the real and the finite—everything beautiful and ethical being here included. And on the other hand, when the concept is posited negatively, the subjectivity of the individual is present in empirical form, and the domination is not that of the intellect but is a matter of the natural strength and weakness of the subjectivities opposed to one other. Above this absolute finitude and absolute infinity there remains the absolute as an emptiness of reason, a fixed realm of the incomprehensible, of a faith which is in itself nonrational [*vernunftlos*], but which is called rational because the reason that is restricted to its absolute opposite recognizes something higher above itself from which it is self-excluded.

In the form of eudaemonism the principle of an absolute finitude has not yet achieved perfect abstraction. For on the side of infinity, the concept is not posited in purity; because it is filled with content it stays fixed as happiness. Because the concept is not pure, it has positive equality with its opposite; for its content is precisely the same reality, which is manifoldness on the other side [the side of finitude]—but on the side of infinity it is posited in conceptual form. Hence there is no reflection on the opposition, which is to say that the opposition is not objective: the empirical is not posited as negativity for the concept nor the concept as negativity for the empirical nor the concept as that which is in itself negative. When abstraction achieves perfection, there is reflection on this opposition, the ideal opposition becomes objective, and each of the opposites is posited as something which is not what the other is. Unity and the manifold now confront one another as abstractions, with the result that the opposites have both positive and negative aspects for one another: the empirical is both an absolute something and absolute nothing for the concept. In the former perspective the opposites are the preceding empiricism; in the latter they are at the same time idealism and skepticism. The former is called practical philosophy, the latter theoretical philosophy. In practical philosophy, the empirical has absolute reality for the concept, that is, it has absolute reality in and for itself; in theoretical philosophy knowledge of the empirical is nothing.

The fundamental principle common to the philosophies of Kant, Jacobi, and Fichte is, then, the absoluteness of finitude and, resulting from it, the absolute antithesis of finitude and infinity, reality and ideality, the sensuous and the supersensuous, and the beyondness of what is truly real and absolute. Within this common ground, however, *these philosophies* form antitheses among themselves, exhausting *the totality of possible forms of this principle*. The Kantian philosophy establishes the objective side of this whole [subjective] sphere: the absolute concept existing strictly for itself as practical reason, is the highest objectivity within the finite realm, and it is absolute as ideality postulated in and for itself. Jacobi's philosophy is the subjective side. It transposes the antithesis and the identity, postulated as absolute, into the subjectivity of feeling, into infinite longing and incurable grief. The philosophy of Fichte is the synthesis of both. It demands the form of objectivity and of basic principles as in Kant, but it posits at the same time the conflict of this pure objectivity with the subjectivity as a longing and a subjective identity. In Kant the infinite concept is posited as that which is in and for itself and as the only thing philosophy acknowledges. In Jacobi, the infinite appears as affected by subjectivity, that is, as instinct, impulse, individuality. In Fichte, the infinite as affected by subjectivity is itself objectified again, as obligation and striving.

So these philosophers are as completely confined within eudaemonism as they are diametrically opposed to it. It is their exclusive, their only artic- ulate tendency, their programmatic principle, to rise above the subjective and empirical and to justify the absoluteness of reason, its independence from common existence [*Wirklichkeit*]. But since this reason is simply and solely directed against the empirical, the infinite has a being of its own only in its tie with the finite. Thus, although these philosophies do battle with the empirical, they have remained directly within its sphere. The Kantian and Fichtean philosophies were able to raise themselves to the concept certain- ly, but not to the idea, and the pure concept is absolute ideality and empti- ness. It gets its content and dimensions quite exclusively in, and hence through, its connection with the empirical. In this way their pure concept is the ground of that very same absolute moral and philosophical [*wis- senschaftlich*] empiricism for which they reproach eudaemonism. Jacobi's philosophy does not take this detour. It does not first sunder the concept from empirical reality and then let the concept get its content from this very same empirical reality because outside of it there is nothing for the concept but its nullification. Instead, since the principle of his philosophy is straightforward subjectivity, Jacobi's philosophy is straightforward eudae-monism, except that it is tinged with negativity. For whereas to eudae-monism thought is not yet the ideal realm, the negative of reality, Jacobi's philosophy does reflect on thought and holds it to be nothing in itself.

The philosophy of Locke and the doctrine of happiness were the earlier philosophical manifestations [*Erscheinungen*] of this realism of finitude (to which the nonphilosophical manifestations, all the hustle and bustle of con-temporary civilization, still belong). Locke and the eudaemonists trans-formed philosophy into empirical psychology. They raised the standpoint of the subject, the standpoint of absolutely existing finitude, to the first and highest place. They asked and answered the question of what the universe is for a subjectivity that feels and is conscious by way of calculations typical of the intellect, or in other words, for a reason solely immersed in finitude, a reason that renounces intuition and cognition of the eternal. The philoso-phies of Kant, Jacobi, and Fichte are the completion and idealization of this empirical psychology; they consist in coming to understand that the infinite concept is strictly opposed to the empirical. They understood the sphere of this antithesis, a finite and an infinite, to be absolute: but [they did not see that] if infinity is thus set up against finitude, each is as finite as the other. They understood the eternal to be above this [sphere of] opposition, beyond the concept and the empirical; but they understood the cognitive faculty and reason simply to be that sphere. Now a reason that thinks only the finite will naturally be found to be able to think only the finite; and reason as impulse and instinct will naturally be found not to be able to think the eternal.

The idealism of which these philosophies are capable is an idealism of the finite; not in the sense that the finite is nothing in them, but in the sense that the finite is received into ideal form: they posit finite ideality, i.e., the pure concept, as infinity absolutely opposed to finitude, together with the finite that is real, and they posit both equally absolutely. (In its subjective dimension, that is, in Jacobi's philosophy, this idealism can only have the form of skepticism, and not even of true skepticism, because Jacobi turns pure thinking into something merely subjective, whereas idealism consists in the assertion that pure thinking is objective thinking.)

The one self-certifying certainty [*das an sich und einzig Gewisse*], then, is that there exists a thinking subject, a reason affected with finitude; and the whole of philosophy consists in determining the universe with respect to this finite reason. Kant's so-called critique of the cognitive faculties, Fichte's [doctrine that] consciousness cannot be transcended nor become transcendent, Jacobi's refusal to undertake anything impossible for reason, all amount to nothing but the absolute restriction of reason to the form of finitude, [an injunction] never to forget the absoluteness of the subject in every rational cognition; they make limitedness into an eternal law and an eternal being both in itself and for philosophy. So these philosophies have to be recognized as nothing but the culture [*Kultur*] of reflection raised to a system. This is a culture of ordinary human intellect which does, to be sure, rise to the thinking of a universal; but because it remains ordinary intellect it takes the infinite concept to be absolute thought and keeps what remains of its intuition of the eternal strictly isolated from the infinite concept. It does so either by renouncing that intuition altogether and sticking to concept and experience, or by keeping both [intuition and concept] although unable to unite them—for it can neither take up its intuition into the concept, nor yet nullify both concept and experience [in intuition]. The torment of a nobler nature subjected to this limitation, this absolute opposition, expresses itself in yearning and striving; and the consciousness that it is a barrier which cannot be crossed expresses itself as faith in a realm beyond the barrier. But because of its perennial incapacity this faith is simultaneously the impossibility of rising above the barrier into the realm of reason, the realm which is intrinsically clear and free of longing.

The fixed standpoint which the all-powerful culture of our time has established for philosophy is that of a reason affected by sensibility [*Sinnlichkeit*]. In this situation philosophy cannot aim at the cognition of God, but only at what is called the cognition of human being. This so-called human being and its humanity, conceived as a rigidly, insuperably finite sort of reason, form philosophy's absolute standpoint. Human beings are not a glowing spark of eternal beauty, or a spiritual focus of the universe, but an absolute sensibility. They do, however, have the faculty of faith so that they can touch themselves up here and there with a spot of alien super-sensuousness. It is as if art, considered simply as portraiture, were to express its ideal aspect [*ihr Idealisches*] through the longing it depicts on an ordinary face and the melancholy smile of the mouth, while it was strictly forbidden to represent the gods in their exaltation above longing and sorrow, on the grounds that the presentation of eternal images would only be possible at the expense of humanity. Similarly philosophy is not supposed to present the idea of human being, but the abstract concept of an empirical humanity all tangled up in limitations, and to stay immovably impaled on the stake of the absolute antithesis; and when it gets clear about its restriction to the sensuous—either analyzing its own abstraction or entirely abandoning it[13] in the fashion of the sentimental *bel esprit*—philosophy is supposed to prettify itself with the surface color of the supersensuous by pointing, in faith, to something higher.

Truth, however, cannot be deceived by this sort of hallowing of a finitude that remains what it was. A true hallowing should nullify the finite. If an artist cannot give true truth to what actually exists by casting an ethereal light upon it, and taking it wholly up therein; if he is only able to represent actuality in and for itself—which is what is commonly called reality and truth, though it is neither the one nor the other—then he will take refuge in feeling, in yearning and sentimentality as his remedy against actuality, spreading tears on the cheeks of the vulgar and bringing an "Oh Lord" to their lips. Thus his figures will indeed look away beyond the actual situation toward heaven, but they will do so like bats that are neither bird nor beast, and belong neither to earth nor to sky. There cannot be beauty of this sort without ugliness, nor a moral ethos of this kind without weakness and perfidy, nor such intellect as here occurs without platitude; good fortune cannot come to pass without meanness, nor ill fortune without fear and cowardice, nor any kind of fortune, without being contemptible. In the same way, when philosophy after its own fashion takes up the finite and subjectivity as absolute truth in the form of the concept, it cannot purify them [i.e., the finite and subjectivity] by connecting subjectivity with an infinite [the concept]. For this infinite is itself not the truth since it is unable to consume and consummate finitude [*die Endlichkeit aufzuzehren*].

In philosophy, however, the actual and the temporal as such disappear. This is called cruel dissection destructive of the wholeness of human being, or violent abstraction that has no truth, and particularly no practical truth. This abstraction is conceived of as the painful cutting off of an essential part from the completeness of the whole. But the temporal and empirical, and privation, are thus recognized as an essential part and an absolute in itself. It is as if someone who sees only the feet of a work of art were to complain, when the whole work is revealed to his sight, that he was being deprived of his deprivation and that the incomplete had been un-incompleted.[14] Finite cognition is this sort of cognition of a part and a singular. If the absolute were *put together* out of the finite and the infinite, abstracting from the finite would indeed be a loss. In the idea, however, finite and infinite are one, and hence finitude as such, i.e., as something that was supposed to have truth and reality in and for itself, has vanished. Yet what was negated was only the negative in finitude; and thus the true affirmation was posited.

The supreme abstraction of this absolutized negation is the ego-concept [*Egoität*], just as the thing is the highest abstraction pertaining to position [i.e., to affirmation]. Each of them is only a negation of the other. Pure being like pure thinking—an absolute thing and absolute ego-concept—are equally finitude made absolute. Eudaemonism and the Enlightenment-fuss [*Aufklärerei*] belong to this same level—not to mention much else—and so do the philosophies of Kant, Jacobi, and Fichte. We shall now proceed to a more detailed confrontation of these three philosophers with one another. . . .

82

The Speculative Good Friday

In their totality, the philosophies we have considered have in this way recast the dogmatism of being into the dogmatism of thinking, the metaphysic of objectivity into the metaphysic of subjectivity. Thus, through this whole philosophical revolution the old dogmatism and the metaphysic of reflection have at first glance merely taken on the hue of inwardness, of the latest cultural fashion. The soul as thing is transformed into the ego, the soul as practical reason into the absoluteness of the personality and singularity of the subject. The world as thing is transformed into the system of phenomena or of affections of the subject, and actualities believed in; whereas the absolute as an ob-ject [*ein Gegenstand*][15] and the absolute object [*Object*] of reason is transformed into something that is absolutely beyond rational cognition. This metaphysic of subjectivity has run through the complete cycle of its forms in the philosophies of Kant, Jacobi, and Fichte—other forms that this metaphysic has assumed do not count, even in this subjective sphere. The metaphysic of subjectivity has, therefore, completely set forth [the intrinsic stages of] the formative process of culture;[16] for this formative process consists in establishing as absolute each of the [two] single dimensions [of being and thought, object and subject, etc.] of the totality and elaborating each of them into a system. The metaphysic of subjectivity has brought this cultural process to its end. Therewith the external possibility directly arises that the true philosophy should emerge out of this [completed] culture, nullify the absoluteness of its finitudes and present itself all at once as perfected appearance, with all its riches subjected to the totality. For just as the perfection of the fine arts is conditioned by the perfection of mechanical skills, so the appearance of philosophy in all richness is conditioned by the completeness of the formative process of culture, and this completeness has now been achieved.

There is a direct connection [*Zusammenhang*] between these distinct philosophical formations and [the one true] philosophy—though the linkage is most defective in the case of Jacobi. They have their positive, genuine though subordinate, position within [true] philosophy. This is clear from the results of [our discussion of] infinity in these philosophies. They make infinity into an absolute principle, so that it becomes infected by its opposition to finitude. For they recognize that thinking is infinity, the negative side of the absolute. Infinity is the pure nullification of the antithesis or of finitude; but it is at the same time also the spring of eternal movement, the spring of that finitude which is infinite because it eternally nullifies itself. Out of this nothing and pure night of infinity, as out of the secret abyss that is its birthplace, the truth lifts itself upward.

In [truly philosophical] cognition, infinity as this negative significance of the absolute is conditioned by the positive idea that being is strictly nothing outside of the infinite, or apart from the ego and thought. Both being and thought are one. But, on the one hand, these philosophies of reflection cannot be prevented from fixating infinity, the ego, and turning it into subjectivity instead of letting it directly somersault into the positivity of the absolute idea. By this route infinity fell once more into the old antithesis, and into the whole finitude of reflection which it had itself previously nullified. But on the other hand, the philosophy of infinity is closer to the philosophy of the absolute than the philosophy of the finite is; for although infinity or thought is rigidly conceived as ego and subject, and must, in this perspective, share the same rank as the object or the finite which it holds over against itself, still there is the other perspective in which infinity is closer to the absolute than the finite is, because the inner character of infinity is negation, or indifference.

But the pure concept or infinity as the abyss of nothingness in which all being is engulfed, must signify the infinite grief [of the finite] purely as a moment of the supreme idea, and no more than a moment. Formerly, the infinite grief only existed historically in the formative process of culture. It existed as the feeling that "God godself is dead," upon which the religion of more recent times rests—the same feeling that Pascal expressed in, so to speak, sheerly empirical form: *"la nature est telle qu'elle* marque *partout un Dieu* perdu *et dans l'homme et hors de l'homme"* (nature is such that it *signifies* everywhere a *lost* God both within and outside of human being).[17] By marking this feeling as a moment of the supreme idea, the pure concept must give philosophical existence to what used to be either the moral precept that we must sacrifice the empirical being [*Wesen*], or the concept of formal abstraction [e.g., the categorical imperative]. Thereby it must reestablish for philosophy the idea of absolute freedom and along with it the absolute passion, the speculative Good Friday in place of the historical Good Friday.[18] Good Friday must be speculatively re-established in the whole truth and harshness of its Godforsakenness.[19] Since the [more] serene, less well grounded, and more individual style of the dogmatic philosophies and of the natural religions must vanish, the highest totality can and must achieve its resurrection solely from this harsh consciousness of loss, encompassing everything, and ascending in all its earnestness and out of its deepest ground to the most serene freedom of its shape.

THE RESUMPTION OF THE WHOLE INTO ONE[1]

In lectures at the University of Jena Hegel began to construct a philosophical system, experimenting with a number of approaches during a period of intense creativity from 1801 to 1806. In the earliest of these system outlines (1802–1803), he envisioned a fourfold division rather than the triadic plan (logic, nature, spirit) he arrived at just a year later. Most of these materials have been lost, and we are dependent on information provided by Karl Rosenkranz in Georg Wilhelm Friedrich Hegels Leben *(Berlin, 1844; r.p. Darmstadt, 1969), a work that takes on the character of an indispensable source. Following an introduction consisting of logic or "the science of the idea as such," there would be a philosophy of nature, concerned with the realization of the idea in nature as its "body," and a philosophy of ethical life (*Sittlichkeit*) as the "real spirit" (human beings in their social-political-cultural existence) that the idea generates for itself. For the conclusion to his system, according to Rosenkranz (p. 179), Hegel intended to take up religion as "the resumption of the whole into one, the return to the primitive simplicity of the idea." Religion is no longer regarded merely as part of social or ethical life (as it was in Hegel's Tübingen and Berne writings) but as the highest synthesis of theoretical (logical) and practical (ethical) cognition, and hence as the culmination of the whole system, which begins with the theory of the absolute and ends with the* experience *of the absolute. Here for the first time in Hegel's thought we glimpse the place of religion in relation to the whole of philosophy. Religion rather than purely philosophical knowledge is the culminating moment, but it is to be a new, philosophical religion of the spirit. In later versions of the system, ethics and religion are incorporated into the philosophy of spirit, and religion is regarded not as the final but the penultimate moment (of which Christianity remains the consummate expression), superseded in form (but not content) by speculative philosophy (see text 4). We also glimpse in this essay the rudiments of the structure by which Hegel organized his treatment of religion in the later works.*

No materials on religion survive from this first system in Hegel's own hand. But Rosenkranz provides (pp. 133–41) a summary of and quotations from a lecture fragment dating from this period that describes how Hegel moved from ethical life to religion and found in the latter the culmination of his philosophy. This is one of the most important texts of the Jena period, for it contains ideas of germinal importance for Hegel's treatment of religion in later writings, and it shows the evolving, fluid character of his thought (including some experimentation with ideas derived from Schelling). Rosenkranz's text has been translated by H. S. Harris as an appendix to the "System of Ethical Life" in System of Ethical Life and First Philosophy of Spirit, *ed. and trans. H. S. Harris and T. M. Knox (Albany: State University of New York Press, 1979), pp. 178–86. The translation has been slightly revised in accord with our editorial principles. Harris inserts a few supplementary quotations from Hegel's manuscript provided by Rudolf Haym in* Hegel und seine Zeit *(Berlin, 1857; r.p. Hildesheim, 1962); we have footnoted these. Harris's introduction (especially pp. 6, 81–85) gives a helpful interpretation of this difficult text, as does his book* Hegel's Development: Night Thoughts *(Jena 1801–1806) (Oxford: Clarendon Press, 1983), chap. 4.*

. . . [Hegel] followed out the concept of the religious *cult* as that in which a people comes to its highest self-enjoyment; and he did this in a fashion notable for its simplicity and intelligibility. He claimed that in *religion* the reality of the objective world itself, and subjectivity and particularity along with it, are posited *as superseded.* Where [subjectivity and particularity] are still held on to as *negative freedom* in this highest region of universal rationality, even just as virtuosity is (as he remarked in criticism of Schleiermacher's *Speeches on Religion,* which were epoch-making at the time), then there is no serious intent to let *spirit appear in spiritual shape.* On the contrary it is the essence of religion that spirit is not ashamed of any of its individuals;[2] it does not refuse to appear to anyone, and everyone has power over it, power to conjure it up. The supersession of subjectivity is not the sheer nullification of it, but just the nullification of its empirical individuality, and by this means it is a purification for the absolute enjoyment of [spirit's] absolute essence. For in religion the ideal shape of spirit is real, while its real side is ideal; and in it spirit appears for the individual. Hence it has for the individual above all the shape of an objective [power] which lives and moves in the people as its spirit, and is alive in all of them. In science spirit appears in an objective shape, the shape of being, but it is still spirit that is also subjective. In respect of its *subject matter speculative knowledge [das Wissen] has no particular advantage over religion.* Religion's essence drives spirit back together, out of the extension of empirical existence, into the supreme point of intensity, and sets it forth objectively for intuition, and in this enjoyment it is at the same time real, i.e., it recognizes itself in the individual, and the individual recognizes himself in it.

As the totality of empirical existence setting itself forth *objectively,* the *essence* of God has a *history* for spirit. God's living being is events and actions. The most living God of a people is its *national God,* in whom its spirit appears transfigured; and not just its spirit but also its empirical existence, the untruth and uncertainty of its life, appears as a sum of singular traits. In religion spirit is [found] not in the ideality of philosophical science [*Wissenschaft*] but in connection with reality; so it necessarily has a limited shape, which when fixated for its own sake, makes up the positive side of every religion. The *religious tradition* thus expresses two things at once: on one side the *speculative idea* of spirit, and on the other the limitation

86

derived from the *empirical* existence of the people—not the limitation of the idea in the way that *art* must employ such limitation in general. And since religion, qua religion, must exclude science and art, therefore it is an *activity* which complements art and science; it is the cult which raises subjectivity and freedom to their highest enjoyment, because it *offers up* a part of its singularity to the great spirit in worship[3] and by this sacrifice makes the rest of its property free. Through the reality of the nullification of singularity in the offering, the subject saves itself from the onesidedness of the deception [*Betrug*] that its exaltation is only a matter of thought. This action, the irony toward the mortal and profitable activity of human beings, is reconciliation, the basic idea of religion. Insofar as singularity wants to maintain itself against rational universality, it comes to be in *sin*, it comes to *transgression*. Here spirit is reconciled only as *fate in punishment*. Reconciliation is exalted above punishment and appears therefore as justified necessity.[4] For since reconciliation in general is directed only to spirit and cannot supersede the [causal] chain of determinate existence, *nothing in fate is changed by it*. Only the essence of the actual battle [*Energie des Kampfes*] against fate, as the potentiality of setting at risk the whole range of empirical existence, is also the potentiality of reconciliation with fate, since spirit has torn itself free from fate through the ethical character of the battle.

Religion must, as Hegel expressed it in the style of the nature-philosophy that was then fashionable, come on the scene of world history in the following three forms (in accord with the three universal dimensions of reason and within the bounds of *climatic* modification according to its empirical difference):

1) in the form of *identity,* in the original reconciliation between spirit and its real being in individuality;
2) in the form where spirit begins from the infinite *difference* of its identity and reconstructs from this difference a *relative* identity and reconciles itself;
3) the latter identity, subsumed under the original absolute identity, will posit the being-at-one of reason in its spiritual shape with reason in its real being or in individuality as original, and will posit at the same time its infinite antithesis, and its reconstruction.[5]

In the first dimension, as original reconciliation, religion is *nature religion.* For its pantheistic imagination,[6] nature is in and for itself a spirit and is holy. Its God has not retreated from any element. A curse may have lain on the heads of single individuals, but no universal aspect of nature is abandoned by God. Spirit may be wroth against such peoples at isolated moments, but they are certain of their reconciliation. The daily round of life is a converse with the gods, a reciprocal giving and receiving from them, and every outward motion is full of significance as a word of fate. The

shapes of the gods cannot be resolved into actual things, or historical expla-
nations, or thoughts. The *eternity of the ideals of a beautiful mythology*
rests neither on its perfect artistic beauty, nor on the truth of the ideas that
they express, nor on the actuality that belongs to them, but precisely on the
identity of all of these factors and their *indivisibility.*

In a second period this beautiful world of the gods must pass away,
along with the spirit that enlivens it. It can abide only as a memory. The
unity of spirit with its reality must be rent. The ideal principle must constitute itself in the form of universality, while the real principle sets itself up
firmly as singularity, and nature is left lying between them as a *desecrated
corpse.* Spirit must abandon its dwelling in living nature and raise itself up
as a potency against it. Ethical grief [*Schmerz*] must be infinite. The time of
this grief came when the Romans smashed the living individuality of the
peoples, putting their spirits to flight and destroying their ethical life, before
extending the universality of their lordship over the dismembered singular
parts. At the time of this dismembering for which there was no reconciliation, and of this universality that had no life—in this *boredom of the world*
when peace was lord over all the civilized earth—the original identity had
to rise out of its rent condition, it had to lift its eternal force above its grief
and come again to its own intuition. Otherwise the human race must have
perished inwardly. And the first theater for the *appearance* of ethereal reason, reawakened in the world that had ceased to be nature, had to be the
very people[7] which in the whole course of their existence has been the *most
rejected* of the peoples, because in them the *grief* was bound to be deepest,
and its utterance must have had a truth intelligible to the whole world.

In this way Christ became the founder of a religion, because he uttered
the suffering of his whole world from the inmost depth; he raised the force
of the divinity of spirit above it, the absolute certainty of reconciliation,
which he bore in himself; and by his *confidence* he awoke the confidence of
others. He uttered the suffering of his time, which had become untrue to
nature, in his absolute *contempt* for a nature become *worldly* and his
absolute confidence of reconciliation, *in his certainty that he is one with
God.* The contempt that he expressed towards the world was necessarily
bound to be avenged upon him as his fate by his death; and this death had to
vindicate the contempt of the world and make it the fixed point [of the new
religion]. These two necessary elements had to become the pivot of the new
religion: the expulsion of the gods from nature, hence contempt for the
world; and the fact that in this infinite division a human being still bore
within himself the confidence of being one with the absolute. In this human
being the world was again reconciled with spirit. Since the whole of nature
had ceased to be divine, only the nature of this human being could be divine
and nature could be come *hallowed* again only from him as focus. But

because humanity, being certain that it was not itself divine, could look upon divinity *only* in this human being and had to make the coming of individuality to oneness with absolute spirit hang upon his *personality,* his determinate existence[8] became the starting point of this religion itself. The more striking tendency of this religion was bound at first to be contempt for the world and of the universal which existed as *state;* and the symbol of this contempt was the *cross,* which, being the gallows of the world, was the most shameful and dishonorable thing.[9] A more distinctive or unambiguous[10] signal of absolute division from the world and of total war against it to wipe it out could not be established.

The other side of the infinite grief of this absolute division was its reconciliation in the faith that *God has appeared in human form* and has thus reconciled human nature with himself in this singular shape as the representative of the species. This single human shape expressed in its history the whole history of the empirical existence of the human race; it had to do this in order to be the *national God of the race.* But at the same time it expressed this history only so far as it was the history of God. In other words the principle is infinite grief, the absolute rending of nature. Reconciliation has neither meaning nor truth without this grief. In order for this level [*Potenz*] of religion to exist *it must eternally produce this grief so as to be able to reconcile it eternally.* The empirical condition of the world in which the religion originated was bound to be superseded through the struggle of this reconciling religion, so that the world was really happier and more reconciled, and the religion must in this way surpass itself. So it must bear within itself the principle by which the infinite suffering is aroused in order to reconcile it infinitely. It has this principle, the fate of the world, necessarily in the history of its God who has died the death of a transgressor. The death of a transgressor could itself be just a single death. The view of death as a universal necessity can arouse no infinite religious grief, but he who died on the cross is simultaneously the God of this religion and as such his history expresses the infinite suffering of nature deprived of its gods. The divine was bruised in the *everyday routine of life, the divine was dead.* The thought that God godself had died on earth—that alone expresses the feeling of this infinite grief; just as the thought that God is *resurrected* from the grave expresses its reconciliation. By God's life and death God is humbled, by God's resurrection humanity has become divine. This religion cannot let the infinite grief and the eternal reconciliation depend on the accidental empirical existence of single individuals.[11] It must constitute itself as a cult through which the grief is aroused and the reconciliation shared. Nature religion must leave it to *chance* how far the original reconciliation is alive in a single individual. But the religion that proceeds to the reconstruction of the indifferent harmony must produce that infinite difference by doing violence to nature so as to make it possible for its reconciliation to be a reconstructed one.

This then is what has happened with perfect *wisdom* in the Christian religion. Human being is led up to the grief of the divine death and of the mortality of all life by an infinite sum of *instituted situations,* and then awakened from this death, and hallowed in oneness with the God-man again (in whom the race is reconciled) by the eating of his body and the drinking of his blood, the most inward type of union. The history of God is the history of the whole race and every single human being goes through the whole history of the race. All nature is hallowed again, beginning from the reconsecrated human being; it is a temple of the newly awakened life. *The new consecration is extended to everything.* The lordly authority of the monarch is consecrated by religion; his scepter contains a piece of the holy cross. Every land has been provided with special messengers of God and is marked by their traces. Everyone of them can boast its own sacred history of reconciliation and has *individualized* the new consecration. To every single act and everything in the highest and lowest activities the consecration is given anew that they had lost. The old curse that lay on all things is dissolved; the whole of nature is received into the state of grace and its grief reconciled.

Through this reconstructed religion the other side, the ideality of spirit in the *form of thought,* is added to the only form of spiritual ideality that can exist in nature, namely, *art,* and folk religion must contain the highest ideas of speculation expressed not just as a mythology but in the *form of ideas.* It reveres the absolute in the form of *Trinity:* God as the *paternal principle* being *absolute thought;* then God's reality, the Father in his creation, *the eternal Son,* who, as the divine reality has two sides, the one being that of his genuine divinity, according to which the Son of God is God, the other the side of his singular existence[12] as world; finally the eternal identity of the objective world with the eternal thought, the *Holy Spirit.* Since religion proceeds from the infinite grief, the reconciliation of this grief has this connection objectively at the same time in the reconciled God as love; and the divinity in which this love finds its own felicity must come to be the *Mother of God* herself.

In *Catholicism* this religion has come to be a *beautiful* one. *Protestantism* has superseded the poetry of consecration, the individualization of holiness, and has poured the color of universality over a *patriotically* hallowed nature, transposing the *patria* of religion and the appearing of God into the distance once more—far from the people's own *patria.*[13] It has changed the infinite grief, the sense of life, the confidence and peace of reconciliation into an infinite *yearning.* It has imprinted on religion the whole character of *northern* subjectivity. Since it has in general transformed the whole cycle of grief and reconciliation into yearning, and yearning into thinking and knowing about reconciliation, and since the violence and [external] necessity with which the grief was aroused thus fall away in it, its character as infinite grief and reconciliation became the prey of chance, and this form of religion could pass over into empirical reconciliation with the actuality of existence [*Dasein*] and an unmediated and untroubled immersion in the common round of empirical activities [*Existenz*] and necessities of everyday. The religious exaltation and hallowing of empirical existence, the *Sabbath of the world,* has disappeared and life has become a common unhallowed workaday matter.

Though Hegel at that time considered Protestantism to be just as much a finite form of Christianity as Catholicism (a fact which emerges clearly enough from the above report), still he did not, like many of his contemporaries,[14] on that account go over to Catholicism. He believed rather that through the *mediation of philosophy* a *third* form of religion would emerge out of Christianity. He said in this connection: "Since that beauty and holiness [of Catholic Christendom] has gone under [in Protestant worldliness[15]], it can neither *come back again,* nor can we *mourn* for it. We can only recognize the *necessity of its passing* and surmise the higher thing for which it has to prepare the way and which must take its place. From what we have already said, in other words, it is evident that the reconstruction occurs within the sphere of the antithesis from which the grief came, and the whole form of religion up to this point belongs primarily at the level [*Potenz*][16] of the *relative antithesis,* for nature is hallowed, but not by a spirit of its own; it is reconciled, but it remains for itself a secular thing as it was before. Consecration comes to it from something external. The entire spiritual sphere has not risen up into the spiritual region from its own ground and soil.[17] The infinite grief is permanent in the hallowing, and the reconciliation itself is a sighing for heaven. Once the alien consecration has been withdrawn from Protestantism, spirit can venture to hallow itself as spirit in its own shape, and reestablish the original reconciliation with itself in a *new religion,* in which the infinite grief and the whole burden of its antithesis is taken up. It will be resolved purely and without trouble when there is a free *people* and reason has found once more its reality as an ethical spirit, a spirit which is bold enough to *assume its pure shape on its own soil and in its own majesty.* Every single individual is a blind link in the chain of absolute necessity on which the whole develops. Every single individual can extend his dominion over a greater length of this chain only if he recognizes the direction in which the great necessity will go and learns from this cognition [*Erkenntnis*] to utter the magic word which conjures up its shape. This cognition, which can embrace in itself the whole energy of the suffering and the antithesis which has ruled in the world and all the forms of its development [*Ausbildung*] for a couple of thousand years, and at the same time can raise itself above it all—this cognition only philosophy can give."[18]

3

PHENOMENOLOGY OF SPIRIT
(1807)

Hegel's most famous work was completed rapidly and under duress in the autumn of 1806. Not only was he in need of funds from the publisher, but also Napoleon's army was advancing on Jena. Shortly thereafter Hegel decided to leave Jena for financial and personal reasons; he was not to resume a university professorship until 1816 in Heidelberg. The Phenomenology of Spirit *was intended as an introduction to Hegel's "System of Science," the first main part of which did not appear until the publication of the* Science of Logic *in 1812–1816 while Hegel was headmaster of a* Gymnasium *in Nuremberg.*

The Preface to the Phenomenology *was written after the work was completed and is one of the most lucid presentations of Hegel's philosophy. We have excerpted a portion of it in which Hegel argues that the subject matter of philosophy, "the true" or "the absolute," must be grasped as both* substance *and* subject. *But this is to say that the absolute is* spirit, *for it is precisely spirit that unifies substance and subject, identity and difference, the ideal and the real, thought and life, through a process of absolution (releasement) and resolution (reintegration). The religious name of this absolving spirit is "God," and God must accordingly be understood to become God only through a process that entails "the seriousness, the anguish, the patience, and the labor of the negative."*

Our second selection provides the whole of the Introduction, which explains that the "phenomenology" of spirit is the "science of the experience of consciousness." Consciousness appears in the three basic forms of consciousness, self-consciousness, and reason. Reason takes on the shape of spirit when it achieves ethical and cultural expression (that is, spirit is intrinsically an intersubjective, social category, although the whole process is also spirit); and the highest shapes of spirit are religion (including art) and philosophy (absolute knowing). The journey of spirit through the various shapes of consciousness constitutes for Hegel a veritable itinerarium mentis in Deum: *the phenomenology of spirit is a religious quest, a pilgrimage.*

The chapter on religion (chapter 7 of the Phenomenology*) is Hegel's fullest and most mature exposition of this subject to date. It treats of natur-*

al religion, the religion of art, and the revelatory religion. Natural religion is the earliest form encountered in Hegel's phenomenological history of religions, while the religion of art means Greek religion, and the revelatory religion (die offenbare Religion) *Christianity. Our excerpt provides the opening paragraphs of this chapter and the whole of the section on revelatory religion. Hegel's treatment of the latter in the* Phenomenology *should be compared with that found in the* Encyclopedia *(selection 4) and in the 1824* Lectures on the Philosophy of Religion *(selection 6.4).*

A truly satisfactory translation of the Phenomenology of Spirit *does not yet exist. The first two texts have been newly translated by J. Michael Stewart, and the last two by the editor, from* Phänomenologie des Geistes, *ed. Johannes Hoffmeister (Hamburg: Felix Meiner Verlag, 1952), pp. 19–30, 63–75, 473–80, 521–48. The translations of J. B. Baillie (London: Allen & Unwin, 1949) and A. V. Miller (Oxford: Clarendon Press, 1977) have been compared and have provided helpful guidance. Our translation has evolved from theirs but is quite different in terms of precision and the rendering of technical concepts. The frequent use of italics for emphasis in the German text is retained. The notes are provided by the editor; some are condensed from the critical edition prepared by Wolfgang Bonsiepen and Reinhard Heede (*Gesammelte Werke, *vol. 9 [Hamburg: Felix Meiner Verlag, 1980]).*

THE ABSOLUTE AS SPIRIT

. . . In my view, which can be justified only by the exposition of the system itself, everything depends on comprehending and expressing the true as *subject* no less than as *substance*. At the same time, it should be noted that substantiality includes the universal or the *immediacy of knowledge* itself no less than the immediacy that is *being* or immediacy *for* knowledge.

If conceiving God as the one substance scandalized the age in which God was so characterized, the reason lay in part in the instinctive awareness that in so doing one was only submerging self-consciousness, not preserving it. But in part the opposite view, which holds fast to thinking as thinking, *universality* as such, is the same simplicity, or undifferentiated, unmoved substantiality. And even if, thirdly, thought does combine with itself the being of substance, conceiving immediacy or intuiting as thinking, the question still arises whether this intellectual intuiting does not in turn relapse into inert simplicity and portray actuality itself in a nonactual manner.[1]

Moreover, it is only to the extent that it is the movement of positing its own self, or mediating with its own self the process of becoming other than itself, that the living substance is the mode of being that is truly *subject* or, what amounts to the same, truly actual. As subject, it is pure *simple nega-*

tivity, and for that very reason, the scission of what is simple. In other words, it is only the kind of duplication that sets up oppositions and in turn negates this indifferent diversity and its antithesis. It is only this self-*reinstating* sameness, or reflection in other-being, within itself—not an *original* or *immediate* unity as such—that is the true. The process is that whereby one becomes one's own self, a circular process that presupposes its end and has its end for its beginning, and that is actual only by being carried out and by virtue of its end.

The life of God and the divine cognizing may therefore, if one chooses, be expressed as the play of love with itself;[2] but this idea sinks into the realm of what is merely edifying, and even insipid, if the seriousness, the anguish, the patience, and the labor of the negative are lacking from it. *In itself,* the divine life may well be untroubled identity and unity with itself, such as makes light of otherness and estrangement, and also of the overcoming of estrangement. But this *in-itself* [*Ansich*] is abstract universality, in which the nature of the divine life *to be for itself,* and with it the whole self-movement constituting the form, is left out of account. If the form is declared to be the same as the essence, then it is for that very reason a misunderstanding to suppose that cognizing can rest content with the in-itself or essence but dispense with the form—that the absolute principle or absolute intuition makes it necessary to elaborate the essence, in other words, develop the form.[3] Just because the form is as essential to the essence as the essence is to itself, the essence has to be conceived and expressed not merely as essence, i.e., as immediate substance, or as pure self-envisagement of the divine, but equally as *form,* and in the whole richness of the developed form. Only then is it conceived and expressed as something actual.

The true is the whole. But the whole is nothing other than the essence [*Wesen*] consummating itself through its development. Of the absolute it must be said that it is essentially *result,* that only at the *end* is it what it in truth is; and precisely in this consists its nature, namely to be actual, subject, becoming its own self. However contradictory it may appear that the absolute should be conceived essentially as result, a little consideration will set this appearance of contradiction in its true light. The beginning, the principle, or the absolute, as at first or immediately expressed, is only the universal. Just as, when I say "*all* animals," this expression cannot pass for a zoology, it is equally plain that the words "the divine," "the absolute," "the eternal," and so on, do not express what is contained in them; and it is only such words that in fact express intuition as something immediate. Whatever is more than such a word, even if it is only the transition to a proposition, contains a *becoming-other* that has to be taken back; it is a mediation. But it is just this that is rejected with horror, as if absolute cognition were surrendered when more is made of mediation than simply to say that it is nothing absolute and has no place in the absolute.

This horrified rejection, however, stems in fact from ignorance of the nature of mediation and of absolute cognition itself. For mediation is nothing other than self-moving identity with self, or reflection into self, the moment comprised by the "I's" having being-for-self—nothing other than pure negativity or, reduced to its pure abstraction, *simple becoming*. The "I," or the mediating process involved in becoming generally, is in fact by virtue of its simplicity immediacy coming to be, the immediate itself.

It is therefore a misconception of the nature of reason when reflection is excluded from the true and is not grasped as a positive moment of the absolute. It is reflection that makes the true the result, but it is also reflection that sublates this antithesis between the true's coming-to-be and its result, for this becoming is likewise simple and therefore not distinct from the form of the true, which consists in showing itself as *simple* in the result; becoming is rather just this process of having returned into simplicity.

Though the embryo is indeed *in itself* a human being, it is not so *for itself;* this it only is as fully formed reason, which has *made* itself into what it is *in itself.* Only then does it achieve actuality. But this result is itself simple immediacy, for it is self-conscious freedom which is at peace with itself, which has not set the antithesis on one side and left it lying there, but is reconciled with it.

What has just been said can also be expressed by saying that reason is *purposive activity.* The exaltation of what is supposed to be nature over what is misconceived as thinking, and more especially the repudiation of external purposiveness, has brought the form of *purpose* in general into discredit.[4] In the same way that Aristotle too defines nature as purposive activity, only purpose is what is immediate, *at rest,* the unmoved that *itself sets in motion;* as such it is *subject.*[5] Its power to set in motion, taken abstractly, is *being-for-self* or pure negativity. The only reason why the result is the same as the beginning is that the *beginning* is *purpose.* To put it another way, the only reason why the actual is the same as its concept is that as purpose the immediate contains the self or pure actuality within itself. The realized purpose or existent actuality is movement and unfolded becoming; but it is just this unrest that is the self, and the reason why the self is indifferent to that immediacy and simplicity of the beginning is that it is the result, that which has returned into itself—but what has returned into itself is nothing else but the self, and the self is self-relating identity and simplicity.

The need to represent the absolute as *subject* has found expression in the propositions: *God* is the eternal, the moral world-order, love, and so on.[6] In such propositions the true is just baldly posited as subject, but it is not presented as the movement of reflecting itself into itself. In a proposition of this kind one begins with the word *God.* Of itself, this is a meaningless sound, a mere name; it is only the predicate that says *what God is,* and gives God content and meaning; only when we get to the end of the proposition does the empty beginning become actual knowledge. This being so, it is not clear why one does not speak solely of the eternal, the moral world-order, and so on, or, as the ancients did,[7] of pure concepts, of being, the One and so on, of what is the meaning, without adding the *meaningless* sound as well. But it is just this word that indicates that what is posited is not a being or essence or universal in general, but something reflected into itself, a subject. At the same time this is only anticipated. The subject is taken to be a fixed point, to which the predicates are attached as their support, by a process that pertains to those that have knowledge of the fixed point, and is not regarded as pertaining to the fixed point itself; yet it is only through this process that the content could be presented as subject. The nature of the process is such that it cannot pertain to the fixed point; but once the fixed point has been presupposed, the nature of the process cannot be otherwise, it can only be external. The anticipation that the absolute is subject is therefore not only the actuality of this concept; it even precludes such actuality, positing the concept as it does as a static point, whereas its actuality is self-movement.

Among the various consequences that follow from what has just been said, this one in particular can be stressed, that it is only as science or as *system* that knowledge attains actuality and can be expounded; and furthermore, that a so-called basic proposition or principle of philosophy,[8] if true, is also false, just because it is only a basic proposition or principle. It is for that reason a simple matter to refute it. The refutation consists in bringing out its defective character; but the reason why it is defective is that it is only the universal or principle, the beginning. If the refutation goes to the root of the matter, it is derived and developed from the principle itself, not accomplished by bringing in counter-assertions and random thoughts from outside. The refutation would therefore properly consist in developing the principle and thus remedying its defective character, if it did not lose sight of its true function by paying attention solely to its *negative* action and disregarding the *positive* aspect of what it is about, and what it achieves. The genuinely *positive* exposition of the beginning is at the same time conversely and in equal measure a negative attitude to it, namely to its one-sided form, that of being initially *immediate* or *purpose.* It can therefore be taken equally well as refutation of what constitutes the *basis* of the system, though it is more correct to regard it is as a demonstration that the *basis* or principle of the system is in fact only its *beginning.*

That the true is actual only as system, or that substance is essentially subject, is expressed in the notion that represents the absolute as *spirit*[9]—

the most sublime concept, one appertaining to the modern age and its religion. The spiritual alone is the *actual;* it is essence or that which has *being in itself;* it is that which *relates itself to itself* and is *determinate;* it is *other-being* and *being-for-self,* and what, in this determinacy, or its being outside itself, remains within itself; in other words, it is *in and for itself.* But this being-in-and-for-itself is initially for us or *in itself,* it is spiritual *substance.* It must also be this *for its own self,* it must be the knowledge of the spiritual, and of itself as spirit; that is to say, it must be present to itself as *object,* but immediately no less than as a sublated object, reflected into itself. Only for us is it *for itself,* insofar as it itself generates its spiritual content; but insofar as it is also for itself for its own self, this self-generating, the pure concept, is for it at the same time the objective element, in which it has its determinate being [*Dasein*], and in this way it is in its determinate being for its own self an object reflected into itself. Spirit that, so developed, knows itself as spirit is *scientific knowledge* [*Wissenschaft*]. Such knowledge is its actuality, and the realm it builds for itself is its own element.

Pure self-recognition in absolute otherness, this ethereal element *as such* is the ground and soil of scientific knowledge; in other words, it is *knowledge in general.* The beginning of philosophy presupposes or requires that consciousness should reside in this *element.* But this element itself achieves its own consummation and transparency only through the movement of its becoming. It is pure spirituality as the *universal* that has the manner of simple immediacy; and this simple element, possessing as it does *existence,* is the soil [of scientific knowledge], the kind of thinking that is present only in spirit. Because this element, this immediacy of spirit, is the very substance of spirit, it is the *transfigured essence,* reflection that is itself simple and is for itself immediacy as such, *being,* which is reflection into itself. For its part, scientific knowledge requires of self-consciousness that it should have raised itself into this ethereal element in order to be able to live, and [actually] to live, with and in scientific knowledge. Conversely, individuals have the right to demand that science provide them with the ladder, at least, to this standpoint, should exhibit to them this standpoint within themselves. Their right is based on their absolute independence, which they are conscious of possessing in every shape of their knowing; for in each, whether it is recognized by science or not, and irrespective of the content, their right is the absolute form, that is to say, the *immediate certainty* of themselves and thereby, if this expression be preferred, unconditioned *being.* If the standpoint of consciousness, that of knowing objective things in opposition to oneself, and oneself in opposition to them—if this standpoint is regarded by science as the *other,* and that in which consciousness knows itself to be in self-communion rather as the loss of spirit, so conversely the scientific element is for consciousness a remote beyond in which it no longer possesses itself. Each of these two partial standpoints appears to the other as a perversion of the truth. For natural consciousness to entrust itself, without further ado, to the guidance of science is tantamount to trying just this once, and for what motive it has no idea, to walk on its head; the compulsion to assume this unwonted posture, and move about in it, is a violence it is supposed to do to itself, with no more preparation than there seems to be necessity for it.

Let science be in its own self what it will; relatively to immediate self-consciousness it presents the appearance of being a perversion of the latter, or again, because immediate self-consciousness has the principle of its actuality in the certain knowledge of its own self, science appears to lack actuality, since self-consciousness exists on its own account, outside of science. Science has therefore to assimilate this element of self-certainty, or rather show that it already possesses it, and how. Lacking such actuality, science is only the content as the *in-itself,* the *purpose* that is at first still something *inward,* not as spirit but only spiritual substance. This *in-itself* has to express itself outwardly and become *for itself,* and this means simply that it has to posit self-consciousness as one with itself.

It is this coming-to-be of *science in general,* or of *knowledge,* that is portrayed in this *phenomenology* of spirit. Knowledge as it is initially, or *immediate spirit,* is what is devoid of spirit, i.e., *sense-consciousness.* In order to become genuine knowledge, or to beget the scientific element that is the pure concept of science itself, it has to undertake a long and laborious journey. This process of coming-to-be, as evinced in its content and the shapes of knowing displayed in it, will not be what is commonly imagined by leading the unscientific consciousness up to the level of scientific knowledge; it will also be something different from establishing the foundations of science; least of all will it be like the heady enthusiasm that, like a shot from a pistol, starts straight away with absolute knowledge and makes short work of other standpoints simply by declaring that it takes no notice of them.

The task of leading the individual out from its uneducated standpoint and bringing it to knowledge had to be seen in its universal sense, just as it was the universal individual, self-conscious spirit, whose formative education [*Bildung*] had to be considered. As regards the relationship between them, every moment, as it gains concrete form and a configuration of its own, is evinced in the universal individual. The particular individual is incomplete spirit, a concrete shape in whose whole existence *one* determinateness predominates while the others are present only in blurred outlines. In spirit that has advanced to a higher level, the lower concrete existence has been reduced to an inconspicuous moment; what was previously the crux of the matter is now no more than a trace, its particular shape shrouded and become a mere shadowy outline. Individuals whose substance is spirit at a higher level go through these past stages in the same way that people embarking on a higher science run through the preparatory studies they have long since absorbed in order to bring their content to mind; they recall the recollection of them, without having any lasting interest in them. The single individual must also run through the formative stages of universal spirit as far as content is concerned, but as shapes that spirit has already left behind, as stages on a way that has been worked over and levelled. Thus, we find in regard to factual information that what in former ages engaged the attention of persons of mature mind has sunk to the level of information, exercises and even games for children; and in this pedagogical progress we shall recognize the history of the cultural development [*Bildung*] of the world traced, as it were, in a silhouette. This past existence is the already acquired property of universal spirit, constituting the substance of individuals and, appearing thus, externally to them, making up their inorganic nature. In this respect, education [*Bildung*], viewed from the side of individuals, consists in their laying hands on this element that is already available, making its inorganic nature organic to themselves and taking possession of it for themselves. Looked at from the side of universal spirit as substance, however, what this means is that substance gives itself the self-consciousness that properly belongs to it, brings about its own coming-to-be and reflection into itself.

Science portrays this developmental movement in all its detail and necessity, and also portrays in its configuration what has already sunk to the level of a moment and property of spirit. The goal is spirit's insight into what knowing is. Impatience demands the impossible, namely, the attainment of the end without the means. For one thing, the *length* of the path has to be endured, for each moment is necessary. For another, each moment has to be *lingered over,* because each is itself an individual entire shape and can only be viewed in absolute perspective insofar as its determinateness is regarded as a whole or concrete, or the whole is regarded in the distinctive light conferred by this determination.

Since the substance of the individual, even the world-spirit itself, has had the patience to pass through these forms in the lengthy process of time, and to undertake the enormous labor of world history, in which it bodied forth in each form the entire content of itself, as each is capable of presenting it, and since there is no less laborious way by which it could attain consciousness of itself, individuals cannot by the very nature of the case conceive their substance any more easily. At the same time, they do have less trouble because all this has already been *implicitly* accomplished; the content is already actuality reduced to possibility, its immediacy overcome and the embodied shape presented as an abridged notation, a simple determination of thought. The very fact of being something *thought* makes the content the *property* of substance. Existence has no longer to be converted into the form of *being-in-itself*, but only the in-itself—no longer merely something primitive, nor submerged in existence, but rather present as something *recollected*—into the form of *being-for-itself*. How this is done must be indicated in more detail.

At the standpoint from which we here take up this movement we are spared, in connection with the whole, the necessity of sublating *existence;* what still remains, however, and requires a higher kind of transformation, is *representation* [*Vorstellung*] and *acquaintance* [*Bekanntschaft*] with the forms. The existence that has been taken back into substance is, through that first negation, initially transposed into the element of the self in *immediate* fashion only. So this property it has acquired has still the same character of uncomprehended immediacy, of passive indifference, as existence itself, which in this way has merely passed over into *representation*. At the same time, it is thus something with which the existent spirit is already *acquainted*, which it is finished and done with, so that it is no longer active and thus concerned with it. If the activity that is finished and done with existence is itself only the movement of the particular spirit, the spirit that does not comprehend itself, so conversely knowing is directed against the representation thus formed, against this being-acquainted; knowing is the activity of the *universal self* and the interest involved in *thinking*.

What we are acquainted with, quite generally, just because we are [merely] *acquainted* [*bekannt*] with it, is not known cognitively [*erkannt*]. It is the commonest way of deceiving ourselves, or others, in regard to cognitive knowledge, to assume acquaintance with something and accept it on that account. For all the talk that may accompany it, such knowledge, not knowing how or why it knows, gets nowhere. Subject and object, God, nature, the understanding, the sensible realm, and so on are uncritically made the foundation with which we are acquainted and as something valid, and constitute fixed points from which to set out and to which to return. While they remain unmoved, the movement goes to and fro between them, and so proceeds only on their surface. Similarly, the process of grasping and testing them consists in seeing whether everyone finds what is said of them in their own representation as well, whether the matter seems so to them, and whether they are acquainted with it or not.

The customary way of *analyzing* a representation was in fact nothing else than to transcend the form in which it was an object of acquaintance.[10] To break a representation up into its original elements is to revert to its moments, which at all events do not have the form of the representation as it is encountered, but constitute the immediate property of the self. To be sure, such analysis only arrives at *thoughts*, which are themselves determinations that are familiar, fixed, and inert. But what is thus *separated* and nonactual is itself an essential moment; for it is only by separating or dividing itself, and making itself nonactual, that the concrete becomes self-moving. The activity of separating out is the function of the *understanding* [*Verstand*], the most astonishing and mightiest of powers, or rather the absolute power. The circle that remains self-enclosed, and as substance holds its moments together, is an immediate relationship, one that has therefore nothing astonishing about it. But that what is accidental as such, cut off from its concomitant circumstances, what is bound and is actual only in connection with an other, should attain an existence of its own and a separate freedom—this is the tremendous power of the negative; it is the energy of thought, of the pure "I." Death, if that is what we want to call this nonactuality, is of all things the most dreadful, and to hold fast what is dead requires more strength than anything else. Lacking strength, beauty hates the understanding for expecting of it what it cannot deliver. But the life of spirit is not the life that is afraid of death and keeps itself untouched by devastation, but the life that endures death and maintains itself in it. It attains its truth only when, in utter dismemberment, it finds itself. It is this power, not as something positive that turns away from the negative, as when we say of something that it is nothing or is false, and then being finished and done with it leave it and pass on to something else; on the contrary, spirit is this power only by looking the negative in the face and lingering over it. This lingering over it is the magic power that converts the negative into being. This power is the same as what we earlier called the subject, which by giving determinateness existence in its own element transcends abstract immediacy, i.e., immediacy that merely *is,* and by so doing becomes authentic substance, [i.e.,] being or immediacy whose mediation does not lie outside it but is this mediation itself. . . .

THE SCIENCE OF THE EXPERIENCE OF CONSCIOUSNESS

It is a natural supposition that before proceeding to the proper subject matter of philosophy, namely the actual cognition of what truly is, it is necessary to come to a prior understanding about cognition, which is regarded either as the instrument whereby to lay hold of the absolute or as the medium through which to catch sight of it.[1] There seem good grounds for concern, on the one hand, that there might be various kinds of cognition among which one might be better adapted than another for the attainment of this goal, and thus it is possible to make a bad choice between them; and on the other hand, that, since cognition is a faculty of a specific kind and scope, without a more precise definition of its nature and limits we may grasp clouds of error instead of the heaven of truth. And there is a natural tendency for this concern to give way to the conviction that the whole enterprise that sets out to secure for consciousness by cognition what has being in itself is in its very concept absurd, and that cognition and the absolute are separated from one another by a hard-and-fast dividing line. For if cognition is the instrument whereby to lay hold of absolute being, it immediately occurs to one that the application of an instrument to anything does not leave it as it is on its own account but proceeds to reshape and alter it. Or if cognition is not an instrument of our activity but to a certain extent a passive medium through which the light of truth reaches us, then again we do not receive the truth as it is in itself, but as it is through and in this medium. In both cases we are employing a means that immediately brings about the opposite of its own end; or rather, what is absurd is that we make use of a means at all.

To be sure, it seems open to us to remedy this sorry state of affairs by acquainting ourselves with the way in which the *instrument* operates; for this enables us to remove from the result whatever part of our representation of the absolute, as obtained through the instrument, pertains to the latter, and thus obtain the truth in its purity. This improvement, however, would in fact only bring us back to where we were before. If we remove from a reshaped thing whatever is due to the instrument, then the thing—in this case, the absolute—becomes for us just what it was before this (accordingly superfluous) effort. If the absolute was supposedly just to be brought closer to us through the instrument, without anything being changed in it, like for instance a bird caught by a lime twig, in all probability it would scorn such a trick, were it not in and for itself and of its own volition already present to us. For a trick is what cognition would be in such a case, since with its manifold exertions it gives itself the air of being about some quite different business than merely bringing about the immediate and therefore effortless relationship. Alternatively, if examination of what we imagine to be the *medium* of cognition teaches us the law of its refraction, it is again useless to eliminate this refraction from the result we obtain. For cognition is not the refraction of the ray but the ray itself whereby truth impinges on us, and if this were removed all that would be indicated would be pure direction or emptiness.

At the same time, if the fear of falling into error introduces an element of mistrust into scientific knowledge, which in the absence of such scruples itself sets to work and actually cognizes, it is not clear why conversely we should not mistrust this very mistrust and be concerned as to whether this fear of error is not itself an error. In fact, it presupposes something—indeed a great deal—as truth, and bases its scruples and inferences on what itself needs prior scrutiny to see if it is true. Specifically it presupposes *notions* [*Vorstellungen*] of *cognition* as an *instrument* and *medium*, and also a *distinction between ourselves and this cognition*. But above all it presupposes that the absolute *stands on one side* and *cognition on the other side,* by itself and separate from the absolute, yet something real. In other words, it presupposes that cognition—as outside the absolute and therefore it might seem also outside truth—is nevertheless true, an assumption whereby what calls itself fear of error reveals itself rather as fear of the truth.

This conclusion stems from the fact that the absolute alone is true, or the true alone is absolute. It can be set aside by making the distinction that one type of cognition, though it does not cognize the absolute as scientific knowledge aims to, is still true, and that cognition in general, even if to be sure incapable of grasping the absolute, may nonetheless be capable of other truth. But we eventually see that this kind of beating about the bush leads in the long run to a confused distinction between something that is absolutely true and something that is true in some other way, and that "the absolute," "cognition," and so on are words that presuppose a meaning which has first to be ascertained.

Instead of bothering ourselves with such useless notions and ways of speaking of cognition as an instrument for laying hold of the absolute or as a medium through which we glimpse the truth (for these relationships seem to be what all these notions of a cognition cut off from the absolute, and an absolute cut off from cognition, ultimately amount to)—instead of putting up with the kind of excuses to which the [supposed] incapacity of scientific knowledge gives rise once one assumes such relationships, so as to spare oneself the effort involved in scientific knowledge but at the same time give the impression of being engaged in serious and zealous endeavor—instead of bothering to refute all these notions, we could reject them out of hand as adventitious and arbitrary, while the associated use of words such as "absolute," "cognition," as also "objective" and "subjective" and countless others whose meaning is assumed to be generally familiar, could be regarded as no more than so much deception. For to give out on the one hand that their meaning is generally familiar, and on the other that one possesses their concept oneself, seems more like an attempt to dispense with the important matter, which is precisely to provide this concept. We could with more justification spare ourselves the trouble of taking any notice of such notions and ways of speaking, the intention of which is to provide a defense against scientific knowledge itself, for they constitute merely an empty appearance of knowledge, which vanishes immediately as soon as scientific knowledge comes on the scene.

But in the very fact that scientific knowledge does come on the scene, it is itself an appearance [*Erscheinung*]; in coming on the scene, it is not yet scientific knowledge displayed and unfurled in its truth. In this regard it is a matter of indifference whether we think of scientific knowledge as *itself* the appearance because it comes on the scene *alongside something else,* or call that other, untrue form of knowledge its process of appearing. Scientific knowledge, however, must liberate itself from this show [*Schein*]; and it can only do so by turning against it. For it cannot simply reject a form of knowledge that is not true, as a commonplace way of looking at things, and assure us that it itself is a quite different type of cognition, for which the other type of knowledge is of no account. Nor can it appeal to the intimation of something better within this other. By the former *assurance* it declared its force to lie simply in its *being;* but untrue knowledge likewise appeals to the fact that *it is,* and *assures* us that for it scientific knowledge is nothing. One barren assurance, however, is worth just as much as another. Still less can scientific knowledge appeal to the intimations of something better that are present in untrue cognition, and there point the way to science. For it would, on the one hand, be appealing once again to what merely *is;* and on the other hand, it would be appealing to itself, to the way in which it exists in untrue cognition, i.e., to a bad mode of its existence, to its appearance rather than to how it is in and for itself. This is the reason for undertaking at this point an exposition of knowledge as appearing or phenomenal [*erscheinendes Wissen*].

Now, because the present exposition has only appearing or phenomenal knowledge for its object, it seems itself not to be scientific knowledge, freely moving in its own peculiar shape; but it can be regarded from the latter point of view as the path taken by natural consciousness as it presses forward to true knowledge, or that taken by the soul as it journeys through its successive configurations, as so many stations appointed for it by its nature, so that it may attain to the purity of spirit by becoming, through the complete experience of itself, acquainted with what in its very self it is.

Natural consciousness will show itself to be only the concept of knowing, in other words not real knowing. Since, however, it immediately takes itself rather to be real knowing, this path has a negative significance for it, and what is in fact the realization of the concept counts for it rather as loss of its own self; for on this path it does lose its truth. This can therefore be regarded as the path of *doubt,* or more properly as the path of despair. For what happens on it is not what is usually understood by doubting, a stumbling over this or that presumed truth, followed in due course by a disappearance of the doubt and a return to the truth in question—so that ultimately the matter is taken as it was in the first place. On the contrary, this path is the conscious insight into the untruth of phenomenal knowing, for which the most real is what is in truth only the unrealized concept. Thus, this thoroughgoing skepticism is also not what an earnest zeal for truth and scientific knowledge fancies it has prepared and equipped itself for in their service—namely, the *resolve,* in scientific thinking, not to deliver oneself over to the thoughts of others but to test everything oneself and follow only one's own conviction or, better still, to produce everything oneself and accept only one's own deed for what is true.

The successive configurations that consciousness transverses along this road in fact constitute the detailed history of the education [*Bildung*] of consciousness itself to the level of scientific knowledge. The resolve to follow only one's own convictions represents this educational process in its own simple manner as something immediately over and done with; the path actually taken by consciousness, on the other hand, as opposed to this untruth, is the actual carrying out of the process. To follow one's own conviction is, to be sure, more than giving oneself over to authority; but changing an opinion accepted on authority into one based on one's own conviction does not necessarily change its content and replace error by truth. The only difference between sticking to a system of opinion and prejudice based on the authority of others and one based on one's own conviction lies in the conceit attendant on the latter position. The skepticism that is directed to the whole compass of phenomenal consciousness, by contrast, for the first time equips spirit to examine what truth is; for it brings about a despair in regard to the so-called natural views, thoughts, and opinions (irrespective of whether these are called one's own or someone else's) with which the consciousness that sets about the task of examining *without further ado* is still filled and hampered, thus being in fact incapable of what it wants to undertake.

The *completeness* of the forms of non-real consciousness will be brought about by the very necessity of their advancing and remaining linked together. To make this intelligible, it may be remarked, by way of a general preliminary, that the exposition of untrue consciousness in its untruth is not merely a *negative* procedure. The natural consciousness in general takes such a one-sided view of it; and a mode of knowing that makes this one-sidedness its essence is one of the shapes of incomplete consciousness we shall encounter along the way. This is indeed the skepticism that in the result never sees anything but *pure nothingness* and disregards the fact that this nothingness is in determinate form the nothingness *of that from which it results*. It is only when taken as the nothingness of that from which it derives, however, that nothingness is in fact the true result; it is itself then something *determinate* and has a *content*. The skepticism that ends up with the abstraction of nothingness or emptiness is incapable of getting any further, but must wait and see whether perchance something new comes along, and what it is—in order to throw it into the same empty abyss. But where the result is grasped as it is in truth, as *determinate* negation, a new form has thereby immediately arisen; and the negation provides the transition by means of which advance through the complete series of shapes comes about of itself.

But the *goal* is just as necessarily fixed for knowledge as the series constituting the advance. The goal is where knowing no longer needs to go beyond itself, where it finds its own self, where the concept corresponds to the object, and the object to the concept. The advance towards this goal is consequently also unhalting, and at no earlier station along the way is satisfaction to be found. That which is limited to a natural life cannot by its own efforts go beyond its immediate existence, but it is driven beyond it by something else, and this being torn out of existence is its death. Consciousness, however, is, for its own self, its *concept,* and so immediately transcends what is limited—and since this latter belongs to it, transcends its own self. Along with the singular is posited for consciousness the beyond, be it only, as in spatial intuition, *beside* what is limited. Consciousness thus suffers this violence at its own hands; it spoils its own limited satisfaction. When it feels this violence, fear may well make it draw back from the truth and strive to hold onto what it is in danger of losing. But it can find no peace. If it seeks to remain in unthinking indolence, then thought troubles its thoughtlessness, and the restlessness of thought disturbs its indolence. Or if it assumes the form of sentimentality, which assures us it finds everything *good in its kind,* then this assurance likewise suffers violence from reason, which finds something not good precisely insofar as it is a kind. Or again, fear of the truth may hide from itself, and from others, behind the pretext that it is the burning zeal for truth itself that makes it so difficult, even impossible, for it to find any truth other than the only truth of which vanity is capable—that of being always cleverer than any thoughts one derives from oneself or from others. This conceit, which understands how to belittle every truth and turn away from it back into itself, and gloats over this its own understanding, which always knows how to dissolve every thought and instead of any content find only the barren ego—this is a satisfaction that must be left to its own devices, for it flees the universal and seeks only a being-for-self.

In addition to these preliminary and general remarks concerning the manner and the necessity of the advance, it may also be of service to say something about *the method used in the detailed exposition.* This exposition, viewed as a way of *relating scientific to phenomenal knowledge,* and as an *investigation* and *testing of the reality of cognition,* seemingly cannot take place without some presupposition that forms its underlying *criterion.* For testing consists in applying an accepted criterion, and the decision whether what is tested is right or wrong turns on whether it is found to be in conformity with the criterion or not, the criterion itself (including scientific knowledge, were this the criterion) being here accepted as the *essence* or *in-itself*. But here, where scientific knowledge first comes on the scene, neither it nor anything else has yet justified itself as the essence or in-itself; and without something of the sort no testing seems feasible.

This contradiction and the means for its removal will become more specific in form if we first call to mind the abstract determinations of knowledge and truth as they arise in regard to consciousness. Consciousness *distinguishes* something from itself to which at the same time it *relates* itself; another way in which this is expressed is that it is something *for consciousness*. And the determinate aspect of this process whereby something is *related to* or has *being for a consciousness* is *knowledge*. But we distinguish this being-for-another from *being-in-itself;* what is related to knowledge is likewise distinguished from it and posited as also *subsisting* outside of this relationship. The aspect pertaining to this in-itself is called *truth*. What these determinations actually involve need not concern us further here. Since the object of our inquiry is phenomenal knowledge, its determinations too will initially be taken up as they immediately present themselves; and they do seem to present themselves in the manner in which we have apprehended them.

If now we inquire into the truth of knowledge, it seems that we are inquiring what it is *in itself*. Yet in this inquiry it is *our* object, it has being *for us*. What we would get as its *in-itself* would thus rather be its being *for us;* and what we would assert to be its essence would be not so much its truth as only our knowledge of it. The essence or the criterion would lie in us, and would not necessarily have to be recognized by what was to be compared with it, and about which a decision was to be taken as a result of this comparison.

But the nature of the object we are investigating overcomes this dissociation or semblance of dissociation and presupposition. Consciousness furnishes its criterion in itself, and the investigation will therefore be a comparison of consciousness with itself; for the distinction that has just been made falls within consciousness. In consciousness one thing is *for an* other; in other words, consciousness itself possesses the determinateness of the moment constituted by knowledge. At the same time this other is to consciousness not merely *for it*, but also outside this relation, i.e., *in itself;* this is the moment constituted by truth. In what consciousness declares within itself to be the *in-itself* or the *true*, we therefore have the criterion that consciousness itself sets up by which to measure its knowing. If we call *knowledge* the *concept* but the essence or *truth* what subsists or the *object*, then the test consists in seeing whether the concept corresponds to the object. If, however, we call *the essence* or in-itself *of the object the concept*, and conversely by *object* understand it as *standing over against* [*Gegen-stand*], i.e., as it is *for an other*, then the test consists in seeing whether the object corresponds to its concept. Clearly the two procedures are the same. But the essential point to bear in mind throughout the investigation is that these two elements, *concept* and *object, being-for-an-other* and *being-in-itself,* themselves fall within what we are investigating, namely knowledge; and we accordingly do not need to import criteria or resort to *our* bright ideas and thoughts in the course of the investigation. It is by leaving these aside that we succeed in viewing it, the matter at hand [*die Sache*], as it is *in and for itself.*

But not only in this respect—that concept and object, the criterion and what is to be tested, are present in consciousness itself—is a contribution from us superfluous; we are also spared the trouble of comparing the two and actually *testing* them, so that in this respect too, in that consciousness tests *itself,* all that is left for us to do is simply to look on. For consciousness is on the one hand consciousness of the object, and on the other hand consciousness of itself—consciousness of what for it is the truth, and consciousness of its knowledge of the truth. Since both are *for one and the same consciousness,* it is itself their comparison; whether its knowledge of the object corresponds to it or not is a matter *for the same consciousness.* The object, to be sure, seems only to be for consciousness in the way that consciousness knows it; it does not seem possible for consciousness to get, as it were, behind the object, to see how it is *not for consciousness* but *in itself,* nor therefore does it seem possible to test its knowledge against it. But the distinction between the in-itself and knowledge is already present in the very fact that consciousness has knowledge of an object at all; the *in-itself* is one thing *to it* while knowledge, or the being of the object *for consciousness,* is another moment. This ready-to-hand distinction forms the basis of the testing. Where the two moments thus compared do not correspond, it would seem that consciousness must alter its knowledge in order to bring it into conformity with the object; but when the knowledge is altered the object itself is in fact altered for it too, since the knowledge that was at hand was essentially a knowledge of the object, and as knowledge changes so too does the object because essentially it belonged to such knowledge. In this way it comes about for consciousness that what it previously took to be the *in-itself* is not in itself, or was only *in itself for it.* Since then consciousness, by reference to its object, finds its knowledge not to correspond to the object, the object too fails the test; in other words, the criterion for the test changes if that for which it was to be the criterion fails the test, and the test is not only a test of knowledge but also of the criterion of the test.

Insofar as the new and true object arises for consciousness out of it, this dialectical movement that consciousness exercises on itself, in regard to both its knowledge and its object, is none other than what is termed *experi-*

ence [*Erfahrung*]. In this connection there is an element of the process just mentioned that merits special attention, as shedding a new light on the scientific aspect of the ensuing exposition. Consciousness knows *something*, and this object is the essence or *in-itself*. But it is also the *in-itself* for consciousness; and this is where the ambiguity of this true object enters in. We see that consciousness now has two objects, one being the first *in-itself,* the other the *being-for-consciousness of this in-itself*. At first sight the latter seems only to be the reflection of consciousness into itself, a representation not of an object but only of its knowledge thereof. As already indicated, however, the first object, in being known, is altered for consciousness; it ceases to be the in-itself and becomes for it such as is only the *in-itself for it*. But then it is accordingly this, *the being-for-consciousness of this in-itself,* that is the true. In other words, it is this that is the *essence* or the *object* of consciousness. This new object contains the nothingness of the first; it is the experience acquired in regard to it.

This exposition of the course of experience includes a moment by virtue of which it does not seem to coincide with what is customarily understood by experience. For the transition from the first object and the knowledge of it to the other object, *in regard to which* experience is said to have been acquired, was presented in such a way as to imply that knowledge of the first object, or the *for*-consciousness of the first in-itself, itself becomes the second object. It usually seems, on the contrary, that we acquire the experience of the untruth of our first concept *in regard to another* object that we happen to come upon by chance and externally, so that our part in all this is reduced to purely *apprehending* what is in and for itself. On the view outlined above, however, the new object is seen to have come about through a *turning about of consciousness* itself. This way of viewing the matter is our contribution, by means of which the successive experiences of consciousness are raised to the level of a scientific process, a contribution that is lacking for the consciousness we are here considering. But this is in fact again the same circumstance that we were referring to above in regard to the relationship between this exposition and skepticism, namely that none of the results obtained with an untrue mode of knowing can be allowed to collapse into an empty nothingness; on the contrary, it must necessarily be grasped as the nothingness of that *from which it results,* a result that contains whatever truth attaches to the preceding mode of knowing. The way in which this is portrayed here is that since what first appeared as object is reduced for consciousness to a way of knowing it, and the *in-itself* becomes a *being-for-consciousness of the in-itself,* this is the new object, bringing on the scene also a new shape of consciousness, for which the essence is something different from what it was with the preceding shape. It is this circumstance that guides the entire series of shapes of consciousness in their necessary succession. But it is just this necessary sequence itself or the *coming-to-be* of the new object—of which consciousness becomes apprised without knowing how it does so—that proceeds for us, as it were, behind its back. This introduces into its movement a moment of *being-in-itself-or-for-us* that does not present itself for the consciousness that is in the grip of experience itself. However, the *content* of what we see coming to be exists *for it;* and all we comprehend is its formal aspect or pure coming-to-be. What has come to be exists *for it* only as object, while *for us* it exists at the same time as movement and becoming.

By reason of this necessary sequence, this pathway to scientific knowledge is itself already *science,* and accordingly, in the light of its content, the science of the *experience of consciousness.*

The experience of itself that consciousness acquires can, in accord with its concept, comprehend nothing less than the whole system of consciousness, or the whole realm of the truth of spirit. For this reason the peculiar specific character in which the moments of the truth present themselves is not to be abstract, pure moments but moments as they are for consciousness, or as consciousness itself comes on the scene in its relation to them, with the result that the moments of the whole are *shapes of consciousness.* In pressing forward to its true existence, consciousness will reach a point at which it lays aside its show of being burdened with something alien that exists only for it and as an other—a point at which the appearance becomes identical with the essence, so that its exposition coincides with the very point thus attained in the scientific knowledge of spirit properly speaking. And finally, as consciousness itself grasps this its own essence, it will delineate the nature of absolute knowledge itself. . . .

RELIGION[1]

In the configurations hitherto considered—which are distinguished broadly as *consciousness, self-consciousness, reason,* and *spirit*[2]—religion also, as the consciousness of *absolute being* [*das absolute Wesen*][3] in general, has doubtless made its appearance. But that was from the *point of view of the consciousness* that is conscious of absolute being. But absolute being *in and for itself,* the self-consciousness of spirit, has not appeared in those forms.

Already *consciousness,* insofar as it is *understanding,* is consciousness of the *supersensible* or the *inner side* of objective existence [*Dasein*]. But the supersensible, the eternal, or whatever it may be called, is *devoid of selfhood*; it is only, to begin with, the *universal,* which is still a long way from being spirit that knows itself as spirit.

Then there was *self-consciousness,* which came to its final shape in the *unhappy* consciousness: that was only the *anguish* of spirit that wrestled unsuccessfully to reach out again into objectivity. The unity of *individual* self-consciousness with its unchangeable *essential being,* to which this stage attains, remains therefore a *beyond* for consciousness.

The immediate existence of *reason,* which for us issued from that anguish, and the peculiar shapes it assumes, have no religion because the self-consciousness of reason knows or seeks *itself* in the *immediate* present.

On the other hand, in the ethical world we did see a religion, indeed the *religion* of the *underworld.* It is belief in the frightful, unknown night of *fate* and in the Eumenides of the *departed spirit.* The former is pure negativity in the form of universality, the latter the same negativity in the form of individuality [*Einzelheit*].[4] Absolute being is in the latter form indeed the *self* and is *present,* since other than present the self cannot be. But the *individual* self is *this* individual shade, which has separated from itself the universality that fate is. To be sure it is indeed a shade, a *sublated particular self* and thus a universal self. But its negative significance has not yet changed around into the positive significance of the universal self, and therefore the sublated self still has at the same time the immediate significance of this particular and inessential self. But fate devoid of self remains the unconscious night, which does not attain to differentiation within itself or to the clarity of self-consciousness.

This faith in the nothingness of necessity and in the underworld becomes *faith* in *heaven* because the departed self must unite with its universality, must explicate in this universality what it contains and thus become clear to itself. This *kingdom* of faith, however, we saw unfold its content only in the element of thought without the concept, and for that reason it perished in its fate, which was the *religion* of *enlightenment.* In this religion the supersensible beyond of the understanding is reinstated, but in such a way that self-consciousness remains satisfied in this world; and the supersensible, *empty* beyond that is to be neither known nor feared it knows neither as a self nor as power.

In the religion of morality it is at last reestablished that absolute being is a positive content; but the content is bound up with the negativity of the Enlightenment. It is a *being* [*Sein*] that is at the same time taken back into the self in which it remains enclosed, and a *differentiated* content whose parts are just as immediately negated as they are produced. The fate, however, that engulfs this contradictory movement is the self that is conscious of itself as the fate of what is *essential* and *actual.*

The self-knowing spirit is in religion immediately its own pure *self-consciousness.* Those shapes of it that have been considered—true spirit, self-alienated spirit, and spirit certain of itself—together constitute spirit in its *consciousness,* which, confronting its *world,* does not recognize itself therein. But in conscience it brings itself as well as its objective world in general into subjection, as also its representational thinking and its determinate concepts, and it is now self-consciousness at home with itself [*bei sich seiendes*]. Here spirit, *represented as an object,* has the significance for itself of being the universal spirit that contains within itself all essential being and all actuality; yet it is not in the form of free actuality or of independently appearing nature. It has indeed the *shape* or form of [immediate] being because it is the *object* of its consciousness. But because in religion consciousness is posited in the essential character of *self*-consciousness, the shape is perfectly transparent to itself; and the actuality it contains is enclosed and sublated within it just as when we speak of *all actuality:* it is universal actuality as *thought.*

Since then in religion the determination of the proper consciousness of spirit does not have the form of free *otherness,* spirit's *determinate existence* is distinguished from its *self-consciousness,* and its proper actuality falls outside of religion. There is indeed one spirit of both, but its consciousness does not embrace both together, and religion appears as a part of determinate existence, of conduct and activity, whose other part is the life lived in its actual world. Since we now know that spirit in its own world and spirit consciousness of itself as spirit, or spirit in religion, are the same, the consummation of religion consists in the two becoming identical with each other—not only that religion concerns itself with spirit's actuality, but conversely that spirit as self-conscious spirit becomes actual and the *object of its consciousness.*

Insofar as in religion spirit *represents* itself to itself, it is indeed consciousness, and the actuality encompassed within religion is the shape and garment of its representation. But in this representational thinking actuality does not receive its perfect due, namely to be not merely a garment but an independent free existence; and conversely, because it lacks completion within itself it is a *determinate* shape that does not obtain to what it ought to set forth, namely spirit that is conscious of itself. If its shape is to express spirit itself, it must be nothing other than spirit, and spirit must appear to itself or be in actuality what it is in its essential being. Only by so doing would also be obtained what may seem to demand the opposite, namely that the *object* of its consciousness have at the same time the form of free actuality. But only spirit that is object to itself as absolute spirit is conscious of itself as a free actuality to the extent that it remains conscious of itself therein.

Since in the first instance self-consciousness and consciousness proper, *religion* and spirit in its world or the *determinate existence* of spirit, are distinguished from each other, the latter consists in the totality of spirit insofar as its moments exhibit themselves in separation, each on its own account. But the moments are *consciousness, self-consciousness, reason,* and *spirit*—spirit, that is, as immediate spirit, which is not yet conscious of spirit. Their totality, *taken together,* constitutes spirit in its worldly existence generally; spirit as such contains the previous configurations in universal determinations, in the moments just named. Religion presupposes that these have run their full course and is their *simple* totality or absolute self.

The course traversed by these moments is, moreover, in relation to religion, not to be represented [as occurring] in time. Only the whole of spirit is in time, and the shapes, which are shapes of the whole *of spirit* as such, display themselves in a sequence one after the other. For only the whole has true actuality and thus the form of pure freedom vis-à-vis otherness, a form that expresses itself as time. But the *moments* of the whole, consciousness, self-consciousness, reason, and spirit, just because they are moments, have no determinate existence separate from one another.

Just as spirit was distinguished from its moments, we have further, in the third place, to distinguish from these moments themselves their individuated determination. We saw that each of these moments was differentiated again into a course of development all its own and took on various shapes, as for example in consciousness sense certainty [and] perception were distinct from each other. These latter shapes fall apart in time and belong to a *particular whole.* For spirit descends from its *universality* through *determination* to *individuality.* The determination or the middle term is *consciousness, self-consciousness,* etc. But *individuality* is constituted by the shapes assumed by these moments. These therefore exhibit spirit in its individuality or *actuality,* and are distinguished from one another in time, although in such a way that the following moment retains within it the preceding one.

If therefore religion is the consummation of spirit, into which its individual moments—consciousness, self-consciousness, reason, and spirit—*return* and *have returned* as into their *ground,* they together constitute the *determinately existing actuality* [*daseiende Wirklichkeit*] of the whole of spirit, which *is* only as the differentiating and self-returning movement of these its aspects. The process of development *of religion as such* is contained in the movement of the universal moments. But since each of these attributes was exhibited not merely as it determines itself in general but as it is *in and for itself,* i.e., as it runs its course as a whole within itself, therefore what has come to be is not merely the process of development of religion *as such;* rather those complete processes of the *individual* aspects at the same time contain the *determinate forms* of *religion* itself. The whole of spirit, the spirit of religion, is again the movement away from its immediacy toward the attainment of the *knowledge* of what it is *in itself* or immediately, so that the shape in which it appears for its consciousness will conform perfectly with its essence, and it will behold itself as it is.

In this process of development spirit itself therefore assumes *determinate* shapes, which constitute the differences involved in this movement; at the same time a determinate religion has likewise a *determinate actual* spirit. Thus if consciousness, self-consciousness, reason, and spirit belong generally to self-knowing spirit, then the *determinate* forms that were specifically developed within consciousness, self-consciousness, reason, and spirit belong to the *determinate* shapes of self-knowing spirit. From the shapes belonging to each of its moments, the *determinate* shape of religion picks out the one appropriate to it for its actual spirit. The *one* distinctive feature that characterizes the religion penetrates all aspects of its actual determinate existence and stamps them with this common character.

In this way, the arrangement of the shapes that have hitherto appeared differs from the way they appeared in their own order. On this point we shall observe briefly at the start what is necessary. In the series we have considered, each moment, exploring its own depths, formed itself into a whole within its own peculiar principle; and cognition was the depth or the spirit in which the moments having no other subsistence of their own possessed their substance. But this substance has now come forth; it is the depth of spirit that is certain of itself, which does not allow the individual principle to become isolated and to make itself a whole within itself; rather, gathering and holding together all these moments within itself, it advances within this total wealth of its actual spirit, and all its particular moments take and receive in common into themselves the same determinateness of the whole. This self-certain spirit and its movement is their true actuality and the being-*in-and-for-itself* that belongs to each individually.

Thus while the previous linear series in its advance marked the retrogressive steps in it by knots, but continued itself again from them in a single line, it is now, as it were, broken at these knots, these universal moments, and falls apart into many lines, which, gathered up into a single bundle, combine at the same time symmetrically so that the similar differences in which each took shape in its own sphere meet together.

For the rest, it is self-evident from the whole exposition how this coordination of universal directions, just mentioned, is to be understood. It is superfluous to remark that these differences are to be grasped essentially only as moments of the process of development, not as parts. In actual spirit they are attributes of its substance, but in religion they are rather only predicates of the subject. Similarly, all forms as such are indeed contained *in themselves* or *for us* in spirit and in each spirit. But as regards spirit's actuality, the main point is solely what determinate character it has in its *consciousness,* in which specific character its expresses itself, or in which shape it knows its essence.

The distinction that was made between *actual* spirit and spirit that knows itself as spirit, or between itself as consciousness and as self-consciousness, is sublated in the spirit that knows itself in its truth; its consciousness and its self-consciousness are harmonized. But since religion is here first of all *immediate,* this distinction has not yet returned into spirit. What is posited [at first] is only the *concept* of religion; in this the essential element is *self-consciousness,* which is conscious of being all truth and contains all of actuality within this truth. This self-consciousness has, as consciousness, itself as an object. Spirit that has to begin with an *immediate* knowledge of itself is thus spirit to itself in the *form* of *immediacy,* and the specificity of shape in which it appears to itself is that of [pure and simple] *being [Sein].* This being, to be sure, is *filled* neither with sensation nor with a manifold material, nor with any other sort of one-sided moments, purposes, or characteristics: it is filled rather with spirit and knows itself to be all truth and actuality. Such *filling* does not conform with its *shape;* spirit as essence is not identical with its consciousness. Spirit is actual as absolute spirit only when it is also for itself in its *truth* as it is in its *certainty of itself,* or when the extremes into which as consciousness it divides itself are for each other in the shape of spirit. The configuration that spirit assumes as object of its consciousness remains filled by the certainty of spirit as by its substance; through this content the object is saved from being degraded to pure objectivity, to the form of negativity of self-consciousness. The immediate unity of spirit with itself is the basis, or pure consciousness, *within* which consciousness breaks up into its constituent elements [subject and object]. In this way spirit, enclosed within its pure self-consciousness, does not exist in religion as the creator of a *nature* in general; rather what it produces in this movement are its shapes as spirits, which together constitute the completion of its appearance. And this movement itself is the process of development of its complete actuality through its individual aspects, or through its incomplete modes of actuality.

The first actuality of spirit is the concept of religion itself, or religion as *immediate* and therefore *natural religion,* in which spirit knows itself as its object in natural or immediate shape. The *second* actuality, however, is necessarily that in which spirit knows itself in the shape of *sublated natural existence* or of the *self.* This, therefore, is the religion of *art,* for the shape of spirit raises itself to the form of the *self* through the *productive activity* of consciousness whereby consciousness beholds in its object its own act or self. Finally, the *third* actuality sublates the one-sidedness of the first two: the *self* is just as much an *immediate* self as *immediacy* is the *self.* If in the first actuality spirit generally is in the form of consciousness, and in the second in the form of self-consciousness, then in the third it is in the form of the unity of both. It has the shape of *being-in-and-for-itself;* and when it is thus represented as it is in and for itself, it is the *revelatory religion.*

Although spirit has indeed obtained to its true *shape* in this religion, precisely the *shape* itself and its *representation* are still the unvanquished aspect from which spirit must pass over into the *concept,* in order therein completely to resolve the form of objectivity—resolve it in the concept that equally embraces within itself its own opposite. It is then that spirit has grasped the concept of itself, just as we now have first grasped it; and its shape, the element of its determinate existence, in being the concept, is spirit itself. . . .[5]

THE REVELATORY RELIGION[1]

Through the religion of art, spirit has passed from the form of *substance* into that of *subject,* for art *produces* its shape and thus establishes in this shape the *act* or the *self-consciousness* that merely vanishes in the awesome substance and fails to comprehend itself in [the attitude of simple] trust. This incarnation or becoming-human of the divine being begins with the statue, which has in it only the *outer* shape of the self, while the *inner* shape, its activity, falls outside it. But in the cultus the two sides become one. At the same time, in the outcome of the religion of art, this unity in being completed has passed over to the extreme of the self. In the spirit that is completely certain of itself in the singularity of consciousness, all essentiality is submerged. The proposition that expresses this levity runs: "The self is absolute being."[2] The being or substance for which the self was [only] an accident has sunk to the level of a predicate; and in *this self-consciousness* over against which there is nothing in the form of essential being, spirit has lost its *consciousness.*

This proposition, "The self is absolute being," belongs quite obviously to the nonreligious, actual spirit, and we have to recall which shape of spirit it is that gives expression to it. It will contain the movement, and the reversal of it, that lowers the self to a predicate and raises substance to subject. It does so in such a way that the reverse proposition does not *in itself* or *for us* make the substance into subject; or, what is the same thing, it does not reinstate substance in such a way that the consciousness of spirit is led back to its beginning, to natural religion; rather, this reversal is one that is brought about *for* and *by self-consciousness* itself. Since the latter consciously gives itself up, it is maintained in its emptying or divestment [*Entäußerung*] and remains the subject of substance; but since it is likewise self-divested, it still has the consciousness of this substance. In other words, since by its sacrifice it *brings forth* substance as subject, this subject remains its own self. In the first of the two propositions, the subject merely disappears into substantiality, and in the second the substance is merely a predicate; and both sides are thus present in each with contrary inequality of value. Here, however, the result achieved is the union and permeation of the two natures in which both are, with equal value, *essential* and at the same time only *moments*. Hence it is that spirit is both *consciousness* of itself as its *objective* substance and simple *self-consciousness* remaining within itself.

The religion of art belongs to the ethical spirit that we earlier saw perish in the *condition of right* or *legal status*,[3] i.e., in the proposition, "The self as such, the abstract person, is absolute being." In ethical life, the self is absorbed in the spirit of its people; it is universality that is *filled*. But *simple individuality* raises itself out of this content, and its levity refines it into a person, into the abstract universality of right. In the latter, the *reality* of ethical spirit is lost; and having lost all content, the spirits of the individual peoples are gathered into a single pantheon—not into a pantheon of representation whose powerless form lets each spirit go its own way, but into the pantheon of abstract universality, of pure thought, which disembodies them and imparts to the spiritless self, to the individual person, a being that is in-and-for-itself.

But this self has through its emptiness let the content go free. It is only *within itself* that consciousness is essence or being [*Wesen*]; its own *determinate existence* [*Dasein*], the legal recognition of the person, is an unfulfilled abstraction. What it possesses, therefore, is rather only the thought of itself; in other words, in the way that it *is there* [*da ist*] and knows itself as object, it is what *lacks actuality*. Thus it is only the Stoic *autonomy of thinking,* which passes through the movement of the skeptical consciousness to find its truth in that shape which we have called the *unhappy self-consciousness.*

The latter knows what the validity of the abstract person amounts to in actuality and equally in pure thought. It knows that such validity is rather a complete loss; it is itself the conscious loss of itself and the divestment of its knowledge from itself. We see that this unhappy consciousness constitutes the counterpart and completion of the comic consciousness that is perfectly happy within itself. Into the latter all divine being returns—the complete *divestment* of *substance*. The unhappy consciousness, on the other hand, is conversely the tragic fate of the *certainty of self* that aims to be in and for itself. It is the consciousness of the loss of all *essentiality* in *this certainty* of itself, and of the loss of even this knowledge of itself—the loss of substance as well as of self. It is the anguish that finds expression in the harsh words, *God is dead.*[4]

Under the [Roman] legal status, then, the ethical world [of the Greeks] and the religion of that world are submerged in the comic consciousness, and the unhappy consciousness is the knowledge of this *total* loss. It has lost the worth it attached to its personality both as immediate and as mediated or *thought*. Trust in the eternal laws of the gods is silenced, just as the oracles, which pronounced on particular questions, are dumb. The statues are now only stones from which the living souls have flown, just as the hymns are words from which faith is gone. The tables of the gods provide no spiritual food and drink, and from their games and festivals human beings are no longer aware of their joyful unity with the [divine] being. The works of the muse now lack the power of the spirit, for spirit has gained certainty of itself from the crushing of gods and humans. They become what they are for us now—beautiful fruit already plucked from the tree, which a friendly fate has offered us as a maiden might set the fruit before us. The actual life in which they existed is no longer there, neither the tree that bore them, nor the earth and elements that constituted their substance, nor the climate that gave them their peculiar character, nor the cycle of the seasons that governed the process of their growth. So fate does not restore their world to us along with those works of art, nor the spring and summer of ethical life in which they blossomed and ripened, but only the veiled recollection of that actuality. Our active enjoyment of them is not therefore an act of worship whereby our consciousness might attain to its perfect truth and fulfillment; rather it is an external activity, the wiping off of some drops of rain or specks of dust from these fruits, and in place of the inner elements composing the actuality of the ethical life that environed, created, and inspired these works, we erect in intricate detail the scaffolding of the dead elements of their outward existence (language, historical circumstances, etc.)—and we do all of this not to enter into their life but only to represent them to ourselves. But just as the maiden who offers us the plucked fruit is more than the nature that directly provides them in all their conditions and elements (tree, air, light, etc.), since in a higher way she gathers all this together into the light of her self-conscious eye and her gesture in offering the gifts, so too the spirit of the fate that presents us with these works of art is more than the ethical life and actuality of that people. For it is the *inwardizing in us* or *re-collecting* [*Er-Innerung*] of the spirit that was in them still *externalized* [*veräußert*]—it is the spirit of the tragic fate that gathers all those individual gods and attributes of substance into the one pantheon, into the spirit that is itself conscious of itself as spirit.

All the conditions for its production are at hand, and this totality of its conditions constitutes the *coming to be,* the *concept,* or the *intrinsic* production of it. The sphere of artistic creations embraces the forms of divestment or externalization of the absolute substance. It is in the form of individuality as a thing, or as an object *subsisting* for sense consciousness—as pure language or the coming to be of the shape whose determinate existence does not go outside the self and is a purely *vanishing* object; as immediate unity with universal self-consciousness in its inspiration, and as mediated in cultic activity; as corporeal embodiment of the self in the form of beauty; and finally as determinate existence elevated into *representation* and expanded into a world that finally gathers itself into a universality that is likewise *pure certainty of itself*. These forms, and on the other side the *world* of the *person* and of right, the destructive ferocity of the released elements of the content, as well as the *thoughtful* person of Stoicism and the restless disquiet of the Skeptical consciousness—these compose the periphery of shapes that surround, expectantly and impatiently, the birthplace of spirit as it becomes self-consciousness. The anguish and longing of the unhappy consciousness that permeates them all forms their center and is the common birth pang of spirit's emergence—the simplicity of the pure concept, which contains these shapes as its moments.

Spirit has in it the two sides that are represented above as two reverse propositions: the one is this, that *substance* divests or empties itself of itself and becomes self-consciousness; the other is the reverse, that *self-consciousness* divests itself of itself and makes itself into an objective thing [*Dingheit*] or a universal self.[5] Both sides have in this way encountered each other, and through this encounter their true union [has] come about. The divestment of substance and its coming into self-consciousness expresses its transition into its opposite, the unconscious transition of *necessity*, or in other words, that substance is *in itself* self-consciousness. Conversely, the divestment of self-consciousness expresses that it is *in itself* the universal being or essence, or—because the self is pure being-for-self that remains at home with itself in its opposite—that substance is self-consciousness *for itself*, and just for this reason is spirit. Of this spirit, which has abandoned the form of substance and enters into determinate existence in the shape of self-consciousness, it may be said—if we wish to employ relationships derived from natural generation—that it has an *actual mother* but an *implicit* father. For *actuality* or self-consciousness and *implicitness* as substance are its two moments, through whose reciprocal divestment, each becoming the other, spirit comes into determinate existence as their unity.

Insofar as self-consciousness one-sidedly grasps only *its own* divestment, even though its own object is thus for it at once both being and self and it knows all existence to be spiritual in nature, nevertheless true spirit has not yet come to be for it. This is because being in general or substance has not yet for its part *implicitly* divested itself and become self-consciousness. In that case, then, all existence is spiritual in nature only from the *standpoint of consciousness*, not in itself. Spirit is in this way only *imagined* into existence; this imagining is the *visionary dreaming* [*Schwärmerei*] that insinuates into both nature and history, into the world and the mythical representations of earlier religions, another, inner meaning than that which lies on the surface, and in the case of religions, another meaning than the one known in them by the self-consciousness whose religions they were. But this meaning is one that is borrowed, a garment that does not cover the nakedness of the appearance and secures no faith and respect; it is no more than the dark night and self-delusive rapture of consciousness.

If the meaning of the objective is not, therefore, to be mere imagination, it must have being *in itself,* i.e., it must *in the first place* arise in consciousness as springing from the *concept* and must come forth in its necessity. It is thus that self-knowing spirit has arisen for us, namely, through the cognition of the *immediate consciousness,* or of the consciousness of the *subsisting* object, through its necessary movement. This concept, which as immediate has also the shape of *immediacy* for its consciousness, has in the *second place* given itself the shape of self-consciousness *in itself,* i.e., by just the same necessity of the concept by which *being* or *immediacy,* the empty object of sense consciousness, divests itself and becomes "I" for consciousness. But the *immediate in-itself* or *subsisting necessity* is itself different from the *in-itself that thinks* or the *cognition of necessity*—a difference that at the same time, however, does not lie outside the concept, for the *simple unity* of the concept is *immediate being* itself. The concept is at once the self-divesting or coming to be of *intuited necessity,* and also in this necessity is present to itself, knowing and comprehending the necessity. The *immediate in-itself* of spirit, which gives itself the shape of self-consciousness, means nothing other than that the actual world spirit has attained to this knowledge of itself. It is then too that this knowledge first enters its consciousness, and enters it as truth. How that came about has already been established.

That absolute spirit has given itself *implicitly* the shape of self-consciousness, and therefore has also given it for its *consciousness*—this now appears as the *faith of the world* that spirit *is there* as a self-consciousness, i.e., as an actual human being, that spirit is [present] for immediate certainty, that the believing consciousness *sees, feels,* and *hears* this divinity.[6] Thus it is not a matter of imagination; it is *actual in the believer.* Thus consciousness does not set out from *its* inner life, from thought, and combine *within itself* the thought of God with existence; rather it starts from an existence that is immediately present and recognizes God in it.

The moment of *immediate being* is present in the content of the concept in such a way that the religious spirit, in the return of all essentiality into consciousness, has become a *simple* positive self, just as the actual spirit as such in the unhappy consciousness was just this *simple* self-conscious negativity. The self of the existing spirit has therefore the form of complete immediacy; it is posited neither as something thought, nor as something represented, nor as something produced, as is the case with the immediate self in natural religion, and also in the religion of art. Rather this God is beheld immediately and sensuously as a self, as an actual human individual; only thus *is* God self-consciousness.

This incarnation of the divine being, its having essentially and immediately the shape of self-consciousness, is the simple content of the absolute religion. Here the [divine] being is known as spirit, or this religion is the consciousness of the [divine] being that it is spirit. For spirit is knowledge of itself in its divestment: spirit is the being that is the process of retaining identity with itself in its otherness. This however is substance insofar as substance is at the same time reflected into itself in its accidents—not indifferent to them as something inessential, or present in them as in an alien element; rather in them it is *within itself,* i.e., insofar as it is *subject* or *self.*

Consequently in this religion the divine being is *revealed.* Its revelatoriness [*Offenbarsein*] consists manifestly in this, that what it is, is known. But it is known precisely in its being known as spirit, as essence that is essentially *self-consciousness.* For there is something hidden from *consciousness* in its object if the latter is for consciousness an *other* or something *alien,* and if consciousness does not know its object as *itself.* This hiddenness ceases when absolute being as spirit is the object of consciousness, for here the object has the form of *self* in its relationship to consciousness; i.e., consciousness knows itself immediately in the object, or is manifest to itself in the object. Consciousness is manifest to itself only in its own certainty of itself; its object is the *self,* but the self is nothing alien; rather it is inseparable unity with itself, the immediately universal. It is the pure concept, pure thinking or *being-for-self,* immediate *being* and thus *being for another,* and as this *being for another* it returns immediately into itself and abides with itself; it is therefore what is truly and alone revelatory. The good, the righteous, the holy, creator of heaven and earth, etc.—these are *predicates* of a subject, universal moments that have their support on this point, and only exist when consciousness goes back into thought.

As long as it is *they* that are known, their ground and essence or the subject itself is not yet manifest; and similarly the *determinate qualities* of the universal are not *this universal* itself. The *subject* itself, however, and thus also *this pure universal,* is manifest as *self;* for this self is just the inwardness that is reflected into itself and is immediately given—the self-certainty of that self for which it is given. The true shape of spirit is to be in its very *concept* the revelatory; and this shape, its concept, is alone its very essence and substance. Spirit is known as self-consciousness, and to this self-consciousness it is immediately manifest, for spirit is this self-consciousness itself. The divine nature is the same as the human, and it is this unity that is beheld.

Here then we find as a fact that consciousness, or the mode in which essential being is for itself, its shape, is the same as self-consciousness. This shape is itself a self-consciousness; it is thus at the same time an *existing* object, and this [existing] *being* has just as immediately the significance of *pure thinking,* of absolute being.

The absolute being, when it is there as an actual self-consciousness, seems to have *descended* from its eternal simplicity, but in fact it has in doing so attained for the first time its *highest* being [*höchstes Wesen*].[7] For it is only when the concept of essential being [*Wesen*] has attained its simple purity is it both the absolute *abstraction,* which is *pure thinking* and thus the pure singularity of the self, and at the same time *immediacy* or [existing] *being* [*Sein*], on account of its simplicity. What is called sense consciousness is just this pure *abstraction;* it is the kind of thinking for which *being* is the *immediate.* The lowest is thus at the same time the highest; the revelatory that has come forth entirely on the *surface* is precisely therein the *most profound.* That the supreme being is seen, heard, etc., as an existing self-consciousness—this is in fact the consummation of its concept; and through its consummation this being is immediately *there* in its very essence.[8]

This immediate existence [*Dasein*] is at the same time not solely and simply immediate consciousness; it is religious consciousness. This immediacy means not only an *existing* self-consciousness but also the purely thought-constituted or absolute *essential being,* and these meanings are inseparable. What we are our conscious of in our concept—that [existing] *being* [*Sein*] is *essential being* [*Wesen*]—is the same as what religious consciousness is aware of. This *unity* of being and essence, of *thinking* that is immediately *existence,* is both the *thought* of this religious consciousness, or its *mediated* knowledge, and equally its *immediate* knowledge. For this unity of being and thought is *self*-consciousness and is itself *there,* or the *thought* unity has at the same time this shape of what it is. Here, therefore, God is *revelatory* as *God is; God is there* as God is *in godself;* God is there as spirit.[9] God is attainable in pure speculative knowledge alone, and *is* only in that knowledge, and is only that knowledge itself, for God is spirit; and this speculative knowledge is the knowledge of the revelatory religion. Speculative knowledge knows God as *thinking* or as pure essential being, and it knows this thinking as [existing] being and as determinate existence, and existence as the negativity of itself, hence as self, *this* self and the universal self: just this is what the revelatory religion knows.

The hopes and expectations of preceding ages pressed forward solely to this revelation, this vision of what absolute being is, and the discovery of themselves therein. This joy of beholding themselves in absolute being comes into self-consciousness and seizes the whole world. For it is spirit, it is the simple movement of those pure moments, which expresses just this: that only when essential being is beheld as *immediate* self-consciousness is it known as spirit.

This concept of spirit knowing itself as spirit is itself the immediate concept and is not yet developed. Essential being is spirit, i.e., it has appeared, it is revelatory. This first revelatoriness is itself *immediate;* but the immediacy is likewise pure mediation or thinking, and it must therefore portray this as such in immediacy itself.

Looking at this more precisely, spirit, in the immediacy of self-consciousness, is *this individual* self-consciousness as contrasted with *universal* self-consciousness. This individual is an exclusive "one" who has the still unresolved form of a *sensuous other* for the consciousness *for which* he is there. This other does not yet know spirit as its own; in other words, spirit as an *individual* self is not yet equally the universal self, the all-self. Or again, its shape does not yet have the form of the *concept,* i.e., of the universal self, of the self that in its immediate actuality is at the same time sublated, is thought and universality, without losing its actuality in this universality. But the proximate and immediate form of this universality is not yet the form *of thought* itself, *of the concept as concept,* but rather the universality of actuality, the allness of the self, and the elevation of determinate existence into representation—just as in general, and to cite a specific example, the sublated *this* of *sense* is first of all a thing of *perception* and not yet the *universal* of the understanding.

This individual human being, then, as whom absolute being is manifest, accomplishes in himself as an individual the process found in *sensuous being.* He is the *immediately* present God; consequently his *being* passes over into *having been.* The consciousness for which he has this sensible presence ceases to see and hear him; it *has* seen and heard him; and it is only because it *has* seen and heard him that it itself becomes a spiritual consciousness. Or in other words, just as formerly he arose for consciousness as a *sensuous existence,* so now he has arisen *in the spirit.*[10] For a consciousness that sees and hears him in sensuous fashion is itself only an immediate consciousness, which has not sublated the disparateness of objectivity, has not taken it back into pure thought; it only knows this objective individual, but not itself, as spirit. In the disappearance of the immediate existence of what is known as absolute being, immediacy acquires its negative moment. Spirit remains the immediate self of actuality, but as *the universal self-consciousness* of the [religious] community, a self-consciousness that rests on its own substance, just as in it this substance is universal subject. The complete whole of the individual subject is not the individual by itself but along with the consciousness of the community, and what the subject is for this community.

The *past* and *distance* are, however, only the imperfect form in which what is immediate is mediated or posited; it is dipped only superficially in the element of thought, is maintained only in a sensuous mode, and is not made one with the nature of thought itself. It is raised only into the realm of *representation,* for this is the synthetic connection of sensuous immediacy with its universality or thought.

This *representational form* constitutes the determinacy in which spirit is conscious of itself in its community. This form is not yet the self-consciousness of spirit that has advanced to its concept as concept; the mediation is still incomplete. This connection of being and thought is defective, therefore, because spiritual being is still burdened by an unreconciled split into a here and a beyond. The *content* is true, but all of its moments have, when placed in the element of representation, the character of not being grasped together [*begriffen*] but of appearing as completely independent aspects related to each other *externally.* In order that the true content should also obtain its true form for consciousness, a higher formative development of consciousness is necessary; it must raise its intuition of the absolute substance into the concept and equate its consciousness with its self-consciousness *for itself*—just as this has happened for us or *in itself.*

This content is to be considered in the manner in which it is [present] in its consciousness.[11] Absolute spirit is *content*, and is so in the shape of its *truth.* But its truth consists not merely in being the substance of the community or its *in-itself,* nor merely in coming forth out of this inwardness into the objectivity of representation, but in becoming actual self, reflecting itself into itself, and being subject. This, then, is the process that spirit accomplishes in its community; this is the life of spirit. What this self-revealing spirit is *in and for itself* is not, therefore, brought out by having its rich life in the community unwound, as it were, and reduced to its original threads, to the notions, say, of the primitive community, or even to what the actual human being [Christ] has spoken. This reversion to the primitive is based on the instinct to get at the concept, but it confuses the *origin,* in the sense of the *immediate existence* of the first appearance, with the *simplicity* of the *concept.* What results from thus impoverishing the life of spirit, and clearing away the community's representation and its action with regard to it, is not the concept but mere externality and individuality, the historical mode of immediate appearance, and the spiritless recollection of a presumably individual figure and its past.

Spirit is the content of its consciousness at first in the form of *pure substance,* or it is the content of its pure consciousness. This element of thought is the process of descending into existence or individuality. The middle term between them is their synthetic connection, the consciousness of passing into otherness, or representation as such. The third term is the return from representation and from other-being, or the element of self-consciousness itself.

These three moments constitute spirit. Its resolution into representational thinking consists in its being in a *determinate* mode; but this determinacy is nothing other than one of its moments. Its comprehensive movement consists in diffusing its nature throughout each of its moments as in an element [in which it lives]; since each of these circles terminates in itself, the reflection of one circle into itself is at the same time a transition to another. *Representation* constitutes the middle term between pure thought and self-consciousness as such, and is only *one* of the determinate forms. At the same time, however, as we have seen, its character—that of being a synthetic connection—is diffused throughout all these elements and is their common characteristic.

The content itself that we have to consider has partly been met with already as the representation of the *unhappy* and the *believing* consciousness. But in the former it has the character of a content *produced* from *consciousness* and for which it *yearns,* a content in which spirit cannot be satiated or find rest because it is not yet its own content *inherently* or as its *substance*. In the believing consciousness, by contrast, the content is regarded as the self-less *being* of the world or as the essentially *objective* content of representation, of a representation that flees from actuality altogether and consequently lacks the *certainty of self-consciousness,* which is separated from it partly as the conceit of knowledge and partly as pure insight. The consciousness of the community, on the other hand, possesses the content as its *substance,* just as the content is its *certainty* of its own spirit.

Spirit, represented at first as substance in the *element of pure thought,* is thus immediately the simple and self-identical, eternal essential being, which does not, however, have this abstract *meaning* of essential being but rather the meaning of absolute spirit.[12] Yet spirit consists in being not a meaning, not the inner, but the actual. Therefore, simple, eternal essential being would be spirit only in empty words if we went no further than the representational expression, "simple, eternal essential being." Simple essential being, however, because it is an abstraction, is in fact the *negative in itself,* and indeed the negativity of thought, or negativity as found in *essential being* per se; that is, it is absolute *distinction* from itself or the pure process of its becoming other. As *essential being* it is only *in itself* or for us; but since this purity is just abstraction or negativity, it is *for itself,* or it is the *self,* the *concept.* It is thus *objective;* and since representational thinking grasps and expresses as an *event* what has just been expressed as the *necessity* of the concept, it is said that the eternal being *begets* for itself an other. But in this otherness it has likewise returned immediately into itself; for the distinction is distinction *in itself,* i.e., it is immediately distinguished only from itself and is thus the unity that has returned into itself.

Thus there are three moments to be distinguished: *essential being; being-for-self,* which is the otherness of essential being and for which that being is [object]; and *being-for-self* or self-knowing *in the other.* Essential being beholds only itself in its being-for-self; it remains only with itself in this divestment. The being-for-self that shuts itself out from essential being is *essential being's knowledge of itself.* It is the word that when spoken leaves behind the speaker, divested and emptied; but it is just as immediately perceived and heard, and only this self-perceiving and hearing is the determinate existence of the word.[13] Thus the distinctions that are set up are just as immediately resolved as made, and just as immediately made as resolved; and the true and the actual consists precisely in this circling movement within itself.

This movement within itself expresses the absolute being as *spirit.* Absolute being that is not grasped as spirit is merely an abstract void, just as spirit that is not grasped as this movement is merely an empty word. When its *moments* are grasped in their purity, they are the restless concepts that only *are* in being in themselves their own opposite, and in finding their rest in the whole. But the *representational* thinking of the community is not this *conceptual* thinking. It has the content without its *necessity;* and instead of the form of the concept it brings into the realm of pure consciousness the natural relationships of father and son.[14] Since even when thinking it proceeds in a representational fashion, essential being is indeed manifest to it, but the moments of this being, owing to this synthetic representation, partly fall of themselves apart from one another so that they are not related to each other through their own concept, while partly this representational thinking retreats from its pure object and connects itself only externally to it. The object is revealed to it by something alien, and in this thought about spirit it does not recognize itself or the nature of pure self-consciousness. Insofar as the form of representation and of those relationships derived from nature must be transcended, and especially the method of taking the moments of the movement that spirit is as isolated immovable substances or subjects instead of transient moments—this transcendence is to be regarded as a compulsion of the concept, as we pointed out earlier in connection with another aspect. But since it is only an instinct, it misunderstands itself, rejects the content along with the form, and, what comes to the same thing, degrades the content to an historical representation and an heirloom of the tradition. In this fashion only the purely external element of faith is preserved, and as something dead and devoid of knowledge, while the *inner element* of faith has disappeared, because this would be the concept that knows itself as concept.

Absolute spirit as represented in the element of pure essential being is indeed not *abstract* pure essential being, for the latter, just because it is only a moment within spirit, has sunk to the level of being an *element* of spirit. The portrayal of spirit in this element, however, has inherently the same defect of form that *essential being* as such has. Essential being is what is abstract and thus the negative of its simplicity, an other; likewise *spirit* in the element of essential being is the *form* of *simple unity,* which on that account is just as essentially a process of becoming other. Or, what is the same thing, the relation of eternal being to its being-for-self is the immediately simple relation of pure thought. In this *simple* beholding of itself in the other, the *otherness* is not therefore posited as such: it is the distinction that in pure thought is immediately *no distinction*—a recognition of *love* wherein the lovers are by their very nature not *opposed* to each other. Spirit that is expressed in the element of pure thought is essentially this, to be not merely in this element but to be *actual,* for in its concept lies *otherness* itself, i.e., the sublation of the pure thought-constituted concept.

The element of pure thought, because it is abstract, is itself rather the *other* of its own simplicity, and thus it passes over into the element proper to *representation*—the element in which the moments of the pure concept acquire a *substantial* existence in relation to each other and are *subjects* as well, which do not exist in indifference toward each other, merely for a third, but, being reflected into themselves, break away from each other and confront each other.

Therefore the merely eternal or abstract spirit becomes *an other* to itself. It enters into existence, and directly into *immediate existence.* Thus it *creates* a world.[15] *Creation* is the word employed by representation for the *concept* itself in its absolute movement, or for the fact that what is absolutely expressed as the simple or as pure thinking, because it is abstract, is rather the negative and hence opposed to itself, *the other* of itself; or because, to put it yet another way, what is posited as *essential being* is simple *immediacy* or *being,* but as immediacy or being lacks self, and therefore, lacking inwardness, is *passive,* a *being-for-others.* This *being for another* is at the same time *a world.* Spirit in the determination of *being for another* is the quiet subsistence of the moments formerly enclosed within pure thought, and is thus the dissolution of their simple universality and their dispersion into their own particularity.

The world, however, is not merely this spirit cast out and dispersed into the plenitude [of natural existence] and its external ordering; rather, since spirit is essentially the simple self, this self is equally present in the world: it is the *existing* spirit, the individual self that has consciousness and distinguishes itself as other or as world from itself. This individual self, as at first posited in immediate fashion, is not yet *spirit for itself;* thus it *exists* but not

127

as spirit, it may be called *innocent* but not yet *good*. In order that it may in fact be self and spirit, it must at first become an *other* to itself, in the same way that eternal being manifests itself as the process of becoming self-identical in its otherness. Since this spirit is first determined as immediately existing or as dispersed into the multiplicity of its consciousness, its becoming other is the withdrawal *into itself* of knowledge as such. Immediate existence turns into thought, or merely sensuous consciousness into the consciousness of thought; and indeed, because it is thought that emerges from immediacy or is *conditioned,* it is not pure knowledge but the thought that has otherness in it, and thus is the self-opposed thought of *good* and *evil.* Humanity is represented in such a way that this simply *happened* and was not necessary—namely, that humans lost the form of harmonious unity by plucking the fruit of the tree of knowledge of *good* and *evil,* and were driven from the state of innocence, from nature offering its bounties without toil, from Paradise, from the animal garden.[16]

Since this withdrawing into itself of existing consciousness immediately destroys its harmony with itself, *evil* appears as the first state of existence of the inwardly withdrawn consciousness. And because the thoughts of *good* and *evil* are utterly opposed, and this opposition is not yet resolved, this consciousness is essentially only evil. At the same time, however, just because of this opposition, there is also present the *good* consciousness opposing the evil one, and their relation to each other. Insofar as immediate existence changes into *thought*—and *being-within-self* is on the one hand itself a thinking, while on the other hand the moment of the *othering* of essential being is more precisely determined in it—[because of this double aspect] the emergence of evil can be shifted further back out of the existing world into the primary realm of thought. Thus it may be said that it is the first-born Son of Light who fell because he withdrew into himself, but that in his place another was immediately created.[17] Forms of expression such as "fallen" and "Son," which belong merely to representation and not to the concept, degrade the moments of the concept to the level of representational thinking, or transfer representational images into the realm of thought.

In the same way, it makes no difference if we coordinate a multiplicity of other shapes with the simple thought of *otherness* in eternal being and transfer the *withdrawal into self* into them. This coordination must at the same time be approved, since by means of it the moment of *otherness* simultaneously expresses diversity, as it should—not indeed as plurality in general, but as determinate diversity, so that one part, the Son, is that which is simple and knows itself to be essential being, while the other part is the divestment of being-for-self, and only lives to praise that being. To the latter part, then, may also be assigned the taking back again of the divested being-for-self and the withdrawal into self of evil. Insofar as otherness falls into two parts, spirit might, as regards its moments—if these are to be counted—more precisely be expressed as a quaternity; or, because the multiplicity again breaks up into two parts, namely one part that has remained good and the other that has become evil, it might even be expressed as a quintity.

Counting these moments, however, can be regarded as utterly useless, since, for one thing, what is distinguished is just as much only *one*—namely the *thought* of distinction, which is only one thought—as it is *this* differentiated element, the second over against the first. For another thing it is useless to count because the thought that grasps the many in the one must be dissolved out of its universality and distinguished into more than three or four distinct components. This universality appears, in contrast to the absolute determinacy of the abstract unit, which is the principle of number, as indeterminacy in relation to number as such, so that we could speak only of number in general, not of a specific number of distinctions. Thus it is quite superfluous to think here of numbers and counting at all, just as in other respects the mere distinction between magnitude and multitude is unconceptual and says nothing at all.

Good and *evil* were the specific distinctions of thought that we have found. Since their opposition is not yet broken down, and they are represented as essential realities of thought, each of which is independent by itself, human being is a self lacking essential reality, the synthetic soil of their existence and conflict. But these universal powers [of good and evil] belong all the same to the self, or the self is their actuality. Accordingly it comes about that, just as evil is nothing other than the withdrawal into self of the natural existence of spirit, conversely good steps into actuality and appears as an existing self-consciousness. That which in the pure thought of spirit is only hinted at as the *othering* of the divine being here comes nearer to its realization for representational thinking; it consists for the latter in the self-humiliation of the divine being, its renunciation of its abstraction and unactuality. The other aspect, evil, is taken representationally as an event extraneous to the divine being. To grasp evil within the divine being itself *as God's wrath* is the supreme and severest effort of representational thinking as it struggles with itself, an effort that remains fruitless because it lacks the concept.[18]

The alienation [*Entfremdung*] of the divine being is thus posited in twofold fashion: the self of spirit and its simple thought are the two moments whose absolute unity spirit itself is. Its alienation consists in the two falling apart from each other, and in one having an unequal value vis-à-vis the other. Thus this disparity is twofold, and two connections arise that have in common the moments just given. In the one, the *divine being* counts as what is essential, while natural existence and the self count as what is unessential and to be sublated. In the other, by contrast, *being-for-self* counts as what is essential, and simple divinity as the unessential. Their still empty middle term is *determinate existence* in general, the bare commonality of their two moments.

The resolution of this antithesis takes place not so much through the conflict between the two moments that are represented as separated and independent beings. Just in virtue of their *independence* each must *implicitly,* through its own concept, resolve itself in itself. The conflict begins where both cease to be these minglings of thought and independent existence, and where they confront each other only as thoughts. For then, as specific concepts, they exist essentially only in an opposed relationship; as independent, by contrast, they have their essentiality outside the opposition. Their movement is therefore their own free and independent movement. If then the movement of both is an *intrinsic* movement, since it is to be regarded in the two sides themselves, it is initiated by that side which, in contrast to the other, has the character of being-in-itself. This is represented as a voluntary action, but the necessity of its divestment resides in the concept that being-in-itself, which is so determined only in opposition, has therefore no genuine subsistence. Thus it is that the side that has no being-for-self but rather simplicity as its essence is the one that divests itself, enters into death, and is thereby reconciled with itself as absolute being. For in this movement it presents itself as *spirit;* abstract being is alienated from itself, it has natural existence and the actuality of selfhood. Thus its otherness or its sensuous presence is taken back again by the second othering and is posited as sublated, as *universal.* Essential being has thereby come to itself in this presence; the immediate existence of actuality has ceased to be something alien or external when it is sublated or universal. This death is therefore its arising as spirit.

The sublated immediate presence of essential being as self-conscious has the form of universal self-consciousness. This concept of the sublated individual self that is absolute being immediately expresses, therefore, the constitution of a community that, having tarried hitherto in the realm of representation, now returns into itself as the self; and spirit thus passes over from the second of its determinative elements, that of representation, into the *third,* that of self-consciousness as such.[19]

If we consider further the sort of procedure that representational thinking adopts as it moves along, we find it said in the first place that divine being takes on human nature. Here it is already *asserted* that *implicitly* the two are not separate—just as in the statement that the divine being divests itself *from the beginning,* and that its determinate being or existence withdraws into itself and becomes evil, it is not asserted but *implied* that *in itself* this evil existence is not something alien to it. Absolute being would be only an empty name if in truth there were an [absolute] *other* for it or a *fall* from it.[20] The moment of *being-within-self* rather constitutes the essential moment of the *self* of spirit.

That this *being-within-self* and the *actuality* that follows from it belong to essential being itself—which is for us a *concept* and insofar as it is a concept—appears to representational consciousness as an incomprehensible *event*. The *in-itself* assumes for such consciousness the form of *indifferent being*. The thought, however, that those moments of absolute being and self-subsisting self that seem to flee from each other are not separate, *also* appears in this representational thinking—for it does possess the true content—but such thinking comes later, in the divestment of the divine being, which becomes flesh.[21] The representation is in this way still *immediate* and thus not spiritual, i.e., it knows the human shape of the [divine] being at first only as a particular, not yet a universal, shape. The representation becomes spiritual for this consciousness in the movement whereby this configured being [i.e., divine being in human shape] again sacrifices its immediate existence and returns into essential being: only when essential being is *reflected into itself* is it spirit.

The *reconciliation* of divine being with the *other* as a whole, and specifically with the *thought* of this other, namely *evil,* is thus set forth here representationally. If this representation is expressed *conceptually* by saying it consists in the fact that *evil* is *implicitly the same* as good, or that divine being is *the same* as nature in its entire extent, or that nature separated from divine being is simply *nothing*[22]—then this must be looked upon as an unspiritual mode of expression that inevitably leads to misunderstandings. If evil is *the same* as goodness, then evil is just not evil and goodness is not good; rather both are really done away with—evil as such, a being-for-self subsisting within itself, and goodness, a selfless simplicity. If both are in this way expressed in terms of their concept, their unity is at once apparent; for being-for-self subsisting within itself is simple knowing, and selfless simplicity is precisely pure and inwardly subsisting being-for-self. Hence if it must be said that good and evil in accord with their concept—i.e., insofar as they are not good and evil—are *the same,* then to the same extent it must be said that they are *not* the same but rather are utterly *different;* for simple being-for-self, or again pure knowing, are in themselves equally pure negativity or absolute difference.[23]

It is only these two propositions that complete the whole, and when the first is asserted and maintained, it must be countered by clinging to the other with invincible stubbornness. Since both are equally right, both are equally wrong; and their wrongness consists in taking such abstract forms as "the same" and "not the same," "identity" and "nonidentity," to be something true, fixed, actual, and in resting on them. Neither the one nor the other has truth; the truth is just their movement, the process in which simple sameness is abstraction and hence absolute difference, while the latter, as difference in itself, also differs from itself and thus coincides with itself. Precisely this is the case with the *sameness* of the divine being and nature in general, and human nature in particular: the former is nature insofar as it is not essential being; the latter is divine in its essential being. But it is in spirit that the two abstract sides are posited as they are in truth, namely as *sublated* [*aufgehoben,* both annulled and preserved]—a positing that cannot be expressed by the judgment, by the spiritless word *is* that forms the copula of the judgment. In the same way nature is *nothing outside of* its essential being; but this nothing itself *is* all the same: it is the absolute abstraction, thus pure thinking or being-within-self, and with the moment of its opposition to the spiritual unity it is *evil.* The difficulty people find in these concepts is due solely to holding fast to the *is* and forgetting the thinking in which the moments just as much *are* as *are not*—they are only the movement that is spirit. It is this spiritual unity, or the unity in which the distinctions are [present] only as moments or as sublated, that is known to representational consciousness as that reconciliation spoken of above. And since this unity is the universality of self-consciousness, the latter has ceased to be representational, and the movement has turned back into self-consciousness.

Spirit is thus posited in the third element, in *universal self-consciousness;* spirit is its *community.* The movement of the community as the self-consciousness that has distinguished itself from its representational form is to *bring forth explicitly* what has been established *implicitly.* The dead divine man or human God is *implicitly* the universal self-consciousness; he has to become this *for this self-consciousness.* Or since this self-consciousness constitutes one side of the representational opposition, namely the side of evil, which takes natural existence and individual being-for-self as essential reality, this aspect, which is represented as independent and not yet as a moment [of the spiritual whole], has, on account of its independence, to raise itself in and for itself to spirit, or to portray in its own self the movement of spirit.

This aspect is *natural spirit.* The self has to withdraw from this natural existence and go into itself, which means to become *evil.* But this aspect is already *implicitly* evil: withdrawing-into-self consists in *convincing oneself* that natural existence is evil. Representational consciousness depicts this as a *determinately existing* process of becoming evil, resulting in the evil state of the world, as well as a *determinately existing* reconciliation on the part of absolute being. In *self-consciousness* as such, however, the form of the representational content is considered only as a sublated moment, for the *self* is what is negative and hence a *knowing,* a knowing that is a pure act of consciousness within itself. This moment of the *negative* must in like manner find expression in the content. That is to say, since essential being is *implicitly* reconciled with itself and is a spiritual unity in which what are parts for representational thinking are *sublated* or are *moments,* we find that each of representation's parts takes on a signification *opposed* to what it had before. Each meaning finds its completion in the other, and in this way the content becomes for the first time a spiritual content. Since the determinacy of each is just as much its opposite, unity in otherness or the spiritual [relationship] is achieved—just as opposed meanings were united previously for us or *in themselves,* and even the abstract forms of *the same* and *not the same,* of *identity* and *nonidentity,* were sublated.

If then for representational consciousness the *inwardizing* of the natural self-consciousness was *determinately existing evil,* in the element of self-consciousness this inwardizing is the *knowledge* of *evil* as something that is *intrinsic* in determinate existence. This knowledge is of course an origin of evil, but only an origin of the *thought* of *evil,* and it is therefore recognized as the first moment of reconciliation. For as a withdrawal into itself out of the immediacy of nature, which is defined as evil, it is a forsaking of that immediacy and a dying to sin.[24] It is not natural existence as such that is forsaken by consciousness, but natural existence that is at the same time known as evil. The immediate movement of *withdrawal-into-self* is just as much a mediated movement. It presupposes itself or is its own ground; that is, the ground of withdrawal-into-self is that nature already has implicitly withdrawn into itself. Because of evil, humanity must withdraw into itself, but *evil* is itself this withdrawal. This first movement is for that very reason only immediate, or the *simple concept* of the movement because it is the same as what its ground is. The movement or the becoming-other must therefore first appear in its proper form.

Beside this immediacy, therefore, representational *mediation* is necessary. The *knowledge* of nature as the untrue existence of spirit, and this inwardly developed universality of the self, is *in itself* the reconciliation of spirit with itself. This *in-itself* obtains for the nonconceiving self-consciousness the form of an *existing being,* something that is *represented to it.* Conceptual comprehension [*Begreifen*] thus is not for it a grasping [*Ergreifen*] of this concept, which knows sublated natural existence to be universal and therefore to be reconciled with itself; rather it is a grasping of the representational idea that the divine being is reconciled with its determinate existence through an *event,* the event of the self-diremption of the divine being through its historical incarnation [*geschehene Menschwerdung*] and its death. The grasping of this representational idea now expresses more precisely what was previously called, in representational form, spiritual resurrection, or the process by which the divine being's individual self-consciousness becomes universal, becomes the community. The *death* of the divine man *qua death* is *abstract* negativity, the immediate result of the process that comes to an end only in the universality of *nature.* In spiritual self-consciousness, death loses its natural signification; it passes into the conception that has just been mentioned. Death is transfigured from what it immediately signifies, the nonbeing of *this individual,* into the *universality* of the spirit, which lives in its community, dies there daily and daily rises again.

Thus what belongs to the element of *representation*—namely, that absolute spirit as *an individual,* or rather as *a particular,* places before us [*vorstellt*] the nature of spirit in its determinate existence—is here transposed into self-consciousness itself, into the knowledge that maintains itself in its *otherness.* This self-consciousness does not actually *die,* as the *particular person* is *represented* to have *actually* died; rather its particularity dies away in its universality, i.e., in its *knowledge,* which is essential being reconciling itself with itself. The immediately preceding *element of representation* is thus here affirmed as sublated: it has returned into the self, into its concept. What was in the former only existing being has become subject. By this very fact the *first element* too, *pure thinking* and the eternal spirit within it, are no longer simply beyond the representational consciousness and the self; rather the return of the whole into itself consists just in containing all moments within itself. When the death of the mediator is grasped by the self, this means the sublating of his *objectivity* or his *particular being-for-self;* this *particular* being-for-self has become universal self-consciousness.

On the other side, the *universal* just for this reason is self-consciousness, and the pure or unactual spirit of bare thought has become *actual.* The death of the mediator is the death not only of his *natural aspect,* of his particular being-for-self: what dies is not only the already dead husk stripped of its essential being, but rather the *abstraction* of the divine being. For the mediator, insofar as his death has not yet completed reconciliation, is something one-sided, which takes as *essential being* the simplicity of thought as opposed to actuality. This extreme of the self does not yet have equal worth and value with essential being; it first gets this as spirit. The death of this representation contains at the same time the death of the *abstraction of the divine being,* which is not yet posited as a self. This death is the anguished feeling of the unhappy consciousness that *God godself* is *dead.*[25] This harsh saying is the expression of the most interior knowing that has simply itself as object, the return of consciousness into the night in which I = I, a night that no longer distinguishes and knows anything outside of it.[26] This feeling is thus in fact the loss of *substance* and of its standing over against consciousness; but at the same time it is the pure *subjectivity* of substance, or the pure certainty of itself that it lacked when it was object, or immediacy, or pure essential being. This knowledge is thus *spiritualization,* whereby substance becomes subject, by which its abstraction and lifelessness have expired, and substance has thereby become *actual,* simple, and universal self-consciousness.

In this way, then, spirit is spirit knowing its *own self.* It knows *itself;* that which is for it an object *is,* or its representation is the true, absolute *content.* The content, as we have seen, expresses spirit itself. It is at the same time not merely a *content* of self-consciousness, and not merely an object *for it;* it is also *actual* spirit. It is this because it passes through the three elements of its nature; this movement through its whole self constitutes its actuality. Spirit is what moves itself: it is the subject of the movement and likewise *the movement* itself, or the substance through which the subject passes. We saw how the concept of spirit emerged when we entered into the sphere of religion: it was the movement of spirit certain of itself, which forgives evil, and in so doing puts aside its own simplicity and rigid unchangeableness; it was, expressed differently, the movement in which things that are absolutely *opposed* recognize themselves as *the same,* and this recognition breaks out into the "yes" with which one extreme meets the other. The religious consciousness to which absolute being is manifest *beholds* this concept and sublates the *distinction* between *itself* and *what it beholds.* Just as it is subject, so also it is substance, and thus it *is* itself spirit just because and to the extent that it is this movement.

But the community is not yet consummated in this its self-consciousness. Its content is generally put before it in the form of *representation,* and this tension applies also to its *actual spirituality,* its return out of its representational forms, just as the element of pure thought was burdened by it. The community also is not aware of what it is: it is the spiritual self-consciousness that is not an object to itself as such, or does not unfold itself into a consciousness of itself. Rather to the extent that it is consciousness, it has those representations that we have considered.

We see self-consciousness at its last turning point becoming *inward* to itself and attaining to *knowledge of its being-within-self.* We see it divesting itself of its natural existence and attaining pure negativity. But the *positive* meaning remains an *other* for devotional consciousness—the meaning that this negativity or pure *inwardness* of *knowledge* is just as much the *self-identical essential being,* or that substance herein attains to being absolute self-consciousness. Devotional consciousness grasps this aspect—namely that the pure inwardizing of knowledge is *in itself* absolute simplicity or substance—as the representation of a state of affairs that comes about not in virtue of its *concept* but as the action of an *alien* satisfaction.[27] In other words, it does not grasp the fact that this depth of the pure self is the force by which *abstract essential being* is drawn down from its abstraction and raised into selfhood by the power of this pure devotion. The action of the self thus retains toward it this negative signification because self-divestment on the part of substance is taken by the self to be something [only] *implicit;* the self does not at once grasp and comprehend it or find it as such in its *own* action.

Since this unity of essential being and the self has been *implicitly* brought about, consciousness also has this *representation* of its reconciliation, but [only] as representation. It attains satisfaction by *externally* attaching to its pure negativity the positive signification of the unity of itself with essential being. Thus its satisfaction remains itself hampered by the opposition of a beyond. Its own reconciliation therefore enters into its consciousness as something *distant,* something in the distant *future,* just as the reconciliation accomplished by the other *self*[28] appears as something in the distant *past.* Just as the *individual* divine human being has an *implicit* father and only an *actual* mother, so also the universal divine human being, the community, has for its father its *own doing* and *knowing,* but for its mother *eternal love,* which it only *feels* but does not behold in its consciousness as an actual, immediate *object.* Thus its reconciliation is in its heart, but with its consciousness still ruptured and its actuality still shattered. What enters into its consciousness as the *in-itself* or the aspect of *pure mediation* is the reconciliation that lies beyond; while what appears as *present,* as the aspect of *immediacy* or of *existence,* is the world that has yet to await its transfiguration. The world is to be sure *implicitly* reconciled with its essential being, and regarding this *essential being* it is known of course that it recognizes the object as no longer alienated from it but as equivalent with it in love. But for self-consciousness this immediate presence still does not have a spiritual shape. Thus the spirit of the community is separated in its immediate consciousness from its religious consciousness—which declares indeed that neither of these *in itself* is separated from the other; but this is an *in-itself* that is not realized, or has not yet become an equally absolute being-for-self.

4

ENCYCLOPEDIA OF THE PHILOSOPHICAL SCIENCES (1817, 1827, 1830)

The Encyclopedia *is the only complete compendium of Hegel's philosophical system. He prepared it for use in conjunction with his lectures, which became expositions of the thesis paragraphs of the printed text. The first edition was published in 1817, less than a year after Hegel's arrival in Heidelberg. In 1818 he was called to Berlin as the successor to Fichte, and there his lectures on the topics covered by the* Encyclopedia *greatly expanded. A second edition was issued in 1827, nearly twice the length of the first; and a third in 1830, only modestly revised from the second. The three main parts of the* Encyclopedia *are the Science of Logic (a shortened version of the book published in 1812–1816 and partly revised shortly before Hegel's death), the Philosophy of Nature (the only published version of this portion of Hegel's system), and the Philosophy of Spirit.*

The third part, the Philosophy of Spirit, is in turn divided into three sections: Subjective Spirit (anthropology, phenomenology of spirit, psychology), Objective Spirit (right, morality, ethical life), and Absolute Spirit (art, revealed religion, philosophy). The first two forms of spirit, which specify human existence in its individual and social manifestations, are transcended and unified in the third, which is the richest and most inclusive of Hegel's categories, encompassing divinity and humanity, the infinite and the finite, the ideal and the real, the spiritual and the natural: it is the whole, the true, the free. In art the absolute is known principally in the shape of sensible intuition (Anschauung); in religion, in that of spiritual representation (Vorstellung); and in philosophy, in that of the speculative concept (Begriff). While the forms of knowledge differ, the content is the same.

The organization of this section of the Encyclopedia *goes back to the first edition of 1817, although the content was considerably revised in 1827. The organization is a modification of that found in chapters 7 and 8 of the* Phenomenology of Spirit, *where Hegel treats in succession "natural religion," "the religion of art," "the revelatory religion," and "the absolute knowing" of philosophy. The section on "art" in the* Encyclopedia *includes as a subtext references not only to "the religion of art" proper, namely Greek religion, but to several of the so-called natural religions as well. In the lectures on the philosophy of religion, this material was expanded greatly to become the section called "determinate religion." Hegel did not lecture in Berlin on the paragraphs on "Objective Spirit" and "Absolute Spirit" in the* Encyclopedia *as such; rather he gave separate and extensive lecture courses on the philosophy of right, the philosophy of art, the philosophy of religion, and the history of philosophy. The* Encyclopedia *continued to be used as a text for lectures on logic and metaphysics, philosophy of nature, and philosophy of subjective spirit.*

The selection in this volume is provided in a new translation by J. Michael Stewart and the editor, based on the 3rd edition of 1830 as edited by Friedhelm Nicolin and Otto Pöggeler, Enzyklopädie der philosophischen Wissenschaften im Grundrisse *(Hamburg: Felix Meiner Verlag, 1959), and compared with the new critical edition of this text edited by Wolfgang Bonsiepen and Hans-Christian Lucas in* Gesammelte Werke, vol. 20 *(Hamburg: Felix Meiner Verlag, 1992). The editorial notes draw upon the critical apparatus of both editions. The translation adheres to the German text in its frequent use of italics. The earlier English translation by William Wallace,* Hegel's Philosophy of Mind *(Oxford: Clarendon Press, 1894, r.p. 1971) has been consulted. The indented passages following the thesis paragraphs are "remarks" provided by Hegel in the later published editions.*

ABSOLUTE SPIRIT: ART, REVEALED RELIGION, PHILOSOPHY

§ 553

The *concept* of spirit has its *reality* in spirit. For this reality, in identity with the concept, to exist as *knowledge* of the absolute idea, what is necessary is that the *implicitly* free intelligence should in its actuality be liberated to its concept in order to be its fitting *shape*. Subjective and objective spirit have to be seen as the road along which this aspect of *reality* or existence develops.

§ 554

Absolute spirit, while an *identity* that is eternally self-contained, is likewise an identity that is returning and has returned into itself; [it is] the one and universal *substance* as spiritual, the primal division [*Urteil*] *into itself* and *into a [mode of] knowing for which* it exists as substance. *Religion,* as this highest sphere may in general be designated, is to be seen as proceeding from and located in the subject no less than as proceeding from absolute spirit, which is [present] as spirit in its community.

As has already been noted, neither here nor anywhere else can faith be opposed to knowledge; on the contrary faith is a [mode of] knowing—a particular form of knowledge.[1] The fact that today so little is known of God and so little store is set on God's objective being, while there is all the more talk of religion, i.e., God's indwelling on the subjective side, and no call for truth as such—this does at least contain the correct principle that God has to be apprehended as spirit in its community.

§ 555

The subjective consciousness of absolute spirit is essentially an inward process whose immediate and substantial unity is *faith* in the witness of the spirit as the *certainty* of objective truth. Faith, as at once this immediate unity and containing the unity as a relationship of these different aspects, has in *devotion*—the implicit or more explicit [act of] worship [*Kultus*]— passed over into the process of sublating this antithesis into a spiritual liberation, by this mediation *authenticating* that initial certainty and achieving its concrete determination, namely reconciliation, the actuality of spirit.

A. ART
§ 556

As *immediate* (the finite aspect of art) this knowledge takes shape [in two ways]. On the one hand, it breaks up into a work of external everyday determinate existence [*Dasein*],[2] into the subject that produces the work and the subject that perceives and venerates [it]. On the other hand, it constitutes the concrete *intuition* [*Anschauung*] and representation of *implicitly* absolute spirit as the *ideal*. [This is] the concrete shape, born of subjective spirit, in which its natural immediacy [is] only a *sign* of the idea, for the expression of which the informing spirit works such a transfiguration that the shape shows it and it alone—the shape of *beauty*.

§ 557

The sensuous externality attaching to the beautiful—the *form* of *immediacy* as such—is at the same time its *determinacy of content*. Alongside its spiritual character, divinity [*der Gott*] has at the same time the character of a natural element or determinate existence—it contains the so-called *unity* of nature and spirit, i.e., the immediate form, that of intuition. This is not the spiritual unity in which the natural is posited only as ideal, as sublated, and the spiritual content would be related only to itself; it is not the absolute spirit that enters this consciousness. On the subjective side the community is to be sure an ethical community because it knows its essence as spiritual, and its self-consciousness and actuality are elevated to substantial freedom in it. But burdened as it is with immediacy, the freedom of the subject is only a matter of custom, lacking the infinite inward reflection and subjective inwardness of *conscience*. This determines also the further development of devotion and worship in the religion of fine art.[3]

§ 558

To arrive at the intuitions it has to produce, art needs not only an external given material, including also subjective images and representations; for the expression of spiritual import, it also needs the given forms of nature with a signification that art must divine and possess. Of all such configurations the human is the highest and the authentic one because only in it can spirit have its corporeality and thus its intuitable expression.

> This disposes of the principle of the *imitation of nature* in art, in respect to which no agreement is possible on the basis of such an abstract opposition—[in other words] so long as the natural is taken only in its externality and not as the characteristic, meaningful natural form signifying spirit.

§ 559

Absolute spirit cannot be made explicit in such single shapes. The spirit of fine art is therefore a limited folk spirit [*Volksgeist*] whose implicit universality breaks down into an indeterminate polytheism as steps are taken to further define its richness. With the essential limitedness of its content, beauty in general achieves only an imbuing of the intuition or image by what is spiritual. It achieves something formal, so that the content of the thought or representation, [together] with the material it uses for its devising, can be of the most varied and even inessential kind, yet the work itself can still be something beautiful and a work of art.

§ 560

The one-sided nature of *immediacy* on the part of the ideal involves the opposite one-sidedness (§ 556) that the ideal is something *made* by the artist. The subject is the *formal element* in the activity, and the *work of art* is only an expression of divinity when no sign of subjective *particularity* is found in it, but rather the import of the indwelling spirit has been conceived and has issued forth without admixture and unspotted by the contingency it involves. But since freedom extends no further than thought, the activity filled with this indwelling import, the *enthusiasm* of the artist, is like an alien power within him under which he is *bound* and passive. [Artistic] *production* has on its part the form of *natural* immediacy; it belongs to the *genius* as to this *particular subject*—and is at the same time a labor concerned with technical understanding and mechanical externalities. The work of art is therefore just as much a work of free and arbitrary will, and the artist is the master of the god.

§ 561

In being thus fulfilled, *reconciliation* initially appears in such a way that it is accomplished immediately in subjective self-consciousness, which is thus self-confident and cheerful, but lacking in depth and in awareness of its antithesis to the being that subsists in and for itself. Beyond the accomplishment of *beauty* in *classical* art that occurs in such reconciliation, lies the art of *sublimity*,[4] *symbolic* art, in which the configuration suited to the idea is not yet found. Rather thought is portrayed as going outside itself and wrestling with the shape as a negative attitude toward it, yet at the same time seeking to mold itself to it. The purport or content thereby shows that it has not yet reached infinite form, is not yet known and known to itself as free spirit. The content exists only as the abstract god of pure thinking or a striving toward it, a striving that throws itself around restlessly and unreconciledly in all manner of shapes, incapable of finding its goal.

§ 562

The other way in which the idea and the configuration are mutually unsuited, however, is that the infinite form, subjectivity, is not, as in the first extreme, merely superficial personality but its innermost element; and divinity is known not as simply seeking its shape or contenting itself in an external shape, but rather as finding itself only within itself and so giving itself its adequate shape only in the spiritual. In this way *romantic* art[5] abandons the idea of showing divinity as such in its external shape and by means of beauty; it presents it as only condescending to appearance and as inwardness in an externality from which it at the same time disengages. Thus the external can appear here as contingent in relation to its meaning.

Philosophy of religion has the logical necessity, in the progressively determinate features that belong to the being that is known as the absolute, to discover to which features cultic practices initially correspond. It has also to discover how worldly self-consciousness, consciousness of what is the highest human vocation, and consequently the nature of a people's ethical life, the principle of its right, of its actual freedom and its constitution as well as of its art and science—how all of this corresponds to the principle that forms the substance of a religion. That all these elements in a people's actuality constitute one systematic totality, that one spirit creates and informs them—this is an insight that provides the basis for the further insight that the history of religions coincides with world history.

Regarding the close connection between art and the religions, it may be especially noted that *fine* or *beautiful* art [*die schöne Kunst*] can only belong to those religions in which *concrete spirituality* is the principle—spirituality that has become inwardly free but is not yet absolute. In those religions in which the idea has not yet become manifest and is known in its free determinacy, the need for art does indeed make itself felt in order to bring the representation of *essential being* [*Wesen*] to consciousness in intuition and fantasy.[6] Indeed art is the sole organ in which the abstract content, inwardly unclear and made up of a confused mixture of natural and spiritual elements, can seek to bring itself to consciousness. Yet this art is defective. Because its content is so defective, the form is defective too, for it is by reason of the content that the content does not contain the form immanently within itself. Its portrayals have an aspect of tastelessness and spiritlessness because its inmost element is still contaminated with a lack of spirituality and thus lacks the power freely to transmute the external part into significant shape. *Fine* art on the contrary is conditional on the self-consciousness of free spirit and thus on the consciousness of the dependence of the sensuous and merely natural upon spirit; it makes the natural wholly into the expression of spirit. Thus it is the inner form that gives utterance to itself alone.

This involves the further, more profound consideration that the advent of art portends the decline of a religion that is still bound to sensuous externality. At the very time it seems to give religion the highest degree of clarity, expressiveness, and brilliance, it has raised it above its limitedness. In the sublime divinity to which the work of art succeeds in giving expression, the genius of the artist and of the spectator finds itself at home with their own sense and sensibility, satisfied and set free; the intuition and consciousness of free spirit is vouchsafed and attained. Fine art has for its part accomplished the same as philosophy—spirit has been cleansed of its lack of freedom. That religion in which the need for fine art, and just for that reason, is first generated, contains in its principle an other-worldly element that is lacking in thought and is sensuous; the images that are *venerated* [by it] are the hideous images of idols, regarded as wonder-working talismans that point to an other-worldly, spiritless objectivity—and bones perform a similar or even better service than such images.[7] But fine art is only a stage in liberation, not the supreme liberation itself.

Genuine objectivity, which obtains only in the element of *thought,* the element in which alone pure spirit is for spirit and liberation is accompanied by reverence, is also lacking in the sensuous beauty of the work of art, and still more in that external, hideous sensuousness.

§ 563

Fine art (like the religion peculiar to it) has its future in authentic religion. In and for itself the limited content of the idea passes into the universality that is identical with infinite form. Intuition, the immediate knowing that is tied to sensuousness, passes into the knowing that mediates itself inwardly, into a determinate existence that is itself knowing—into *revelation*. In this way the content of the idea has for its principle the characteristic of free intelligence, and as absolute *spirit is for spirit*.

B. REVEALED RELIGION[8]
§ 564

It lies essentially in the concept of authentic religion—i.e., the religion whose content is absolute spirit—that it should be *revealed,* and, what is more, revealed *by God*. Knowledge, the principle by which substance is spirit, is what is *self-determining* as the infinite form that subsists for itself; therefore it is nothing other than a *manifesting*. Spirit is only spirit insofar as it is *for* spirit, and in the absolute religion it is absolute spirit that no longer manifests abstract moments of itself but its very own self.

The ancient notion of Nemesis, according to which the divine and its action in the world was grasped by the still abstract understanding solely as a *leveling* power, destroying what was high and great—this was opposed by *Plato* and *Aristotle* on the grounds that God is not *jealous*.[9] This can likewise be opposed to the modern assurances that humanity cannot know God. These cannot be called more than assurances and are all the more illogical when they are made within a religion that is expressly called the *revealed* religion; for according to them it would rather be the religion that contains *nothing revelatory* of God, a religion in which God has *not* revealed godself. In this way its adherents would be "the Gentiles who do not know God" [1 Thess. 4:5]. If the word "God" is to be taken at all seriously in religion, then it is from God, the content and principle of religion, that the definition must begin. If God is denied the possibility of self-revealing, then the only thing left to be said of God is to ascribe to God *jealousy*. But if the word *spirit* is to have its full meaning, this includes self-revealing.

If one considers how difficult it is to have knowledge of God as spirit—a knowledge that [can] no longer be content with the facile representations of belief but proceeds to thought (initially to reflective understanding but then it must go on to conceptual thinking)—in light of this difficulty it is not too surprising that so many people (especially theologians whose vocation it is to concern themselves with such ideas) succumb to the temptation to take a short cut and thus have willingly

accepted whatever they are offered for the purpose. There is nothing easier to accept than the conclusion that human beings know nothing of
God. To grasp what God is as spirit, rightly and in specific terms of
thought—this calls for profound speculation. First and foremost it
embraces the following propositions: God is only God to the extent that
God knows godself; God's self-knowing is, further, a self-consciousness
in humanity and humanity's knowledge *of* God, which proceeds to
humanity's self-knowing *in* God. (See the thorough exposition of these
propositions in the work from which they are cited: *Aphorisms on
Knowing and Not-Knowing, etc.* by C.F. G—l, Berlin 1829.[10])

§ 565

When the immediacy and sensuousness of shape and knowledge are sublated, absolute spirit is, in respect to content, the spirit of nature and of [finite]
spirit subsisting in and for itself, while in respect to form it subsists primarily for the subjective knowledge of *representation [Vorstellung]*. On the one
hand, representation imparts to the elements of its content independence,
making them presuppositions of each other and phenomena *following one
another,* a web *of happenings* understood in terms of *finite reflective categories.* On the other hand, this form of finite representation is sublated in
faith in the one spirit and in the devotion of worship.

§ 566

In this separating the *form* parts from the *content;* and in the form the different moments of the concept divide into *particular spheres* or elements in
each of which the absolute content presents itself: (α) as eternal content
abiding with itself in its manifestation; (β) as differentiation of eternal
being from its manifestation, which through this differentiation becomes
the phenomenal world into which the content enters; (γ) as infinite return of
the alienated world and its reconciliation with eternal being, the latter's
withdrawal from the phenomenal into the unity of its fullness.[11]

§ 567

(α) In the moment of *universality [Allgemeinheit]*, the sphere of pure
thought or the abstract element of *essential being,* it is absolute spirit that is
at first what is *presupposed*—although not remaining closed off but, as *substantial power* in the reflective category of causality, the *creator* of heaven
and earth. Yet in this eternal sphere absolute spirit rather begets only *itself*
as its *son,* and at the same time remains in original identity with this differentiated element as what has the characteristic of differing from universal
being; it eternally sublates itself, and by this mediation of the self-sublating

144

mediation it is the first substance essentially as *concrete individuality* and subjectivity—it is *spirit*.

§ 568

(β) In the moment of *particularity* [*Besonderheit*], of judgment or primal division [*Urteil*], this concrete eternal being is what is *presupposed,* and its movement [is] the coming to be of *appearance,* the falling apart of the eternal moment of mediation, of the only Son, into an independent opposition: on the one hand is heaven and earth, elemental and concrete nature, and on the other hand, standing in *relationship* to it, is spirit, which therefore is *finite*. Finite spirit, as the extreme of inherent negativity, makes itself independent and becomes evil; it is that extreme by its relation to a nature that stands over against it and by its own resulting naturalness. Yet, amid that naturalness, it is, when it thinks, directed toward the eternal, but for this reason stands in external relationship to it.

§ 569

(γ) In the moment of *individuality* [*Einzelheit*[12]] as such, namely of subjectivity and the concept itself, in which the antithesis of universality and particularity has returned to its *identical ground,* the place of *presupposition* is taken, first, by the *universal* substance as actualized out of its abstraction into an *individual* self-consciousness. This individual,[13] as *immediately identical* with essential being, transposes him who in the eternal sphere is called the Son into [the sphere of] temporality, and in him evil is portrayed as *implicitly* sublated. Further, this immediate and thus sensuous existence of what is absolutely concrete is portrayed as putting itself in judgment and expiring in the anguish of *negativity*—in which, as infinite subjectivity, it has become identical with itself and, as absolute return from that negativity and as universal unity of universal and individual essentiality, has become *for its own sake* the idea of spirit as eternal, yet *living* and present in the world.

§ 570

Secondly, this objective totality[14] is the implicit *presupposition* for the *finite* immediacy of the individual subject. For such a subject therefore it is at first an *other,* something *intuited*. But it is the intuition of *implicit* truth; and through the witness of the spirit within it the subject, because of its immediate nature, at first determines itself for itself as nought and evil. But then in accord with this example of its truth, and by means of faith in the unity, therein *implicitly* accomplished, of universal and individual essentiality, the subject is also the movement to divest itself of its immediate natural determinateness and its own will, and to merge with that example and its *implicitness* [*Ansich*] in the anguish of negativity and so recognize itself as united with essential being. This being, thirdly, brings about through this mediation its own indwelling in self-consciousness and is the actual presence of the spirit that exists in and for itself as universal spirit.

§ 571

These three syllogisms, which constitute the one syllogism of the absolute mediation of spirit with itself, are also its revelation, a revelation that makes the life of spirit explicit in the cycle of concrete shapes of representation. From its separation into parts with a temporal and external sequence, the unfolding of the mediation coalesces in its result, where spirit closes in unity with itself, to yield not merely the simplicity of faith and devotional feeling, but also *thought*. In the immanent simplicity of thought, the unfolding still has its expansion, yet is known as an indivisible coinherence of the universal, simple, and eternal spirit within itself. In this form of truth, truth is the object of *philosophy*.

If the result—spirit subsisting *for itself* in which all mediation has been sublated—is taken in a merely *formal,* contentless sense, so that spirit is not at the same time known as subsisting *in itself* and developing objectively, then its infinite subjectivity is a merely formal self-consciousness that knows itself inwardly as absolute. This is *irony,* which can make every objective content null and *vain,* and is itself emptiness and vanity, determining itself from itself and thus producing a contingent and fanciful content. It remains master of itself, is not bound by the content, and, with the assurance of standing at the very summit of religion and philosophy, relapses rather into hollow arbitrariness. Only to the extent that the pure infinite form, the self-manifestation that is centered on itself, throws off the one-sidedness of the subjective in which it is the vanity of thought, is it free thought, which at the same time has its infinite characteristic in the absolute content that subsists in and for itself, and has this content as an object in which it is also free. To this extent thought is itself merely the formal element of the absolute content.

C. PHILOSOPHY
§ 572

This science is the unity of art and religion. The intuitional mode of art, external in point of form, with its subjective production and its splintering of the substantial content into many independent shapes, is not merely held together so as to form a whole in the *totality* of religion, with its falling apart as it unfolds in representation and its mediation of what has unfolded.

It is also combined into a simple spiritual *intuition* and then raised in this intuition to *self-conscious thought*. This knowledge is then the *concept* (cognized by thought) of art and religion, in which the diverse elements in the content are recognized as necessary, and what is necessary as free.

§ 573

Philosophy is thus defined as a cognizing of the necessity of the *content* of the absolute representation as well as of the necessity of two *forms: on the one hand* immediate intuition and its *poetry,* and the mode of representation it *presupposes,* that of objective and external *revelation; on the other hand,* first the subjective entry into self, and then the subjective departure [from self] and the identification of *faith* with the presupposed object. This cognition [*Erkennen*] is thus a *recognition* [*Anerkennen*] of this content and its form, as well as a *liberation* from the one-sidedness of the forms and their elevation into the absolute form, which determines itself to become the content and remains identical with it, and thus is the cognition of that necessity which subsists in and for itself. This movement, which is philosophy, finds itself already accomplished when at the close it grasps its own concept, that is, only *looks back* upon its knowledge.

This might seem to be the place to treat the *relationship of philosophy to religion* in a specific exposition. Everything turns on the difference between the forms of speculative thought and those of representation and reflective understanding. But it is the whole course of philosophy and of logic especially that enables us not only to recognize this difference but also to judge it or rather to develop and direct its nature in light of these categories themselves. Only on the basis of recognizing these forms can we acquire the genuine conviction that the content of philosophy and religion is the same, leaving out the further details of external nature and finite spirit, which fall outside the sphere of religion. But religion is the truth *for all of humanity,* and faith rests on the *witness of the spirit,* which as witnessing is spirit in humanity. Insofar as it is driven to explicate itself, this witness, in itself substantial, forms initially into the cultural pattern that matches its worldly consciousness and understanding; in this way the truth becomes subject to the terms and conditions of finitude generally. This does not prevent spirit, even in the use of sensible representations and finite categories of thought, from retaining its content (which as religious is essentially speculative) in regard to the truth, doing violence to and acting *inconsistently* toward such representations and categories. By this inconsistency spirit corrects their defects. Nothing therefore is easier for the understanding than to demonstrate contradictions in the exposition of faith, and thus to prepare triumphs for its principle, formal *identity*. If spirit yields to this finite reflection that has called itself reason and philosophy (i.e., rationalism), it finitizes the religious content and makes it in fact nothing. Religion then has a perfect right to defend itself against such reason and philosophy and to treat them as enemies. But it is another matter if religion sets itself against comprehending reason and philosophy in general, and specifically against a reason and philosophy that are speculative in content and therefore religious. Such an opposition proceeds from lack of insight into the difference indicated and the value of the spiritual forms in general, and in particular the forms of thought; or to be more precise, from lack of insight into the distinction of the content, which may be the same in both, from those forms. It is on the ground of form that philosophy has been reproached and accused by the religious side, just as conversely its speculative content has resulted in the same charges being leveled against it by a self-styled philosophy—and by an empty piety. It has *too little* of God in it for the former, too much for *the latter*.

The charge of *atheism,* which often used to be brought against philosophy—that it has *too little* of God—has grown rare. All the more common, however, is the charge of pantheism, that it has *too much* of God.[15] So much is this the case that it is treated not so much as a charge but as a proved fact, or as a bare fact that needs no proof. Piety in particular, which with its pious air of superiority fancies itself free to dispense with proof, abandons itself—in concert with the empty philosophy of the understanding, to which it is so firmly resolved to be opposed, but on whose habit of mind it is in fact wholly based—to the assertion (as though it were merely mentioning a well-known fact) that philosophy is the "all-one" doctrine or pantheism. It must be said that it was more to the credit of piety and theology when they accused a philosophical system (e.g., Spinozism) of atheism rather than pantheism, although the former accusation at first glance looks more cruel and invidious. The charge of atheism, however, presupposes a definite representation of a *full and real* God, and arises because the representation does not detect in the philosophical concepts the peculiar forms to which it is itself attached. Philosophy can indeed recognize its own forms in the categories of religious representation as well as its own content in the religious content, which therefore it does not disparage. But the converse is not true: the religious mode of representation does not apply the critique of thought to itself and does not comprehend itself, and is therefore in its immediacy exclusive.

To impute pantheism instead of atheism to philosophy is part of the modern habit of mind—of the new piety and the new theology. For them philosophy has *too much* of God—so much so that (according to their claim) God is all and all is God. This new theology, which makes religion only a subjective feeling and denies any cognition of God's nature, thus retains nothing more than a God *in general* without objective characteristics. Without interest of its own for the concrete, fulfilled concept of God, it treats it only as an interest that *others* once had, and hence treats what belongs to the doctrine of God's concrete nature as something merely *historical* [*historisches*]. The indeterminate God is to be found in all religions. Every kind of piety—that of Hindus toward asses, cows, etc., or the Dalai Lama, that of Egyptians toward oxen—is always veneration of an object that despite its absurdities also contains the generic abstract, *God in general*. If this view needs no more than such a God, so as to find God in everything called religion, it must at least find such a God recognized even in philosophy, and thus can no longer accuse it of atheism. The mitigation [*Milderung*] of the charge of atheism into that of pantheism has its ground therefore in the superficial representation to which this mildness [*Mildigkeit*] has attenuated and emptied God. Because this representation clings to its abstract universality, *from which* all determinate characteristics are excluded, such characteristics belong only to the undivine, the worldly existence of things, which is thus left standing in *fixed undisturbed substantiality*. With such a presupposition, even in face of the *universality that subsists in and for itself,* which is maintained of God in philosophy and in which the being of external things has no truth, people cling now as before to the view that *worldly things nonetheless retain their being,* and that it is these things that constitute what is determinate in the divine universality. They thus change that universality into what they call *pantheistic: everything is* (empirical things without distinction, whether regarded more highly or lowly), everything possesses substantiality, and this being of worldly things is God. It is only their own stupidity and their consequent falsification of concepts that gives rise to the notion and allegation of pantheism.

But if those who give out that a certain philosophy is pantheism are unable and unwilling to see this—for it is just this insight into concepts that they refuse—they should above all have verified the alleged fact that *any one philosopher* or *any human being* [has] really ascribed substantial reality, subsisting in and for itself, to *all* things and regarded them as God—that such a notion has ever come into the head of anyone but themselves. This allegation I will further elucidate in this exoteric discussion, and the only way to do so is to set down the evidence. . . .[16]

I refrain from accumulating further examples of the religious and poetic representations that are customarily called pantheistic. Of the philosophies to which this name is given, for example the Eleatic or Spinozistic, it has been noted earlier[17] that, far from identifying God

149

with the world and making God finite, these philosophies rather attribute no truth to this *all*. Consequently, they should more accurately be called *monotheism,* and in regard to their representation of the world, *acosmism.* They would be most accurately defined as the systems that grasp the absolute as *substance* and nothing more. Of the Oriental and especially the Islamic modes of representing God, we may rather say that the absolute appears as the *utterly universal genus* that dwells in the species or existences, but in such a way that these have no actual reality. The defect of all these modes of representation and systems is that they do not proceed to define substance as *subject* and as *spirit*.

These modes of representation and systems originate from the one need common to all philosophies and religions alike to obtain a representation of God and then of the *relationship* between God and the world. In philosophy it is more clearly recognized that the relationship of God to the world is determined by the definition of God's nature. The reflective understanding begins by rejecting all those modes of representation and systems, whether they spring from the heart, imagination, or speculation, that express the interconnection of God and the world. In order to have God pure in faith or consciousness, God is separated as essence from appearance, as infinite from finite. But after this separation, the conviction also arises as to the *relation* of appearance to essence, the finite to the infinite, and so on, and thus arises the reflective question about the nature of this relation. It is in the reflective form that the whole difficulty of the matter lies. This relation is called *incomprehensible* by those who wish to know nothing of God's nature.

The conclusion of philosophy is not the place, even in an exoteric discussion, to waste a word on what it means to *comprehend* or *conceive*. But since the view taken of this relation is closely connected with the view taken of scientific knowledge generally and with all the accusations made against it, it may also be recalled in this connection that although philosophy certainly has to do with *unity* in general it is not, however, with abstract unity, mere identity, and the empty absolute, but with *concrete* unity (the concept), and that in its whole course it has to do with nothing else. Thus every stage in its advance is a *distinctive determination* of this concrete *unity,* and the deepest and last of the determinations of unity is that of absolute spirit. Of those who judge philosophy and wish to express an opinion about it, it would have to be supposed that they focused on these *determinations* of *unity* and took the trouble to become acquainted with them, and that they at least knew that these determinations include *a great number* and a great diversity. But they show so little acquaintance with this matter and even less concern with it that whenever they hear of *unity*—and *relation* at the same time involves *unity*—they go no further than a wholly abstract, *indeterminate unity,* and lose sight of the chief point of interest, namely the manner in which unity is determinate. Thus all they can say about philosophy is that dry identity is its principle and result and that it is the system of identity. Sticking fast to this unconceptual thought of identity, they have in truth grasped absolutely nothing of concrete unity, the concept and content of philosophy, but rather its opposite. They proceed in the philosophical field as those physicists do in the physical field who likewise may well know that they are faced with diverse sensible properties and materials (or usually *only* materials since properties get transformed into materials for such physicists), and that these materials also stand in *relation* to one another. Now the question is, What kind of relationship is this? The distinctiveness of all natural, inorganic, and living things, and the entire difference between them, rests solely on the *diverse determinacy of this unity*. But instead of recognizing this unity in the diverse ways it is determinate, ordinary physics (including chemistry) grasps only one, the most external and the worst [form of unity], namely *composition,* applies only it in the whole range of natural structures, and thus makes it impossible to grasp any of them.

The aforementioned shallow pantheism is the direct result of this shallow identity. Those who employ this invention of their own to censure philosophy suppose from their consideration of the *relation* of God and the world that this category, *relation,* gives rise to the one, but only the *one moment,* in fact the moment of indeterminacy—*identity*. Thus they remain stuck in this halfway house of comprehension and assert what is factually false, that philosophy maintains the identity of God and the world. And since, for them, both the world and God have the same solid substantiality, they conclude that in the philosophical idea God is *composed* out of God and the world. Such then is the notion that they have of pantheism and that they ascribe to philosophy. Those who in their thinking and comprehension of thoughts do not pass beyond such categories import them into philosophy, where they are entirely out of place. Thus they infect it with the disease against which they subsequently raise an outcry.[18] They avoid all the difficulties that emerge in comprehending the relation of God to the world, and they do so at once and very easily by confessing that for them this relation involves a contradiction of which they have no understanding; consequently they have to acquiesce in the wholly *indeterminate representation* of such a relation and of the more precise forms it takes such as omnipresence, providence, etc. In this sense *faith* means no more than not proceeding to a determinate representation, being unwilling to enter further into the content. That persons and classes of untrained intellect are satisfied with indefinite representations is what one expects; but when a person of trained intellect and with an interest for reflective study is satisfied with indefinite representations in matters acknowledged to be of higher and even supreme interest, it is hard to decide whether the thinker is really *in earnest* about the subject. If, however, those who cling to this bare understanding were *in earnest* about maintaining (for example) God's *omnipresence,* in the sense that they visualized faith in it in the form of a specific representation, in what difficulty would they be involved by their faith in the *genuine reality* of sensible things? Unlike Epicurus, they would hardly be willing to have God dwell in the interspaces of things, i.e., in the pores of the physicists, such pores being the negative that is supposed to exist *along side* the materially real.[19] This *along side* would give them their pantheism of spatiality—their "all," defined as the mutual externality of space. But since they would attribute to God, in God's relation to the world, an efficacy on and in filled space and on and in the world, they would have the infinite splintering of the divine actuality in infinite materiality. The faulty notion they call pantheism or the all-one doctrine would in fact only be the necessary consequence of their faulty notions of God and the world. To put this sort of thing, such as the stale talk about unity or identity, on the shoulders of philosophy, shows such a recklessness for justice and truth that it can only be explained by the difficulty of getting into one's head thoughts and concepts—i.e., not abstract unity but the multiple shapes of its determinacy. When factual assertions are put forward and the facts are thoughts and concepts, it is indispensable to get hold of their meaning. But it is no longer necessary to satisfy even this requirement now that it has long been a *foregone* conclusion that philosophy is pantheism, a system of identity, an all-one doctrine, so that a person who might be unaware of this fact is treated as either ignorant of a known matter or prevaricating for a purpose.

Because of this chorus I have felt myself obliged to speak more extensively and exoterically about the outer and inner untruth of this alleged fact. For it is only possible in the first instance to speak exoterically of the external comprehension of concepts as mere facts—which is to exchange concepts for their opposite. The esoteric contemplation of God and identity, as of cognition and concepts, is philosophy itself.

§ 574

This concept of philosophy is the *self-thinking* idea, the knowing truth (§ 236)—the logical idea [*das Logische*] with the signification that it is universality *attested* in concrete content as in its actuality. In this manner science has returned to its beginning: its *result* is the logical idea but as a *spiritual principle* [*das Geistige*]. Out of the presupposing judgment in which the concept was only *implicit* and the beginning was something immediate, and thus out of the *appearance* that it initially had in it, the logical has arisen into its pure principle and thus also into its element.

§ 575

It is this appearing that originally provides the basis for the further development. The first appearance is furnished by the *syllogism* that has the *logical* as basis and starting point, with *nature* for the middle term, which couples *spirit* with the logical.[20] The logical becomes nature, and nature becomes spirit. Nature, which stands between spirit and its essential being, does not to be sure separate them into extremes of finite abstraction, nor does it separate itself from them as something independent, embracing as other only others. For the syllogism is defined *in the idea,* and nature is defined essentially as only a transition point and negative moment, and *implicitly* as the idea. But the mediation of the concept has the external form of *passing over,* and science that of the course of necessity, so that only in the one extreme is the freedom of the concept posited as its closing with itself.

§ 576

In the *second syllogism* this appearance is sublated to the extent that the syllogism is already the standpoint of spirit itself, which is what mediates the process, *presupposes* nature, and couples it with the *logical.* It is the syllogism of spiritual *reflection* in the idea. Science appears as a subjective *knowing,* of which freedom is the aim, and which is itself the way to produce it.

§ 577

The third syllogism is the idea of philosophy, which has *self-knowing reason,* the absolute universal, as its *middle term*—a middle that divides itself into *spirit* and *nature,* making the former its presupposition as the process of the *subjective* activity of the idea, and the latter its universal extreme as the process of the *implicitly* [yet] objectively existing idea. The *primal self-dividing* [*Sich-Urteilen*] of the idea into the two appearances (§§ 575, 576) determines them as *its* (the self-knowing reason's) manifestations. In it there is a unification of two aspects: that it is the nature of the thing [itself], the concept, that moves forward and develops; and that this movement is no less the activity of knowing. The eternal idea that exists in and for itself is eternally active, engendering and enjoying itself as absolute spirit.

ARISTOTLE, *METAPHYSICS*, XII.7[21]

"But thinking [*noēsis*], which exists purely for itself, is a thinking of what is most excellent in and for itself; and the more thinking exists purely for itself, the more it is thinking the most excellent.

"But thought [*nous*] thinks itself by taking up what is thought [*noēton*]. Thought becomes thought by making contact and thinking, so that thought and the object of thought are the same. For what takes up the object of thought [*noēton*] and [therefore] being [*ousia*] is thought [*nous*]. Thought acts when it possesses [its object] so that [its own activity] is more divine than the deity that thinking reason supposes itself to have. Speculation [*theōria*] is thus what is most enjoyable and best. If God is always in that enjoyable state in which we sometimes are, then God is to be wondered at; if in a better state, to be wondered at all the more. But that is just how God is.

"However, God also has life. For the activity [*energeia*] of thought is life. But God is activity; activity directed to itself is God's most excellent and eternal life. We say that God is an eternal life, and the best life. So God acquires life and permanent, eternal existence. For that is God."

5

FOREWORD TO HINRICHS'S *RELIGION* (1822)

In this essay Hegel returns to the theme of his early work Faith and Knowledge *(selection 2.1). He is no more sanguine now than he was before about the reconciliation of these elements, which it is the task of speculative philosophy of religion to accomplish in light of the failure of theologians to do so. Hegel's target is no longer simply the Kantians but Friedrich Schleiermacher, whose* Christian Faith *or* Glaubenslehre *was published the preceding year. Perhaps Hegel viewed the popular title of this work as ironic in view of the inability (from his perspective) of a theology of feeling actually to reconcile* Glaube *(faith) and* Lehre *(doctrine, teaching, knowledge)—if faith means not merely subjective certainty and personal appropriation but also the objective* credo, *the content of the church's confession of God, its truth-claims. Can these claims be subjected to rational critique and reconstruction without abandoning their fundamental content? Can faith and reason be reconciled without either being decimated?*

The foreword Hegel wrote for the work of a former student and future disciple is one of the most lucid and succinct statements of his mature position on these questions. It serves as a helpful introduction to the 1824 lectures on philosophy of religion (selection 6), which build on several of its themes. It is of added importance because it is one of Hegel's few published *statements on religion during the Berlin years; most of his effort was in the form of lectures, although he did publish revised editions of the* Encyclopedia *in 1827 and 1830, wrote a lengthy review of a theological work in 1829, and was preparing for publication his lectures on proofs of the existence of God when he died in 1831. Our translation has been made by J. Michael Stewart from H. F. W. Hinrichs,* Die Religion im inneren Verhältnisse zur Wissenschaft *(Heidelberg, 1822), pp. i–xxviii. A. V. Miller's translation of this material for an appendix to* Beyond Epistemology: New Studies in the Philosophy of Hegel, *ed. Frederick G. Weiss (The Hague: Martinus Nijhoff, 1974), pp. 227–44, has been compared. Merold Westphal's introduction to the appendix (pp. 221–27) is helpful. Recently the whole of Hinrichs's book, including Hegel's foreword, has been translated with a critical commentary by Eric von der Luft,* Hegel, Hinrichs, and Schleiermacher on Feeling and Reason in Religion *(Lewiston, N.Y.: Mellen Press, 1987), and this too has been studied.*

THE RECONCILIATION OF FAITH AND REASON

The opposition of faith and reason, which for centuries has occupied the attention not only of scholars but also of the world, may seem to have lost some of its importance in our day, indeed almost to have disappeared. If that were in fact the case, our age would perhaps have to be congratulated for this. For the nature of that opposition is such that the human spirit cannot turn aside from either of its two sides; each shows itself rather to be rooted in its inmost self-consciousness, so that if they are understood to be in conflict, the security of spirit is shaken and its condition becomes one of the unhappiest scission. Were the conflict of faith and reason to have disappeared, however, and passed over into a reconciliation, it would depend essentially on the nature of this reconciliation to what degree our age should be congratulated.

For there is also a peace born of indifference to the depths of spirit, a peace made up of frivolity and barrenness. In such a peace what offends may appear removed, while it is only set aside. What is only overlooked or looked down upon, however, is not for that reason overcome. On the contrary, were the deepest, genuine needs not to be satisfied in reconciliation, were the sanctuary of spirit not to obtain its right, the implicit scission would remain, and the enmity would fester all the more deeply within; unbeknown to, and having no cognizance of, its own self, the damage would be all the more dangerous.

An unsatisfactory peace may have come about if faith has become devoid of content and nothing has remained of it but the empty shell of subjective conviction—and [if] on the other side reason has renounced the cognition of truth, and spirit is left no issue other than one partially in appearances and partially in feelings. How should there then be the possibility of any great discord between faith and reason if neither of the two any longer comprises any objective content, and thus any object of dispute?

By faith I do not, of course, mean the merely subjective fact of being convinced, which relates only to the form of certainty and leaves it still undecided whether this being convinced has any content, and, if so, what; nor do I mean merely the creed, the church's confession of faith, which is compiled in words and writing and can be adopted orally, in representation and memory, without having penetrated the inner core, without having been identified with the certainty human beings have of themselves, with human self-consciousness. In accord with the genuine, ancient sense of the word, I reckon faith as consisting in the one moment no less than the other, and I locate it in the fact of their being combined in undifferentiated unity. The community (church) is in a happy state if the opposition within it is confined purely to the formal difference I have referred to, and if it is not the case either that the human spirit establishes out of itself a content of its own in opposition to the content of the church or that the truth established by the church has become an external content, such as leaves the Holy Spirit indifferent toward it. The church's own inner activity will consist primarily in the education of the human being, in the matter of internalizing the truth, which initially can be given only to representation and memory so that the mind may be carried away with it and permeated by it, and self-consciousness may find itself and its essential security only in that truth. The fact that these two sides are not united with each other either in immediate fashion or permanently and securely in all determinations, but rather that the immediate certainty of oneself is divorced from the authentic content, pertains to the way in which such permanent education becomes apparent. The certainty of oneself is, to begin with, natural feeling and natural will, together with the opinions and idle notions that correspond to them. But the genuine content at first impinges on spirit externally, in words and letters. Religious education unites the two so that the feelings that human beings have only immediately in natural fashion lose their force, and so that what was mere letters becomes its own living spirit.

For this transformation and unification of what is at first external material is immediately confronted with an enemy with which it has to deal; it has an immediate opponent in what it must presuppose, natural spirit, precisely because it is free spirit, not a natural life, that is to be engendered, and because free spirit exists only as a reborn spirit. This natural enemy, however, is spontaneously overcome by the divine idea, and free spirit is released. So the struggle with natural spirit is only a matter of appearance in the finite individual. The individual, however, gives rise to yet another enemy—an enemy that does not originate in the mere naturalness of human being but rather in its supersensuous essence, *in thinking:* thinking is the primal state of inner being itself, the mark of human beings' divine origin, that by which they are distinguished from animals, and what alone is the root of their nobility no less than of their degradation. For animals are capable neither of nobility nor of degradation. If thinking makes itself independent to the point where it becomes dangerous to faith, a higher, more stubborn struggle is engaged than the former struggle, involving only the natural will and the simple consciousness that does not yet stand up for itself. This thinking is then what has been called human thinking, one's own understanding, finite reason, and it is rightly distinguished from the thinking that, although it is within human being, is nonetheless divine, from the understanding that seeks not its own but the universal, from the reason that knows only the infinite and eternal to be what alone has being, and contemplates it as such.

It is, however, unnecessary for this finite thinking to be immediately opposed to the teaching of faith. Its endeavor will be initially directed rather within this teaching and presumably in favor of religion, to adorn, support, and honor it with its discoveries, curiosities, and ingenuities. In such an endeavor it comes about that the understanding adjoins to the teachings of faith a multitude of determinations as inferences or preconditions, grounds and aims—determinations that are finite in their import but can easily be attributed equal dignity, importance, and validity with the eternal truth itself because they appear in immediate conjunction with it. As at the same time their import is only finite, and they are thus equally open to counter-arguments and objections, in order to be maintained they are apt to need external authority and become a field for human passions. Produced in the interest of finitude, they are not supported by the testimony of the Holy Spirit, but by finite interests.

Absolute truth itself, however, when it appears, enters into a temporal configuration together with its external conditions, conjunctions, and circumstances. This automatically surrounds it with a multiplicity of local, historical, and other positive material. Because the truth *is,* it must appear and be apparent; its manifestation belongs to its eternal nature itself, which is inseparable from it, so much so that such separation would destroy it, namely, reduce its content to an empty abstraction. But what pertains to the momentary, local, external ancillary essence [*Beiwesen*] must be clearly distinguished from the eternal appearance that inheres in the essence of truth, in order not to confuse the finite with the infinite or what is indifferent with what is substantial. In regard to this aspect the understanding finds new scope for its efforts and the finite material begins to proliferate for it; and in the way in which this ancillary essence coheres together it finds immediate inducement for assigning to its singular features the dignity of the truly divine, elevating the frame to the dignity of the work of art it surrounds—in order to demand for the finite histories, events, circumstances, representations, commandments, and so forth the same reverence, the same *faith,* as for what is absolute being or eternal history.

It is in these aspects then that the *formal meaning of faith* begins to come to the fore, namely that faith is in general a *taking-as-true* [*Fürwahrhalten*]. (The inner nature of what is to be counted as true may be whatever it likes.) This is the same taking-as-true that is appropriate and valid in the everyday things of ordinary life, its conditions, relationships, and events or other natural modes of existence, properties, and qualities. If the criteria on which faith is based in such cases are sensuous external perception or direct inner feeling, the testimony of others and trust in them, etc., it should be possible in this regard to distinguish a conviction—a taking-as-true mediated by *reasons*—from faith as such. But this distinction is too insubstantial to maintain a preference for such conviction as opposed to mere faith. For the so-called reasons are nothing other than the designated sources of what is here called faith.

Of another kind, however, in regard to this general taking-as-true is a distinction relating to the material and in particular the use made of it. Since those finite and external histories and circumstances that lie within the orbit of religious faith are connected to the eternal history that constitutes the objective foundation of religion, piety creates from this material its manifold constructions, inspirations, and teachings in regard to worldly relationships, individual destinies and situations, and for the most part or entirely finds its representations and the whole range of its education attached to the sphere of histories and doctrines that surrounds the eternal truth. It is from such a sphere, as from a book that has become a popular favorite, that people have derived their consciousness about all further circumstances of their mental life and life in general, and also find the medium through which they raise their actuality to the religious viewpoint. At all events such a sphere merits, to say the least, the greatest respect and reverent treatment.

Now it is one thing if such a sphere is used in all innocence by pious sentiment alone and employed for such sentiment, and quite another if it [is] grasped and secured by the understanding and is presented to the understanding of another in such a way that it purportedly is valid for the latter as a rule and a firm basis for taking-as-true. Thus the second understanding is supposed to subject itself only to the first, even if this subjection is called for in the name of divine truth.

Such a call in fact accomplishes its own opposite. Since it is not the divine spirit of faith but the understanding that demands the subjection of the understanding to itself, it is the understanding that is entitled thereby to have the principal word in divine matters. By contrast to the dead letter and the arid learning of orthodoxy, the better sense has a divine right. Thus it happens that the more this finite wisdom expands in regard to divine matters, and the more it lays weight on the external historical element and on the inventiveness of its own sagacity, so much the more has it worked against the divine truth and against its own self. It has brought forth and acknowledged the opposite principle to the divine truth, and disclosed and prepared a wholly different foundation for cognition; and on this foundation the infinite energy that the principle of cognition possesses within itself, wherein lies at the same time the deeper possibility of its future reconciliation with true faith, will turn against being confined to that finite realm of the understanding and destroy its claims to aspire to be the kingdom of heaven.

Indignant at the contradictory nature of this pretention to let finitudes and externalities be recognized as the divine, and equipped with the weapon of finite thought, it is the better sense that on the one hand as *enlightenment* has established and maintained the *freedom of spirit,* the principle of a spiritual religion, but on the other hand as solely abstract thinking has *been ignorant how to make any distinction* between determinations of a merely finite interest and determinations of *the truth* itself. This abstract understanding has thus turned against *all* determinacy; it has completely emptied the truth of all content, and kept nothing over for itself except on the one hand the purely negative itself, the *caput mortuum* of a merely abstract *essence,* and on the other hand finite material. This finite material is in part what the understanding has obtained for itself from the divine content, reducing such material itself to the externality of merely common historical events, to local opinions and particular points of view. However, thinking cannot, in principle, be inactive. Nothing can be obtained [*holen*] or recovered [*erholen*] from or in that God, for such a God has already been made inwardly completely hollow [*hohl*]. God is the unknowable, for cognition is concerned with content, determination, movement, whereas what is empty is devoid of content, indeterminate, without life and action in itself. The teaching of truth consists solely in being a teaching about God and in making manifest God's nature and occupation. In dissolving all this content, however, the understanding has again put God under wraps and reduced God to what God was previously, in the time of mere longing, namely the unknown. Thinking activity is therefore left with no material other than the finite material previously mentioned, but *with the consciousness and the determination* that it is nothing but temporal and finite material. All it can do is to expatiate on such material and find satisfaction in vanity, to shape and turn what is vain in a multitude of ways, and to bring a great mass of it before itself in learned fashion.

To spirit, however, which cannot abide this vanity, is left only yearning; for that wherein it wanted to satisfy itself is something *other-worldly.* It is shapeless, devoid of content or determination. Only shape, content, and determination make something exist for spirit, only they make it reason, actuality, life, make it in and for itself. But that finite material is only something subjective, and incapable of furnishing import for the empty eternal. The need inherent in spirit as it again seeks after religion is therefore more specifically characterized by the fact that it demands an import that exists in and for itself, a truth that does not pertain to the opinions and conceits of the understanding, but is *objective.* All that this need still requires in order to attain satisfaction is *to be driven back into feelings.* Feeling is still the only way in which religion can be present; in the higher shapes of its existence, in the form where it *represents* a content and *holds it as true,* reflection always participates, and reflection has driven itself to the point of negating all objective determination.

Such are in brief the main features of the process taken by formal reflection in religion. The system of hair-splitting, metaphysical, casuistical distinctions and definitions into which the understanding split up the solid content of religion, and to which it ascribed the same authority as is possessed by the eternal truth, is the first evil, and one that originates in religion itself. But the other evil, however much it initially appears to be the opposite, is already grounded in this first standpoint and no more than a further development of it. It is the evil consisting in the fact that thinking comes on the stage as independent and uses the formal weapons to which that massive, arid lack of content owes its origin, and which thinking itself owes to that first concern, in order to turn against itself, attaining its final principle, pure abstraction itself, distinctionless supreme being. It is of interest for philosophical consideration to note specifically this unexpected shift of reflection itself into something hostile to its own work—a shift that is at the same time a determination inherent in reflection itself.

The evil into which the Enlightenment has brought *religion* and *theology* can accordingly be defined as the lack of *a known truth, an objective content, a doctrine of faith* [*Glaubenslehre*[1]]. Properly speaking, however, of religion only can it be said that it suffers from such a lack, for there is no longer any theology if there is no such content. Theology is reduced to a matter of historical erudition, coupled with the arid exposition of some subjective feelings. Yet the declared result is what has happened from the religious side with respect to the reconciliation of faith and reason. It must still be mentioned that *philosophy* too, for its part, has offered to assist in such a settlement, and in like manner.

For the privation into which philosophy has sunk shows itself no less as a lack of *objective content*. Philosophy is the science of thinking reason, while religious faith is the consciousness of and the absolute taking-as-true of the reason provided for representational thinking; and the material for philosophical science has become as impoverished as for faith.

The philosophy by which the standpoint of the universal cultivation of thought has been primarily established in recent times, and which has rightly called itself *critical* philosophy, has done nothing other than to have reduced the concern of the Enlightenment, which was initially directed to concrete representations and objects, to its [own] simple formula. This philosophy has no content and result other than what has issued from the rationalizing understanding we have been considering. *Critical* or *Kantian* philosophy is, to be sure, no less than the *Enlightenment* something that its *name* brands as obsolete. And it would be a mistake nowadays still to blame those authors (including scientific authors on theological, religious, and moral subjects) who call themselves philosophers—and also those who write on political affairs, laws, and constitutional matters—for the view that what might appear to pertain to philosophy in their writings is Kantian philosophy. It would be equally mistaken to seek to attribute the *Enlightenment* too to the rationalizing theologians, and still more to those who locate religion in subjective feelings. Who has not refuted or improved Kantian philosophy, and yet still today proceeds as a knight to defend it? Who has not progressed further? But if one examines the achievements of these authors—philosophers, moralists, and theologians (the last of which commonly protest against nothing so strongly as against the desire to produce something philosophical)—one straightaway recognizes only the same principles and results, which however already appear here as *presuppositions* and *recognized truths*. "You will know them by their fruits" [Matt. 7:16]. The fact of standing wholly and exclusively on the highway of contemporary representations and prejudices does not prevent one from arrogantly claiming that one's trivialities, dredged up from the general stream, are wholly original insights and new discoveries in the field of science and spirit.

What is in and for itself, and what is finite and temporal—these are the two basic categories that must occur in a doctrine of truth. And the import of such a doctrine depends on how these two aspects are grasped and established, and what attitude toward them is assigned to spirit. With this in mind, let us consider the truths of the philosophy of our time—truths that are so much taken as recognized that no further words need be wasted over them.

One of the absolute presuppositions in the culture of our time is that human beings *have no knowledge of truth*. The Enlightenment understanding has not so much achieved consciousness and articulation of this result as it has given rise to it. As already mentioned, its starting point has been to free thinking from the fetters of that other understanding—which planted its finitudes in the soil of the divine doctrine itself and wished to enlist absolute divine authority in the service of this its rampant growth of weeds—and to establish the freedom won by the religion of truth and made its abode. Thus it has in the first place had the will to attack error and superstition, and what it has genuinely succeeded in destroying is not, to be sure, religion but that pharisaical understanding which has been clever about things of another world in the manner of this world and has deemed it possible to call its clevernesses doctrine of religion. It has wished to avoid error only in order to make room for *truth*; it has sought and recognized eternal truths, and furthermore located the dignity of human beings in the fact that *for them,* and for them alone, not for animals, *such truths exist.* From this viewpoint these truths are seen as what is firm and objective as opposed to subjective opinion and the impulses of feeling, and opinion and feelings are seen as essentially subordinate to the insight of reason and guided by it if they are to have any justification.

The *consistent* and *autonomous* development of the principle of the understanding leads, however, to grasping determination and consequently all content solely as a finitude, and so destroying the configuration and character of the divine. Objective truth, which was supposedly the goal, has been brought down more unconsciously to the decimated, desiccated condition that Kantian philosophy had brought only to consciousness and needed to proclaim as characterizing the goal of reason. Accordingly *the identity of the understanding* is declared by this philosophy[2] as the highest principle, as the ultimate result not only for cognition itself but for its object—the *void* of atomistic philosophy, God devoid of all determination, having no predicates or properties, elevated to *what is beyond* knowing, or rather lowered to the lack of any content. This philosophy has given to this understanding a correct awareness of itself, that it is incapable of cognizing truth; but inasmuch as it conceived spirit as this understanding and nothing more, all it came up with was the general proposition that human beings can have no knowledge of God or for that matter of whatever *is in itself*—as if there could ever be absolute objects, and a truth, outside God. If religion locates the honor and the salvation of human beings in the cognition of God, and its own benefit in having communicated this cognition to them and having disclosed the unknown being of God, this philosophy, in monstrous contrast to religion, degrades spirit to the modest state of cattle as far as its highest vocation is concerned, except that spirit unhappily possesses the advantage of still being conscious of its ignorance, whereas cattle in fact possess the much purer, genuine, in other words quite unsophisticated modesty of ignorance. This result may doubtless now be regarded as having, with few exceptions, become a universal prejudice of our culture. It is of no help to have refuted Kantian philosophy or destroyed it; the progress and presumptions of progress beyond it may have busied themselves with much else in their own way, but they are only the same worldly wisdom as that of Kantian philosophy, for they deny to spirit the capacity and the vocation for objective truth.

The *other* principle of this wisdom directly associated with it is that inasmuch as spirit, though admittedly knowing, is denied the truth, it can deal only with phenomena, with finitudes. The church and piety have frequently taken the worldly sciences to be suspicious and dangerous, indeed not uncommonly hostile to them, and viewed them as leading to atheism. A famous astronomer is supposed to have said that he had searched the whole heavens and been unable to find any God there.[3] Worldly science is in fact directed to cognition of the *finite;* since its endeavor is to climb into what lies within the finite, causes and grounds are the last thing with which it is concerned. But these causes and grounds are essentially analogous to what is to be explained, so it is at the same time only finite forces that fall into its domain. It may be the case that these sciences do not carry their cognitions over into the realm of the eternal, which is not only something supersensible, for those causes and forces too, the inner element created by the reflective understanding and cognized in its fashion, are not something sensible; they are not concerned with such a mediation. Even so, the science of the finite is in no way prevented from conceding a divine sphere. Over against such a higher sphere it is of course quite natural to acknowledge that what only enters consciousness through the senses and the reflective understanding is a content that is nothing in and for itself, but only an appearance. But if such a thing as cognition of the truth is renounced, then cognition has only *one foundation,* that of appearance. From this standpoint, even the endeavors of cognition with a teaching that in other respects it recognizes as divine cannot be concerned with *the teaching itself* but only with its external environment. The teaching for its part remains beyond the field of interest of spiritual activity; and no insight, faith, or conviction regarding it can be sought, for its content is assumed to be unattainable. The concern of intelligence with the teachings of religion must therefore be limited to their phenomenal aspects and seize on external circumstances. Its interest must become *a historical [historisch] interest,* one where spirit is concerned with past events, something remote from itself, and *in which it itself is not present.* Whatever the earnest endeavor of erudition, industriousness, sagacity, etc., discloses is likewise called truth, and a sea of such truths is brought to light and propagated; but these are not truths such as are required by the earnest spirit of religion for its satisfaction.

Now if what is *this-worldly* and *present for spirit* is this broad realm of vanity and appearance, while what is in and for itself withdraws from spirit into an empty beyond, where can spirit still find a place in which it would encounter the substantial, where the eternal would come in contact with it, and where it could achieve union with it and the certain knowledge and enjoyment of such union? Only in the *region of feeling* can the impulse to truth take refuge. Only in the veiled guise of sensation[4] can consciousness still tolerate what is rich in import and does not vacillate in the face of reflection. This form lacks the objectivity and determinacy called for by knowledge and self-conscious faith, but which the understanding has known how to bring to nothing, and in the face of which (by very reason of this danger) the religious attitude [*Religiosität*] is merely dismayed and consequently withdraws into this veiled guise that seems to offer thought no opening for dialectical attack. In such a religious attitude, if it is based on genuine need, the soul will be able to find the peace it demands by endeavoring to complement, in intensity and inwardness, what it lacks in content and extent of faith.

It is still possible to adduce, however, as the *third general prejudice,* the supposition that feeling is the genuine and even the only form in which the religious attitude preserves its authenticity.

This religious attitude is, in the first place, no longer naive. Spirit requires as a matter of principle, because it is spirit, that what exists in feeling should also be present for it in representation, that there should be something sensed corresponding to sensation, and that the vitality of sensation should not remain a motionless concentration but should at the same time be a concern with objective truth. It should then, as occurs in a cultus, move on to actions that point to what spirits have in common in religion and (like the concern with truths) nourish religious sensation, keeping it in the truth while affording it the enjoyment of such truth. But to reach out in this way toward a cultus, as toward a set of doctrinal beliefs, is no longer compatible with the form of feeling. In the shape we are here considering, the religious attitude has rather taken refuge from development and objectivity in feeling, and has in polemical fashion declared feeling to be the sole or the predominant form.

It is here then that the danger of this standpoint, and its conversion into the opposite of what the religious attitude seeks in it, originates. This is an aspect of the utmost importance, which can only be touched on briefly; in this connection I must refer only to the most general matters, without going further into the nature of feeling. There can be no doubt but that feeling is a soil that, indeterminate on its own account, at the same time includes what is most diverse and most in conflict. On its own account feeling is natural subjectivity, no less capable of being good than evil or pious than godless. Now if what was formerly called reason [*Vernunft*], but what in fact was finite understanding [*Verstand*] and its mode of rationalizing [*Räsonnement*], is made the deciding criterion in regard both to what I am to deem true and to what is to be my maxim for action, and if it is to be feeling that is to provide the basis for deciding what I am and what is valid for me, then even the semblance of objectivity contained at least in the principle of the understanding has disappeared. For according to this principle, what is to be valid for me must nonetheless rest on a universally valid ground, on something that exists in and for itself. In all religion, as in all ethical common life among human beings, in the family as in the state, the divine that exists in and for itself, the eternal, the rational, is valid in even more determinate fashion as an *objective law,* and this objective law is thus valid as the *prime element* through which alone feeling obtains a firm footing and its authentic direction. Natural feelings are supposed rather to be determined, corrected, and purified through the teachings and practice of religion and through the firm principles of ethical life, and from these foundations only to be brought into *feeling,* which is thereby *made* something correct, *religious, moral.*

"*Natural humanity* does not perceive [the things that pertain to] the spirit of God and cannot recognize them, for they must be spiritually judged."[5]

But natural humanity is human being in its natural feelings, and it is just this human being that according to the doctrine of subjectivity is supposed to know nothing, yet be the only one, [precisely] as natural humanity, to perceive the spirit of God. Admittedly the feelings of natural humanity *also* include a feeling of the divine, but the natural feeling of the divine is one thing, the spirit of God something different. And what other feelings are not also found in human hearts? Even the fact that natural feeling is a feeling of the divine does not inhere in feeling as natural feeling. The divine is only in and for spirit, and spirit consists, as has been said above, in not being a natural life but being reborn. If feeling is supposed to be the basic determination of the human essence, then human beings are equated with animals, for it is the property of animals to find their vocation in feeling and to live in accord with feeling. If religion in human beings is grounded solely on a feeling, such feeling has rightly no other characteristic than to be the *feeling of their dependence;*[6] and a dog would then be the best Christian, for the dog carries this feeling most strongly within itself, and its life is spent primarily in it. The dog also has feelings of redemption if its hunger is satisfied by a bone. But spirit finds liberation, and the feeling of its divine freedom, rather in religion. Only free spirit has, and can have, religion. What is constrained in religion is the natural feeling of the heart, particular subjectivity; what becomes free in it, and in this very way comes into being, is spirit. In the worst religions—those in which servitude, and so superstition, is strongest—elevation to God provides human beings with the locus in which to feel, intuit, and enjoy their freedom, infinitude, universality, namely the higher things that do not stem from feeling as such but from spirit.

If we speak of religious, ethical, and other feelings, we shall of course have to say that these are genuine feelings. And since it is on this basis that we have arrived at this standpoint, if mistrust or rather contempt and hatred for thinking (the misology of which Plato spoke long ago[7]) have attained this point, it becomes almost the obvious course to find in feelings on their own account the locus for what is authentic and divine. It admittedly would not be necessary, especially in regard to the Christian religion, to see as the origin of religion and truth no more than a choice between understanding and feeling. And what the Christian religion adduces as its source, the higher divine revelation, must already have been put aside for one to be limited to that choice, and then, after rejecting the understanding and thought in general, to seek to base a Christian teaching on feelings.

Since, however, feeling in general is supposed to be the seat and source of what is authentic, the essential nature of feeling is overlooked, that it is of itself a *mere form,* of itself indeterminate, and can comprise any content. There is nothing that cannot be felt and is not felt. God, truth, and duty are felt, as are evil, falsehood, and wrong. All human states and relationships are felt; all representations of one's own relationship to spiritual and natural things become feelings. Who would endeavor to name and enumerate all feelings, from religious feeling, the feeling of duty, sympathizing, etc., down to envy, hatred, pride, vanity, joy, sorrow, sadness, and so forth? The very diversity, still more the opposing and contradictory nature of feelings, leads ordinary thinking to the correct conclusion that feeling is only something formal and cannot be a principle for a genuine determination. Moreover it is no less correct to conclude that if *feeling* is made the principle all that is needed is to leave it to the *subject* to decide *which* feelings it wants to have. It is the absolute indeterminacy feeling gives itself as standard and justification—i.e., arbitrary free will, the choice to be and do as it pleases and to make itself the oracle of what is deemed of value, what kinds of religion, duty, and right are deemed of high value.

Religion, like duty and right, will become and also ought to become an affair of feeling and enter into the heart, the same way that freedom in general descends into feeling and a feeling of freedom comes about in human being. But it is a completely different matter whether a content such as God, truth, or freedom is created out of feeling, whether these objects are to have feeling as their justification, or whether conversely such objective content is deemed valid in and for itself and first enters heart and feeling: it is only from this content that feelings derive not only their content but also their determination, their orientation and justification. On *this difference of attitude* everything depends. On it rests the divorce between on the one hand old-fashioned honesty and faith, genuine religious sentiment and ethical life, which makes God, truth, and duty *the prime element,* and on the other hand the perversity, the conceit, and the absolute selfishness that has arisen in our time and makes one's own will, opinion, and inclination the rule governing religious sentiment and right. Obedience, discipline, and faith in the old sense of the term are sentiments that cohere with and derive from the former attitude, while vanity, conceit, shallowness, and pride are the feelings that derive from the latter attitude, or rather it is these feelings of the solely natural human being from which this attitude originates.

What has been said above could have provided the material for a far-ranging exposition, such as I have already in part given elsewhere, covering several aspects of the material, while in part this is not the place for such an exposition.[8] Let the foregoing remarks be no more than reminders of the viewpoints that have been highlighted in order to denote more precisely what constitutes the evil *of our day* and consequently *its need.* This *evil,* namely the *contingent* and *capricious* nature of *subjective* feeling and its opinions, combined with the *culture of reflection,* which claims that spirit is *incapable of knowing truth,* has from ancient times been called *sophistry.*

This is what merits the nickname of *worldly wisdom,* which has recently been given fresh publicity by Herr Friedrich von Schlegel;[9] for it is a wisdom in and of what is usually called the *world,* of what is contingent, untrue, and temporal. It is the vanity that makes what is vain, the contingency of feeling and the whimsical nature of opinion, the absolute principle of what is right and duty, faith and truth. To be sure, we often have to hear these sophistical presentations termed philosophy. Yet this doctrine itself is at odds with the practice of applying the name of philosophy to it, for it can frequently be heard claiming *that it has nothing to do with philosophy.* It is right in wishing to know nothing of philosophy; in this way it expresses an awareness of what in fact it wants and is. Philosophy has ever been engaged in combating sophistry; all that sophistry can take from philosophy is the formal weapon, the culture of reflection, but it has nothing in common with it in regard to content, for its very being is to shun everything objective in respect of truth. Nor can it use to gain as a content the other source of truth—insofar as truth is an affair of religion—namely the holy scriptures of revelation; for this doctrine recognizes no other ground than the vanity of its own asserting and revealing.

As regards the *need* of our time, however, it emerges that the *common* need of *religion* and *philosophy is directed* to a *substantial, objective content of truth.* To the extent that religion for its part and in its manner regained respect, reverence, and authority vis-à-vis the arbitrary forming of opinion, and made itself a nexus of objective faith, doctrine, and also worship, this far-reaching self-examination would at the same time have to take the contemporary empirical condition in its multifarious tendencies into consideration, and thus it would be not only out of place here but also in general not merely philosophical in nature. In regard to one part of the business of satisfying this need, however, the two spheres of religion and philosophy come together. For this can at least be mentioned, that the development of the spirit of the times has resulted in *thinking* (and the way of viewing things connected with thinking) becoming for consciousness an *indispensable criterion* of *what consciousness* is to accept and recognize as *true.* It is here a matter of indifference to establish to what extent it would be only one part of the religious community that would be unable to continue living, i.e., existing spiritually, without the freedom of thinking spirit, or to what extent it is rather the whole of those communities in which this higher principle has reared itself for which the form of thinking, developed to whatever level, is henceforward an indispensable demand of their faith. Development and return to principles may occur at a multitude of levels; for in order to express itself in popular fashion, thinking may be placed in the position of reducing particular cases, propositions, etc., to one *immanent, universal proposition,* which is relatively speaking the *basic proposi-*

tion for the material that is made dependent on it in consciousness. What is thus at one level of the development of thought a basic principle, something irreducibly firm, at another level needs once more to be further reduced to yet more general, deeper basic propositions. But the basic propositions are a content held fast by consciousness in conviction, a content to which its spirit has witnessed, and which is now indistinguishable from thinking and one's own selfhood. If the basic propositions are surrendered to rationalizing, we have noted above the deviation by which they are replaced by subjective opinion and arbitrariness and culminate in sophistry.

But the mode and manner of conviction that occurs in religion can retain the shape of what is properly called *faith,* though it must be borne in mind that faith too must not be represented as something external to be offered mechanically; in order that it may be living and not a servitude, faith essentially needs the testimony of the indwelling spirit of truth and must have been implanted in one's own heart. If, however, religious need has been permeated with the element of the basic principles, then it is inseparable from the need and activity of thought, and in this respect religion requires a *science* of religion—a theology. Whatever in theology goes beyond (or only in theology deserves to go beyond) the general familiarity with religion that pertains to any member of each and every culture, that science has in common with philosophy. Thus it was that *scholastic theology* came into being in the Middle Ages—a science that developed religion in the direction of thinking and reason and endeavored to grasp the most profound doctrines of revealed religion in thinking fashion. As compared with the lofty aim of such a science, that mode of theology is very backward which locates the scientific distinction between it and the general teaching of religion merely in the historical element that, in all its breadth and length and its boundless individual details, it adds to religion. The absolute content of religion is essentially something present, and it is therefore not in the external addition of previously taught historical material but only in rational cognition that spirit can find the further material, present to it and free, that can satisfy its external need to think and so add infinite form to the infinite content of religion.

Scholastic theology fortunately did not yet have to fight the prejudice with which philosophizing on the topic of religion currently has to fight, namely that the divine cannot be *conceived,* or rather that the very concept and the kind of cognition that conceives demotes God and the divine attributes to the domain of finitude and by so doing annihilates them. The honor and worth of thinking cognition had not been abased to that extent; on the contrary, it had been left unimpaired, still unaffected. It was only modern philosophy itself that so misunderstood its own element, the concept, and brought it into such discredit. It did not recognize the infinitude of the concept and confused it with finite reflection, the understanding—so much so that only the understanding is supposed to be able to think, while reason is supposed not to be able to think but only to know immediately, i.e., only feel and intuit and so only *know in sensuous fashion.*

The ancient Greek writers represented divine justice in terms of the gods opposing and abasing whatever raises itself up, whatever is happy and excellent. Purer thought of the divine banished this image: Plato and Aristotle teach that *God* is *not jealous* and does not withhold from human beings knowledge of godself and of the truth.[10] What would it be but *jealousy* for God to deny to consciousness the knowledge of God? In so doing God would have denied to consciousness all truth, for God is alone what is true. Whatever else is true and may seem to have no divine content is only true to the extent that it is grounded in God and known from God; in other respects it is a temporal appearance. The cognition of God and of truth is the only thing that raises human beings above animals, that sets them apart and makes them happy, or rather, according to Plato and Aristotle as well as Christian doctrine, blessed.

It is the quite distinctive phenomenon of our time to have reverted at the pinnacle of its culture to the ancient notion that God is uncommunicative and does not reveal the divine nature to human spirit. Within the sphere of the Christian religion this assertion of the jealousy of God is all the more striking in that this religion is and seeks to be nothing other than the *revelation* of what God is, and the Christian community is supposed to be nothing other than the community into which the Spirit of God is sent and in which this spirit—for the very reason that it is spirit, not sensuousness and feeling, not a representing of what is sensuous, but thinking, knowing, cognizing, and because it is the divine Holy Spirit—is only the thinking, knowing, and cognizing of God, and leads its members into cognition of God. Without this cognition what would the Christian community still be? What is a theology without cognition of God? Just what a philosophy is without cognition of God, a noisy gong and a clanging cymbal! [1 Cor. 13:1.]

Inasmuch as my friend, who for the first time presents himself to the public with the following work, wished me to preface it with a foreword, I had, in so doing, to concentrate in the first place on the attitude that an endeavor such as a speculative contemplation of religion adopts in regard to what initially confronts it on the surface of the time. In this foreword I thought it necessary to remind the author himself what kind of reception and favor he had to look for from a state of affairs in which what calls itself philosophy (and may well constantly refer to Plato himself) no longer has any inkling of the nature of speculative thinking, of contemplation of the idea—where in both philosophy and theology there swaggers the *beastlike ignorance of God* and the *sophistry of this ignorance* that substitutes individual feeling and subjective opinion for the doctrine of faith as the principles governing rights and duties. It is a situation in which the writings of Christian theologians such as *Daub* and *Marheineke*[11] experience the vilest calumny at the hands of insipidity and ill-will. These are writings that still maintain the teaching of Christianity as well as the right and honor pertaining to thought, and in which the principles of reason and ethical life are defended and grounded through the concept against those doctrines that destroy the ethical cohesion of human beings and the state as well as religion. . . .[12]

6

LECTURES ON THE PHILOSOPHY
OF RELIGION (1824)

Hegel lectured for the second time on philosophy of religion in the summer semester of 1824, making partial use of a copy of his lecture manuscript from 1821, heavily revised and amended with additional notations. An excellent transcription was made by K. G. von Griesheim and serves as the basis of our text. The lectures in 1824 differed in many respects quite radically from those in 1821 and represented for Hegel a breakthrough to the fully speculative conception and treatment of religion. The breakthrough was provoked largely by Hegel's response to the challenge of Schleiermacher's theology of feeling and subjectivity as articulated in Der christliche Glaube, *the first volume of which appeared while Hegel was lecturing in 1821, and the second volume in 1822. Hegel was also able to draw on insights attained in writing the Foreword to Hinrichs's philosophy of religion of 1822 (the preceding selection). Although a fully systematic treatment of all the topics was not attained by Hegel until the lectures of 1827 and 1831, those of 1824 were the richest in content and have a vital, fluid, experimental quality. We provide the full main text of the Introduction and Part III (The Consummate Religion), and brief selections from Parts I (The Concept of Religion) and II (Determinate Religion). A one-volume paperback edition of the lectures of 1827 is available from the University of California Press (1988); thus for the present volume it seemed appropriate to provide excerpts from the lectures of 1824. (The lectures of 1831 cannot be reconstructed from presently available sources, and the lecture manuscript of 1821 is not suitable for the purposes of this volume.)*

Source: Lectures on the Philosophy of Religion, *edited by Peter C. Hodgson, translated by R. F. Brown, P. C. Hodgson, and J. M. Stewart, 3 vols. (Berkeley and Los Angeles: University of California Press, 1984–87), 1:113–47, 310–28; 2:233–38; 3:163–247. In the selections for this edition the textual apparatus is omitted and editorial notes are abbreviated. References to God are rendered gender-inclusive and a few other minor revisions are made to the translation.*

INTRODUCTION: ON THE PHILOSOPHY OF RELIGION
Preface

I have deemed it necessary to devote a separate section of philosophy to the consideration of religion. Let us first consider how the philosophy of religion is connected with philosophy in general; this is tied up with the question of our present-day interest in religion and philosophy; and this in turn is linked to the relationship of the philosophy of religion, and of philosophy, to positive religion.

To begin with, we must recall in general the object that we are dealing with in the philosophy of religion. Our object is the object of religion itself; it is the supreme or absolute object. The philosophy of religion has as its goal, as its content, the region in which all the riddles of the world, all the contradictions uncovered by profound thought, are resolved, and in which every pain of feeling is dissolved and healed, the region of eternal rest, of truth. Human beings are truly human through consciousness—by virtue of the fact that they think and by virtue of the fact that they are spirit. This gives rise to manifold images and configurations, i.e., the sciences, the arts, political interests, the relationships that are connected with human freedom and will. From here flows all that brings them respect, satisfaction, honor, and happiness, all these interests have their center, find their end and their beginning, their truth, in one thought, in the thought of God. God is known in religion; God is the sustaining center, which breathes life into all these configurations in their existence. If we consider this object [God] in relation to others, then we can say that it *is* strictly for its own sake; it has no such relation [to others] and is strictly in and for itself *the unconditioned,* the free, the unbounded, that which is its own purpose and ultimate goal.

Religion appears as what is occupied with this object. Occupation with this ultimate, final end is thus unreservedly free and is therefore its own end since all other aims go back to this final end; though previously valid for themselves, they disappear in the face of it, no other aim holds out against it, and all are resolved in it. Occupation with this object is fulfilling and satisfying by itself, and desires nothing else but this. Hence it is the absolutely free occupation, the absolutely free consciousness. This occupation is the consciousness of absolute truth; as a mode of sensibility it is the absolute enjoyment we call blessedness, while as activity it does nothing but manifest the glory of God and reveal the divine majesty. For the peoples have generally regarded this occupation, their religious consciousness, as their true merit, as the sabbath of life in which finite aims, limited interests, toil, sorrow, unpleasantness, earthly and finite cares—in which all the unpleasantness and misery of the everyday world—waft away in devotion's present feeling or in devotion's hope. All of it wafts away into a kind of past. Psyche drinks from this river of forgetfulness,[1] and in its doing so earthly cares and worries waft away, and the whole realm of temporality passes away into eternal harmony.

This image of the absolute that religious devotion has before it can have a greater or lesser degree of present liveliness, certainty, and enjoyment, or can be presented as something longed or hoped for, something far off, otherworldly. But it is never isolated, for it radiates into the temporal present. Faith is cognizant of it as the truth, as the substance of present existences; and this content of devotion is what animates the present world, what operates effectively in the life of the individual, ruling over one's commissions and omissions, over one's volition and action. This is the representation that religion has of God generally, and the philosophy of religion makes this content the content of a particular treatment.

1. The Relation of the Philosophy of Religion to the Whole of Philosophy

Since I have deemed it necessary to give it this separate treatment, I must remark that it had previously escaped my notice that *theologia naturalis* was an object of the Wolffian philosophy,[2] which introduces the nature of God into the content of philosophy. However, Wolff's treatment stays within the bounds of the metaphysics of the understanding [*Verstand*] then current, and is to be viewed rather as a science of the understanding than as one of rational thinking. This manner of approach does not seem to alter the fact that this science could not have the same goal as ours. But it called itself essentially "theology," and its content and object was God as such. Our object, however, is not just God as such; the content of our science is religion. In regard to that concrete science we can say that, because it was only a science of the understanding, its concept of God was restricted to the sterile result of an abstract being [*Wesen*] of the understanding.[3] To the extent that God is grasped as a being of the understanding, God is not grasped as spirit; to the extent that God is grasped as spirit, however, this concept includes the subjective side within it, the side that is introduced into this concept when it is defined as religion.

Our concern here is therefore not with God as such or as object, but with God *as God is [present] in God's community*. It will be evident that God can only be genuinely understood in the mode of God's being as *spirit,* by means of which God makes godself into the counterpart of a community and brings about the activity of a community in relation to God; thus it will be evident that the doctrine of God is to be grasped and taught only as the doctrine of *religion*. Regarding the relationship of the two sciences in general, a further point to be noted is that our science is not differentiated from philosophy. Philosophy in general has God as its object and indeed as its only proper object. Philosophy is no worldly wisdom, as it used to be called; it was called that in contrast with faith. It is not in fact a wisdom of the world but instead a cognitive knowledge of the nonworldly; it is not cognition of external existence, of empirical determinate being and life, or of the formal universe, but rather cognition of all that is eternal—of what God is and of what God's nature is as it manifests and develops itself.

To this extent, then, we have here the same object generally as in philosophy pure and simple; but there is also a difference.

In philosophy the supreme [being] is called the absolute or the idea, and it is superfluous to go back any further. In the Wolffian philosophy this supreme [being] is called *ens*[4] or thing, and it promptly announces itself as the sort of abstraction that does not in principle correspond to our representation of God. In more recent philosophy[5] the absolute is not merely an *ens* of this kind, for it is not so completely abstract; but what we call the *absolute* and the *idea* is still not for that reason synonymous with what we call *God*.

In order to make the difference plain we must first consider what "meaning" itself means. When we ask what this or that "means," we are asking two different questions, in fact two opposite questions. In the first place we call what we have in mind—the significance, purpose, or general thought of the expression or work of art in question—"the inner." This is what we are asking for. But the inner is *universal* representation or determinateness; it is *the thought* in general. When we ask in this way what God is, what the expression "God" means, we want the thought; it is the thought that is supposed to be delivered up to us—the representation we no doubt have. Consequently it signifies that the concept should be delivered up, and so what we call in philosophy the "absolute" or the idea is of course the meaning. What we want to know is the absolute, the idea, the conceptualized nature of God, the nature of God grasped in thought, or the logical essence of the same. This is one meaning of "meaning," and to this extent what we call the "absolute" is synonymous with the expression "God."

But there is another sense in which we ask, when the opposite is what is wanted, namely, when we start from pure categories of thought and not from representation. It may be that spirit is not at ease in the categorial definition chosen, that it is not at home there and asks what this pure category of thought can mean. For example, there is the category of the unity of subjective and objective, or of the unity of the real and the ideal; we may understand each of the terms on its own account, may know what "unity," "objective," "subjective," and the like are, and yet we can very well say that we do not understand the category in question. In a case of this kind, if we ask what it means, the "meaning" is the opposite of what it was before. What is wanted here is an intuition or a representation of the thought-category, an example or an accompaniment of the content that has so far only been given in thought. Our expression "example" contains the representation and intuition of this already. If we find a thought-content of this kind difficult, the difficulty lies in the fact that we have no representation of it. It becomes clear to us through the example, and [we] say that now we know what such a thought-content means. Spirit is thus for the first time present to itself in this content.

When we begin in this way from the representation of God and ask for the meaning, what is wanted on the one hand is the idea of God, the absolute, the being [*Wesen*] grasped in the concept; and this meaning is coincident with the logical idea. But God is this: not merely to be *in* godself, but to be just as essentially *for* godself. God is spirit, not finite spirit but absolute spirit. That God is spirit consists in this: that God is not only the being that maintains itself in thought but also the being that appears, the being that endows itself with revelation and objectivity.

Although we consider the idea of God in this way in the philosophy of religion, we at the same time also have before us the mode of God's representation. God represents only godself, and does so only to godself. This is the aspect of the existence of the absolute. Thus in the philosophy of religion we have the absolute as our object not merely in the form of thought but also in the form of its manifestation. Thus the universal idea is to be grasped in its utterly concrete meaning, which involves the characteristic of appearing, of revealing itself. This aspect of existence, however, is itself to be rethought in philosophy and grasped by thought.

But [pure] philosophy in its customary divisions [first] considers the logical idea, the idea as it [is] in thought, not just for our thoughts but in the way that the content is thought itself or the categories of thought themselves. Beyond that, philosophy points to the absolute in its process of production, in its activity—and this activity is the absolute's path in coming to be for itself, in becoming spirit. God is thus the result of philosophy, a result that is recognized not merely to be the result but to be eternally producing itself, the act of production and equally the beginning of the first [step]. These determinate configurations of the idea or of the absolute—nature, finite spirit, the world of consciousness—are embodiments of the idea; but they are determinate configurations or particular modes of appearance of the idea. They are configurations in which the idea has not yet penetrated through to itself in order to be as absolute spirit.

In the philosophy of religion we consider the idea not merely in the way it is determined as idea of pure thought, nor yet in its finite modes of appearance, but as the absolute, or as the logical idea—except that at the same time we also consider it in the way this idea appears and manifests itself, though in its *infinite appearance* as spirit. Spirit is what manifests itself, what appears but is infinite in its appearance; spirit that does not appear *is not;* it reflects itself back within itself. This then, in general, is the position of the philosophy of religion vis-à-vis the other branches of philosophy. God is the result of the other branches: in the philosophy of religion this end is made the beginning. *That God* (as result) *appears* is what we make into our particular object—God as the *utterly concrete idea* together with its infinite appearance, which is identical with the substance, with the essence [of reality]; this is the content, the specification of this content.

This is the content of the philosophy of religion, expressed abstractly. We treat this content with our thinking reason, and the definition of our treatment as thoughtful [*denkend*] brings us to the topic of how the philosophy of religion stands with reference to our contemporary needs, i.e., its relationship to the theology of our time, to the church, and to the representation of God.

Thus far we have considered philosophy of religion as the treatment of the concrete idea of the divine in rational form, as the conceptualizing cognition of God. Now we turn to its relationship to our contemporary needs, to the contemporary view of religion and God.

2. The Position of the Philosophy of Religion vis-à-vis the Needs of Our Time[6]

If we call the cognition or knowledge of God "theology" generally, whether we approach it from the standpoint of philosophy or from that of theology in the narrower sense, we seem at first to be treading the same path as the theology that used to be called rational theology. It is the universal highroad or the universal mode in which what is known of God is said of God. We know namely that in the Christian church and chiefly in our Protestant church there was set down a *doctrinal system* [*Lehrbegriff*], a content that was universally valid and universally accepted as the truth, as [stating] what God's nature is. This content has generally been called the creed: in the subjective sense, what is believed, and objectively, what is to be known as content in the Christian religion, what God godself has revealed that God is. This content can be called *dogmatics:* the doctrinal system of the church, the content [of its teaching] concerning what God's nature [is] in relationship to humanity and in the latter's relationship to God. (New definitions have been added to this old *symbolum,* which nonetheless are not our concern here.) In the Protestant church the doctrinal system is at the same time supposed to be based essentially upon the Bible; it does not exist merely in the spirit of the church but also has an external footing in the Bible.

Later on, so-called [pure] thinking turned against this content in the name of "Enlightenment." It left the doctrinal system in place and also left it the Bible as foundation, but arrived at its own divergent views and sought to interpret the word of God in a different way. This took place in the guise of exegesis. Because exegesis draws upon reason for counsel, what happened is that a so-called *rational theology*[7] came into being, opposed to the doctrinal system in the form established by the church. In part, this was the church's own doing, in part it was the doing of [the thinking] to which the church is opposed. In this rational theology it is exegesis that plays the primary role. Here exegesis takes over the written word, interprets it, and professes only to make the understanding of the word effective and to remain faithful to it.

But where interpretation is not mere explanation of the words but discussion of the content and elucidation of the sense, it must introduce its own thoughts into the word that forms the basis [of the faith]. There can only be mere interpretation of words when all that happens is that one word is replaced by another with the same scope. If interpretation is *elucidation,* then other categories of thought are bound up with it. A development of the word is a progression to further thoughts. One seemingly abides by the sense, but in fact, new thoughts are developed. Bible commentaries do not so much acquaint us with the content of scripture as with the mode of thought of their age.

In a commentary the sense of the word is supposed to be indicated. But indicating the sense means bringing the sense out into consciousness, into representation; and this other representation makes its influence felt in the exposition of what the sense is supposed to be. The most sharply opposed views are exegetically demonstrated by theologians on the basis of scripture, and in this way so-called holy scripture has been made into a wax nose.[8] All of the heresies have appealed to scripture, as has the church.

Since a so-called theology of reason arose and was produced in this manner, we can on the one hand say that we find ourselves on common ground [with it], that reason has to be a factor; and if the interpretation that emerges is supposed to be in accordance with reason, then we can here claim the right to develop religion freely and openly out of reason, without taking as our starting point the specific word [of scripture]. It is therefore at this point that we consider the nature of God and of religion in general.

This rational theology has on the whole been called the theology of the Enlightenment. Pertinent here, however, is not merely this kind of theology but also the kind that leaves reason aside and expressly rejects philosophy, and then erects a religious doctrine from the plenitude of its own argumentative power. Though biblical words lie at its basis, to be sure, *private opinion* and *feeling* still remain the controlling factor. It very often happens that philosophy is set aside in the process, that philosophy is represented as something ghostlike that must be ignored because it is uncanny. Philosophy, however, is nothing other than cognition through reason, the common feature in the cognition of all human beings; and to the extent that one rejects philosophy, one rejects with it the very principle of the common rationality of spirit, in order to leave the door open to "private reason."

In the rational theology of more recent times the principal role is played by this way of looking at things, bringing reason into the lists against itself and combating philosophy on the grounds that reason can have no cognition of God.[9] The consequence is that no meaning for the expression "God" remains in theology any more than in philosophy, save only the representation, definition, or abstraction of the supreme being—a vacuum of abstraction, a vacuum of "the beyond." Such is the overall result of rational theology, this generally negative tendency toward any content at all in regard to the nature of God. The "reason" of this kind of theology has in fact been nothing but abstract understanding masquerading under the name of reason, and it has ventured as far in this field as has the reason that claimed the possibility of cognition for itself. The result is that one only knows in general *that* God is; but otherwise this supreme being is inwardly empty and dead. It is not to be grasped as a living God, as concrete content; it is not to be grasped as spirit. If "spirit" is not an empty word, then God must [be grasped] under this characteristic, just as in the church theology of former times God was called "triune." This is the key by which the nature of spirit is explicated. God is thus grasped as what God is for godself within godself; God makes godself an object for godself (the Son); then, in this object, God remains the undivided essence within this differentiation of godself within godself, and in this differentiation of godself loves godself, i.e., remains identical with godself—this is God as spirit. Hence if we are to speak of God as spirit, we must grasp God with this very definition, which exists in the church in this childlike mode of representation as the relationship between father and son—a representation that is not yet a matter of the concept. Thus it is just this definition of God by the church as a Trinity[10] that is the concrete determination and nature of God as spirit; and spirit is an empty word if it is not grasped in this determination.

But when modern theology says that we cannot have cognition of God or that God has no further determinations within godself, it knows only that God *is* as something abstract without content, and in this way God is reduced to this hollow abstraction. It is all the same whether we say we cannot have cognition of God, or that God is only a supreme being.[11] Inasmuch as we know [only] *that* God is, God is the *abstractum*. To cognize God means to have a definitive, concrete concept of God. As merely having being, God is something abstract; when [God is] cognized, however, we have a representation with a content. If the representation to the effect that God is not to be cognized were substantiated through biblical exegesis, then precisely on that account we would have to turn to another source in order to arrive at a content in regard to God. Whether it is substantiated by the

Bible must be left to the theologians. Although we may seem to be sharing common ground with rational theology (because our definition of God is that of thinking reason), in what follows we shall nonetheless see that rational theology is precisely the staunchest opponent of philosophy. In this respect it is a need of the present day to be cognizant of God through thinking reason, and thereby to obtain a living, concrete representation of the nature of truth. The result of rational theology is expressed by saying that we cannot be cognizant of the truth. God is truth. But to the extent that human beings have faith in their own dignity, in the dignity of their spirit, and have the courage of truth and freedom, they are driven to seek truth. Truth is no empty shell [but] something concrete, a fullness of content. It is this fullness that modern theology has emptied out. Our intention, however, is to regain such a fullness by means of the concept.

It is to be noted that there is a type of theology that wants to adopt *only a historical attitude* toward religion; it even has an abundance of cognition, though only of a historical kind. This cognition is no concern of ours, for if the cognition of religion were merely historical, we would have to compare such theologians with countinghouse clerks, who keep the ledgers and accounts of other people's wealth, a wealth that passes through their hands without their retaining any of it, clerks who act only for others without acquiring assets of their own. They do of course receive a salary, but their merit lies only in keeping records of the assets of other people. In philosophy and religion, however, the essential thing is that one's own spirit itself should recognize a possession and content, deem itself worthy of cognition, and not keep itself humbly outside.

This is therefore the relationship [of the philosophy of religion to the theology of our time]. In view of this plague the more explicit need that arises is that of regaining, for the true, essentially through philosophy, a fullness, a concept, and an import.

3. The Relationship of the Philosophy of Religion to Positive Religion[12]

In the third place, finally, theology is not merely rational theology, which brings it only to the abstraction of the I, to this emptiness or lack. There is still a theology that has a content—a content consisting of the church's doctrine—which we call the content of a positive religion. The philosophy of religion seems at first to stand on the same side [with what] is called rational theology, but it is in fact opposed to it; and it seems to be even more opposed to the theology that holds to the church's positive doctrine. But just as in the first relationship the reverse is the case, so here, too, it will be shown that the philosophy of religion is infinitely closer to positive doctrine.

The antithesis of reason and faith, as it used to be called, is one that arose long ago in the Christian church;[13] the church often feared the destruction of its doctrine by philosophy and on that account was hostile to it. But rational theology is hostile to philosophy because a content might be able to gain entry through philosophy, and for that reason it declares every elucidation of the content to be an obfuscation.

Regarding the relationship of the philosophy of religion to the church's doctrine (insofar as this doctrine [*Lehre*] is not that emptiness [*Leerheit*] but has solid content), it is to be noted that there cannot be two kinds of reason and two kinds of spirit,[14] a divine and a human reason or a divine and a human spirit that would be strictly distinct from one another, as if their essence were strictly opposed. Human reason, human spiritual consciousness or consciousness of its own essence, *is* reason as such [*Vernunft überhaupt*], is the divine within humanity. Spirit, insofar as it is called divine spirit, is not a spirit beyond the stars of beyond the world; for God is present, is omnipresent, and strictly *as spirit* is God present in spirit. God is a living God who is effective, active, and present in spirit. Religion is a begetting of the divine spirit, not an invention of human beings but an effect of the divine at work, of the divine productive process within humanity. What has emerged as religion, and is a product of the divine spirit, shows itself first as faith. So we must have faith that what has emerged in the world is precisely reason, and that the generation of reason is a begetting of the spirit and a product of the divine spirit itself. The expression "God rules the world as reason" would be irrational if we did not concede that among the peoples nothing is higher than religion [and that it is] the divine spirit that has accomplished everything in them.

We should also mention as a historical note that in the Catholic church, particularly in former times, there was no such separation between philosophy and church doctrine, for Scholastic philosophy was the philosophy of the church. Speculative philosophy has, in fact, been more in evidence in the Catholic church than in the Protestant. This cleavage first occurred in the Protestant church.

4. Preliminary Questions[15]

We could now proceed to deal with the object, with the thing itself. But it seems necessary on external grounds to discuss certain preliminary questions first, questions that must seemingly be disposed of before we can advance to the science [of the philosophy of religion] proper. Such questions are bound to occur to us; they must do so if we are familiar with the culture of our time, i.e., with the philosophical culture and with the interests of theology. There are viewpoints, preliminary questions, and modes of representation, which seem to make it necessary that, before we proceed to the philosophy of religion, it must be recognized and shown that such a science exists. There are views that reject it, that deem it impossible. Hence we have to discuss such positions; we do not do so, however, in order to resolve these preliminary questions, but rather to show that we have to leave these views aside, and that what is essential in them comes within the purview of our science itself and is settled there.

Therefore, with reference to the content of these major views, in the *first* place what we have before us is not religion in general but what we call a positive religion, a religion that is acknowledged to have been revealed by God and to rest upon an authority higher than human authority, and which for that reason appears sublime, outside the domain of human reason. The initial difficulty in this view is that we would first have to argue for reason's entitlement and capacity to concern itself with such truth and such teaching of a religion as purportedly lies beyond the domain of human reason. We certainly agree that reason must enter into relation with what is called religion. In this respect we can proceed in the traditional way. It has been said, and is still said,[16] that positive religion exists on its own account, that we are to offer no opinion on its doctrines [but simply] are to respect and esteem them. On the other side stands reason or comprehending thought, and never shall these twain come into contact or reason make connection with those teachings of the revealed religion. This was how they wanted to preserve the freedom of philosophical investigation in former days. They said it is a subject matter by itself that should do no harm to positive religion, but they subordinated its results to the teaching of positive religion. We do not want to give our investigation this posture. In and for itself it must be viewed as only a pretense; i.e., it is false that both of these—both belief in, standing fast in, positive religion, and free philosophical investigation—can subsist peacefully alongside one another. There is no ground for supposing that faith in the content or in the doctrine of positive religion can still persist when reason has convinced itself of the contrary. The church has been both correct and consistent in not allowing this comparison to be made. Human spirit in its innermost aspect, [in its] conviction about the nature of God, is not, in this most inward conscience, the sort of divided thing in which the two sides of a contradiction could subsist—faith [on one side and] a reason on the other that had achieved results deviating from this teaching of positive religion. This, then, is the first preliminary question, in which the right of reason is to be demonstrated, its right to concern itself with the [positive] teachings of religion.

The *second* preliminary question relates to an impression, a proposition or a view, regarding what reason and cognition are, that can almost be regarded as the focal point of the plague of the present age. Those mentioned in the preceding sphere only contend that reason cannot cognitively apprehend the truth of God's nature; they do not deny the possibility of cognizing other truths, since for them only the highest truth is uncognizable. According to the second position, however, reason is entirely debarred from cognitively apprehending truth at all. Its contention is that if cognition relates itself to spirit in and for itself, to life, to the infinite, it only produces errors, and that reason must forgo all claims and all attempts to grasp any aspect of the infinite affirmatively; for through comprehension the infinite is annulled and downgraded to the finite.[17] This result in regard to reason, this denial of reason, is supposed to be a result of rational cognition itself. The first thing we have to do, according to this tendency, is to investigate the cognitive subject beforehand, in order to establish cognitively its capacity to have cognition of God and thereby to establish the possibility of a philosophy of religion.

Because knowledge of God does not fall within the comprehension of reason, there coheres with this standpoint the view that consciousness of God is rather sought only in the form of *feeling*—that religion has feeling as its source, and that the relationship of the human spirit to God is to be confined only to the sphere of feeling and is not to be transposed into thought or into comprehension. Surely if God and divine things are excluded from the realm of necessary and substantial subjectivity, if knowledge is excluded from this realm, then nothing remains but the realm of contingent subjectivity; that is the realm of feeling.[18] If in regard to God we could appeal only to feeling, then we would have to wonder how any kind of objectivity is still attributed to this content, i.e., to God. The materialistic views have been more consistent in this respect. They have regarded spirit and thought as something merely material, a combination of material forces; they have reduced spirit and thought to feeling and sensation, and accordingly taken God and all representations [of God] as products of feeling, and denied objectivity to God. The result is then atheism. God is thus a product of feeling, of my weakness—a product of pain, hope, fear, joy, cupidity, and so forth. What is rooted only in my feeling *is only for me;* what is in my feeling is what is mine, but it is not what is his [God's?], is not independent in and for itself. It seems necessary therefore to show beforehand that God is not simply rooted in feeling, is not merely *my* God. The former metaphysics, therefore, always used to begin by proving that there is a God, that God is not merely rooted in feeling, that God is not merely something subjective but is something objective.[19]

Connected to this is then the *fourth* preliminary question, inasmuch as one starts by demonstrating that there is a God—that there are not mere feelings of God but an objective God, that God *is,* that God is an *object.* Proving God turns out to be the summons to the philosophy of religion. One might suppose that our inquiry must also begin at this point.

It may appear as though the other sciences hold over philosophy the advantage that their object is already acknowledged in and for itself. In arithmetic, numbers are conceded in advance; in geometry, space; in medicine, illnesses. The object of philosophy is not, and should not be, of this kind. Since its object is not something already granted, philosophy, and more specifically philosophy of religion, must first demonstrate its object. From this it would follow that before philosophy exists it should prove that it exists, that it is. It would have to prove its existence prior to its existence.

These then are the preliminary questions that must be settled first, so it seems, and the very possibility of a philosophy of religion depends upon their being settled. But if these points of view are valid (i.e., that conceptual thought has no relationship to positive religion, or that religion is only a feeling), then philosophy of religion is directly impossible, since in order to show its possibility those hindrances must first be eliminated. So it seems at first glance, and a brief accounting needs to be given of why we are pushing these preliminary questions to one side. Why we do so must be briefly sketched in its main features, in order to remove this difficulty. The initial demand is that we should first investigate reason generally, the cognitive capacity or conceptual thought, before proceeding to cognition. This demand is involved in all of these views. We picture the project of cognition as though it were something that came about by means of an *instrument* with which one wants to grasp the truth. On closer consideration, the demand that we should first cognize this instrument is inappropriate, however plausible it may seem. The critique of the cognitive capacity is a stance taken by Kant's philosophy and by our time. It was believed that a great discovery had been made at this point, but, as so often happens in life, the belief was a mistake. Just when people think they have done the cleverest thing is when they have done the silliest.

Reason is to be investigated—but how? It must be investigated rationally, it must be cognized. This is possible only through rational thinking, through rational cognition; any other way it is impossible. This demand directly involves a requirement that annuls itself. If we ought not to begin philosophizing until we have cognized reason rationally, then we cannot begin at all, for in cognizing we *are* comprehending rationally; but we are supposed to relinquish this rational comprehension, since it is precisely reason that we are supposed to cognize. This is the same demand as that Gascon makes who does not want to go into the water until he is able to swim.[20] To learn to swim one must go into the water. Once cannot make cognition into one's object without thereby behaving cognitively at the same time.

Here in the philosophy of religion it is more precisely God, or reason in principle, that is the object. God is essentially rational, is rationality that is alive and, as spirit, is in and for itself. When we philosophize about religion, we are in fact investigating reason, intelligence, and cognition; only we do so without the supposition that we will get this over first, apart from our [real] object; instead the cognition of reason *is* exactly the object, is what it is all about. Spirit is just this: to be for itself, to be for spirit. This is what finite spirit is; and the relationship of finite spirit or of finite reason [to infinite spirit or reason] is engendered within religion itself and must be dealt with there. Also pertinent here is the distinction between a science and conjectures concerning a science. These conjectures are contingent; but insofar as they are thoughts containing viewpoints relating to the matter, they must fall within the treatment itself, though in their proper order and where they are necessary; then they are not [just] contingent bubbles of thought that arise within us. The other factor is that the viewpoints underlying these questions, insofar as they are involved in the matter, are brought up along with [the evolution of] the content itself. In this way those viewpoints even occur within religion itself, and we thus come to the relationship of reason to positive religion.

The [infinite] spirit that makes itself an object gives itself essentially the shape of a *representation,* of something given, of something appearing to the other [finite] spirit *for which* it is. Spirit appears for the other as something given, something coming to it in a higher mode; and therein lies the necessity that the relationship of spirit [to spirit] comes to be a positive religion. Spirit comes to be for itself in the shape of representation; the positive aspect of religion is brought forth in the shape of [spirit's being] the other *for* the other, *for which* spirit is. Similarly, the definition of religion— according to which it is *cognitive,* is the activity of reason or the activity of conceptualization and thought—lies within religion itself; this cognitive attitude toward God falls within religion itself, just as the standpoint of feeling does. Feeling, too, must show itself in religion. Feeling is the subjective aspect, what pertains to me as this single individual. When I feel I thereby appeal to myself, and thus relate myself back to my singular subjectivity; others can have other feelings and thereby appeal to themselves, too. With thinking, on the other hand, we are on common ground. Both this standpoint [of *thinking*] (inasmuch as God gives godself this ultimate singularization of thisness, [becoming] the object for a cognizing activity and the object for a thinking activity) and [*what is*] *thought* (inasmuch as God thus gives godself the relationship of God to the feeling subject) must be treated within religion.[21] Thus the determination that God *is,* the determination of what has being in and for itself, this determination of [God's] being, is a determination that falls essentially within the treatment of religion, within the treatment of the nature of its object.

5. Survey of the Stages of Our Discussion

The more precise division of our treatment is as follows. The first topic is the concept of religion itself in general; the second is the necessary or determinate religion, religion in its determinateness; the third is religion in its infinitude, the absolute religion as existing. The concept of religion is not yet religion in the way it exists, while determinate religion, just because it is determinate, does not yet correspond to the concept. Religion contains within itself the infinite absolute content. Determinate religion does not correspond to this content, for it is finite. The infinite religion is what first corresponds to the concept; it is the consummate religion, i.e., the Christian religion.

I. THE CONCEPT OF RELIGION[22]

We have to consider the moments [of the concept] in more detail. Taken in its speculative, absolute sense, the concept of religion is the concept of the spirit that is conscious of its essence or of itself. The mode and manner of consciousness, the way that spirit itself is for itself or is objective to itself, is, as a rule, *representation,* and thus absolute consciousness is *religion.* It is *philosophy* to the extent that spirit is conscious of itself not in the mode of representation but in that of *thought.* This is now the *speculative concept,* spirit conscious of itself.

Now, speaking more precisely, the following moments are contained in this concept. First, we consider the determinateness, the metaphysical content, the pure thought of it. Second, because it is a consciousness, pure thought does not stay pure but enters into the distinction of consciousness. In this consciousness we have two sides, the object and the subject for which this object is; this is the standpoint of finite spirit within religion. Spirit rules in religion. According to its concept, in and for itself, spirit is infinite, and spirit rules insofar as it differentiates itself inwardly; but as the inwardly self-differentiating spirit that gives itself consciousness, as spirit in relation to an other within its distinction, it is finite. And it is just from this standpoint of finite spirit that we are to consider the shape in which its essence is object to it. The *first* moment is therefore the *substantial* one, the *second* the standpoint of *consciousness,* while the *third* is the sublating of this finite standpoint of consciousness, the uniting of both sides, the *cultus.* The concept of religion [is] the substantial basis of religion, the substance that is one. The standpoint of consciousness is the subordinate moment of difference. Then there is the return to the first, substantial standpoint. [First] the concept is for us, [though] in actuality it is what is *inward;* at the second stage it *appears* as object, as something *external;* only at the third stage is it *one,* does it become *cultus.* These three moments belong to the idea of religion in general, to religion insofar as it is idea. The first is the *abstract* concept, the second the process or the *realization* of the concept, and the third the *identity* of the first two.

II. DETERMINATE RELIGION

What is second, then, is that we have to consider determinate religion, religion in its determinateness. The route from abstract to concrete is based on our method, on the concept, or rather on the nature of the concept. The fact that the concept resolves to determine itself, that absolute spirit resolves to be in a determinate mode, we can present in the following manner. Spirit *is* in the most *concrete* sense. The absolute or highest being belongs to it. But spirit is, and this being belongs to it, only insofar as it is *for* itself, i.e., insofar as it posits itself or brings itself forth; for it *is only as activity*. It is not immediate; natural things are immediate and abide in this [immediate] being. Spirit's being is not immediate in this way, but only as self-producing, as making itself for itself. Spirit comes to itself; this is a movement, an activity, a mediation of itself with itself. It involves distinctions and directions, and this succession of directed movements is the path by which spirit comes to itself, for spirit is itself the goal. The absolute goal is to recognize itself, to be for itself. That it cognizes itself, that it is as object for itself, that it grasps itself in the complete intuition and complete consciousness of itself, is object to itself in the way that it is in itself, and comes to complete cognition of itself—this goal is its true goal. This process by which spirit produces itself or comes to itself, this path it takes, contains distinguishable determinations and distinct moments. The path is not yet the goal. Spirit does not reach the goal without having traversed the path, is not at the goal from the outset; that which is most perfect [i.e., complete] must traverse the path *to* the goal. Something cannot be perfect from its very beginning, but only when it attains itself, attains its goal. Therefore spirit is this process and is perfect only at its goal. At the stations of its process spirit is not yet perfect; its consciousness concerning itself is not yet authentic; it is not yet manifest to itself according to its truth; it is revealed to itself only at its goal. Inasmuch as spirit is essentially this activity of self-production, these are stages of its consciousness, but it is conscious of itself only according to these stations. These distinct stages now yield the determinate religions; [a determinate] religion is a consciousness of universal spirit that is not yet for itself as absolute. This consciousness, at each stage, of the spirit that has not yet penetrated to itself, is spirit's determinate consciousness but not yet absolute consciousness; i.e., it is determinate religion. We therefore have to consider the determinate religions, imperfect as they are, because they are stages of the path of spirit. It is the very nature of spirit itself that it forges this path, for *it is* only through the fact that it *becomes for itself.*

We now have to consider these determinate religions in three ways. *First,* we must look at the determinateness of any such religion as a pure determination of thought, i.e., we must consider its metaphysical concept. What will present itself to us in this metaphysical determinacy is the con-

tent that, in the older tradition of philosophy—[for example, in the] Wolffian philosophy—took the form of the "proofs of the existence of God." We
shall consider in more detail how this form of "giving proofs" is deficient
and faulty. In more recent times we no longer hear of these "proofs," since
"proof" as such is only a procedure of the understanding, [whereas] here
only speculative reason suffices. Besides being representations, these
"proofs of God's existence" also have a certain content, a thought-content,
and it is noteworthy that these different proofs correspond to the different
stages of determinate religion. (The fact that there are a number of proofs[23]
already speaks against them, since a proof must on its own account be adequate and exhaustive if it is suited to the nature of its object.) Therefore the
different proofs of God's existence have a content; and it is precisely the
different stages of the determinacy of religion that are expressed by their
similarly determinate thought-content. In other words, the succession of the
different determinate religions is contained in the succession of proofs. This
is a higher justification for these very proofs of God's existence, as we shall
see. (It is easy to recognize their negative aspect, but difficult to recognize
their affirmative import.) [Thus] the first step is [that we give an account of]
the thought-determinacy of God and simultaneously of the determinacy of
the finite and its sublation, in the course of which, by means of sublation,
the very representation of God is supposed to arise—and we hold fast the
pure thought-determinacy of religion, of a specific stage of religious consciousness.

The *second* step is that we consider the shape or the *representation of
this determinacy,* i.e., what shape this determinacy must have. Religion is
such a consciousness insofar as in religion there occurs that determinacy of
consciousness for which the object is on the whole a represented object and
not a conceived object; in other words, the subjective consciousness is a
representing and not a conceiving consciousness (the latter is philosophy).
We have to show that, in order to make itself capable of being represented,
spirit must advance to the form wherein it is a subjective consciousness of
something represented.

The *third* aspect is the *particular cultus,* the church of such a religion—
the cultus or the mode of unification of the thought-determinacy and the
representation. The historical side of religion (i.e., of the religions) is then
linked especially with these two aspects, the modality of the shape and of
the cultus. For it should be noted, in connection with determinate religion,
that these determinacies, of which we take cognizance one after another [in
logical order], have also been necessarily present in the world. When we
consider the sequence of the determinate religions under the guidance of
the concept, as ruled and determined by the concept, the sequence of the
historical religions emerges for us from it, and thus we have the history of

religions before us at the same time. For what is *necessary* through the concept must have *existed,* and the religions, as they have followed one another, have not arisen in a contingent manner. Instead it is spirit that governs what is inward, that has brought it forth. It is not the work of chance, and it is absurd to see contingency here. Therefore the religions, in the way they have followed one another in history, are not determined externally but instead by the concept itself; they are determined by the very nature of spirit itself, which has forced itself into the world in order to bring itself to consciousness of itself. Inasmuch as we consider the consciousness of spirit and these determinate religions according to the concept, this is a purely philosophical treatment, but at the same time also a treatment of what *is.* Philosophy on the whole does not consider *what is not;* only *what is, is rational.* ([I mean] what *actually* is, not the merely phenomenal or the merely existing.)

III. [THE REVELATORY RELIGION][24]

The third stage is that in this very course of the determinate religions the concept loses its finitude, loses this inadequacy of its existence, which it has in consciousness; it sublates its own untruth and comes to be as it is, arrives at genuine consciousness of itself. This is then the *revelatory* or *manifest religion,* and not only the *revealed* religion—manifest, whereas formerly religion was always still veiled, was not in its truth. The fact that what we cognize as the concept of religion is also the content of *this* religion holds good to begin with in the mode of representation. The content of religion itself is found in a religious mode. Only when the time had come[25] did spirit become manifest; for the very movement of spirit, this path upon which it alone posits itself as spirit, whereby it becomes all things as spirit and arrives at the goal, is a path that falls within existence and hence in time. Religion is for the universal consciousness, the nonphilosophical consciousness, for consciousness of spirit generally; and thus for this general consciousness spirit is an object in a sensible mode, in representation; only in philosophy is spirit an object as concept.

This is therefore the general survey of our procedure. This procedure will to a certain degree be a theodicy.[26] Spirit is not only an abstract, otherworldly spirit, but living and contemporary spirit, [which] is present within consciousness and is effective. For this very reason spirit itself has to appear within consciousness and to pass through the [mode of] appearance, in order then *to be for itself.*

THE SPECULATIVE CONCEPT OF RELIGION

Part I of Hegel's philosophy of religion is "The Concept of Religion." In the 1824 lectures it is divided into two main sections called "Empirical Observation" and "The Speculative Concept of Religion." Our selection begins with the transition between these two sections.[1]

"Empirical Observation" was initially intended as merely introductory to the proper treatment of the concept of religion, but it grew into nearly three-fifths of the whole of Part I, and insufficient time remained for an adequate treatment of the "Speculative Concept." But the time was not wasted, and the material is rich and suggestive. For in this "introduction" Hegel sets out to show that the "empirical approach," which starts with religion as it is given in immediate experience, and which limits itself to finite categories of consciousness, can never arrive at what is distinctively religious, namely the relationship *of finite and infinite spirit. This is not to say that immediate experience is irrelevant. On the contrary, it represents the beginning of all knowledge—but it is only the beginning of knowledge, not the totality of it. Religion finally is not merely an empirical reality, something that can be exhaustively accounted for in terms of sense-based experience or immediate self-consciousness; rather it is a "speculative" reality because it is a "mirroring"* (speculum) *of the absolute precisely in the religious relationship to the absolute, precisely in the feeling and consciousness of the absolute. Therefore religion can be properly or adequately grasped only speculatively, not empirically. Hegel was indebted to Schleiermacher for forcing a recognition of the experiential dimension of all religion, but Schleiermacher himself did not move beyond this dimension.*

Hegel's method in "Empirical Observation" is not itself empirical. Rather he offers what might be described as a phenomenology of the empirical approach, viewing religion as it appears to empirical consciousness, showing how this point of view arrives at its own limits and must be transcended. The stages of religious consciousness identified by Hegel are immediate knowledge *(the faith or certainty that God is),* feeling, reflection *(in the form of* understanding *and* representation*), and finally* reason *or* thought. *By progressing through these stages, religious consciousness becomes aware of the antithesis between oneself as a finite, feeling, particular subject and God as the infinite, independent, universal object. It is these distinct elements that constitute the religious relationship. But how is such a relationship between the finite and the infinite possible? From the point of view of empirical observation, only two options present themselves: either God remains what is totally other and beyond, the negation of finitude, of which I can have no cognitive knowledge; or finitude itself is what is exhaustively real and good, existing solely for itself. Finitude is related either* negatively *to God or* affirmatively *to itself; it cannot be relat-*

ed affirmatively to God. Finitude attempts to bridge this gulf in the form of "reflective" knowledge, which appears philosophically as "understanding" and religiously as "representation," but from this point of view the infinite remains either an incomprehensible beyond or a mere projection of the finite. Only from the point of view of reason or thought is it possible to conceive the infinite as that which "overreaches" the finite, both encompassing and transcending it as an "affirmative infinitude." Here the perspective shifts from finite consciousness to the infinite self-mediation of spirit. There is no way of "passing over" from the finite to the true infinite unless the infinite itself constitutes the passage; but this is already the speculative insight.

1. Transition to the Speculative Concept [2]

We have now attempted to arrive at religion by the path of observation, and so we have come to the consciousness of the antithesis of the finite and the infinite, and to the standpoint where consciousness is ultimate, so that the finite *this* maintains itself and makes itself into the one and only affirmative.

The observer finds this standpoint and sticks to it. Then he says that there is only a relationship of this kind to be found, and it is therefore impossible to know anything about the absolute, or God, or the truth. This "impossibility" is based on the fact that no such entity is perceived in the observing consciousness. We should notice here that "possibility" and "impossibility" are taken in a determinate sense; a definition of this kind concerns the inner core, or concept, of an object, what the object is in itself generally. So if anything is to be said about possibility or impossibility, it must be decided by the nature of the concept in question. From the point of view of the observing consciousness, however, there can be no discussion of the inner core or of the concept, for from this standpoint consciousness renounces any cognizance of what pertains to the inner core; it has before it only what falls within external consciousness as such. But possibility and impossibility do not fall within this sphere. More exactly, this standpoint pretends that the observing consciousness will in the end be found to be that from which the concept arises. The possible will be just what arises from experience, while what runs counter to experience will be the impossible.

In reference to this point it must be said that observation arbitrarily limits itself to the sphere of finite consciousness; there are in fact other spheres that can be observed—not just this one, whose content is merely finite versus finite. Consciousness remains free to make other observations in another sphere, in which the affirmative relationship of consciousness to what has being in-and-for-itself is contained. Hence it is capricious to stick at the point where one can observe only that in virtue of which the finite is set against the finite, so that this posited infinite is in fact nothing but a finite and subjective [entity]. To be precise, religious consciousness can be observed—[either] in the form of naive religiosity or devotion, or in that of religious cognition—and this yields a different result from that reached at the standpoint of finite consciousness. The observation can be conducted upon others or upon the very ones who wish only to occupy the standpoint of finite consciousness. If cognition is limited to this standpoint, it may well be that religious sensibility,[3] the heart, devotion, is more affirmative than consciousness insofar as consciousness is a determinate, cognizant, and observing consciousness. The two can be distinguished—this possibility must be conceded. This is the standpoint of cognition, and I must here weigh my consciousness against what I am in and for myself as spirit.

All that I know, all that affects my consciousness, is contained in me myself. So when this possibility is conceded, it must be noted that the conviction that spirit has only a negative relationship to the content, to God, vitiates sensibility and ruins devotion. The conviction of consciousness that it has only a negative relationship to God ruins religious sensibility itself. For *thinking* is the source, the very ground upon which God, or the universal in general, *is:* the universal is in thought, *only* in thought, and for thought. This thinking, spirit in its freedom, supplies the content of truth, the concrete deity, and delivers it to sensibility; its content is what sustains sensibility in regard to religiosity. If we hold firmly in our thinking consciousness that there is no affirmative relationship to God, then all content goes out of sensibility. Its very stuff is taken from it. If the thinking sphere empties itself, then sensibility too is without content, in the same way that I cannot use my eyes without a light source. If light is taken away in the physical realm, I cannot have the sensation of seeing. Similarly, I can have no religious sensation if this content is not present in the territory of religion. If the content is denied in this realm, and banished from it, then there is present no longer that which yields the characteristic of sensibility. Hence, if it may on the one hand be granted that there can be more in devotion than there is in the religious consciousness, this [extra element] could be observed; on the other hand, it is caprice or ineptitude that what is present either in one's own consciousness or in that of others should not be observed. In point of fact, however, this caprice or ineptitude does not come on the scene for the first time at this juncture, but rather when the decision is taken *merely* to observe. This limits observation to the sphere of finitude, for observing means being related to something external, something that is to be and to remain external for me. But it is only externally posited. That which is external to itself is the finite. If I adopt the standpoint of pure observation, then *ipso facto* I have something before me that is in itself an external object, existing on its own account; in other words, it is the finite in general. The external [thing] is not just external to me, but to itself; it is the finite. I can observe thinking, even speculative thinking, or religion or philosophy—but thinking *is* only for the thinker himself. Similarly, if I want to observe piety, that too is present only for the pious; just as thinking is only for the thinker, so religion is only for the religious, that is, for those who actually are what at the same time they observe. In the case we have here the observer is not by any means *merely* observing; rather he is outside the object in a relationship such that what is observed is not simply something external, and the observer is not simply an observer, nor merely in a negative relationship to the object observed.

It follows, then, that in order to find the ground of religion we must abandon the abstract relationship of observation; we must renounce this empirical standpoint for the very reason that it is only this standpoint of observation. It is therefore the case that the determinations of reflection, of the finite, posit the determinations of the infinite. But the infinite is itself posited only as negative. Reflection does, to be sure, go so far as to require that the finite should be posited as finite, but we have shown that this demand must be made only in reference to the affirmative.

With this we make the transition to the treatment of the speculative concept of religion.

2. Definition of the Concept of Religion[4]

We will now consider the speculative concept of religion, the only ground (it has already defined itself) on which religion can be at home. Its basic defining character, as we have seen, is just the affirmative relation of consciousness, which exists only as the negation of negation, or as the self-sublating of the determinate [moment] of the antithesis—and hence the self-sublating of just those determinations that reflection takes to be independent, hard and fast. To this degree the ground of religion is what is called the *rational* [sphere], and more precisely the *speculative* [sphere]. But religion is not therefore something abstract, as thus defined, not just an affirmative relation of consciousness to the universal in general. Religion is not just this abstract determination. If it were merely an abstract determination of this sort, all further content would lie outside it, or, if we posited this abstraction in the field of the actual as well, there would still have to be some other actuality alongside this abstraction and outside religion.

For the affirmative relation to the universal, to what is true, is the relation to right, to ethics, to something true, to the true generally. The standpoint of religion, then, is in principle precisely the affirmative relation of consciousness, consciousness generally; it is [the affirmation] that the truth with which consciousness is actively related *embraces all content within itself*. Hence this relation of consciousness to this truth is itself the highest level of consciousness, its absolute standpoint.[5]

What we have just said we could let stand as the concept of religion in general. But in philosophy it is necessary to demonstrate the *necessity* of this standpoint, the *genesis* of the concept that is advanced here as a definition; or we must indicate precisely the place where the necessity of this standpoint, of this content, which is spoken of as religion, resides.

We could, for example, establish some [principle] regarding religion and prove that this is the situation in our representation of it; but there are other representations of religion, and in principle our representation cannot be the criterion of what is in and for itself true. What we have to do, then, is to give some account of the necessity of the content, and to show that the content is necessary in itself and in principle; once this is done we can say in more detail, "This content is religion"; and we need not worry whether others find another content, or other determinations, in their representation of it. That will not matter to what we are discussing then, for we are concerned with content, and disagreement could only be about whether something pertaining to the representation is religion or not. The content, however, is valid in and for itself if its necessity is firmly established. To say "This is religion," is just one type of arbitrariness.

First, then, we must give an account of what "necessity," and "showing the necessity of something," means. There is a content of which we say, "This is religion." As regards necessity, we know this much, that if the necessity of something is to be demonstrated, one has to start from *something else,* from which, by virtue of its nature, one arrives at a certain content, and that which follows [from what] one began with is termed "necessary."

But it is clear that if we want to start with religion, this other content lies behind us. Moreover, if we view necessity in this way, it includes the definite moment of mediation, so that the content, which is thereby defined, which we call religion, appears as mediated or as resulting from something else; but this definition, being one-sided, appears to be inappropriate if religion is to be the highest level, if it is intrinsically the first standpoint, which is not posited through [the mediation of] another, but must be posited purely and simply through itself. In this way we become involved through this "other side" in an inadequacy; but this inadequacy, this process according to which necessity has the appearance of something mediated through something else, is sublated as soon as we consider true necessity. Or [in other words], it is a feature of rational necessity that it cancels this [mere] show and lifts itself up to the affirmative.

In this respect three stages in the process must be kept in mind: (1) necessity is a process in which what is called religion is in the situation of deriving its content from something other and of being posited; (2) the stage where the one-sidedness of this relationship, this mode of necessity (that even religion is the sort of thing that emerges from something else) is shown to be self-sublating, with the result that what we have defined as necessity (a positing emanating from another) is a process contained within religion itself; (3) the determinations of these forms within religion itself are to be noted.

If the concept of religion is to be further elucidated, an additional prior remark is called for. Since, as we have said, the necessity of religion occurs within religion itself, it is also the case that the concept of religion will be generated within religion itself; and the syllogistic outcome of religion, the true religion, is the one which produces the consciousness of itself, the one which has for its object what religion is.

The concept of religion must be expressed. Religion is a consciousness of the absolutely universal object. If, however, we have so far used the term "consciousness," this word expresses only the side of the *appearance* of spirit. Insofar as I have a consciousness, I am actively related to an object. I am thus defined as relationship; but it is the essence of spirit not to be *merely* in relationship, not to be a connecting of two sides. Consciousness encompasses [only] the finite. Here I am the knower, the subject, which is implicitly spirit; the other side, the object, remains standing independently over there. Spirit is not merely in the relational mode, and does not merely have the form of consciousness. It is precisely in abstracting from this relationship that we can speak of spirit, and consciousness is then encompassed as a moment within the being of spirit. So it is in speaking of *spirit* that we intend to use the term "spirit" instead of "consciousness"; thus in using it we have an affirmative relationship of *spirit* to *absolute spirit*. Where we have spoken in this way, we have in mind the relationship of spirit [to spirit] as such. But this is not merely a [separable] connection between [finite] spirit and absolute spirit; rather it is what is essential, it is inner connectedness. Absolute spirit is itself that which connects itself with what we have put on the other side to distinguish it. Thus, on a higher plane, religion is this idea, the idea of spirit that relates itself to itself, *the self-consciousness of absolute spirit*. Within this its *self-consciousness,* there falls also its *consciousness,* which was previously defined as relationship. Thus in the highest idea, religion is not the affair of the single human being; rather it is essentially the highest determination of the absolute idea itself.

I have now set forth the concept of religion provisionally.

In that spirit differentiates itself implicitly, the finitude of consciousness comes into play. The consciousness of spirit, for which [absolute] spirit is, is finite consciousness—but this finite consciousness is a moment of absolute spirit itself. Absolute spirit is what differentiates and determines itself, i.e., it posits itself as finite consciousness. Consequently it is not from the standpoint of finite consciousness that we consider religion. Already, even in this superficial consideration of it, the [absolute] idea is developing itself.

3. The Necessity of the Religious Standpoint

The next point [to be discussed] is the *necessity* of this standpoint. In fact absolute spirit is in its consciousness a knowing of itself: if it knows something else, then it is no longer absolute spirit. So it is this definition of which we speak. This definition is here maintained from the standpoint of religion in order that this content may be the absolute truth, simply the whole truth, so that this idea encompasses within it all plenitude, all the riches of thought, all the riches of known truth; it constitutes the sole substance and truth of this wealth. Furthermore it is maintained in order that the absolute idea may alone be this truth; all things have their truth only in it, as moments of its life and activity. These assertions that this content of religion is the absolute truth—this [is] what is to be proved, what has to be demanded. This deduction lies outside our science. To prove that this content is the absolute truth means nothing other than to demonstrate its necessity. Necessity involves our starting with something else. So the procedure used in the proof of the content has as its first step the exhibiting of the content as the result of another content.

First we must indicate where this procedure is to be found, and, second how it is structured, what it looks like. The other that is taken as a starting point is nothing else but what we call, quite generally, the *finite world,* and the *consciousness* of the finite world. This provides the general starting point from which the result is necessarily inferred. (Concerning this necessity, it will be noted later that it is an essential moment in absolute spirit itself.) What must be shown therefore is the transition from a finite starting point to a more or less abstract, absolute content. This transition can be kept on an abstract plane, or developed more fully, and in such a way that the development occurs through thought, through the concept. This transition occurs in the [movement of] spirit, but it may do so abstractly or in a more developed way. The transition is more abstract when we have expressed the content of nature as the universal, or as negation of the negative, as essentially containing this mediation within itself. In this way it is possible to make the transition from the finite to the absolute. As Vanini says, a single straw suffices to prove the existence of God.[6]

But if the process is accomplished in all relevant detail by progressive development, determined by the concept, then what we have is philosophy in general, or, more specifically, the philosophy of religion; and the unmediated [starting point] is in that case *nature* in general. So we must [first] show how the *logical* [*idea*] unlocks itself in the resolve[7] to become nature, to pass over into nature and lose itself in this externality. The next stage in philosophy is the consideration of nature [itself], a beginning [having been] made with the logical. The treatment based on the *concept* presents itself as this movement: the indwelling concept of nature sublates the externality in which the concept exists as nature; as contradictory to the concept, this externality is dissolved and the concept takes upon itself a higher, more appropriate mode than the natural externality in which it has reality as nature. The treatment of nature exhibits its progression as a sequence of steps or moments, and thus shows how the concept, which exists in nature only implicitly, breaks through its "rind" and comes forth to makes its appearance, until it gets to the point of being explicit, of appearing as it is. Or, what comes to the same thing, nature recollects itself; it is its destination [that it should] go back into its center, or that the center should emerge into external existence. What results is *spirit* in general. *The necessity of nature is to posit spirit as its truth,* that spirit *is* its truth. In nature the concept is lost in externality. Nature is the eternal emergence and dissolution of this externality. Nature has the implicit destination of becoming spirit.

Spirit generally—the truth of nature—that is what spirit is. Spirit in its immediacy is finite, natural spirit; it has potentialities, that is, it is initially no more than the abstract concept of itself. It is the abstract identity of its concept and its appearance. Nature is implicitly idea; thus it is for us when we contemplate it in thought. Those two aspects, its being as idea for us, and as idea in itself, fall apart in nature; in spirit there is this identity, this being *for* itself what it is *in* itself. [There is the potential] that it might be, like nature, idea implicitly; but [there is also the fact] that what it is in itself also appears to it, i.e., the idea exists in its appearance. The consideration of finite spirit, then, has as its result the idea of absolute spirit.

Thus it is through this process [*Gang*] of the cognizing concept that the content of which we have spoken, absolute spirit conscious of itself, is exhibited as necessary, as the truth of all things, as the absolute truth into which, precisely through itself, all this other content returns. Philosophy, then, is the methodical proof that this content is what is genuine, that it is the absolute truth. This is the process that lies before [i.e., precedes] our science; so we have to presuppose this result here. If we did not presuppose it, we would have to expound philosophy as a whole. This is the only way in which the demonstration can be carried out, the proof that this content is the absolute truth.

The second point to remark upon about this process is that it is still one-sided: it has a distorted and false character, namely, the determination that we begin with something else, either with the logically abstract or with concrete being, with nature, finite being. Because we begin from something else of this kind, this very content does not appear as absolute but as a *result*. The process seems to have this distorted aspect implicit in it, but *absolute truth cannot be a result; it is what is purely and simply first, unique.* It is what takes up simply everything into itself—the absolute plenitude in which everything is but a moment. In this connection it should be noted that, even though the process appears initially as a mediating process, nevertheless it is in this result itself that the one-sidedness is abolished: the result casts off its position as result and develops a *counterthrust,* so to speak, against this movement.[8] To be more precise, the process is so defined that even this starting point, the first [moment] from which we begin—whether it be the logical abstraction of being or the finite world, the [moment] which appears to be immediate, and therefore to be something that is not posited—is itself posited in the result *as* something posited and no longer as something immediate; it is reduced from an immediate to a posited [status], so that absolute spirit is what is true, rather [than that first moment].

In this final result, then, *absolute spirit,* conscious of itself, *is the first and alone true.* But there is also this in it: the fact that nature, the finite world, is posited, that it is something posited, is therefore one moment in this spirit, in this content itself. It is not only consistent with the method (or the external modality of our proceeding) that this immediacy, nature, appears as something posited, and that the immediate sublates itself in this way; but also this pertains essentially to the result itself, it belongs to its content. [This content is] the positing of [a moment] such that it [first] appears as something immediate and second retains this quality of being posited, of sublating itself and of going back to its truth.

Thus, therefore, what we have posited, this process of necessity, is the first moment. But the other moment, the positing of something immediate, is equally a determination in the absolute content itself. Together they make up a single movement, a mediating [process] which comes together with itself; together these two moments make up the activity of God within godself. It is from this standpoint that the first process comes before us, but also the second moment that appears as immediate—a nature, a finite world is posited. This happens within the idea, as the activity and movement of the idea itself. This is nothing else but [what is meant by] the popular statement that "God creates the world." In other words, God posits the world as something that is other, distinct from God (hence something naturally posited); [yet] the world is [also] what continues to belong to God and to be posited by God, so that it has the movement of betaking itself back to God.

What we have said so far, then, about this process is in the first place that it shows itself as a process outside religion; but that, second, this process is a moment within religion itself. Inside religion, however, it has a shape and form different from what it had in that first mode, wherein it is, so to speak, merely innocent with respect to God. Here God is strictly the first [moment]. And this is just what is implied in the idea of absolute spirit. We have to consider these moments as they are conceived in relation to this idea. Spirit is *for itself,* that is, it makes itself the object, it is what subsists on its own account over against the concept; it is what we call generally the world, or nature. This diremption constitutes the first moment. The second one is that this object returns to its source, and this movement constitutes the divine life as a whole. Thus spirit as absolute is initially what shows itself, what appears to itself, it is a being-for-itself that has being on its own account. That is why it is first what appears. But appearance as such is what nature is; spirit is not only what appears, what has being, for us; it is what-has-being-for-itself, what-appears-to-itself, and with that, consciousness as such is posited. So what we initially regard as necessary is [present] as a moment within spirit itself. We have that necessity in its very essence within religion too—not as an immediate existence but essentially as an appearing of the idea, not as the being but as the appearance of the divine. This then is the relationship of *necessity* to our content, and it is this relationship of necessity to it that supplies our content with its *definition,* or yields the concept of what our object is.

With respect to that object, we could now say that we have established the *concept* of it, and that we are in a position to pass on to its *exposition.* It is to be noted that the exposition of this concept is nothing other than that *the concept develops itself into the idea,* and that we *contemplate* this *realization of the concept as the idea.*

4. The Realization of the Concept of Religion[9]

The concept of religion that we have given is still highly abstract at this point, still confined to very general terms. It might be demanded that we should set it forth in a more concrete form; but the more concrete mode of the concept is in fact a producing, a bringing forth, of the concept *through itself.* As a concept it is abstract; but it is the concept itself that makes itself concrete, consummating itself as a totality, so that this concept itself comes to be the object. The simple concept that we have established is *the self-consciousness of absolute spirit,* its self-consciousness of being *for itself* as spirit. *For itself* it is spirit: this is the respect in which there lies a distinction in its being, and this [distinction] is the moment of *natural life* in general. In common speech this means that God is the unity of the natural and the spiritual; but the spirit is at the same time *lord* over nature, so that the natural and the spiritual are not of equal weight in this unity—which indeed is such that the unity is spirit itself. Spirit is not some *tertium quid* wherein the two are neutralized; rather the absence of difference between them is itself spirit. Spirit *is* spirit and nature. It is on the one hand one side of the union, and on the other hand what also *overreaches* the other side; hence it is the unity of itself and an other. Consequently, our further exposition will be nothing but the laying out of the further concrete determinations of spirit.

The concept of God, then, is the concept of the idea. This content must develop itself as idea; and the exposition of the philosophy of religion displays nothing but this development of the concept of the idea. The more detailed moments of it display for us at the same time the more detailed subdivisions or forms in which religion has to be considered; this characterization of the development of the idea is what supplies the pattern of the general sections into which our exposition breaks up.

We have defined the idea as the absolute unity of the spiritual and the natural, and the spiritual as the substantial, so that the "other" is only something posited by spirit and sustained within it. This idea comprises the following moments:

(1) the *substantial,* absolute, subjective *unity* of both moments: the idea in its self-equivalent affirmation;[10]

(2) the *differentiation* itself, the being for one and for an other—these two moments [as distinct];

(3) the self-positing of what is differentiated in this *absolute affirmation.*

The first two moments are those of the concept, the ways in which the connection of the spiritual and the natural are contained in the concept. Further, they are not merely moments of the concept, but are themselves the two sides of the differentiation—what is then termed the second moment.

This second moment is what, in [the realm of] spirit, is *consciousness.* Consciousness is a positing of two that are supposed to be distinct, but this is nothing else than what has been stated, namely this differentiation of the moments themselves. This differentiation takes on the character of a relationship, and in this way the two moments constitute the content of the two sides of the relationship. In consciousness one side is the solid, substantial unity of the idea—God as having being, the God that has being as a self-relating unity. The other side of the distinction is the act of differentiating itself, which is consciousness, the side for which the other, the solid unity, exists; this side consequently takes on the character of being finite. God is thereby determined as an object, as appearance, as having being and appearing for consciousness. God does not merely have being, but inasmuch as God has being *for an other,* God is appearing. God is not to be grasped as [a being] that is enclosed within itself and that does not appear, [but rather] as *spirit.* A God who is not appearing is an abstraction. The essential moment is self-differentiation; and precisely thereby an other is posited. This differentiation, or the aspect of consciousness, has to be grasped in a reversion to the *absolute affirmation*—an appearing which elevates itself just as eternally to the truth of appearance. As we have said, the differentiation contains both moments, the substantial unity and the differentiation. Accordingly, that substantial unity is [only] one aspect of the relationship, for God *is* only as spirit: God is essentially for an other and to appear to God's other. The return of the differentiated to the absolute affirmation constitutes the third moment. It is these three moments that must be accounted the reality of the concept.

These two aspects are also to be defined thus: the first, the unity, is the *theoretical* aspect, the mode of God's *appearance,* the mode of *representation* of what has being, the objective, the representation of divine appearance and divine being. The second is the *practical* aspect, the activity of *sublating the rupture,* the aspect of form, the form of *freedom,* which is what *subjectivity* is as such; here, then, what we have to consider is subjectivity, self-consciousness in motion, in its characteristic activity and behavior. The first aspect is that of the *representation* of God, and the second that of the *cultus.* The two are connected; the definition that pertains to God pertains also to consciousness in its connection with the cultus.

The text continues with two subsections: (a) "The Theoretical Relationship: The Representation of God"; (b) "The Practical Relationship: The Cultus." The first is devoted, however, not to religious knowledge per se but to a survey of different modalities of the "appearance" of God in the history of religion, from nature religion to the Christian religion. The second addresses three topics: faith and its verification as the characteristic cognitive activity of the cultus; the question of "pantheism"; and determinate forms of the cultus in the history of religion. Thus Part I ends by surveying themes to be addressed in Part II, "Determinate Religion." But these contents scarcely correspond to the form envisioned by Hegel.

DETERMINATE RELIGION: INTRODUCTION

The Introduction to Part II, "Determinate Religion," in the 1824 lectures (excerpted below) contains a classification similar to that found in the 1821 manuscript. The classification makes it clear that in 1824, as in the other lecture series, Hegel initially envisioned a threefold structure, namely, immediate religion or nature religion (greatly expanded in content from 1821), the religion of spiritual individuality (Jewish and Greek religion), and the religion of expediency (Roman religion). In the actual execution, however, Roman religion is treated quite briefly and as the third stage of the religion of spiritual individuality. It is evident that Hegel changed his plan in midcourse from a threefold to a twofold structure. This permitted him to argue that the religions of spiritual individuality correspond to three forms of nature religion "in inverse order," Jewish religion corresponding to Persian, Greek religion to Hinduism, and Roman religion to the religion of ancient China. The latter pair are the most regressive, and determinate religion is seen to curve back in upon itself in an apotheosis of finitude. On this schema, which is found only in the 1824 lectures, Christianity becomes the

201

third moment in the dialectic of the religions, which moves from the reli-
gions of nature, to those of finite spirit, to that of infinite spirit.

The content of "Determinate Religion" expanded enormously from the
1821 manuscript (139 printed pages) to the 1824 lectures (280 pages,
about a third longer than Parts I and III together). In the intervening years
Hegel assimilated a large amount of material from the history of religions,
especially in the areas of primitive religion ("the religion of magic") and
Oriental religions (Hinduism, Buddhism, Chinese religion, Persian reli-
gion, Egyptian religion). His interpretation of Greek and Roman religion
did not change fundamentally after 1821, but a growing appreciation and
more positive assessment of Judaism was evident.

The organization of "Determinate Religion" remained fluid and was
altered significantly in each of the four lecture series; even in 1831 Hegel
had not arrived at a satisfactory form, and consequently it is difficult for
him to persuade us that what is involved is a "necessary classification that
follows objectively from the nature of spirit." Indeed, the discrepancy
between the introductory outline and the actual execution of the 1824 lec-
tures suggests that what is involved has more the character of imaginative
conceptual play on the part of the author.

The first thing is to classify these determinate, ethnic religions;[1] however,
the particular forms that have to be considered under this heading only need
to be defined in a general way at first.

1. The initial [form of] religion is *immediate religion, natural religion,*
nature religion; it is the unity of the spiritual and the natural. God is
[always] the content, but at this stage it is God in the natural unity of the
spiritual and the natural. The natural mode is what characterizes this form
of religion generally; but it also has a great variety of shapes. All these
shapes are together called *nature religion;* we say that at this stage spirit is
still identical with nature, that consciousness remains one with nature; and
to that extent natural religion is the religion of unfreedom.

2. The second stage is the religion of *spiritual individuality* or *subjectiv-*
ity; it is here that the subject's spiritual being-for-self begins. The principal,
or first, or determining element is thought, and the natural state is reduced
to a mere semblance, something accidental over against what is substantive, related to it; the natural becomes merely material, or corporeality for
the subject, or is simply what is determined by the subjective. Two forms of
this religion need to be distinguished.

Inasmuch as spiritual being-for-self is emerging, it is that which is
adhered to purely for itself. There is therefore just the one eternal God, who
has his being only in thought; and natural life, being generally, is only
something posited, something that as such stands opposed to God, but has

no substantiality over against God and has being only through the essence of thought.

In the second form [of the religion of spiritual individuality] the natural and the spiritual are united—not, however, in the way they were in their immediate union, not like that, but in the kind of union where it is simply subjectivity that determines and combines the corporeal in union with itself, so that in this union the corporeal is only its organ, its expression, and displays itself as the appearing of the subject.

This is therefore the religion of divine appearing, of divine corporeality, materiality, and naturalness, but in such a way that this materiality is the appearing of subjectivity—in other words, that here in this corporeality the self-appearing of subjectivity is made manifest; it appears not only for other but for itself. Natural life is thus the organ of the subject, whereby it makes itself appear. This spiritual individuality is therefore not the unlimited individuality of pure thought; it has only spiritual character. Thus on the one hand, the natural is determined as the body in regard to the spiritual realm; on the other hand, the subject is determined as finite because it employs the body in this way.

The first moment or form [of the religion of spiritual individuality] is the religion of sublimity, or the Jewish religion, while the second is the religion of beauty, or the Greek religion.

3. Third, there is the religion in which the concept, or in general a content determined for itself, a concrete content, has its beginnings; this content is *purpose,* fulfilled content, it is subserved by the general powers of nature or the gods of the religion of beauty. Moreover, it is a concrete content that embraces such determinacies within itself; it is the determinant, so that the previously isolated powers are made subject to one purpose. The mode in which the concept first appears is that of external, finite purpose, external conformity to purpose or *expediency.* Absolute conformity to purpose belongs to the idea of spirit, where the idea is its own purpose and there is no other purpose save the concept of spirit itself, namely, the infinite, absolute final purpose, the concept that realizes itself. At this stage the spiritual is indeed the purpose; this moment has within it the inwardly concrete determinations, but its inwardly concrete determination is still finite, having a particular content; it is a particular purpose, which for that very reason is not yet spirit's relatedness to itself.

These [then] are the three forms [of determinate religion]:

1. Nature religion in general, to which the *Oriental* religions all belong, wholly consisting as they do in this unity of nature and spirit and the mingling of them both.[2]

2. The religion of the spiritual for itself, as subjectivity in general that has being abstractly on its own account, the religion of pure thought and of

the spiritual corporeality that is set apart and determined in itself, namely, *Jewish* and *Greek* religion.

3. The religion of external conformity to purpose or expediency, namely, *Roman* religion, forming the transition to the absolute religion.

This classification must not be taken in a merely subjective way; rather it is a necessary classification that follows objectively from the nature of spirit. In the mode of existence that it assumes in religion, spirit in its naturalness is initially natural religion; the next stage is where the reflection of spirit into itself comes on the scene. Spirit becomes inwardly free, and this is the beginning of being-for-self—the subjective generally, which, however, does not yet have its freedom within itself but first emerges from the unity of nature, to which it is still related: this is the conditioned becoming-free of spirit. The third stage, then, is where spirit inwardly gets hold of itself, has the will to achieve inward self-determination, and accordingly appears in such a way that there is purpose, something that is purposive on its own account, but what is inwardly purposive is also at first still finite and limited. The last stage, then, is the absolute, where the spirit is for itself.[3] Such are the basic characteristics that constitute the moments in the development of the concept of spirit, and are at the same time moments of the concrete concept. Spirit accordingly *is* this process.

These stages can be compared to the stages of human life. The child is still in the first, immediate unity of will and nature (both its own nature and that which surrounds it). The second stage [is] youth, this individuality, this becoming-for-self, this spirituality blossoming into life, still setting no particular purpose for itself but questing, searching this way and that, paying heed to everything that comes its way, taking heart from it. The third stage, maturity, is that of work for a particular purpose, to which adults subject themselves, to which they devote their strength. Hovering above maturity, finally, the fourth stage is old age, the age of thought, having the universal before itself as infinite purpose, recognizing this purpose—the age that has turned back from particular forms of activity and work to the universal purpose. These characteristics are those that are logically determined by the nature of the concept. Ultimately, in the concept, in the idea, it becomes evident that the first immediacy does not have being as immediacy but is itself only something posited: the child, for instance, is itself something produced.

CHRISTIANITY: THE CONSUMMATE RELIGION

The full text of Part 3 of the 1824 lectures is given below. Hegel made use of phenomenologically descriptive terms to designate the world religions. For Christianity he commonly employed three: die vollendete Religion *("the consummate religion"), die offenbare Religion ("the revelatory religion"), and die absolute Religion ("the absolute religion"). The new German/English edition prefers the first since it is the one found on the title page of the third part of Hegel's lecture manuscript and its occurs more frequently in the body of the texts of all the lecture series. However, the heading in Griesheim's transcription of the 1824 lectures is "the revelatory religion," and this title is given greater prominence in these lectures than in the others. "Revelatory" (offenbar) points to the process of "making open" or "manifesting," as contrasted with something that has been "revealed" (geoffenbart) in historical, positive fashion. The 1827 lectures make the point that Christianity is both the "revelatory" and the "revealed" religion.*

Hegel himself did not use the title "the absolute religion," but this expression occurs in the texts of the lectures as well, although less frequently. It might be assumed that "consummate" (or "final," "perfect," "complete") and "absolute" mean approximately the same thing, but there are differences of nuance. "Consummate" suggests that Christianity is the product of the historical evolution of spirit and in this sense belongs within the history of religions. "Absolute" should not be taken in the sense of something that is fixed and immutable; rather, for Hegel, "the absolute" is what "absolves," that is, "releases" or "sets free" the other from itself. The absolute is and constitutes relationality, and absolute spirit is what encompasses all relationality within itself. Christianity as the consummate or absolute religion encompasses and fulfills the truth of all other religions. This is a classic instance of what is now called religious inclusivism; the option of a genuine religious pluralism was scarcely on the horizon in the early nineteenth century, but Hegel did recognize that truth emerges historically in a plurality of forms.

Introduction

I. THE CONSUMMATE RELIGION

This is the *consummate religion,* the religion that is the being of spirit for itself, the religion in which religion has become objective to itself. We have called religion the consciousness of God, the consciousness of the absolute being [*Wesen*]—and that is the concept of this religion. Consciousness is inward differentiation, spirit that differentiates itself. Now, therefore, God is [present] as consciousness, or the consciousness of God means that finite consciousness has its essential being, this God, as its object; and it knows the object as its essential being, it objectifies it for itself. In the consciousness of God there are two sides: the one side is God, the other is that where consciousness as such stands. With the consciousness of God we arrive directly at one side, which is what we have called religion. This content is now itself an object. It is the whole that is an object to itself, or religion has become objective to itself. It is *religion* that has become objective to itself—religion as the consciousness of God, or the self-consciousness of God as the return of consciousness into itself.

This religion is precisely what we have called *spirituality*. "Spirit" means precisely not what immediately is, but what is objectively for itself. Spirit is *for* spirit in such a way that the two are distinct. They are defined by their contrast: the one as universal, the other as particular; the one as inner, the other as outer; the one as infinite spirit, the other as finite spirit. This distinction *is* religion, and at the same time religion is the sublation of this distinction, i.e., the self-consciousness of freedom—a spirituality which was there *for us* in all the preceding formative stages of religion, but which is now the *object*. The single self-consciousness finds the consciousness of its essential being in it; hence it is free in this object, and it is just this freedom that *is* spirituality—and this, we say, is religion. In other words, spirit is now the object. Spirit has been all along an object for us that stands neither [solely] on the finite nor on the universal side; rather this *relationship* of spirit to spirit—this alone is religion. It is religion, then, that has now become what is objective in that the object of finite consciousness is known as spirit by spirit; this one substance is the absolute truth for itself, the truth of everything, inasmuch as the universal is the absolute power in which everything is negated; it is posited as organic, not only as substance but as subject. The freedom of self-consciousness is the content of religion, and this content is itself the object of the Christian religion, i.e., spirit is its own object. This absolute being distinguishes itself at one and the same time into absolute power and subject; it communicates itself in what is distinguished from it while at the same time remaining undivided, so that the other is also the whole—all this, along with its return to itself, is the concept of religion. [It] constitutes the totality of spirituality, it is the very nature of spirituality. This concept is the absolute idea, which has previously been [an object] for us in our study of religion, and [is] now itself the object [for itself]; spirit is identical with spirit.

In this religion, religion has become objective to itself; the object or content by means of which religion is fulfilled, what is objective for it, is now its *own* definition, namely that spirit is [present] only *for* spirit. Universal and singular spirit, infinite and finite spirit, are here inseparable; their absolute identity is religion, and absolute religion is the awareness of just this content. Since we have expressed it initially in this form, one can say that what is at issue here, the whole, the absolute, *is* religion. One can say this in contrast with defining what is at issue—the absolute, the essential—as the majesty of God; for the latter implies that we know God only as an object that stands over and above us for all time, that we know about this object, are cognizant of it.

At first sight, what theology is about is the cognition of God as what is solely objective and absolute, what remains purely and simply separate from subjective consciousness. Therefore God is an external object—like the sun or the sky—but still a thought-object. An external object of consciousness exists where the object permanently retains the character of something other and eternal. In contrast with this, we can designate the concept of absolute religion as follows: what is involved here, the essence of what is involved, is not this external object but religion itself, i.e., the unity of this object with the subject, the way in which it is in the subject.

We can regard the present age as concerned with religion, with religiosity, or with piety, in which no regard is had for what is objective. People have had various religions; but—[according to] the present dogmatics,[1] at least—that does not matter, as long as they are pious. We cannot know God as an object, we cannot cognize God, and it is the subjective attitude that is important. This standpoint has been recognized in our earlier discussion, and we have already spoken of its one-sidedness. It is the standpoint of the age, and at the same time it is a very important advance, which has validated an infinite moment; for it involves the recognition of the consciousness of subjectivity as an absolute moment. There is the same content on both sides, and this being-in-itself of both sides is religion. The great advance of our age is that subjectivity has been recognized as an absolute moment; thus subjectivity is an essential category. But everything depends on how we define it.

In the first place, this *must* be viewed as a great advance. For as we take it up first in the determination of consciousness, religion is so constituted that its content flees into the distance, and seems at least to remain far off. Consciousness is [the awareness] that there is an object that is simply determined as an other and remains over against me, e.g., a mountain, sun, sky. In this characterization of consciousness, the [religious] content flees into the distance and remains remote. Religion may have whatever content it likes. When fixed at the standpoint of consciousness, its content is one that stands over and above it, and even when the specifications of supernatural revelation are added, the content still remains simply given and external to us. Along with a representation of this sort—that the divine content is merely given, inaccessible to reason, that our role is to comport ourselves passively in faith, etc.—[there is another one, namely,] that all of this is not the sole standpoint of the religion of consciousness, and that there is still room for the subjectivity of sensibility, of feeling, the subjectivity that is the result of sensibility and divine worship. The devout submerge themselves in their object with their heart, devotion, and will; thus at the pinnacle of devotion they have sublated the separation. For their consciousness, this devotion or intensity can be considered a separation if the Spirit of God, the grace of God, is something alien to humanity, something it must allow to come upon it—an alien thing working in it, which it must allow to come upon it, in relation to which it is merely something passive and dead. Thus, as we have already noted, even in what I have called the standpoint of consciousness, there also occurs this elevation, this non-alien condition, this submersion of spirit in the depth that is no depth or the remoteness that is absolute nearness and presence instead. In contrast with this, then, there is separation, which has a different shape: the finite subject confronts the object as absolute spirit. This separation can be represented as the standpoint of the consciousness or feeling of the individual. It is against this separation that the objection is raised that what is involved here is religion as such, i.e., the subjective consciousness that wills, inwardly senses, and purposes what is divine. Thus it is in the subject that this inseparability of subjectivity and of the other, which appears as objective, exists. The validating of this subjectivity is the important thing, or [the recognition] that this subjectivity is absolutely essential for the whole sphere of the religious relationship. Thus this standpoint elevates subjectivity into the essential characteristic of the whole range of the religious relationship. There is a rather close bond between it and the freedom of spirit, in that spirit has reestablished its freedom, and there is no standpoint within which it is not at home but stands opposed to [something like] a rock. That is what is important in this definition. It is inherent in the concept of the absolute religion that it is the religion that is objective to itself, the one where religion *is* what is objective. But this is only the concept of religion; the consciousness is something else. Consciousness can have this concept as something otherworldly. This concept is one thing and the consciousness of it is another.

Hence in the absolute religion too, the concept may be this implicitly, and yet consciousness [as such] may be unfree; the third moment is the consciousness of what this concept is in itself. This is the aspect that has emerged and come to consciousness in the determination that it is religion which is here involved. But the concept—yes, even the concept—is itself still one-sided when taken as merely implicit; that is how it is in this one-sided form. Subjectivity itself here becomes one-sided or has the character of just one of the sides, is merely infinite form, pure self-consciousness. That is to say, subjectivity is pure knowledge of itself, but a knowledge that is, on its own account, contentless, void of content. It has no content because religion as such is grasped only in its implicit potential. It is not the religion that is objective to itself, but only a religion whose form is not yet self-determining and self-regulating, able to provide its own content. What has no objectivity has no content.

But to the extent that religion is without content, it must still *have* a content, for it is the right of what is true always to be, although it can, to be sure, have either a truthful or a disguised form. But because the content is not self-determined through subjectivity, because it is not religion itself that is objective to itself, this content has a contingent, empirical, finite character, and a similarity with Roman times arises. The period of the Roman emperors has much similarity with our own.[2] Just because [the subject] is abstract, it is finite. This is the highest pinnacle we have reached, namely, that religion [is] what is empirical, arbitrary, contingent, etc. The result is that this freedom, which has a contingent content, is only one that allows a beyond to subsist as a [goal] of yearning; it simply denies spirituality as such, or what we call the standpoint of consciousness. In this way it repudiates the essential moment of spirit and this is spiritless subjectivity. It is what is richest in spirit—but [in that] there is still reversal into what is poorest in spirit.

We have said that religion is here its own content; inasmuch as it is the content, what is objective, this means that what it contains *is* religion. The beyond is the object, and religion as religion is only the one side, whose content stands on the side of finite subjectivity.

Thus the absolute religion has essentially the character of *subjectivity* or of *infinite form,* which is equivalent to substance. This subjectivity—we may call it knowledge, cognition, pure intelligence—is infinite form, the infinite elasticity of substance that enables it to dirempt itself inwardly and make itself its own object. Hence the content is an organic content because it is this *infinite,* substantial *subjectivity* that makes itself into the object and content. In this antithesis one side is termed the finite and the other the infinite. The infinite side—God as spirit—is when God remains above, when God is not [present] as the living spirit of God's community, [but then] God is characterized in only a one-sided way as object. This is the first point in the definition of the concept [of this religion].

This is the concept. It is the concept of the idea, of the absolute idea. The reality is now that spirit is *for* spirit, has itself as its object.

2. THE REVELATORY RELIGION

The second point in the definition is that this religion is the *revelatory religion.* God reveals godself. As we have seen, "revealing" refers to the primal division [*Urteil*] of infinite subjectivity or infinite form; it means determining oneself to be for an other. This revealing of self-manifesting belongs to the essence of spirit itself. *A spirit that is not revelatory is not spirit.* It is said that God has created the world and has revealed godself. This is spoken of as something God did once, that will not happen again, and as being the sort of event that may either occur or not occur: God could have revealed godself, God could have created the world, or not; God's doing so is one of God's capricious, contingent characteristics, so to speak, and does not belong to the concept of God godself. But it is the essence of God as spirit *to be for an other,* i.e., to *reveal* godself. God does not create the world once and for all, but is the eternal creator, the eternal act of self-revelation. This *actus* is what God is; this is God's concept, God's definition.

[True] religion is thus revelatory inasmuch as it is spirit *for* spirit. It is the religion of spirit—not a secret that has to remain closed but rather is open or revelatory and has to be for an other, but for an other that is only momentarily so. God is this process of positing the other and then sublating it in God's eternal movement. Thus the essence of spirit is to appear to itself, to manifest itself. [If we ask,] "What is revealed?" the answer is that what God reveals is this infinite form that we have called subjectivity; i.e., it is the act of determining or positing distinctions, of positing content. What God reveals in this way is that God *is* manifestation, i.e., the process of constituting these distinctions within godself. It is God's nature and God's concept eternally to make these distinctions and at the same time to take them back into godself, and thereby to be present to godself. The content that becomes manifest [*offenbar*] is what is revealed [*geoffenbart*], namely, that God is for an *other* but [also] eternally for *godself.* This is what is specified by "revealing."

3. THE RELIGION OF TRUTH AND FREEDOM

Thirdly, therefore, this religion is the religion of *truth* and the religion of *freedom.* For "truth" means that in what is objective we are not relating to something alien. "Freedom" expresses the very thing that truth is, but with a logical character of negation. The [consummate] religion is the religion of truth: it is precisely *spirit* that is for spirit, and it is so *for* spirit. Spirit is its presupposition; we begin with spirit. In this way spirit is identical with itself, it is the eternal intuition of itself; i.e., it is simultaneously comprehended only as a result, an end. In this way it is both what presupposes itself and the result, and it *is* only an end—as this self-differentiation, this act of presupposing itself. Truth consists in the mutual adequacy to each other of what we have characterized as subject and object. That spirit as object *to itself* constitutes the reality, the concept, the idea: this is the truth.

Likewise, it is the religion of freedom. In the abstract, freedom means relating oneself to something objective without its being something alien. This is the same definition as that of truth, except that in the case of freedom the categorial moment of the negation of difference or of otherness is emphasized, and freedom therefore appears in the form of reconciliation. Reconciliation begins with differentiated entities standing opposed to each other—God, who confronts a world that is estranged from God, and a world that is estranged from its essence. [They are] in conflict with one another, and [they are] external to one another. Reconciliation is the negation of this separation, this division, and means that each cognizes itself in the other, finds itself in its essence. Reconciliation, consequently, is freedom and is not something quiescent; rather it is activity, the movement that makes the estrangement disappear.

All of these [moments]—reconciliation, truth, freedom—constitute a universal process, and thus cannot be expressed in a simple proposition except one-sidedly. One can express it in a more determinate fashion by saying that it is posited in a religion that a representation of the unity of divine and human nature occurs. God has become human: this therefore is a revelation. This unity is to be regarded as implicitly [present], but as revealed it is *only* what is implicit. Yet it is the movement that consists in being eternally brought forth, and this bringing forth is *liberation, reconciliation,* which is only possible precisely through what is implicit. The *substance* that is identical with itself is this unity, which as such is the foundation; but as *subjectivity* it is what brings forth. We may accept this as the concept of this religion.

That this idea is absolute truth—this is the result of the whole of philosophy. In its pure form it is what is logical, but is also the result of considering the concrete world. This is the truth: that nature, life, spirit are completely organic—i.e., that everything that exists on its own account is itself just the mirror image of this idea, such that the idea presents itself in each thing as singularized, as a process involving it, so that it manifests this unity in itself. But what is singularized is not a single [entity].

4. RELATION TO PRECEDING RELIGIONS

The general relation [of the consummate religion] to the preceding religions has been expounded from the beginning [of these lectures] and follows from what has just been said. First we had *nature religion,* i.e., religion from the standpoint of *consciousness* alone. In the absolute religion this standpoint is still [present], but only momentarily, as a transitory moment, whereas in nature religion it was the essential determination. In nature religion God is represented as an other, in a natural configuration— sun, light, mountain, river—so that the [divine] is defined as an other; or in other words religion has only the form of consciousness.

The second form was that of *spiritual religion,* but it was the religion of the spirit that remains finitely determined; to this extent it is the religion of *self-consciousness.* Here we saw absolute power, or necessity: the One who is absolute power and who is wisdom only in an abstract sense is not yet spirit because he is only abstract power—not absolute subjectivity with respect to his content but only abstract necessity, simple, abstract self-possession.[3] Abstraction constitutes finitude, and it is the particular powers and gods, defined according to their spiritual content, that first constitute the totality.[4]

The third form, which we are now considering, is the *religion of freedom,* the religion of the self-consciousness (or of the consciousness) that is *self-contained,* for in it there is equally both the objectivity of spirit and the freedom of self-possession: this is [*its*] definition of consciousness. *Freedom* is the [true] definition of self-consciousness.

I. The Metaphysical Concept of God[5]

We now proceed to the *abstract, metaphysical* concept. The *concrete* concept of this sphere [i.e., the consummate religion] is that spirit is *for* spirit and that it is itself spirit only in this way. The two sides into which spirit differentiates itself are both spirit, together they are the totality, and just this is its reality now. With the metaphysical concept, however, all we have before us is the pure, *abstract* concept in its determinations or moments, without these being this totality, without their having this concrete content. Therefore what now constitutes the metaphysical concept is that the content is the *concept,* the pure concept, and that we only have to discuss the pure concept—but it is also real per se. Concretely the pure concept is the concept that is for itself; in other words, the concreteness of spirit means that spirit inwardly differentiates itself into itself, inwardly opposes itself and sets itself as another spirit over against itself. The definition we have here is that we have the pure concept, which realizes itself, which is in itself real; and we here call this determination merely "reality"—in other words, [it has] also to be defined vis-à-vis the concept as either being or existence [*Existenz*]. But there is a content in it, too—and this content is God, but God as represented, not God as spirit internally developed; and we shall see that it is the pure concept. In appearance, however, we have the concept of God—the fact that it is the concept of God that *realizes* itself; but, as we shall see, what ultimately matters here is the general relationship of the concept to reality or to being.

The content seems to be a determinate concept; [it seems that] the discussion is about the concept of God, and that God's being follows from God's concept. And it seems, at first, that we are discussing a determinate or specific concept of God, not the concept generally. But we shall see that this content "God" dissolves itself, that it essentially has the meaning of the *unity* of the concept; i.e., it has the meaning both of the pure concept and of reality, and of the unity of the two.

The metaphysical concept is the concept of God and the unity of that concept with reality. In the form of the proof of God's being [*Sein*], of the determinate being [*Dasein*] of God, of the existence [*Existenz*] of God, what we have is a proof which is just this transition or mediation: that God's being follows from God's concept. This is what is called the *ontological proof.*

It should be noted that in the other proofs we proceeded from finite being, which was the immediate, and from it we concluded to the infinite, the genuine being that appeared for us in the form of infinitude, necessary, absolute power, the power that is at the same time wisdom, and posits its own end inwardly. But here our starting point is the concept, and the transition is from the concept to being. Both ways are necessary, and in order to demonstrate this unity it is necessary to begin both from being and from the concept, for the identity of the two is what is genuine. Both the concept and being (determinate being, the world, the finite) are one-sided determinations, and only in the idea is their truth to be found, i.e., the truth that they are both *posited*. Neither of them must be defined solely as the term that permanently has the initiative or is the origin; they must rather be portrayed as passing over into the other, i.e., each of them must be a posited term. In this way each displays itself as a transition into an other, or as a moment, so that it must be demonstrated of both of them that they are *moments*. This transition has two opposite meanings: each term is portrayed as a moment; i.e., on the one hand, as what has being, it is something that passes over—essentially it is by passing over from the immediate to the other (so that each of them is reduced to something merely *posited*); on the other hand, each term also has the significance that it is posited by something else, it is brought forth. For if a determination is shown to have been brought forth, then it has equally been shown to be merely something set up. In this transition each term sets itself down as something transient, not genuinely primitive. The other is then what has issued forth from it. Hence the one side is movement, the passing over from finite to infinite, but so too is the other.

Now we see the transition from concept to being. Here the argument begins from the concept, and more directly from the concept *of God*. The transition to being is to be demonstrated from this content, or from this concept. This is the first point; but secondly it must at once be said that the category of "being" is in fact totally impoverished; it is the relation of self-identity, abstract equality with self, the ultimate abstraction—affirmation, indeed, but in its ultimate abstraction, completely indeterminate immediacy and self-reference. So if there were nothing more in the concept of God, or [in] the concept as such, then at least this utterly poor abstraction must belong to it. For the concept itself is defined only as infinitude or, in a more concrete sense, as the unity of universal and particular, as the universality that particularizes itself and so returns into itself. Thus this negation of the negative is the sublation of the difference, this relation to self *is* being, taken abstractly. This determination, this self-identity, is *ipso facto* essentially contained in the concept.

In the third place it must be said that the transition from concept to being is of the utmost importance and holds the deepest interest for reason. To grasp this relationship of concept to being is also the special concern of our time. We must now explain in more detail the reason why this transition or relationship is of such interest. The appearing of this antithesis between concept and being is a sign of *subjectivity,* a sign that subjectivity has attained its being-for-self and has arrived at totality. The essential characteristic of the revelatory religion is the form through which substance is spirit. This antithesis of concept and being appears so difficult and endless because reality—this one side that we have called the side of subjective spirit—because finite spirit has arrived inwardly at the comprehension of its infinitude. Only when the subject is the totality and has inwardly attained this freedom, this infinitude that belongs to it, only then is it being. Then it is the case that *this* subject is indifferent to *this* being, that the subject is *for itself* and being stands over against it as an indifferent other. Then, too, the other is a thing-in-itself, something that stands over against it, a reality that exists outside it. This is the specific reason why the antithesis can appear to be endless; and at the same time, therefore, the impulse to resolve the antithesis is present in the subject. The requirement that this antithesis—this other—should be resolved is directly involved in the subject's totality, but the task of sublating it has become infinitely difficult just because the antithesis itself is so endless, and the other, as something out there beyond it, is so entirely free.

This then is the grandeur of this standpoint, the standpoint of the modern world: that the subject has so sunk itself within itself that the finite knows itself as infinite and in this infinitude it is afflicted with finitude, is afflicted with this antithesis that it is driven to resolve. The question now is how it is to be resolved. This antithesis pertains to modern times. How is it to be resolved? I am the subject, I am free, I am a person for myself, and outside me there is a world. Precisely because I am free, I freely let that other go from me too, the other that is "out there" and remains so. The ancients did not arrive at this antithesis, they did not come to this estrangement. To reach it is the highest capacity of spirit, and to be spirit is nothing but the grasping of this antithesis, the comprehending of oneself infinitely within it. The way the standpoint is given for us now is that we have the *concept* of God on the one side, and on the other side, set against the concept, we have *being.* What is required, therefore, is the mediation of the two, in such a way that the concept, which is self-contained infinitude, resolves itself into being, and that being is *conceived* from the concept. What this proof requires is that what is purely and simply other, the contrary of the concept, should proceed from the concept. The way this happens, and the form that it has for understanding, must now be briefly expounded.

As we have already said, the shape that this mediation takes is what is called the ontological proof of the existence of God, the argument that takes the concept of God as its starting point. But what is the concept of God? The concept of God is fixed as follows: God is the most real of all beings, the conceptual sum of all reality;[6] God can only be grasped affirmatively, God is inwardly determined, a content, but one that is to contain no limitation; God is the whole of reality but is only reality, without limitation; but in fact this leaves us with only a dead abstraction, as we remarked earlier. The second point is [to show] that this concept is possible, that it contains no contradiction, and [this] is shown according to the canon of the understanding. About this second point it is said that being is a reality, while nonbeing is a negation, a lack, utterly antithetical. Being is therefore reality, and hence it figures among the real predicates of God. God contains all reality; being is a reality; therefore God also contains this reality, being.[7]

The next point is Kant's objection to this proof, an objection that has become universal, a refutation of the proof that all the world takes for granted. Kant says, to be precise, that on the one hand we have the concept of God—but that we cannot "pluck" [*herausklauben*] being from this concept, for being is something other than the concept. The two are distinguished and opposed to each other; therefore the concept cannot contain being; "being" stands opposed to it. He goes on to say that "being" is not a "reality." Being is not a reality, therefore it is not contained in the concept of God, so that it is not a determination of content, or predicate. Being is no predicate and therefore not a "reality." Whether I imagine a hundred thalers or actually possess them makes no difference; the concept is one and the same whether I possess them or imagine them.[8] Kant thus takes the content as that which *constitutes* the concept; it is not what is *contained* in the concept. One can say this, to be sure, if one understands by "the concept" the determination of content, and distinguishes that from the *form,* which contains thought on the one side and being on the other. All content is thus on the side of the concept, and being is the other to this content. What this amounts to is (briefly) that the concept is not being and the two are distinct; this is the basic notion, to which frequent reference has already been made. We have no cognition of God, we know nothing of God; to be sure, we can form concepts of God, but the fact that we form a representation of this kind does not mean that these concepts are so. This, then, is what the Kantian destruction of the proof reduces to.

We know quite well, of course, that one can build castles in the air, but that this does not bring them into existence. Thus the argument has a popular appeal, which is why Kant has, in the general judgment, produced a refutation [of the ontological argument].

Anselm of Canterbury, a thoroughly learned philosophical theologian of the twelfth century, set forth the proof as follows. God is what is most perfect, the conceptual sum of all reality; but if God is merely a representation, merely a thought or concept, God is not what is most perfect, for we regard as perfect only that which is not merely represented, but also has being.[9] This is entirely correct, and it is a presupposition that underlies all philosophy. If it is permitted to make presuppositions, this presupposition is one that all persons hold within themselves, namely, that what is only represented is only imperfect, and only what also has reality is perfect. Now God is what is most perfect, therefore God must be real, God must have being, just as God is concept. Our notions include both the view that concept and representation are different, and likewise the view that what is merely imagined is very imperfect, whereas God is also what is most perfect. Kant does not demonstrate the difference between concept and being; it is merely accepted in popular fashion. We grant its validity where we can appeal to sound human sense, [i.e., where we speak] of imperfect things and representations.

To establish the case more soundly, [the following] remark must be made regarding this form, whether we mean the form of the Anselmian proof or the form of the argument adduced in the proof nowadays. The latter runs as follows: God is the conceptual sum of all forms of reality; consequently God also includes being. This is entirely correct. Being is so poor a determination that it belongs immediately to the concept. The other point, however, is that being and concept are also different from one another. Being and thinking, the real and the ideal, reality and ideality, are different from and opposed to each other. True difference is also opposition in any case, and the task therefore is to sublate this antithesis. The unity of the two determinations has to be demonstrated in such a way that it results from the negation of the antithesis, and it is shown that being is contained in the concept. [To talk of] this reality as "unrestricted" is only to utter empty words, mere abstractions. So the first step is that the determination of being is exhibited as affirmatively contained in the concept; this then is the unity of concept and being.

But in the second place they are also different from each other; thus their unity is the negative unity of the two, and the task now is to sublate the difference. The difference must be spoken of also, and what has to be done is to establish and demonstrate the unity *after* this differentiation. This demonstration is the task of logic. That the concept *is* the movement by which it determines itself to be, that it is this dialectical movement of self-determination into being, or into its own opposite—this logical dimension is a further development, which we do not find in the ontological proof— and this is where it is defective.

Let us now consider first the form of the Anselmian proof and then compare with it the view of the present time.

Concerning the form of Anselm's thought, we have remarked that his argument goes that the concept of God *presupposes* reality because God is what is most perfect. Another point to notice is this: I have said that the essential thing, the first point at issue, is the transition from concept to reality, i.e., that the concept objectifies itself and that, properly speaking, it makes no difference whether what has to realize itself is the concept of *God*—although it seems that this necessity can only hold good [for] God. The point is that the concept objectifies itself for itself.

So, then, that God is what is most perfect is presupposed. But when God is only posited in the imagination, without reality, then God is not that; and it is when measured against what is most perfect that the mere concept of God appears to be deficient. The criterion is the concept of perfection, and by that criterion God as mere concept, thought, the subjectivity of this content of God, is inadequate. God is supposedly what is most perfect; God in the form of thought does not correspond to this. God is what is most perfect; it is this then [that is here presupposed].

The second thing to note in this connection is that the "perfect" is only an indeterminate notion [*Vorstellung*].[10] What is it then to be perfect? For it to be something determinate, the perfect must be defined. The definition of what is "perfect" we can see immediately in what is counterposed to the referent of this notion. For what is imperfect is just the mere thought of God, and hence the perfect is the unity of the thought (or the concept) with reality. Thus this unity is here presupposed. The perfect, therefore, is not mere subjective being but objectivity.

The third point is that since God is posited as what is most perfect, God has no further definition [in the argument]. God is only what God is; God is only what is perfect, and what is perfect is the unity of the concept with reality. God only *is* as such, and this is God's determinateness. Hence it is evident that the only thing that is properly relevant here is this unity of concept and reality. This unity is the definition of perfection and of God godself at the same time. It is also in fact the definition of the idea in general; but it is only the abstract idea, and certainly there is more than that involved in the definition of God.

The second point [regarding what has just been said] about Anselm's way of [abstracting] the concept is that its presupposition is in fact the unity of concept and reality. This is why the proof cannot afford satisfaction for reason, since the presupposition is precisely what is at issue. That this presupposition should now be proved, that the concept sublates its one-sidedness, that it determines itself implicitly, objectifies itself, realizes itself, this is a further insight which [needs] first to have emerged from the nature of the concept. This insight, which is not present—and could not occur—in Anselm or even in later times, is an insight into the extent to which the concept itself sublates its one-sidedness. This is one of the most important points.

The other thing [we said we would do] is to compare Anselm's position with the view of our own time, which derives in particular from Kant. According to this view, to say that we think is to say this: that we intuit and we will, and our willing and intuiting is accompanied by thinking. We think too, we comprehend too; a human being is a concrete [being] of sensation, and also a rational [being]. Secondly, so we are told, the concept of God—the idea as such, the infinite, the unlimited in general—is *only* a concept that we make for ourselves; we should not forget that it is only a concept and its place is in our heads. Why do we say, "It is only a concept, it is the indeterminate, and hence it is only something imperfect"? The concept is something imperfect inasmuch as thinking, conceiving, is only one quality, one human activity among others. That is to say that we measure our comprehension by the reality that we have before us, and by concrete human beings. To be sure, human beings do not just think, they are also sentient, and even in thought they can have sensible objects. In fact this is the merely subjective aspect of conceiving, that we only find it to be imperfect on account of the criterion we have, since this criterion is the concrete human being. One might also say that the concept is declared to be only a concept and that the sensible is declared to be reality. What we can grasp with our hands, what we see, feel, or sense, this is what we call reality—a sensory datum, something sensed. So reality is also what we have sense awareness of—so far as that goes. One could assert this, and indeed many people do say it. They acknowledge as actual only what they sense; however, the fact that there are people who ascribe actuality only to the sensible, not to the spiritual, is not such a terrible tragedy. It is the concrete human nature, the total subjectivity of human beings, that hovers before their eyes as the whole and [that they] take as a yardstick. By that standard, conceiving is conceiving and nothing more.

When we now compare the two, Anselm's pattern, his thought, and the thought of the present day, what they have in common is the fact that they both make presuppositions. Anselm presupposes perfection, which in itself is still indeterminate, while the modern view presupposes concrete humanity as such in a general sense. Compared with perfection on the one hand and this empirically concrete unity on the other, the concept is seen as something one-sided and unsatisfying. In the thought of Anselm the definition of perfection also has, in fact, the sense that it is the unity of concept and reality. Later on, in Descartes and in Spinoza too,[11] God is the first reality; in God we find the absolute unity of thought with space, *cogito ergo sum,* absolute substance—it is the same in Leibniz too.[12] What we thus have on one side is the presupposition of what is concrete in fact, as the unity of thought and being; and measured by this standard, the subjective concept appears defective. The modern view insists that this is as far as we can go, to say that the concept is only the concept, the concept is as it were placed on one side, and does not correspond to the concrete. Anselm, on the other hand, says we must give up wanting to let the subjective concept stand as something firm and independent; on the contrary, we must get away from this one-sidedness and [begin from] the unity of subjective and objective in general.

Both views have in common that they have presuppositions; the difference is that the modern view is based on the concrete, while the metaphysical, Anselmian view is based on absolute thought, the absolute idea, which is the unity of concept and reality. The old view is superior insofar as it takes the concrete to be not empirical human beings and empirical actuality but thoughts. It does not take its stand on the claim that we must hold fast to the imperfect, adhere to the subjective concept; [instead it takes its stand on] a concept that is at the same time reality. There is an unresolved contradiction in the modern view because both what is concrete and the one-sided subjective concept are accepted as valid. Now in recognizing the concrete, we have already passed beyond the subjective concept. But it is the subjective concept that is valid and must be accepted as something subjective; one must stand by it, one must not pass beyond it. Thus the older view is at a great advantage in that it is founded on the idea; in one respect the modern view is more advanced, in that it posits the concrete as unity of the concept and reality, whereas the former view took its stand upon an abstract form of perfection. But on the other hand [it has] lapsed into the empirical way of looking at things. Certainly Descartes and Spinoza made further progress in the defining of "the perfect." But in saying that substance is the unity of concept and being, Spinoza [and Descartes[13]] were merely presupposing it to be so, and not proving it. It is only thinking that has that unity immediately before it.

II. The Development of the Idea of God[14]

Our next step is to proceed to concrete representation, to the development and more specific determination of the idea.

We have defined the metaphysical concept as the concept that realizes itself, the one that is itself real; the whole of finitude subsists within it. God is the absolute idea, the fact that reality matches the concept. What we have called reality in the metaphysical concept is now reality as such, being, etc. But, more precisely, it is not *natural* being. In nature religion, "being" was naturalness in general—the sky, the sun, etc. The reality we are now speaking of constitutes the determinateness of God. It is not something natural. Similarly, God's determinateness is not constituted by a predicate or a plurality of predicates. "Predicates" (characteristics such as wisdom, justice, goodness) are not, to be sure, natural and immediate; but they are stabilized by reflection—[each predicate is] a content that has attained through reflection the form of universality, of relation to self. Thus each determinate content has become just as immovable, just as rigidly *for itself*, as the natural content was to begin with. About the natural we say, "It is." These "predicates" are just as self-identical as [natural] immediacy. The predicates do not correspond to the reality of the concept; the reality of the concept is more precisely the first [natural] reality, namely, that the concept in itself is real, wholly free totality, free totality present to itself. The one side, spirit, the subjective side, the concept, is itself the idea, while the other side, reality, is likewise the whole or spirit, posited at the same time as distinct. Reality is thus the reality of the idea itself, in such a way that each side is the idea, the free idea, present to itself, so that spirit, this idea, knows itself, is present to itself. It is real, places itself vis-à-vis [itself] as another spirit, and is then the unity of the two. And this is what the idea *is*.

The next point is to explicate the idea [of God in its self-development] as follows. Universal spirit—the totality that it is—posits itself [*setzt sich*] in its three determinations, i.e., it develops itself, realizes itself; and it is complete only at the end, which is at the same time its presupposition [*Voraussetzung*]. At first, it is in itself as the totality; [then] it sets itself forth [*setzt sich voraus*], and likewise it *is* only at the end.[15]

We thus have to consider spirit in the three forms, *the three elements,* into which it posits itself. These three forms are: (1) Eternal being, within and present to itself—the form of *universality.* (2) The form of *appearance,* that of *particularization,* of being for others. (3) The form of return from appearance into itself, the form of *absolute singularity,* of absolute presence-to-self.[16]

It is in these three forms that the divine idea explicates itself. Spirit is the divine history, the process of self-differentiation, of diremption and return into self; it is the *divine* history and therefore is to be viewed in each of the three forms.

These three forms are also determined as follows in regard to *subjective consciousness.* The first form [is determined] as the element of *thought,* that God is in pure thought as God is in and for godself; God is manifest but not yet issued forth into appearance—God in God's eternal essence, present to godself, yet manifest. The second form is that God is [present] in the element of *representation,* in the element of particularization, that consciousness is entrapped in its relation to the other; this is appearance. The third element is that of *subjectivity* as such. Partly this subjectivity is immediate subjectivity, disposition, thought, representation, sensation, but also it is partly a subjectivity that is the concept, i.e., it is thinking reason, the thinking of free spirit, which is inwardly free only through the return [into itself].

We can also explain these three forms as follows. We can say that these histories take place as it were in different *locales.* Thus the first divine history is *outside the world,* it is not in space, but outside finitude as such— God as God is in and for godself. The second locale is the *world,* the divine history as real, God having God's determinate being in the world. Thirdly there is the *inner place,* the community, first of all in the world, but also the community insofar as it simultaneously raises itself to heaven, or already has heaven within itself on earth—the community which, as the church, is full of grace, and in which God is active and present.

We can then define these three elements differently in regard to *time.* Thus the first element is God outside of time, God as the eternal idea in the element of the pure thought of *eternity,* but eternity only in the sense in which it is set against time. This time that is in and for itself explicates itself by unfolding into past, present, and future. The second element is the divine history as appearance, but as a *past* time; it is [there], for appearance means something that is, that has being, but it has a mode of being that has been reduced to mere show. As appearance it is an immediately determinate being, which is simultaneously negated; this is the past—exactly what is called history, which proves itself to be mere appearance by the very fact that it is *only* history. The third element is the *present,* but only the limited present, not the eternal present as such but the present that distinguishes past and future from itself. This is the element of heart and mind, of imme- diate subjectivity—the spiritual "now" as it is in this [single] individual. But this present has also to be the third element; the community raises itself to heaven as well. So it is a present that raises itself, it is essentially recon- ciled, brought to consummation through the negation of its immediacy, consummated in universality, but in a consummation that is not yet achieved, and which must therefore be grasped as *future*—a now of the pre- sent that has consummation before its eyes; but because the community is posited now in the order of time, the consummation is distinguished from this "now" and is posited as future. These are the three universal ideas in which we have to consider the divine history.

It should be noted that I have not made the distinctions that I made pre- viously between *concept, figure,* and *cultus*;[17] in the subsequent treatment we shall in fact see how the relationship [among the forms of the divine idea also] enters into the cultus. In general it may be remarked that the ele- ment in which *we* exist is [that of] the Spirit. Spirit is simply self-manifes- tation, it *is* utterly *for* itself. So as it is grasped, it is never found alone but always has the character of being utterly manifest or of being for an other, for its *own* other, i.e., for the side that is finite spirit. And the cultus is the relationship of finite spirit to absolute spirit. Accordingly, we at once find before us the cultic aspect in each of these elements.

In this connection we have to distinguish between how the idea is for the *concept* in the various elements and how this comes to *representational* expression. Religion is universal and does not exist only for educated, conceptual thought, for philosophical consciousness; instead the truth of the idea of God is manifest for representational consciousness and it has this necessary characteristic: that it *must* be universal[ly accessible] for representation.

A. THE FIRST ELEMENT: THE IDEA OF GOD IN AND FOR ITSELF

The first element in which we have to consider the idea of God is the element of thought, the idea in its eternal present, as it is for free thought, the thought whose basic character is to be untroubled light, or identity with itself. This is an element that is not yet burdened by other-being.

In this element too a defining character is necessary because thinking *in general* is different from *conceptual* thinking as such. The eternal idea is in and for itself in thought, as the idea in its absolute truth. Therefore religion essentially has a content, and the content is an object. Religion is *human* religion, and (among its other modes) human consciousness is *thinking* consciousness, so that the idea must also be [available] for thinking consciousness. But it is not only in this way (not just among other modes) that the human being is a thinker. It is in thinking that humanity truly exists for the first time. The universal object, the essence of the object, *is* only for thinking, and since in religion God is the object, God is such essentially for thinking. God is *object* just as spirit is consciousness, and God is *for thinking,* because it is God who is the object.

It is not for sensory or reflective consciousness that God can have being *as God,* i.e., in God's eternal essentiality in and for itself. God's *appearance* is another matter: appearance *is* for the sentient consciousness. But if God were *merely* in sensation, human beings would stand no higher than the animals; to be sure, God also is for feeling, but only in God's appearance. Nor is God this or that limited content for the argumentative consciousness (the thinking of the well-ordered understanding). God is not that kind of content either. God is therefore essentially *for thought.* This is what we have to say if we take the subjective, the human, as our starting point. But we also arrive at precisely the same point if we begin with God. Spirit only is as a self-revealing, a self-differentiation *for spirit.* This [other] spirit, for which it *is,* is the eternal idea, thinking spirit, spirit in the element of its freedom. In this field God is the act of *self-revealing* because God is spirit; but God is not yet the act of *appearing.* Thus it is of the essence that God is for spirit.

The second point to note is that spirit *thinks* spirit. In this pure thinking there is initially no difference that divides them; there is nothing between them. Thinking is pure unity with itself, where all obscurity and darkness disappears. This thinking can also be called pure *intuition,* as the simple activity of thinking, such that between the subject and object there is no [difference] and, properly speaking, subject and object are not yet present. This thinking has no limitation, it is this wholly universal activity, and the content is only the universal itself. *Thinking* is simply *knowing.*

The third point is that the absolute diremption is also differentiation. How does this come about? Thinking as *actus* is indeterminate. The very first distinction is for the two sides we have seen to be distinguished as the two modes of the principle, according to the starting point adopted. One side, that of subjective thinking, is the movement of thinking insofar as it begins from immediate, singular being and elevates itself therein to the universal, to the infinite, as we have seen it do in the first proofs of the existence of God. To the extent that it has arrived at the universal, thinking is unlimited; its end is infinitely pure thinking in which all the mist of finitude has disappeared. At that point it thinks God: all particularity has disappeared, and thus religion, the thought of God, begins. The second side is that which adopts the other starting point, which proceeds from the universal, from the result of the first side—a result that is also movement—from the universal, from thinking, from the concept; and hence it consists in differentiating itself inwardly, but keeping the difference *within itself* in such a way that it does not disturb the universality. The universality is here one that has a distinction within itself, yet is in harmony with itself. This is the abstract content of thinking, i.e., it is abstract thinking, it is the result that has elevated itself.

The two sides stand opposed to each other as follows. The first and simpler mode of thinking is also a process, an inward mediation; but this process goes on outside it, it is so to speak beyond it, behind this thought. Only insofar as the thought has elevated itself does religion begin. Thus there is in religion pure, motionless, *abstract* thinking; the concrete, on the other hand, pertains to its *object,* for this is the thinking that starts from the universal, differentiates itself [from it], yet is in harmony with it. This concrete element is the object for thinking simply as such. So this thinking, as such, is abstract thinking and therefore it is *finite* thinking; for the abstract is finite. The concrete is the truth, the *infinite* object.

Regarding the content more specifically, the following remarks need to be made. We have long been familiar with them, so we can be brief. There is little to be said about them, and we need only call to mind what is essential.

In the first place, God is spirit; in God's abstract character God is defined as universal spirit that particularizes itself. This is the absolute truth, and the religion that has this content is the true religion. In the Christian religion this is what is called the *Trinity*—it is "triune" insofar as number categories are applied. It is the God who differentiates godself but remains identical with godself in the process. The Trinity is called the *mystery* of God; its content is mystical, i.e., speculative. But what is for reason is not a secret. In the Christian religion one *knows,* and this is a secret only for the finite understanding, and for the thought that is based on sense experience. There the distinctions are immediate, and natural things are accepted as valid; this is the mode of externality. But as soon as God is defined as spirit, externality is sublated, and for sense this *is* a mystery; for sense everything is external to everything else—objects change, and the senses are aware of them in different ways. The changing is itself a sensible process, occurring in time. The sun exists: once it did not exist, some day it will not exist—all these states are external to one another in time. The being [of a thing] is *now,* and its nonbeing is separated from now; for time is what keeps the determinations apart from one another, external to one another. For the understanding too [nonbeing] is other [than being]; thus the understanding, like the sensible [realm], is a holding fast to abstract characteristics in such a way that each exists on its own account. The negative is distinct from the positive; so for the understanding it is something else.

Certainly, when we say "Trinity" or "triune," the unfortunate formal pattern of a number series (1, 2, 3) comes into play. Reason can employ all the *relationships* of the understanding, but only insofar as it destroys the *forms* of the understanding. And so it is with the Trinity. Hence the very word "triune" is an extreme of misuse as far as the understanding is concerned—for it believes the mere fact of the formula being used establishes its rights; but to use it as one does here to say "three equals one" is to misuse it. Consequently it is an easy matter to point out contradictions in such ideas, distinctions that go to the point of being opposites. Everything concrete, everything living contains contradiction within itself; only the dead understanding is identical with itself. But the contradiction is also resolved in the idea, and the resolution is spiritual unity. The living thing is an example of what cannot be grasped by the understanding. "God is love" is an expression very much to the point: here God is present to sensation; as "love" God is a person, and the relationship is such that the consciousness of the One is to be had only in the consciousness of the other. God is conscious of godself, as Goethe says,[18] only in the other, in absolute externalization. This is spiritual unity in the form of feeling. In the relationship of friendship, of love, of the family, this identity of one with the other is also to be found. It is contrary to the understanding that I, who exist for myself and am therefore self-consciousness, should have my consciousness rather in another; but the reconciliation [of this conflict] is the abstract content—the substantial, universal *ethical* relationship as such.

The second remark is a reflection upon the foregoing. We can find traces of the Trinity in other religions. They occur, for example, in the Trimurti or in the triad of Plato, while Aristotle says: We believe we have invoked the gods completely only when we have invoked them three times.[19] But wherever else we turn, we encounter only imperfect definitions. In Plato,[20] the "one" and the "other" and the "mixture" are wholly abstract in character, while in the Trimurti the wildest mode [of fanciful imagination] has entered into play, and the third moment is not that of spiritual return, for, as Siva, it is merely alteration, not spirit.[21]

A further point is that in the Christian religion it is not merely asserted that God is triune but also that God subsists in *three persons*. This is being-for-self taken to the extreme, the extreme being not only *one* but *person*, personality. Being a person is the highest intensity of being-for-self. Here the contradiction seems to be pushed so far that no resolution, no mingling of one person with another, is possible. But just this resolution is expressed in the assertion that God is *only* one; the three persons are thus posited merely as a transient moment or aspect. "Personality" expresses the fact that the antithesis is to be taken as absolute, that it is not a mild one, and it is only when it is pushed to this extreme that it sublates itself. Of this too we have a representation. In love and friendship it is the *person* that maintains itself and *through* its love achieves its subjectivity, which is its personality. But in religion, if one holds fast to personality in the abstract sense, then one has three gods, and subjectivity is likewise lost. Infinite form, infinite power is then all there is to the moment of divinity. Furthermore, if one holds fast to personality as an unresolved [moment], one has *evil*. For the personality that does not sacrifice itself in the divine idea is evil. It is precisely in the divine unity that personality, just as much as it is posited, is posited as resolved; only in appearance does the negativity of personality appear distinct from that whereby it is sublated.

The Trinity has also been brought under the relationship of Father, Son, and Spirit. This is a childlike relationship, a childlike form. The understanding has no other category, no other relationship that would be comparable with this in respect of its appropriateness. But we must be aware that this is merely a figurative relationship; spirit does not enter into this relationship. "Love" would be more suitable, for the spirit [of love] is assuredly what is truthful.

There is a third point that we must not overlook, because it has given rise to many so-called heresies. As we have said,[22] the abstract God, the Father, is the universal, what is all-encompassing, what is One. We are now on the level of spirit; the universal here includes everything within itself. The other, the Son, is infinite particularity, the [realm of] appearance; the third, the Spirit, is singularity as such. But we must be aware that all three are spirit. In the third, we say, God is the Spirit; but the Spirit is also "presup-posing,"[23] the third is also the first. It is essential to hold on to this; it is explained by the nature of the [logical] concept. We encounter it in every goal and every kind of life process. Life maintains itself; self-maintenance means entering into differentiation, into the struggle with particularity, [the organism] finding itself distinguished from an inorganic nature, and its going outwards. Thus life is only a result because it has produced itself and is a product; moreover if we are asked, "What is produced?" the answer is that what is produced is the life process itself, i.e., life is its own presuppo-sition. This is just what the universal consists in: that it works through its process and that the process gives rise to nothing new; what is brought forth is already [there] from the beginning. It is the same with loving and being loved in return. Insofar as love is present, its utterance and all the activities to which it gives rise, whereby it is simultaneously brought forth and sup-ported, merely confirm it. What is brought forth is already there: the confir-mation of love is a confirmation whereby nothing comes forth save what is already there. Similarly, spirit sets itself forth,[24] it is the initiating.

The differentiation that the divine life goes through is not an external [process] but must be defined solely as internal, so that the first, the Father, is to be grasped just like the last [the Spirit]. Thus the process is nothing but a play of self-maintenance, a play of self-confirmation.

This definition is important in that it provides the criterion for evaluating many representations of the essence of divinity, and for appraising and rec-ognizing their deficiencies. We must recognize where they are defective, and the defect arises especially from the fact that this definition is often overlooked.

I have already pointed out that hints and traces of the idea of God, which essentially is the Trinity, emerged most notably shortly before and after the time when the Christian religion appeared on the scene—the church called these other views heresies. These are the Gnostic representations, which arise from the need to *cognize* God.[25] Philo, a Jewish Platonist, defines God as the *on,* as what has being, in other words the hidden God who is unknow-able, uncommunicative, inconceivable. If the first [the Father] is defined as what is only abstractly universal, and [all] determinations are allowed to come only *after* what is universal, *after* the *on,* then this first is, to be sure, inconceivable because it is without content; anything conceivable is con-crete and can *be* conceived only inasmuch as it is determined as a moment. The defect lies here, therefore, in the fact that the first is not itself grasped as entire totality. The second definition is as the Logos, *Nous,* that which reveals itself, the [first] mover, which posits differentiation, the moment of determining generally. In respect of this second definition there is a great diversity of representations—the Son of God, Sophia, Wisdom the archetype of humanity, the First Man, the eternal one, heavenly revelation of the godhead, thinking, effective power. This is the second, and is a genuine distinction that touches the quality of both; but it is still one and the same substance, so the distinction is after all just a superficial one, though defined as a difference of persons.

According to another representation, the first is the *buthos,* the abyss, the depths, the *aiōn,* the eternal one whose dwelling is in the inexpressible heights, and who is exalted above all contact, from whom nothing can be developed, the principle, the father of all essence and all existence. The first is termed *propatēr,* Father only mediately, *proarchē,* before the beginning. The revealing of this abyss, this hidden God, is defined as self-contemplation, i.e., reflection into self, concrete determination in general. Self-contemplation begets, it is in fact the begetting of the only-begotten; this begetting is how the eternal becomes comprehensible, because it is here that it achieves determination. Thus this *monogenēs,* the only-begotten one, also signifies the *Father,* the principle that grounds all essentiality etc. The defect in all these representations is that what is first is not grasped in the determination of totality, as what is last [also].

As we have seen, the content is an object for pure thinking, for the finite, subjective spirit, which is here still posited in the form of infinitude, of pure intuition, of *thinking*. This relationship must be considered in greater detail. On the one side, then, we have an absolute content, the eternal idea. This is *object,* and it is object *essentially*. Self-revelation, being object for godself, is what God essentially is. God is the concrete, the idea; for pure thinking God is object, the simple directing and concentrating of thought—in other words, pure devotion. For this thinking there is only this object, the absolute truth, before which it is simply in awe—not fear but awe. In pure thinking there is nothing to be feared, all mortality and dependence are already surrendered and removed as negated and vanishing. It is a simple and pure relationship, to which the name of reverence can be applied. This concrete [relationship] is on the one hand pure thinking; on the other it is the same thought as absolute power, essentially concrete within itself, absolute plenitude; hence the relationship to what is absolutely true is one of freedom, one of blessedness, the blissful intuition of absolute truth.

When we engage in reflection on this relationship, we see the inequality between the two sides, namely that subjective spirit is defined as universal thinking, not as concrete within itself; what is concrete within itself, the genuine idea, is the object. That for which the idea is, is only pure intuition, this universal thinking, and God only is for thinking. This thinking is not conceptual because it is abstract. It is not posited as activity, not posited as *concrete;* and the concrete object that it must be posited as, is the *truth.* Spirit bears witness unto spirit, but this spirit that bears witness to what is true is not yet posited concretely; therefore finite spirit only *receives,* the content is only something *given.* Because it is not posited as concrete in itself, [spirit] relates to itself in the sentient mode, and this is the more precise definition of the finitude of spirit. Our reflection continues as follows: that spirit, because it is finite in this way, is not *active;* it does not possess itself because it is not concrete. Reverence is its object, its essence, and hence, although it is blissful in the presence of its truth, it still does not have the character of the concrete posited with respect to itself.

This is the standpoint of the first element in general; we can now proceed to the second element.

B. THE SECOND ELEMENT: REPRESENTATION, APPEARANCE

This is the element of representation as such or of appearance.

1. DIFFERENTIATION

a. Differentiation within the Divine Life and in the World

We can say that the absolute idea—the way it is determined as an object, subsisting in and for itself—is complete. On its subjective side, however, this is not so; it is neither complete in itself—[for] it is not [yet] concrete— nor is it complete as consciousness with respect to what it has as its object. It is not reflected into self, it is not posited as *differentiated.* The subject does not view itself in the divine idea. This is the second element; it is what is lacking in the first relationship, and it has now to be supplied. In this second element the subjective aspect comes on the scene as such—and with it comes *appearance.* In its development the subjective aspect contains the ground of [true] religion, namely, the need for truth. The Christian religion begins with truth itself; this truth is God, and God is truth; and it is from God that truth first passes over to the subject. This second aspect must now be defined more closely.

There are two sides from which the definition must be grasped. First from the side of the *idea:* from this side we have said that spirit in the categorial determination of universality posits itself in that of particularity; but this new category is still the eternal idea; God is the entire totality. Or we can say that it is the *Son* that is to be analyzed; he unites these two determinations. [He is] the difference—but in love, and in the Spirit, or posited also as being identical with the idea in the form of universality. Other-being is the first determination, while the second is that this in-itself of the other is also the divine idea. In the process of analysis the two determinations are initially to be posited as distinct—but only for an instant, as it were, since they are not truly distinct. Both in its being and in its being distinguished the concept includes the fact that what is being has negation, it is only a moment, and is sublated too. It is representation that holds these two sides apart—otherwise it would not be a real representation. [Indeed,] it is also the awareness that negation, the implicit being of the divine idea, is a true moment as well; but representation holds the two sides apart in time: now [the other is] estranged and [has] fallen away, and then [the divine idea] comes forth vis-à-vis this other-being.

The other side is what we have defined as *finite spirit*. Finite spirit is here pure thinking and has in view the truth, the eternal truth, to which its relationship is that of thinking. This thinking is its result, its end. Finite spirit begins from immediacy, it raises itself from the sensible to the infinite, to the element of thinking. But in fact it is not the *result* of thinking; on the contrary, thinking exists only through movement, through the process of elevation. And spirit is intrinsically the process of elevation. It is this process we now have to consider.

From the first standpoint, the relationship is that God in God's eternal truth is represented as a state of affairs in time, for the blessed spirits ("that the morning stars may praise me," etc.).[26] This relationship is thus expressed as a state of affairs in *time,* although for the object it is the *eternal* relationship of thinking. Later on, what is termed a "fall" occurred. This is the positing of the second standpoint—on the one hand it is the analysis of the Son, the keeping apart of the two moments that are contained in him. Jacob Boehme represented it as the fall of Lucifer, the firstborn, and the begetting of another son in his place.[27] This happened in heaven in the eternal idea, as it were. Thus in the analysis of this other the other is itself contained, though not posited. But then the other side is what we have termed subjective consciousness, finite spirit; the other side is that subjective consciousness as pure thinking is in itself the process, that it has begun from immediacy and has elevated itself to the truth. This is the second form.

At this point we enter the determinacy of *space,* of the finite world and finite spirit, or—to express it more precisely—we begin upon the positing of determinations *as* determinations, the positing of a distinction that is momentarily held fast. This is a going forth—the appearing of God in [the realm of] finitude. For finitude is properly the separation of what in itself is identical but is maintained in separation. From the other side, however, from the side of subjective spirit, this is posited as pure thinking; but in itself pure thinking is result, and it is to be posited the way it is, implicitly as this movement. In other words, pure thinking has to go into itself, and for that reason it posits itself first as *finite*.

The first thing we have to consider is this movement. As a going into itself the subjective consciousness of self consists in its being *for* itself what it is *in* itself. In itself it is this process, so this process has to be for it. But when what it is in itself is *for* it, the need for its reconciliation arises. Since it is for itself in this way, and is first posited as subject, there arises the need that subjectivity too should be present for it in the divine idea, that it should know subjectivity within the idea. In the first relationship, subjectivity is not yet posited for the subjective consciousness, because it is not yet conceptual knowing. The other aspect, then, is that the need is *satisfied,* in other words that God *appears* for the subjective consciousness in the shape of subjectivity, of immediate consciousness. These are the two aspects that we now have to consider.

b. Natural Humanity

In the first place, subjective consciousness is posited as it is. As spirit it consists on the one hand in starting from immediacy and raising itself to pure thinking, to the infinite, to the knowledge of God. When one considers this in its determinate form, it contains what we know from the Christian religion. First, consciousness has to enter into itself, it has to become concrete, become what is in itself; hence it starts from immediacy, and through the sublation of this immediacy it elevates itself to thinking. This means that its true nature is to abandon its immediacy, to treat it as a state in which it ought not to be: as immediately natural human beings, we *ought* to regard ourselves as being what we *ought not* to be. This has been expressed by saying that human beings are *evil by nature,* i.e., they ought not to be the way they immediately are; hence they are as they ought not to be.

In the condition of human immediacy two characteristics are present: first, there is what humanity is implicitly, human talents and rationality, spiritual potential, the image of God, nature as what is intrinsic within us; and second, there is natural being, the fact that human rationality has not yet developed. What is lacking here is that humanity is [only] *implicitly* rational and spiritual; this is precisely the deficiency, for spirit ought not to be implicitly spirit—it is spirit only because it is so *explicitly.* Nature is only implicitly rational; this implicit potential constitutes its laws. For this reason it is *only* nature. Humans on the other hand ought to be spirit *explicitly,* not merely spirit *implicitly;* their merely implicit potential, their natural being, must be sublated. This sublation comprises two different things. All that has to be sublated is the *form* of implicit being; the absolutely primordial, that humanity *is* implicitly spirit, is what maintains itself, what abides, just as the goal or end maintains itself in the divine idea. We can therefore rightly say, on the one hand, that because human beings are implicitly spirit, they are *good* "by nature." But this is not yet "being good," for human beings are not yet what they ought to be. Immediacy is what a human being ought *not* to be, what has to be sublated.

So this first definition of the human condition is expressed by saying that "by nature" we are evil. This is a troublesome expression and can produce many false impressions. The crucial thing is that human beings are "by nature" such as they ought not to be; humanity ought to be spirit, but natural being is not spiritual being. We should notice that certain objections to this view immediately occur to us. Children are not evil, and this definition does not seem to fit many peoples and individuals. No. Children are innocent; and that is because they have no will and they are not yet accountable. It pertains to evil to be able to decide, to have a will, to possess insight into the nature of actions. Inasmuch as the will is established through the process of growing up, it appears initially as caprice, which can will what is good just as easily as it can will evil, and by no means wills only evil according to its nature. But, of course, we cannot appeal to empirical, particular conditions at all. As regards the condition of the child, it is one of innocence, neither good nor evil. A human being, however, ought not to be like a child: adults are not innocent in this sense but must be responsible for what they do. That the condition of childhood also includes will is an empirical fact, but a child is still not what is meant by a "human being," for human beings possess insight, their will has been trained. The adult ought not to remain in the condition of childhood.

As for the second point, that the will is caprice and can will good or evil, this caprice is in fact not the genuine will. It becomes will only insofar as it comes to a decision, for insofar as it still wills merely this or that, it is not genuine. The natural will is the will of appetite, or of inclination; it wills the *immediate* but it does not yet will *this* [particular act]. For it to be rational will, there must be a consciousness that has some knowledge of the universal, and the will itself must have insight that the law is what is rational. What is demanded of human beings is that they should not exist as natural will, that they should not be just what they are by nature. Certainly the concept of willing is also what is called "human nature." But the concept of willing is something else; as long as human beings still exist in this "nature," they are only *implicitly* will, not yet actual will, they do not yet exist as spirit. This is the general situation, the special aspects of which must be left out of consideration; it is only within a particular condition [of culture] that we can speak of what pertains to the sphere of morality—this does not concern the nature of spirit.

Now comes another objection to the view that the will is evil. There is something wrong here, in that when we view humanity concretely, and speak of will, this concrete, actual will cannot merely be something negative. The evil will, however, is posited to be merely evil volition. This is just an abstraction, and even if we are not by nature what we ought to be, we are still implicitly rational, still implicitly spirit—this is what is affirmative in us. But we have to realize this, we have to go further, and the fact that we are not by nature what we ought to be refers therefore only to the form of our willing. The essential point is that humanity is implicitly spirit. That which is implicit persists, and in the surrender of the natural will, the *concept* is what persists, it is what produces itself. What spirit is implicitly is no longer something implicit, it is something that has been *produced*. If we contend on the other side that the will is evil by nature, then we are speaking of the will considered only negatively; thus we also have this concrete [reality] in mind, which this [negative] abstraction contradicts. So much is this the case that if we set up the devil, we have to show that there must be something affirmative in him; and Milton's devil—his strength of character, energy, and consistency—appears far better, far more affirmative, than many of his angels;[28] in a concrete [reality] affirmative characteristics must emerge at once.

In all of this it is forgotten that when we speak of human beings, these are human beings who have been educated and trained by customs, laws, etc. We are told, people aren't so bad after all, just look around you. But these are people with ethical and moral training, already reconstructed and put into a certain pattern of reconciliation. The main point is that such conditions, like that of childhood, are not to be looked for [empirically]. In religion, as in the portrayal of truth, what is essentially represented is rather the unfolded history of what humanity is. It is a speculative mode of treatment that dominates here; the abstract distinctions in the concept are presented one after another. If educated and cultured human beings are to be considered, then the transformation, reconstruction, the discipline through which they have passed, the transition from natural volition to true volition, must be visible in them, and their immediate, natural will must be seen to be sublated in all that. The first definition [of humanity], therefore, is that human beings in their immediacy are not what they ought to be.

c. Knowledge, Estrangement, and Evil

The second point is that they ought to *regard* themselves in this way; the fact of being evil is then set in the relationship of being *looked at*. This can then easily be taken to mean that it is only with reference to *cognition* that human beings are posited as evil, with the implication that such consideration is a kind of external demand or condition, so that if people do not regard themselves in this way, then the other characteristic—the fact that they *are* evil—falls away as well.

Since such consideration is made into a duty, one may imagine that this alone is the essential thing, and that without it there is no content either. In the second place, the relationship involved in it is also stated in such a way as to imply that it is the consideration or the cognition that *makes* people evil, so that consideration and cognition [themselves] are what is evil, and that [therefore] such cognition is what ought not to exist [because it] is the *source* of evil. The coherence between being evil and cognition lies in this representation. This is a point of essential importance.

The more precise way of representing this evil [condition] is to say that human beings become evil by cognizing, or, as the Bible represents it, that they have eaten of the tree of knowledge of good and evil [Gen. 3:5-6]. Through this story cognition, intelligence, and theoretical capacity come into a closer relationship with the will, and the nature of evil comes to more precise expression. Against this it may be said that it is in fact cognition that is the source of all evil, for knowledge or consciousness is the only act through which separation is posited at all—negation, evil, and cleavage, the more specific categories involved in being-for-self as such. Human nature is not what it ought to be: it is cognition that discloses this and brings forth the mode of being in which human beings ought not to be. Natural humanity is not as it should be; this "should" is the human concept, and that humanity does not conform to it first emerges in the separation, in the comparison with what humanity is in and for itself.

It is cognition that first posits the antithesis in which evil is to be found. Animals, stones, and plants are not evil: evil first occurs within the sphere of rupture or cleavage [*Entzweiung*]; it is the consciousness of being-for-myself in opposition to an external nature, but also in opposition to the objective [reality] that is inwardly universal in the sense of the concept or of the rational will. It is through this separation that I exist for myself for the first time, and that is where the evil lies. Abstractly, being evil means singularizing myself in a way that cuts me off from the universal (which is the rational, the laws, the determinations of spirit). But along with this separation there arises being-for-self and for the first time the universally spiritual, laws—what ought to be. So it is not the case that [rational] consideration has an external relationship to evil: it is itself what is evil. Inasmuch as it is spirit, humanity has to progress to this antithesis of being-for-self as such. Humans must have their antithesis as their objective—what for them is the good, the universal, their vocation. Spirit is free; freedom has the essential moment of this separation within itself. In this separation being-for-self is posited and evil has its seat; here is the source of all wrong, but also the point where reconciliation has its ultimate source. It is what produces the disease and is at the same time the source of health.

d. The Story of the Fall

We can now compare this more specifically with the way in which it all happens in the story of the fall. In this story sin is described by saying that Adam and Eve ate of the tree of knowledge, etc. This gives rise to the cognition, cleavage, and separation through which good first comes to be for humanity, but therewith evil also. According to the story, it is forbidden to eat of the tree, so evil is represented formally as the transgression of a divine command. In this way the rise of consciousness is posited; but at the same time it is to be represented as a standpoint that ought not to be, and where we ought not to rest, a standpoint that must be sublated; for we ought not to stand fast in the cleavage involved in being-for-self.

Moreover, the serpent says that by eating the fruit of the tree Adam and Eve will become like God, and this appeals to human pride. God later communes with godself, saying, "Behold, Adam has become like one of us" [Gen. 3:22]. So the serpent did not lie, for God confirms what it said. The explication of this text has been the occasion of much labor, and some have gone so far as to explain what God says as irony.[29] The higher explanation, however, is that by this "Adam" the second Adam, or Christ, is understood.[30] Cognition is the principle of spirituality, and this—as we said—is also the principle by which the injury of the separation is healed. It is in this principle of cognition that the principle of divinity is also posited, which through a further process of adjustment must arrive at the reconciliation, the authentic state of humankind. The story says moreover that humanity has received natural punishments, natural ills [Gen. 3:16-19]; this is an uncertain content, but in any case Adam's labor is a consequence of his cognition. Animals do not labor; the act of laboring is at the same time the stamp of humankind's higher spiritual nature. We are also told that Adam and Eve were driven out of Paradise so that they would not also taste of the tree of life [Gen. 3:22-24]. This means that although individuals arrive at cognition, each remains a single [being] and hence a mortal one.

One more characteristic has to be added. For in this separation human beings are defined as being for themselves. As consciousness, being-for-self is self-consciousness; it is infinite self-consciousness, abstractly infinite, because [the independent being] is conscious of its freedom, its wholly abstract freedom. This is the infinite presence-to-self [*Beisichsein*] that did not come to consciousness in this way in the earlier religions, where the antithesis did not progress to this absoluteness, this depth. Because this has now happened, human dignity is simultaneously raised to a much higher plane. Because of it the subject acquires absolute importance and becomes an essential object of the interest of God, since it is a self-consciousness that has being on its own account. As this pure inward certainty of itself, it is formal subjectivity. To be sure, it is abstract—but it is abstract being-in-and-for-self. This comes forth in the shape that human being as spirit is *immortal*, the object of divine interest, elevated above finitude, dependence, and external conditions, [having] the freedom to abstract from everything. This implies that humanity is outside the range of mortality. Just because its antithesis is infinite, it is in religion that the immortality of the soul is such an important moment.

"Mortal" means something that can die, while whatever can reach a state into which death does not enter is "immortal." When we say "combustible" and "incombustible," combustion is only a possibility that impinges on the object externally. The determination of being is not a possibility of this kind but an affirmatively defined quality that a thing already possesses in itself. Hence the immortality of the soul must not be imagined as though it first emerges into actuality at some later time; rather it is a present quality. Spirit is eternal, and for this reason it is already present; spirit in its freedom does not lie within the sphere of limitation. As pure knowing or as thinking, it has the universal for its object—this is eternity. Eternity is not mere duration but *knowing*—the knowing of what is eternal. Hence the eternity of spirit is brought to consciousness at this point, in this cognition, in this very separation that has attained to the infinitude of being-for-self, which is no longer entangled in the natural, the contingent, the external. Now this inner eternity of spirit is what spirit is implicitly to begin with; but the very next standpoint, where we are at present, is that spirit ought not to be the way that it is as merely natural spirit, but rather the way it is in and for itself. Spirit should contemplate itself, and this gives rise to its rupture. But it ought not to remain at this point where its being [for itself] is not the way it is in itself; it should become concordant with its concept, with absolute spirit. At the point of rupture, this [duty] is initially something other, and spirit itself is initially natural will, inwardly ruptured. There is this rupture inasmuch as [there is] a feeling of consciousness of contradiction; and this posits the need for sublating the contradiction—i.e., it posits reconciliation. Here at this standpoint, reconciliation has its own distinctive form.

Human beings must consider themselves as [being initially the way] they ought not to be. From this separation an infinite need arises. In this cognition [of self], in this separation and rupture, the subject, as we have said, here defines itself, grasping itself as the extreme of abstract being-for-self, or abstract freedom; the soul plunges into its depths, right down into its abyss. This soul is the undeveloped monad, the naked monad,[31] the empty soul lacking fulfillment; but since it is implicitly the concept, what is concrete, this emptiness or abstraction contradicts its vocation, which is to be concrete. Thus the universal means that in this separation, which develops as infinite antithesis, this abstractness is to be sublated. Even the abstract ego has a will implicit in it, it is concrete, but the fulfillment that it finds there is the natural will. The soul finds nothing before it but desire, selfishness, etc., in that fulfillment; and it is one of the forms of the antithesis that I, the soul in its depths, and my real soul are so distinct from one another that the real soul is not one that [can be] made to match the concept, and therefore brought back to it, [but one] that finds in itself only natural will. The antithesis in which the real side is further developed is then the *world*, and the unity of the concept thus has the natural will as a whole opposed to it, the will whose principle is selfishness in general, and the actualization of which takes the form of depravity, brutishness, etc. The objectivity that this pure ego has, and that is for it as what is appropriate to it, is not its natural will, nor is it the world. Instead, this appropriate objectivity is just the universal essential being [*das Wesen*], this One who is not fulfilled in the ego and to whom *all* fulfillment [in] the world stands equally opposed.[32]

Now the consciousness of this antithesis, of this separation of the ego and the natural will, is the consciousness of an infinite contradiction. This ego exists in immediate relation with the natural will and with the world, yet at the same time it is repelled from them. This is the infinite anguish, the suffering of the world. A reconciliation can take place at this standpoint, but it is unsatisfactory and one-sided. It consists in an inner equilibrium of the ego, in the way that this ego exists for itself in Stoic philosophy. It knows itself as a thinker, and its object is what is thought, the universal; this is for it absolutely everything, it is the genuine essence for it, so that this universal is valid for it. Something that is thought belongs to the subject, because it is posited by it. But a reconciliation of this kind is itself only abstract; all determination lies outside this thought, which is merely formal identity with itself. An abstract reconciliation such as this cannot and should not take place at the absolute standpoint where we now are. Even the natural will cannot be inwardly satisfied [with it], for those who have comprehended their infinitude cannot be contented either with the natural will or with the state of the world. The abstract depth of this absolute antithesis demands an infinite suffering of the soul and, with it, a reunification that is equally complete.

2. RECONCILIATION[33]

a. The Idea of Reconciliation and Its Appearance in a Single Individual
Such is the nature of the need. The question now is: "How can it be satisfied?" "What is it that effects reconciliation for it?" This reconciliation can come about only by the separation being sublated for it. Both for the need and for the representation, it must turn out that what *seems* incompatible— the infinite and the inner ego [on the one hand], and pure essentiality [*die reine Wesenheit*] or God, and fulfillment [on the other]—is not so, that this antithesis is null and void, and that the truth, or what is affirmative and absolute, is the *unity* of the finite and infinite, the unity of subjectivity, in its various determinations, and objectivity. This is expressed in the determinate form that the resolved contradiction comes into being for the need itself; divine and human nature enter into a unity wherein both have set aside their abstractness vis-à-vis each other. These extremes, divine and

human nature, are not in themselves extremes, but the truth is their identity instead—the unity of abstract, rigid being-for-self and its fulfillment, so that what is concrete is the truth. And to the extent that this stands opposed to concrete divinity, this weak antithesis too is done away with, and there remains the [unitary] determination of divine and human nature. The subject is in *need* of this truth, and this truth must come into being for it. "Divine and human nature" is a puzzling and difficult expression, and the kind of representation we associate with it should be forgotten. What it means is spiritual essentiality [*die geistige Wesenheit*]; in the unity of divine and human nature everything that belongs to external particularization has disappeared—the finite [itself] has disappeared.

The second question is this: "Cannot the subject bring about this reconciliation by itself, through its own efforts, its own activity—so that through its piety and devotion it makes its inner [life] conform with the divine idea, and expresses this conformity through its deeds?" "And further, is this not within the capability [not merely] of a single subject but of all people who genuinely wish to take up the divine law within themselves, so that heaven would exist on earth and the Spirit would be present in reality and dwell in its community?" The question is whether the subject cannot bring this about on its own, as subject. It is commonly believed that it can. It is to be noted here that we must bear carefully in mind that the subject we are dealing with is the extreme case—it is the subject that is *for itself*. Subjectivity has the characteristic of *positing*—something is so through *my agency*. This positing and activity happens through my agency, let the content be what it may; so bringing it forth is itself a one-sided determination, and the product is only something posited. It abides as such only in abstract freedom. In other words, the question is whether or not the subject can produce this result through its own positing activity. And this is always one-sided.

This positing must essentially be a *presupposing,* in such a way that what is posited is also something implicit. The unity of subjectivity and objectivity—this divine unity—must be a presupposition for my positing. For only then does the latter have a content; otherwise it remains subjective and formal. This is the way in which it gains for the first time true, substantive content. By taking on the character of a presupposition, it loses its one-sidedness; with the signification of a presupposition of this kind it enters into possession of this one-sidedness, takes it into itself, and thereby gets rid of it. Kant and Fichte maintain that we can sow, do good only on the presupposition of a moral world order.[34] We do not know whether what we do will prosper and succeed, and we can act only on the assumption that the good bears fruit in and of itself, that this is not simply something posited but is an objective fact in virtue of the very nature of the good. This presupposition therefore constitutes an essential condition [of human action].

The harmony, the resolution of this contradiction, must be represented as something that is in and of itself, it must be a presupposition for the subject. Since the concept cognizes divine unity, it recognizes that God is in and of godself. The one-sidedness that appears as the activity and so forth of the subject is merely a moment [that] simply subsists; it is nothing on its own account but exists only by virtue of this presupposition. The truth must therefore appear to the subject as a presupposition, and the question is how and in what guise the truth can appear at the standpoint at which we now find ourselves, i.e., the standpoint of infinite flight and abstractness. This is the infinite anguish, the pure depth of soul, and it is for this anguish that the contradiction is to be resolved. To begin with, the resolution necessarily has the form of a presupposition because the subject is, as we have seen, a one-sided extreme. More precisely, the subject is now defined as this profound being-within-itself, this flight from reality, this complete withdrawal from immediate existence, from fulfillment. But at the same time this abstraction of the ego is defined, in its reality, as an immediate being. So this subjective [element], this ego, is itself something presupposed too. It does have the aspect of a reality as well, for the idea is the unity of concept and reality, and its reality is determined according to the definition of the concept; here it is subjective reality. The subjective [element] is this profundity involved in the fact that the ego and its fulfillment (the world) is an other. But what is as idea is also actual, and hence it has the determinate character of reality. Empty, naked reality is, as sensible, defined in a strictly exclusive way. Thus there is consciousness, subjectivity and objectivity, objectivity being defined as abstractly as consciousness itself. Consciousness exists in the mode of sensible being; it is simple, abstract being-within-self and does not yet reflect, for reflecting is an inner relating, thinking; reflection is not abstract being-within-self—just as the thinking of Stoicism is not.

This infinite suffering that is wholly unfulfilled is without reflection. Hence for consciousness its sensible content is one that ought not to be, and it still lacks any extended world within itself; so in its infinite depth it relates to itself as sensible consciousness. Therefore, since the truth now has to be *for it,* there is on the one hand the *presupposition* of the unity of divine and human nature, and on the other hand, because it is *sensible* self-consciousness, this unity *appears.* God appears as the concrete God. For this reason the idea appears in sensible immediacy, in sensible presence too, for the form of being for others is the immediate and sensible form.

Consequently God appears in sensible presence; God has no other figure or shape [*Gestalt*] than that of the sensible mode of the spirit that is spirit in itself—the shape of the *singular human being.* This is the one and only sensible shape of spirit—it is *the appearance of God in the flesh.* This is the monstrous reality whose necessity we have seen. What it posits is that divine and human nature are not intrinsically different—God [is] in human shape. The truth is that there is only one reason, only one spirit; we have seen that spirit as finite does not have genuine existence.

The essential aspect of the shape of appearance is thus explicated. Because it is the appearance *of God,* it occurs essentially for the community; it must not and cannot be taken in isolation. Appearing is being for an other; this other is the *community.*

The verification of this appearance has two aspects. The first concerns the *content* of the appearance, which is the unity of the finite and the infinite, the fact that God is not an abstraction but what is utterly concrete. Inasmuch as God is *for consciousness,* the verification of this is from our present standpoint a purely *inner* verification, a witness of the Spirit. Philosophy has to make explicit that the witness is not merely this mute inner one; it has to bring it to light in the element of thinking. This is the one side, the *imago*-aspect of human nature; human beings are the image of God [Gen. 1:26-27].

The second aspect [of the verification] is the one that we have observed earlier, that God, considered in terms of God's eternal idea, *has* to generate the Son, has to distinguish godself from godself, in such a way that what is distinguished is wholly God godself; and their union is love and the Spirit. The suffering of the soul, this infinite anguish, is the witness of the Spirit, inasmuch as spirit is the negativity of finite and infinite, of subjectivity and objectivity being conjoined but still as conflicting elements; if there were no longer any conflict, there would be no anguish. Spirit is the absolute power to endure this anguish, i.e., to unite the two and to be in this way, in this oneness. Thus the anguish itself verifies the appearance of God.

As for the other mode of verification,[35] namely, that God appeared in *this* human being, at *this* time and in *this* place—this is quite a different matter, and can be recognized only from the point of view of world history. It is written: "When the time had come, God sent forth God's Son" [Gal. 4:4]; and *that* the time had come can only be discerned from history.

b. The Historical, Sensible Presence of Christ

The question is now more precisely this: "What content must present itself in this appearance?" The content can be nothing else than the history of spirit, the history of God (which is God godself), the divine history as that of a single self-consciousness which has united divine and human nature within itself—the divine nature in this [human] element.

The first [aspect] of this history is the *single, immediate human being* in all his contingency, in the whole range of temporal relationships and conditions. To this extent this is a divestment of the divine. What is to be seen here is that this aspect is for the community. There is in it the unity of the finite and the infinite, but there is at the same time in this sensible mode a divestment of the idea, and this has to be sublated.

The second point relates to the *teaching*. What must the teaching of this individual be? It cannot be what later became the doctrine of the church or community. The teaching of Christ is not Christian dogmatics, not the doctrine of the church; Christ did not expound what the church later produced as its doctrine. For his teaching evokes sensations through representation, and it has a content. It is this content, which at the highest level is an explication of the nature of God, that has to be initially directed specifically at the sentient consciousness, coming to it as an *intuition*. Hence it is not present as a doctrine, which begins with assertions.

The main content of this teaching can only be universal and abstract, it can only contain abstract and universal [images]. If something new, a new world, a new religion, a new concept of God is to be given to the world of representational awareness, then two aspects are involved. First there [is] the universal soil, and second there is what is particular, determinate, and concrete. The world of representational awareness, insofar as it thinks, can achieve only abstract thinking, it thinks only the universal. It is reserved solely for conceptualizing spirit to cognize the particular from the universal, to let the particular emerge from the concept by its own power. For the world of representational awareness, determinate [reality] and the soil of universal thought are mutually exclusive. So what can initially be produced here by teaching is the universal soil for the concept of God. This can be expressed briefly as the *kingdom of God*.[36] This has been taught: it is the real divinity, God in God's *determinate being* [*Dasein*] in God's *spiritual actuality,* the kingdom of heaven. This divine reality contains already within itself God and God's kingdom, the community—a concrete content. This is the main content.

This teaching, insofar as it cannot initially advance beyond the universal, has in this universal (as an abstract universal) the character of negation vis-à-vis everything in the present world. Insofar as it affirms the universal in this way, it is a *revolutionary* doctrine that partly leaves all standing institutions aside and partly destroys and overthrows them. All earthly, worldly things fall away as valueless, and they are expressly declared to be so. What is brought before the imagination is an elevation to an infinite energy in which the universal demands to be firmly maintained on its own account. This is how we interpret the following sayings. When Christ is among his disciples and his mother and brothers come to speak to him, he asks: "Who are my mother and my brothers? Behold my mother and my brothers! For whoever does the will of God is my brother, and sister, and mother" (Mark 3:31-35). "To another he said, 'Follow me.' But he said,

'Lord, let me first go and bury my father.' But Jesus said to him, 'Leave the dead to bury their own dead; but as for you, go and proclaim the kingdom of God.' Another said, 'I will follow you, Lord; but let me first say farewell to those at my home.' Jesus said to him, 'No one who puts his hand to the plow and looks back is fit for the kingdom of God'" (Luke 9:59-62). All of the relationships that refer to property disappear, but at the same time they inwardly sublate themselves—for if everything is given to the poor, there are no poor any more. Christ says: "Do not be anxious about another day, for each day is anxious for itself."[37] Such concerns, however, are proper for human beings. Family relationships, property, etc., recede in the face of something higher, namely, following Christ. This perfect independence is the abstract, primal soil of spirituality. On the one hand, morality as such has its place at a subordinate level here, and it is nothing peculiar; for the commands of Christ are for the most part already to be found in the Old Testament. On the other hand, *love* is made the principal commandment— not an impotent love of humanity in general but the mutual love of the community,[38] such that no one has any particular purpose [of his or her own]; for this community the universal can consist in the spiritual tie that binds them together.

As for the particular [duties of life], all that is supplied from elsewhere, so to speak, for the representational consciousness. We find quite concrete examples of this in other spheres. In the Islamic doctrine there is merely the fear of God: God is to be venerated as the One, and one cannot advance beyond this abstraction. Islam is therefore a religion of formalism, a perfect formalism that allows nothing to take shape in opposition to it. Or again in the French Revolution, liberty and equality were affirmed in such a way that all spirituality, all laws, all talents, all living relations had to disappear before this abstraction, and the public order and constitution had to come from elsewhere and be forcibly asserted against this abstraction. For those who hold fast to the abstraction cannot allow anything determinate to emerge, since this would be the emergence of something particular and distinct in contrast with this abstraction. (I am bringing in all of this to illustrate how far the representational consciousness can go by itself, and how it can be self-possessed with its own freedom and knowledge in this abstraction; but the particular must come into play in some other way.)

And the particular *is* the determinate aspect that comes into play here in equally distinctive fashion. Although to be sure the soil for it is the universalism of [Christ's] teaching, and some individual traits point to that, still the main point is that this [particular] content does not impinge on our representation through teaching but through sense-intuition. This content is nothing other than the life,[39] passion, and death of Christ.

c. The Death of Christ and the Transition to Spiritual Presence

For it is *this* suffering and death, this sacrificial death of the individual for all, that is the nature of God, the divine history, the being that is utterly universal and affirmative. This is, however, at the same time to posit God's negation; in death the moment of negation is envisaged. This is an essential moment in the nature of spirit, and it is this death itself that must come into view in this individual. It must not then be represented merely as the death of *this individual,* the death of this empirically existing individual. Heretics have interpreted it like that,[40] but what it means is rather that *God* has died, that *God godself is dead.*[41] God has died: this is negation, which is accordingly a moment of the divine nature, of God godself.

In this death, therefore, God is satisfied. God cannot be satisfied by something else, only by godself. The satisfaction consists in the fact that the first moment, that of immediacy, is negated; only then does God come to be at peace with godself, only then is spirituality posited. God is the true God, spirit, because God is not merely Father, and hence closed up within godself, but because God is Son, because God becomes the other and sublates this other. This negation is intuited as a moment of the divine nature in which all are reconciled. Set against God there are finite human beings; humanity, the finite, is posited in death itself as a moment of God, and death is what reconciles. Death is love itself; in it absolute love is envisaged. The identity of the divine and the human means that God is at home with godself in humanity, in the finite, and in [its] death this finitude is itself a determination of God. Through death God has reconciled the world and reconciles godself eternally with godself. This coming back again is God's return to godself, and through it God is *spirit.* So this third moment is that Christ has risen. Negation is thereby overcome, and the negation of negation is thus a moment of the divine nature.

The Son is raised up to the right hand of God. Thus in this history the nature of God, namely, spirit, is accomplished, interpreted, explicated for the community. This is the crucial point, and the meaning of the story is that it is the story of God. God is the absolute, self-contained movement that spirit is, and this movement is here represented in the individual. There are quite a number of ways in which the matter can be represented, which refer to finite, external relationships. In particular a number of false relationships have been introduced: for example, the sacrificial death offers occasion for representing God as a tyrant who demands sacrifice; this is untrue. On the contrary, the nature of God is spirit, and that being so, negation is an essential moment.

As for the *verification* of this individual, this involves essentially the witness of the Spirit, of the indwelling idea, of spirit in itself. Spirit is here brought to intuition; what is given is an immediate *witness of the Spirit to spirit,* which only conceptualizing spirit recognizes in its true necessity. Outward attestations are of a subordinate character and do not belong here.

Essentially the Son is recognized by the community as the one who has been raised to the right hand of God (i.e., that he is essentially a determination for the nature of God itself), not as he who was here in sense experience. So all sensory verification falls away, including miracles in the way in which they fall within the empirically external consciousness of faith. This is another field, another soil, but we readily imagine that the individual [Jesus] must have attested himself through the marvelous phenomenon of miracles and through absolute power over nature, since we humans ordinarily picture God as the power in nature. We have already discussed that. But it may be recalled that Christ himself renounces miracles. He says, "You wish to see signs and wonders."[42] It is not a matter of signs and wonders; Christ renounced them. In any event, this is by its very nature an external, spiritless mode of attestation. We are rightly aware that God and God's power are present in nature in and according to eternal laws; the true miracle is spirit itself. Even the animal is already a miracle vis-à-vis plant life, and still more spirit vis-à-vis life, vis-à-vis merely sentient nature. However, the genuine mode of verification is quite different—it is through power over minds. We must insist that this is the genuine [proof]. But even this power over minds is not an external power like that of the church against heretics; rather it is power of a spiritual type, which leaves spirit's freedom completely intact. This power has subsequently been manifested through the great community of the Christian church. One can say that this again is only an effect and [thus] an external mode [of verification]. But to say this is to fall into self-contradiction, for what is demanded is proof of the *power,* and this consists merely in its effect; the proof of the *concept* requires no verification.

This, then, is what this history is. The first moment is the concept of this standpoint for consciousness; the second is what is given to this standpoint, what actually exists for the community; the third is the transition to the community.[43]

This appearance of God in the flesh occurs in a specific time and in this single individual. Since it is an appearance of this kind, of itself it passes by and becomes past history. This sensible mode must disappear and rise again in the sphere of representation. The formation of the community has just this content—that the sensible form passes over into a spiritual element. The manner of this purification of immediate being preserves the sensible element precisely by letting it pass away; this is negation in the way that it is posited and appears in the sensible individual as such. Only in regard to that single individual is this intuition given; it is not capable of being inherited or renewed. This cannot happen because as "this" event, a sensible appearance is by its very nature momentary, and its destiny is to be spiritualized. It is therefore essentially something that *has been* and it will be raised up into the sphere of representation in general.

For the spirit that has need of it, sensible presence *can* be brought forth again in various ways, in pictures, relics, holy images. There is no lack of such mediations when they are needed. But for the spiritual community, immediate presence (the now) has passed away. At first, then, sensible representation reintegrates the past, which is a one-sided moment for representation; the present includes the past and the future as moments within itself. Hence sensible representation includes the coming again of Christ, which is essentially an absolute return, but then takes [the shape of] a turning from externality to the inner realm—a Comforter, who can come only when sensible history in its immediacy has passed by.[44]

This then is the point relating to the formation of the community, in other words the third point—namely, the Spirit.

C. THE THIRD ELEMENT: COMMUNITY SPIRIT

This is the transition from externality, from appearance, to inwardness. What it is concerned with is subjectivity, the certainty felt by the subject of its own infinite, nonsensible essentiality, the certainty with which it knows itself to be infinite, to be eternal, immortal. Beyond that there is the subject's being filled with the truth, and the fact that this truth is in self-consciousness *as* self-consciousness, that it is not external but is there as the inward truth of thought, as the representation of inwardness as such. At first, subjectivity and the knowledge of its essence is the knowledge of a sensibly present content. This is obviously nonspiritual, transitory; yet it is not merely transitory, but essentially *transitional*—it is a door where one cannot tarry, a form that is destined to be sublated, a form that is defined not merely as past but as belonging eternally to the spiritual nature of God. This is the turning to the inward path, and in this third realm we find ourselves on the soil of spirit as such—this is the *community,* the *cultus, faith.*

We have defined the manifestation of God first as revelatory and second as appearance. The third [moment of manifestation] is knowledge or faith, for faith is also knowledge, but in a distinctive form. This third [moment] we now have to consider.

It consists, then, in the divine content being posited as *self-conscious* knowledge of this content, posited in the element of self-consciousness, of inwardness. On the one hand it is the knowledge that the content is the truth, and [on the other hand] that it is the truth of finite spirit as such—that is to say, the knowledge of it belongs to finite spirit so that finite spirit has its freedom in this knowledge, and is itself the process of casting off its particular individuality and of liberating itself in this content.

Regarding this cultus and community, etc., we have once more three aspects to be considered: (1) the *origin* of the community and the coming to be of faith; (2) the *existence* [*Dasein*] or *subsistence* [*Bestehen*] of the community; (3) the *realization of faith,* which is at the same time the process by which faith passes over [into worldly actuality], the transformation and transfiguration of faith itself.

1. THE ORIGIN OF THE COMMUNITY

The first [aspect] concerns the origin of faith and the community. This lies in the generation and discovery of the doctrine of the Spirit (or better, of the content of this doctrine). Thus it is more precisely the explication of what we have already indicated in general in the process of making the transition to the community.

If we begin by comparing the community with what we have already seen, we first considered the eternal idea in the element of thinking, and second in the element of divestment, in the sensuously external, immediate mode of presentation. It was *we* who considered it in this way, it was *for us.* But if we ask, "Who are 'we'?" we are nothing other than the community itself, subjective consciousness. It is therefore manifest to us, we know about it; hence we are the presupposition, [that] for which it is. But at this point we have ourselves proceeded to the realization of the idea, so that spirit is *for* spirit, and what spirit is for spirit, it is as sense-consciousness. Thus there are two that are for one another. The side that we directly constitute stands now over against us. Just as in a drama the spectators have themselves in the form of the chorus standing objectively over against them, so here the standpoint is that the content is for spirit, and this relationship must be considered in its essence.

Initially this spirit has been defined as sense-consciousness. However, it ought no longer to be for us as it is for consciousness, in this one-sided way. Or, to the extent that we have defined it as sensible, this part of the whole relationship must—if we are at the true standpoint—raise itself to our standpoint, which is that of considering the truth. Such a consideration presupposes the community in actual fact. The origin of the community is the production of the content for the community, for subjective self-consciousness. We have considered the idea first in the element of thinking, and second how it realizes itself outwardly, posits itself in differentiation. In the community, the stages are at first in the opposite order: the community begins with the sensible appearance, and the next step is the discovery of its content, the promulgation of its teaching. In other words, as has been said, the origin of the community lies in the generation of doctrine. Initially the community is immediate self-consciousness, and truth comes to it in this sensible mode as a determination of sense; and it is in moving on from this sensible mode to the attainment of eternal truth that it first raises itself into a community.

Initially, then, the content is for immediate consciousness, where it was possible for the truth to appear in a diversely sensible fashion. For the idea is one in all, universal necessity; actuality can only be a mirror of the idea. The idea, therefore, can issue forth for consciousness from everything; for it is always just the idea that is in these infinitely numerous drops that reflect it back again. The idea is represented, recognized, foreshadowed in the seed, which is the fruit, the ultimate determination of the tree; the seed first dies out in the earth, and only through this negation does the plant spring forth. A story—an intuition, a portrayal, an appearance of this kind—can also be raised by spirit to the level of the universal, and thus the history of the seed or of the sun becomes a symbol of the idea, but only a symbol; these are configurations that, in terms of their peculiar content or specific quality, are not adequate to the idea. What is known in them lies outside of them; their meaning does not exist in them as meaning.

The object that does exist in itself as the concept is spiritual subjectivity, human being. As thinking being it is in itself meaningful; meaning does not lie outside of it. It is all-interpreting, all-knowing, it is not a symbol. Human consciousness, what is specific to humanity, *is* essentially history itself, and the history of the spiritual does not take place in an existence that is not adequate to the idea. Thus what is necessary in regard to humanity is that the thought, the idea, should become objective in the community. Initially, however, the idea is present in the single individual in sense-intuition; this must be stripped away and the meaning, the eternal, truthful essence, must be made to emerge. This is the faith of the nascent community. It began from the individual [founder]; that single human being is transformed by the community, he is known as God—characterized as the Son of God, but entangled in everything finite that pertains to subjectivity as such. Subjectivity itself, the form that is finite, then disappears in the face of substantiality. This is the transformation of the sensible appearance into something spiritual and the knowledge of what is spiritual. It is the community as it begins from faith; but on the other hand, it is the faith that is brought forth as spirit, so faith is at the same time the result. We have now to bring out the different meanings of faith and verification.

Since faith begins from the sensible mode, it has a temporal history before it. What it holds to be true is an outward, ordinary occurrence, and its verification is [by means of] the historical [*historisch*], juridical method of attesting a fact, [which gives] sensible certainty. Or again, the representation of the foundation [of truth] is based on the sensible certainty of other persons regarding certain sensible facts, and it brings other evidence in support of this.

246

The content in this kind of attestation is of a wholly sensible nature—for instance, that Christ lived in Palestine. But faith changes its significance; in other words, it is not merely a question of faith as belief in [what happened at this] time and in this external history, but rather of faith that this man was the Son of God. Thereby the sensible content becomes something quite different; it is transformed into something else, and the demand then is that this latter should be attested. The object has been completely transformed from something that exists sensibly and empirically into something divine, into what is essentially the highest moment of God godself. This content is no longer something sensible, for the transition consists precisely in sublating the sensible. Thus if the demand is made to attest the content as a fact in the same sensory way as before, this way at once proves to be inadequate, because the object is of an entirely different nature.

If one defines the content in such a way that Christ's miracles are themselves sensible phenomena that can be attested in historical fashion, and likewise regards his resurrection and ascension as sensible events, then with regard to the sensible it is no longer a question of the relationship of historical verification to these phenomena, but of the relationship of verification by the senses per se and of sensible events (of both together) to spirit, to the spiritual content. Verification of the sensible, whatever its content, occurs through [sense-]intuition etc. It remains subject to an infinite number of objections because sensible externality lies at its basis; and that is something entirely different from spirit, from consciousness. In such verification, consciousness and object are separated, and this fundamental separation brings with it the possibility of error, deception, and lack of the culture needed to comprehend a fact correctly, so that one can have doubts. A sensible content is in fact one that *cannot* be certain in itself because it is not certain by virtue of spirit as such, because it stands on a different soil and is not posited by the concept. One might suppose that we must get to the root of things by comparing all the evidence and circumstances, or that there must be grounds for deciding in favor of one possibility or the other; but this entire mode of attestation, and the sensible content as such, has to be replaced by spirit. What is to have truth for spirit as spirit, what spirit is to believe, must not be a sensory belief; what is true for spirit is something for which in fact sensible appearance becomes subordinate. Since spirit begins from the sensible and advances [from that] to what is worthy of itself, its relationship to the sensible is at the same time a negative attitude, even though the sensible is its point of departure.

This is a basic characteristic, and it is basic to all cognition insofar as it is directed in any way toward something universal. [For example,] it is well known that Kepler discovered the laws of the heavens.[45] They are valid for us in a twofold fashion; they are the universal. The discovery began from [the observation of] single cases; certain movements were referred back to laws, but these were still only single cases. One might think that millions of other cases were possible, and that there were bodies which do *not* fall[46] in this way; thus even [as applied] to the heavenly bodies this is no universal law. This is, to be sure, how we have initially become aware of the matter; it has come within the ken of our representative capacity. But the interest of spirit is that such a law be true in and for itself; [the concern is] whether [it] is in conformity with reason, i.e., that reason finds its counterpart in the law. Where it does so, it recognizes it to be true in and for itself. By contrast with this cognition on the basis of the concept, cognition through the senses takes on a subordinate place. It is indeed the starting point, the point of departure, and should be gratefully acknowledged as such, but a law of this kind stands on its own feet, and therefore its verification is of another sort. It is the *concept,* and sensible existence is reduced to the level of a dream image, above which there is a higher region with its own enduring content.

The relationship is the same as we have seen in connection with those proofs for the existence of God that begin from the finite.[47] The defect in them is that the finite is grasped only in affirmative fashion; but at the same time the transition from the finite to the infinite is such that the realm of the finite is abandoned, and the sensible is reduced to a subordinate status, to a distant image that now subsists only in the past and in recollection—not in spirit, which is strictly present to itself. Having left that starting point behind, spirit now stands on a soil of quite a different worth. This is the relationship involved in the transition, which should in essence be attended to. Piety can build on whatever opportunity comes to hand; this furnishes its point of departure, but it leaves that behind as it passes over to a spiritual [interpretation]. It has been demonstrated that several of Christ's quotations from the Old Testament are incorrect, so that [the meaning that] derives from them is not grounded in the immediate sense of the words, or the fathers of the church have made something else out of the words. The word was presumably something hard-and-fast, yet spirit makes of it what has truth. In the same way, sensible history constitutes the point of departure for spirit. These two categories [sense and spirit] must be distinguished: the chief thing that matters is spiritual consciousness, the return of spirit into itself.

The church has been right to condemn the attack upon the miracles, the resurrection, etc., because such attacks entail the assumption that these things are what establish that Christ is the Son of God. But this claim stands secure on its own account, even though the miracles, etc., were its point of departure, to be sure.

This transition is what is termed the *outpouring of the Spirit.* It could occur only after the Christ who had become flesh had withdrawn, after his sensible, immediate presence had ceased; then for the first time the Spirit issued forth. What the Spirit alone produces is something else, has another form.

We have arrived, then, at the issuing forth of the Spirit in the community. About this emergence of the spiritual being of the community in this self-conscious spirit, there are two things worthy of note. The first question is, "What does spirit know?" It is itself the object [of its own knowing] because it is spirit. [The second question is,] "What then is its content, what is its teaching?" [Its content is that] this objective spirit, while standing over against the community, also posits itself, realizes itself therein; even as it was first posited objectively, it now posits itself, is posited, subjectively. What objective spirit knows is first of all God, God's essential being. But God does not merely have being in general; God is now a living, active God, the God who possesses activity, who produces godself; God godself is God's activity, God makes godself objective. This objectivity has initially the character of the otherness, the distinctness, the finitude that is termed the Son of God. This is the witness of spirit, that God has a Son, the absolute decree of spirit, which it has not yet conceptually comprehended, but which it testifies immediately from its own nature, in an instinctive manner so to speak. This is the second [moment]; the third is that the Spirit defines itself as the unity of the first two. Only in thought does history first achieve the form by which it has absolute interest for spirit. This third [moment] consists in what was already there in the Son—namely, that spirit is objective for itself, that it objectifies itself as the unity of the first and the second [moments], so that the second [moment], otherness, is sublated in eternal love. But this love expresses initially [i.e., in God made flesh] a relationship, a knowing, a seeing of the one in the other, such that the two extremes remain independent; it expresses an identity in which the two extremes are not absorbed. Now, on the contrary, it is love [itself] that is defined as what is objective; this is the Spirit.

It is possible, in the form of a [particular] religion, to advance basically no further than the representation of the Son and those about him. This is perhaps the case principally in Catholicism, with the result that Mary, the Mother of God, and the saints are exalted, the Spirit being also recognized as spirit, but only entering into the picture, as it were, rather than dwelling in the church and abiding in its decrees. As a result the second [moment] is brought to the fore in its sensible form for sensible imagination, rather than being spiritualized, and spirit does not essentially become an object.

The other side is the converse of this, namely, that now—just as, in the emerging community, doctrine took shape in such a way that the eternal truth is also something known, something posited in and through the community—so also the reverse is true, and finite spirit abides in itself not in an objective way but rather brings forth spirit in itself, begetting itself in its self-consciousness. This exaltation happens by means of the content that we have seen. This content is the mediator, for it is a one-sided view to characterize faith in the form of subjectivity, meaning that the community raises *itself* into the form of self-consciousness, that it has its being in the activity of bringing forth. All activity is mediated: what is to be brought forth must already exist in and for itself. Activity is merely positing, it imparts only the character of being-for-self; spiritual activity is possible only if what is to be posited is presupposed. "Is it possible that this can be done?" means, "Is it already so in and for itself?"

We have seen finite subjectivity taken up into the content. Reconciliation is already implicitly accomplished. This is the representational image of the Spirit, and only by means of this image can reconciliation be brought forth. Thus the activity of the community is already determined by the fact that reconciliation is implicitly accomplished, i.e., that God is spirit. This is the spiritual element of religion, and this content is what the community *brings forth*. It is evident that the community brings forth this doctrine, this relationship within itself, that it cannot be brought forth, so to speak, from the words, from the mouth of Christ, but is produced through the community, through the church. The empirical way in which [this] has happened does not concern us here. The story may be full of the passionate disputes of bishops at church councils and so on—this is of no account. What is the content in and for itself? Only by philosophy can this simply present content be justified, not by history [*Geschichte*]. What spirit does is no history [*Historie*].[48] Spirit is concerned only with what is in and for itself, not something past, but simply what is present. This is the origin of the community.

2. THE SUBSISTENCE OF THE COMMUNITY

The second aspect is its continuation, the subsistence of the community, its self-maintenance. Within itself the community is an eternal becoming that presupposes itself. Spirit is an eternal process of self-cognition in self-consciousness, streaming out to the finite focus of finite consciousness, and then returning to what spirit actually is, a return in which *divine* self-consciousness breaks forth.[49] The community is a process of eternal becoming.

More precisely, in the subsistence of the community, doctrine is already complete, and the individual is merely attracted to a doctrine that is already there in a finished state. It is evident that a doctrine is necessary. The content must be made representationally visible, and it is a content in which what is to be accomplished in the individual as such is accomplished, exhibited in and for itself.

[(1)] The sacrament of *baptism* is the first thing to play a part in this connection. The individual, that is, is already born within the community of the church; he or she is not born in misery and will not be confronted by a hostile world but by a world that is a church, so that each one simply has to be grafted as subject upon a community that already exists as the individual's current environment.

Doctrine comes to the individual through the *authority* of the church. The beginning of all our knowing is and must be authority. Even in the case of sense-knowledge we begin with the authority of being: it is the way it is, immediately, and it is valid for us as such—this is the authority of the sensible. Representational images with which we are familiar are the authorities from which we begin our philosophizing. They are given us as true; they are not our own insight. Our own insight comes only later on through the reworking, assimilation, appropriation, and taking back of this material.

[(2)] This second moment is therefore the assimilation involved in *rebirth* by means of doctrine or teaching. Human beings must be born twice, first naturally, then spiritually, like the Brahmans. Spirit is not immediate; it is only insofar as it engenders itself from itself. That is why there is a grief belonging to the natural state. This rebirth is no longer the infinite melancholy arising from the pangs of birth; but there is also present the antithesis arising from the purely private preoccupations of human beings, their further interests, passions, self-seeking, etc. Only so can they have a natural heart, being other than they should be. The natural heart in which they are imprisoned is the enemy that is to be combated, but in the community this enemy is so determined as to be implicitly overcome.

The representation of a perennial struggle is not here the last word, as it is in the Kantian philosophy, where the strife is unending and the resolution is put off to infinity, so that we must take our stand upon the "ought."[50] Here the contradiction is resolved; hence the nature of spirit also is represented to the individual in such a way that evil is implicitly overcome. It does not have an absolutely independent subsistence, as it does in the eternal struggle between light and darkness of the Persian religion; [nor] is there a mechanically external relationship between the sensible and the rational, as in the Kantian philosophy, where the two realms remain independent.[51] Here the power belongs to spirit; but spirit is the absolute and is what is here known—the awareness that what has happened as such, what has been found to be the case, the natural being of humanity, can be undone. Here there is the awareness that, just as the natural will can be given up, so there is no sin that cannot be forgiven, except for the sin against the Holy Spirit,[52] the denial of spirit itself; for spirit alone is the power that can itself sublate everything. Spirit has only to deal with itself in the element of the soul, of freedom, of spirituality; it does not continue to stand over against natural being or action and deed. Only spirit is free; its energy is not restricted. There is no power that is equal to it or that can come against it; no mechanistic or spiritless relationship is possible.

It is true that there are very many difficulties about this topic, difficulties that arise from the concept of spirit and of freedom. On the one hand there is spirit as universal spirit, and on the other hand human being-for-self, the being-for-self of the single individual. It must be said that it is the divine Spirit that effects rebirth; this is the free grace of God, for everything divine is free. It is not fate or destiny. On the other hand, however, the self-consciousness of the soul stands fast, too, and the question now is to ascertain how much is due to human agency. A *velleitas,* a *nisus* remains to it, but stubborn persistence in [its own contribution to] this relationship is itself what is unspiritual. The first being [of a human, its] self-being, is the concept in itself, implicit spirit; and what has to be sublated is the form of its immediacy, of its singularized, private being-for-itself. This self-sublating and coming to self on the part of the concept is universal nature, in the same way that in the element of thought, spirit that comes to itself is free spirit; but free spirit is unlimited, universal spirit.

(3) The third [moment] in regard to this rebirth is that of *partaking* [*Genuß*]—the consciousness of this divine grace, the consciousness of being a citizen of God's kingdom—what is called mystical union, the sacrament of the Lord's Supper, where human beings are vouchsafed the consciousness of their reconciliation with God in a sensible, intuitable form, the indwelling and lodging of the Spirit within them.

The content of the sacramental actions is also the development of spirit. There are three ways of representing the content of this sacrament. For the content begins from the representation, which is based on the sensible; but the sublation of this sense-element is the certain knowledge, in worship, of the grace of the divine Spirit. What is represented in the sacrament is that Christ is eternally sacrificed and rises again in the heart; this is correct. The eternal sacrifice is the process through which single individuals make themselves their own, the process by which their implicit being passes away. But since they belong to grace and are reconciled, the resurrection of Christ also takes place within them. The differences within the Christian religion are essentially involved in this point.

The first representational image is that Christ is present in the host in a sensible, bodily, unspiritual fashion. He is in this *thing* through the consecration of the priest: the divine is to be found in this externality. This is the view of the Catholics; the divine is literally eaten by the worshipers.

The second view is that God is present only in spirit, in faith, or in a spiritual way: this is the great image of the Lutheran confession. It too begins from eating and drinking, as in the Eleusinian mysteries;[53] the starting point is the consumption of God objectively present. The advance is that the individual worshiper takes up this consumption inwardly, and the sensible is first spiritualized in the subject. The Father is what exists only insofar as it surrenders itself; but it first exists as real spirit, spirit realized, in self-consciousness. The crucial point in this interpretation is that transubstantiation takes place only in the partaking of communion, in faith, and only in a spiritual fashion.

The third view is that the deity is not present here at all, but is only remembered as an image. This is the Reformed view: [the sacrament] is merely a lively recollection of the past, devoid of spirit. It is not divine presence, there is no actual spirituality.

Such are the main considerations regarding the subsistence of the community.

3. THE REALIZATION OF FAITH

The third aspect to be considered is the realization of faith; but this also involves the transformation of the community, its recasting and modification.

The fact is that religion, as we have seen it, is spiritual religion, and the community exists primarily in what is inward, in spirit as such. This inwardness, this subjectivity that is inwardly present to itself, but not inwardly developed, is feeling or sensibility. The community also essentially possesses consciousness and its representations in the form of doctrine, etc., but this brings with it separation and differentiation. The divine objective idea confronts consciousness as something other, which is in part given by authority, in part appropriated in worship. Or again, the moment of communion is just one single moment; or yet again, the divine idea, the divine content, is not intuited, it is only represented. The "now" of communion dissolves in its representation, partly into a beyond, an otherworldly heaven, partly into the past, and partly into the future. But spirit is *simply present to itself;* it demands a fulfilled present, it requires more than merely confused images. It requires that the content should itself be present, or that feeling, sensibility, should be developed and expanded.

Thus over against the community, and the kingdom of God in the community, there stands an *objective reality.* As the external, *immediate* world, this objective reality is the *heart* and the concerns of the heart. Another form of objectivity is that of *reflection,* of abstract thought or understanding; and the third form, the true one, is that of the *concept.* Accordingly, we must consider the manner in which faith *realizes* itself in these three elements.

The realization of faith or of religion in general is simply the *reconciliation* of spirit. Initially, this reconciliation still has an antithesis, and we must consider its relationship to it, the way in which the antithesis is sublated, how the idea takes shape in it and seems in so doing to run the risk of losing itself.

[(1)] The first thing that opposes reconciliation is the natural *heart*. Religious reconciliation proceeds within the heart as that which is most inward and deep. On the other hand, the heart is also something private: it is the *natural* heart, with passions, inclinations, self-seeking, and egoism; hence in its one-sidedness it is forsaken by the universal, removed from faith. The direct reconciliation of the community with this worldliness, a reconciliation that is only immediate, is through the community's taking all these passions, inclinations, etc. up into itself, so that the *church*, which has its existence in its subjects, lets them do as they like, takes them up into itself as they are immediately, and thereby receives into itself all the coarseness and passions, etc. [of human life]. The church is, on the one hand, the struggle with what is worldly; but on the other hand, standing as it does in the existence of a crude world, it falls into worldliness and corruption. So this initial reconciliation has rather the character of the church's corruption.

[(2)] The second [realm] to which the church is related is *reflection*.[54] It is indeed through the contact between the inward and the worldly or finite that reflection, indeed thinking in general, is first awakened, as the mediation of the real, worldly side with the ideal. This proximate and initial reconciliation can only be an abstract one; it is a self-disclosure of the understanding, of reflection, a self-disclosure of the reflection of a universality that is at first the abstract universality of the understanding.

Inasmuch as reflection thus sets [itself] up as a standard, there arises a hostile relationship to the church. Since the church seeks to imprint its image on the understanding, while the understanding imagines itself to be the content of religion, there emerges the sharpest possible apparent conflict. The community has the peculiarity of containing within itself the infinite antithesis between absolute spirit, having being in and for itself, and subjective, single spirit. The latter, in its character as singular self-consciousness, represents the extreme of formal freedom. As such, this extreme is what we have previously called the innermost realm. Over against this innermost realm stands "natural humanity" with all of its private concerns, so that the subject itself is this infinite contradiction. This antithesis is reconciled in and for itself, and the reconciliation is portrayed in religion. Implicitly it is reconciled in the concept too, and this is the subjectivity, the infinitude of the ego within itself, what was previously pointed out as the principle of immortality. Here the realization of faith consists in the fact that this inward element does not remain simply the inward heart, simply the depths of the heart, but develops itself within itself. So if we say that faith grows in the soil of what is most inward, the natural human self is quite distinct from this; and because the innermost element is not [yet]

254

developed within itself, this truth [about faith] is for it a sensible history, a representation of God; it is spiritual truth as merely objective, as a datum.

The requirement is that the inmost element shall develop inwardly itself, that it shall exist for itself as the idea, albeit only as the subjective idea. This is what is meant by saying that faith realizes itself in reflection. What is awakened initially is thinking in general, the demand for the unity of what is inmost with one's own particular worldly life. This is a demand for universality, in the first place for abstract universality. What it produces or manifests by itself is that this infinite inwardness, or pure thinking within itself, turns against authority and demands the form of selfhood with regard to every content that is to be accepted by it as true. Faith is indeed the testimony of the Spirit to the truth. The sensibility of devotion receives and has within itself the fulfillment afforded by the Spirit, but the individual worshipers do not exist for themselves therein; the truth has the form of authority, and the self lacks the determination of its own being-for-self in it.

The second [moment] is that thinking itself then produces hard-and-fast characteristics within itself and by itself. It discovers in the self a content, namely, that it is natural humanity; and since it is the universal, and its activity is that of universality, it extracts the affirmative element from the content and gives it the form of universality. Thus it arrives at hard-and-fast characteristics. For instance, the family relationship [is] a content of this kind—family life or family love, justice in general, contractual provisions, the relation of individuals to official authority, the relations of sovereigns and states. There is the testimony of spirit for these also that they are essential relationships. In human life they become fixed characteristics—the family against celibacy, [property] rights against the poverty enjoined by the church, obedience to civil authority against the blind obedience of the church ([i.e.,] against the demand that one surrender all one's will and know nothing of determinations fixed within oneself and by oneself). Thus, in the second place, reflection also arrives at a hard-and-fast content; the content becomes fixed by obtaining the form of universality and, therewith, the form of identity with itself. Thinking thus enters into an antithesis to the church; it bases itself on fixed determinations; it brooks no contradiction. Whatever contradicts these fixed determinations is invalid; pretensions and ordinances of the church that run counter to them have no validity for it.

Abstract thinking, with its principle of identity, assails the inner content of the church even more violently. This content is concrete; it is the unity of the two [the universal and the particular]—the divine Trinity. This concrete content stands in contradiction to the abstract law of identity. In the same way the relationship of God to humanity, the process of grace, the unity of divine and human nature, the mystical union—[all of these] represent an absolute coupling of opposite determinations. This content is annulled in thought; and reflection then has as its final result the objectivity of identity itself, namely, that God is nothing but the supreme being [*das höchste Wesen*]—which (for the very reason that it is not concrete, without definition, and empty) is simultaneously defined for cognition as what is beyond it. For every determination makes [what is determined] concrete, and cognition is only the knowledge of concrete content. This consummation of reflection is the antithesis of the Christian church.

There are two forms of this abstract unity. [For the first,[55]] what counts as the true is empty unity, something other opposed to cognition. Vis-à-vis the subject, this empty unity is a negation, for the subject knows itself as concrete. Finitude stands on this side of the empty essence. It has become free for itself, and it is of absolute value within itself, it is independent. In this way, finitude is its own criterion of value in various forms, as, for example, the personal uprightness of individuals. The further consequence of this is not only that the objective reality of God is thus removed into the beyond and negated, but also that all other objective determinations, all of the determinations that are valid implicitly and explicitly (and are posited in the world as rights, customs, etc.), explicitly disappear. Since the subject withdraws to the pinnacle of its own infinitude, what is good, just, etc. is contained only within it; it makes good and justice into its subjective decisions, they constitute *its* thoughts. What bodies out this good is then derived from natural caprice, contingency, passion, etc. The [single] subject is simply the consciousness that objectivity is shut up within itself; it is conscious that objective reality has no subsistence; only the principle of identity is valid for this subject. It is an abstract subject, it can be bodied out with any sort of content; it has the capability (so deeply implanted in the human heart) of subsuming each and every content. Thus subjectivity is caprice and the knowledge of its power over everything—its power to produce objectivity, the good, and imbue it with content.

The second form [of abstract unity] is that, vis-à-vis the unity toward which it has stretched out, subjectivity has no being on its own account, and therefore it does not allot to itself an affirmative private sphere; instead its vocation is to submerge itself in the unity of God, of the infinite. Thus the subject has no private purpose, and no absolute purpose other than that of willing itself to exist for this One, and it alone, of making its sole purpose the glory of the one God. This other form is religion: it contains an affirmative relationship to one's essence, which is this One, wherein the subject yields itself up. This religion has in general the same content as the Jewish religion, but the relationship in which human beings stand is broadened. No particularity remains to it; here there is no defining characteristic like the Jewish sense of national value. Here there is no limitation to a particular people; humanity relates itself to the One as purely abstract self-consciousness. This is the characteristic of the *Islamic religion*.[56] In it Christianity finds its antithesis because it occupies a sphere equivalent to that of the Christian religion. It is a spiritual religion like the Jewish, but its God is [available] for self-consciousness only within the *abstract* knowing spirit. Its God is on a par with the Christian God to the extent that no particularity is retained. Anyone, from any people, who fears God is pleasing to God, and human beings have value only to the extent that they take as their truth the knowledge that this is the One, the essential being. The differentiation of subjects according to their station in life or class is sublated; there may be classes, there may even be slaves, but this is merely accidental.

The antithesis consists in the fact that in Christianity spirituality is developed *concretely* within itself and is known as Trinity, as spirit; and that human history, the relationship to the One, is likewise a *concrete* history that begins with the natural will, which is as it ought not to be. The surrender of the natural will and the coming to be of the [spiritual] self takes place through the negation of our [natural] self for the sake of our [spiritual] essence. The religion of Islam, by contrast, hates and proscribes everything concrete; its God is the absolute One, in relation to whom human beings retain for themselves no purpose, no private domain, nothing peculiar to themselves. Inasmuch as they exist, humans do in any case create a private domain for themselves in their inclinations and interests, and these are all the more savage and unrestrained in this case because they lack reflection. But coupled with this is also the complete opposite, namely, the tendency to let everything take its own course, indifference with respect to every purpose, absolute fatalism, indifference to life; no practical purpose has any essential value. But since human beings are in fact practical and active, their purpose can only be to bring about the veneration of the One in all humanity. Thus the religion of Islam is essentially fanatical.

The [stance of] "reflection" that we have been considering is on a par with Islam in that God has no content and is not concrete. In this way the concrete historical content of the life of Christ also disappears; his exaltation to be the Son of God, the transfiguration of self-consciousness, etc. have no place here. The distinction consists in the fact that this independence of Islam [from everything concrete and worldly] is not preserved [by reflection]; here, on the contrary, subjective reflection retains for itself the power to fill out its own contingent free will. This is the religion of the Enlightenment, of reflection, of abstract thinking, which means in fact that the truth cannot be cognized, cannot be known—that it is not there for subjective self-consciousness [proper] but only for its opinion, its contingency, and its pleasure.

The final point is that a reconciliation can also be recognized in this last-mentioned form; thus this last mode of appearing is also a realization of faith. For since all content and all truth perish in this subjectivity that inwardly knows itself as infinite yet remains private, the principle of subjective freedom thereby comes to consciousness in it. What is called inwardness in the community is now developed within itself. It is not only inwardness and conscience, but is the subjectivity that divides, differentiates itself, that is concrete; it knows within itself the universal that it produces from itself. This is the subjectivity that is for itself and inwardly determines itself, the consummation of the subjective extreme to the point of being the self-contained idea. But the deficiency here is that this is only formal and lacks true objectivity; it represents the ultimate pinnacle of formal development without inner necessity. For the true consummation of the idea, what has been differentiated must be set free, must in itself constitute a totality of objective reality.

(3) The third relationship of faith is to the *concept,* to the *idea.* Once reflection has invaded the sphere of religion, thinking or reflection assumes a hostile attitude toward the representational form in religion and toward the concrete content. And once thinking has begun in this way, it does not stop; it carries through, it empties heart and heaven; cognitive spirit and the religious content then take refuge in the concept. Here they must find their justification; thinking must grasp itself as concrete and free, not maintaining the distinctions as merely posited, but letting them go free and in that way recognizing the content as objective.

Philosophy therefore has the task of mediating these two relationships. Religion and the need for religion can take refuge in the form of feeling or sensibility as well as in the concept. It can limit itself to giving up the truth and renouncing all hope of knowing a content, with the result that the holy church no longer has any commonality and splits into atoms, each with its own worldview. For commonality is based on doctrine, but individuals have each their own feeling, their own sensations. It is just this form that does not correspond to spirit, which is resolved to *know.*

Thus philosophy stands between two opposing views. On the one hand it seems to be opposed to the church; because it conceptualizes, it shares with the development of culture and with reflection the refusal to remain bound to the form of representation. Instead, it [advances to the point] of comprehending [the truth] in thoughts; and in the process it also recognizes the necessity of the form of representation. But the concept is the higher form because, even while encompassing the various [representational] forms and acknowledging their legitimacy, it has its own content. So this opposition [to the church] is only a formal one. The other opposition is between philosophy and the Enlightenment. Philosophy is opposed to the [attitude of] indifference toward the content, it is opposed to mere opinion, to the despair involved in its renunciation of the truth, and to the view that it does

CHRISTIANITY: THE CONSUMMATE RELIGION

not matter what content is intended. The goal of philosophy is the cognition of the truth—the cognition of God because God is the absolute truth. In that context nothing else is worth troubling about compared with God and God's explication. Philosophy knows God essentially as concrete, as the spiritual, realized universality that is not jealous but communicates itself. Even light communicates itself. Whoever says that God cannot be recognized is saying that God is jealous,[57] and is not making a serious effort to achieve cognition when he speaks of God. The Enlightenment—that vanity of understanding—is the most vehement opponent of philosophy. It takes it very ill when philosophy demonstrates the rational content in the Christian religion, when it shows the witness of the Spirit, the truth in the most all-embracing sense of the term, is deposited in religion. Thus the task of philosophy[58] is to show forth the rational content of religion.

That was the purpose of these lectures, to reconcile reason with religion in its manifold forms, and to recognize them as at least necessary.

This conceptual cognition of religion is by its nature not universal, but is rather only the cognition of a community.[59] For that reason three stages take shape in regard to the kingdom of the Spirit: the first estate is that of immediate, naive religion and of faith; the second is that of the understanding, the estate of the so-called cultured, of reflection and the Enlightenment; and finally the third estate is the community of philosophy.

NOTES

INTRODUCTION. HEGEL: THEOLOGIAN OF THE SPIRIT

1. Information for this section has been provided by a number of sources, including Franz Wiedmann, *Hegel: An Illustrated Biography,* trans. Joachim Neugroschel (New York, 1968); Jacques D'Hondt, *Hegel in His Time,* trans. John Burbidge (Peterborough, Ontario, 1988); Stephen Houlgate, *Freedom, Truth and History: An Introduction to Hegel's Philosophy* (London and New York, 1991); and Richard Kroner, "Hegel's Philosophical Development," introduction to *Early Theological Writings,* trans. T. M. Knox (Chicago, 1948).

2. Hegel's first child, Ludwig, was born in 1807 to the wife of his landlord in Jena, with whom he had had an affair. Later, after his marriage, Ludwig was taken into Hegel's household and raised as a member of the family. He was a troubled, unhappy boy, who later served in the Dutch army and died in Indonesia in 1831. Hegel himself died before learning of the death of his eldest son.

3. Walter Jaeschke, *Reason in Religion: The Foundations of Hegel's Philosophy of Religion,* trans. J. Michael Stewart and Peter C. Hodgson (Berkeley and Los Angeles, 1990), pp. 1–9.

4. See ibid., pp. 121–28.

5. *Lectures on the Philosophy of Religion,* ed. and trans. Peter C. Hodgson et al. (Berkeley and Los Angeles, 1984–87), 1:84 (1821 lecture ms.). "Service of God" translates *Gottesdienst,* the normal German word for "worship." Hegel played on the literal meaning of the term.

6. Ibid., 1:121–22 (1824 lectures), 154–58, 168 (1827 lectures).

7. Ibid., 3:246–47 (1824 lectures). The variant referring to the "[branch of] philosophy that is theology" derives most likely from Hegel's marked copy of Griesheim's transcript of the 1824 lectures. In this Hegel is drawing on a tradition that goes back to Aristotle, who conceived his "first philosophy" as theology.

8. Ibid., 3:347 (1827 lectures). Here the allusion is to Phil. 4:7.

9. Ibid., 2:252 (1824 lectures); and Hegel's Foreword to Hinrichs's *Religion* (below, p. 170).

10. Hegel praised Daub and Marheineke specifically in this connection at the conclusion of his Hinrichs Foreword (below, p. 171).

11. For a thorough discussion, see Jaeschke, *Reason in Religion,* chap. 4.

12. See Cyril O'Regan, *The Heterodox Hegel* (Albany, 1994), p. 3. O'Regan shows how Hegel's postcritical reconstruction of ontotheology draws upon resources in a heterodox tradition that goes back to Gnosticism, Neoplatonism, and medieval and early modern mysticism (Meister Eckhart, Joachim of Fiore, and Jacob Boehme). Another valuable study, which explores the influence on Hegel's pneumatology of Luther and Lutheran pietism, is Alan M. Olson, *Hegel and the Spirit: Philosophy as Pneumatology* (Princeton, 1992), esp. chap. 3. A considerable portion of Olson's study (chaps. 4–6) is devoted to the relationship between Hegel and Hölderlin, and especially to the impact of the latter's madness on Hegel's interpretation of spirit.

13. O'Regan, *The Heterodox Hegel,* pp. 20–21, 29–30, 45–49.

14. Ibid., pp. 52–54, 56–57.

15. For the etymology of *Geist,* see Steven G. Smith, *The Concept of the Spiritual: An Essay in First Philosophy* (Philadelphia, 1988), pp. 9–11. On the connection between spirit and recognition, see Robert R. Williams, *Recognition: Fichte and Hegel on the Other* (Albany, 1992). My reading of Hegel has been influenced in a number of ways by Williams.

16. This is the beginning of Hegel's later analytic distinction, applied to each of the determinate religions in the philosophy of religion lectures, between abstract concept, concrete representation, and community or cultus.

17. See Jürgen Moltmann's discussion of this matter in *The Spirit of Life: A Universal Affirmation,* trans. Margaret Kohl (Minneapolis, 1992), pp. 157–60.

18. See Raimon Panikkar, *The Cosmotheandric Experience: Emerging Religious Consciousness* (Maryknoll, N.Y., 1993).

19. For the historical religions considered in this bundle, see n. 5 to this selection.

20. This is true of the second (1827) and third (1830) editions as well as the first, although the content of the section on religion was revised and expanded somewhat in 1827. Our translation is of the 1830 edition. On the relation of the *Phenomenology* and the *Encyclopedia* to the *Lectures,* see Jaeschke, *Reason in Religion,* pp. 208–15.

21. Cyril O'Regan discusses the significance of these two arrangements in *The Heterodox Hegel,* pp. 235–37. He points out that the Spirit is the "first among equals" for Hegel, and that Hegelian heterodoxy "swerves" away from traditional christology, pneumatology, and ecclesiology through the impact of mysticism.

22. See *Elements of the Philosophy of Right,* ed. Allen W. Wood, trans. H. B. Nisbet (Cambridge, 1991), p. 20 (incl. n. 22); and *Lectures on Natural Right and Political Science* (Heidelberg, 1817–1818), ed. Hegel Archives with an Introduction by Otto Pöggeler, trans. J. Michael Stewart

and Peter C. Hodgson (Berkeley and Los Angeles, 1995), pp. 221, 242, 247.

23. The linkage with the Roman Empire, couched in almost apocalyptic terms, occurs at the very end of the lectures of 1821. See *Lectures on the Philosophy of Religion,* 3:158–62.

24. See the Editorial Introduction to *Lectures on the Philosophy of Religion,* 3:48–50. In the 1831 lectures, Hegel offered an interesting comparison: the concept sublates its subjectivity and objectifies itself just as, when human beings realize their purposes, what was at first only ideal becomes something real.

25. See *Lectures on the Philosophy of Religion,* 3:27.

26. Cyril O'Regan argues that the expression "inclusive Trinity" is a more adequate term for Hegel's trinitarian elaboration than "economic Trinity." In the classical immanent-economic model, the economic Trinity refers only to God's threefold saving work in the world (the divine *oikonomia*), whereas on Hegel's immanent-inclusive model, the inclusive Trinity *overreaches* the intradivine Trinity, incorporating it as the first moment (the "Father"), while the second moment is creation/incarnation/redemption (the "Son"), and the third moment is divine presence and reconciliation (the "Holy Spirit"). The inclusive Trinity is simply the divine plenitude that Hegel names absolute spirit. See O'Regan, *The Heterodox Hegel,* pp. 72–75. See also Dale M. Schlitt, *Hegel's Trinitarian Claim: A Critical Reflection* (Leiden, 1984), pp. 267–73.

27. See *Lectures on the Philosophy of Religion,* 3:292–93. Hegel refers to Jacob Boehme's interpretation of the fall of Lucifer in both the 1824 and 1827 lectures. The idea of "releasing" is probably indebted to Meister Eckhart.

28. See *Lectures on the Philosophy of Religion,* 1:52–58 (translation principles), and 3:399–408 (glossary).

1. EARLY THEOLOGICAL WRITINGS (1793–1800)

Religion Is One of Our Greatest Concerns in Life (1793)

1. Four pages are missing at this point. The manuscript resumes with the end of a sentence: ". . . setting in motion the [?] of human life." The paragraph continues: "We should not . . ."

2. *Nathan the Wise,* 4.7 (1770)—an enormously influential drama by Gotthold Ephraim Lessing (1729–1781).

3. The full passage to which Hegel refers reads: "Again, although he knew something of the truth and denied the gods, Socrates at the end ordered a cock to be sacrificed to Aesculapius—I think in order to honor his

(Aesculapius's) father, since Apollo had declared Socrates to be the wisest of humans. Careless Apollo! He had testified to the wisdom of a man who denied that the gods existed!" Translated from *Q. Septimi Tertulliani Apologeticum*, ed. C. Pascal and L. Castiglioni (Torino, 1965), pp. 105–6.

4. The reference is apparently to the third of Christian F. Gellert's lectures on morality. Gellert (1715–1769) was best known for his poem "Der Christ." Tertullian had written: "Any Christian workman discovers God (*Deum quilibet opifex Christianus*) and demonstrates his presence, attributing to him everything one looks for in God. And yet Plato can assert that the maker of the universe is not easy to find, and is hard to describe to everyone even when he is found."

5. Here in all likelihood one sheet (roughly eight pages) is missing. Several additional pages are also omitted at this point in the present edition. Hegel goes on at some length with a critique of the Enlightenment and its notion of "understanding," to which he contrasts "true wisdom."

6. Hegel has here "ein pathologisches Prinzip des Handelns." He is following a philosophical convention, owing much to Kant, according to which "pathological" is contrasted with "rational" and has no connotation of disease.

7. H. S. Harris is surely right in translating *hierarchischen* this way.

8. Cf. Harris, *Hegel's Development: Toward the Sunlight, 1770–1801* (Oxford, 1972) p. 498 n. 2, for a variant translation (*Schmerzen:* sorrows) based on certain passages in Hegel's subsequent essays. But given the fragmentary character of Hegel's remark here, the naturalness of the distinction as we have it, and (as Harris notes) its isolated occurrence in this collection of texts, we find neither interpretation conclusive.

9. The Greek phrase *anangkaia tychē* designates necessity, fate, or forture; *moira* refers to one's destiny or lot in life.

10. [*Hegel's note:*] Outside the Christian church a sacrifice was at most a drop of balm for the soul of the offender; his conscience (for surely there is no instance of such a degree of moral corruption among a [more primitive] people) was not so easily pacified.

11. The translators construe subsequent references to "a being" (*ein Wesen*) as masculine whereas in this edition they are converted to the neuter. *Wesen* is masculine in a grammatical but not necessarily a conceptual sense.

12. There is no *b*.

13. The Greek *tēs sophrosynēs* can very well mean, as Hegel has it, "of a well-ordered sensibility," i.e. one that is imbued with temperance.

14. Hegel's reference is to the Stephanus edition of Plato's *Symposium*. Cf. Harris, *Toward the Sunlight*, p. 505n.

15. [*Hegel's addition:*] The father of this genie [*Genius*] is Chronos

(Time), on whom he remains to some extent dependent all his life (temporal circumstances). His mother is the *politeia*, the constitution. His midwife, his wet-nurse, is religion, which enlists the aid of the fine arts, especially music, in order to form the movement of his spirit and body. His is an ethereal being which, though drawn down to earth and held there by a slender thread, resists with the help of a magic spell all attempts to break it, for it is completely entwined in his essence. This thread, whose coarse grain is animal desire, is woven together out of myriad natural fibers. Since with each new fiber he is bound more tightly to nature, he feels so little weighted down that he experiences on the contrary an expansion of his pleasures, a broadening of his life, as he willingly senses these fibers spontaneously enlarge and multiply. Gradually all the finer, more delicate feelings ripen within him, feelings which through social interaction bring him a thousand modulations of delight.

[*Ed.*] This passage occurs in the main text, but as Harris rightly notes, Hegel cancelled the passage "some time after he had written it." Fuss and Dobbins translate *Genius* here and in the following paragraphs as "spirit," but we have changed it to "genie" since it represents a personification and mythologization of the "spirit of the people" [*Geist des Volks*].

16. [*Hegel's note:*] The Occident has concocted for itself a quite different native genie [*Genius*]. His form shows its age—it was never particularly fair—and only a few faint traces of manliness remain. His father is bent with age; and he too is beyond even trying to look about joyfully or to rejoice in his own sense of well-being. Indeed he is so short-sighted that he doesn't have the courage to see any but the littlest things, one at a time. And lacking confidence in his powers, he never ventures anything bold. Iron fetters, cruel and . . .

[*Ed.*] The remainder of this paragraph was evidently never completed and the extant portion was cancelled. It is impossible to tell from the German syntax whether the "he" in the phrase "and he too is beyond" refers to the "native genie" or to his father. Nor can this be definitively determined from the sense of the extant passage.

The Divine in a Particular Shape (1799)

1. In his Introduction to *Early Theological Writings*, trans. T. M. Knox (Chicago, 1948), p. 9. Kroner provides an excellent survey of Hegel's philosophical development, especially in the earlier years. For a detailed analysis of "The Spirit of Christianity and Its Fate," see H. S. Harris, *Hegel's Development: Toward the Sunlight, 1770–1801* (Oxford, 1972), chap. 4.

2. Knox translates this term here and in the following sentences as "the real." In later writings Hegel distinguishes between *Wirklichkeit* (actuality)

and *Realität* (reality), the former encompassing all that is, the whole, the latter referring to the real as opposed to the ideal. The distinction may have little significance in the early writings.

3. A similar reference is found in Hegel's 1821 philosophy of religion lecture manuscript. See *Lectures on the Philosophy of Religion*, ed. and trans. Peter C. Hodgson et al. (Berkeley and Los Angeles, 1984–87), 3:121–22, incl. n. 156.

4. As Nohl indicates in a footnote, Hegel is quoting and criticizing Kant. See the "General Remark" appended to Part 3 of Kant's *Religion within the Limits of Reason Alone,* trans. T. M. Greene and H. H. Hudson (New York, 1960).

5. Hegel quotes loosely here from John 14:9; 17:8; 17:21–26.

6. Cf. Matt. 9:3; John 5:18.

7. Knox translates as "dunghill," but the expression here, *im Kote,* more likely means "hut," "hovel" (*das Kot[e]*), not "mud," "dung" (*der Kot*). The context supports this reading (something large will not fit into something small). In the next sentence, Knox translates *Nuß* as "nest" rather than "nut"; and in the second sentence preceding, he translates *die Armen,* "the poor," as "poor things that they were." These translations unfortunately intensify Hegel's negative attitude toward Judaism. His prejudice shifted to qualified appreciation in the later philosophy of religion lectures. For example, in the lectures of 1827, Hegel says that the Jewish insight into the "spiritually subjective unity" of God is "for us . . . what first merits the name of God" (*Lectures on the Philosophy of Religion,* 2:669). It is probably also the case that, like the Gospel of John upon which he is here so dependent, the Jews represent for Hegel in typological fashion the blindness of humanity as a whole. After all, it is the (Enlightenment) attitude of *Verstand* (intellect) that fails to grasp the unity of the divine and the human.

8. Knox observes that God is the object (*Gegenstand*) of faith, i.e., the one in whom we believe and who stands over against (*gegen-stand*) us. But God is not an object (*Objekt*) as distinct from a subject, because God is spirit or a living consciousness.

9. Hegel translates Greek *hōs* as "until" (*bis*) rather than as the more customary and accurate "while."

10. Hegel quotes here loosely from Matt. 18:3-6, 10, with considerable emendations of his own.

11. Knox annotates: that is, a God who is a person exclusive of other persons and set over against them.

12. The avenging spirits or furies of Greek religion.

13. See G. Keate, *The Pellew Islands,* German translation by G. Forster (Hamburg, 1789), p. xxiv. Hegel referred to this book in a marginal note. Nohl supplies the exact reference.

14. In an earlier section of *The Spirit of Christianity,* Hegel writes: "Universal philanthropy, i.e., the philanthropy which is to extend to all, even to those of whom the philanthropist knows nothing, whom he has not met, with whom he stands in no relation, is a shallow but characteristic discovery of ages which, because their real achievement is so poor, cannot help setting up ideal commands, virtues directed on an *ens rationis,* for the sake of appearing remarkably splendid in such conceptual objects. Love for one's nearest neighbors is philanthropy toward those with whom each one of us comes into contact." See *Early Theological Writings,* pp. 246–47.

15. Knox refers the reader at this point to Hegel's *Philosophy of Right,* § 5 (the most recent English edition is edited by Allen W. Wood and translated by H. B. Nisbet, Cambridge, 1991). Hegel returns to this theme in a later passage of *The Spirit of Christianity* (see *Early Theological Writings,* pp. 288–89n.).

2. JENA WRITINGS (1802–1803)

Faith and Knowledge

1. Hegel is referring to Immanuel Kant's *Religion within the Limits of Reason Alone* (1793).

2. If *an und für sich* is translated less literally, the sentence might read: "Reason, though, had already gone to seed when . . . ."

3. Friedrich Heinrich Jacobi, *Letters on the Teaching of Spinoza* (1796); see *Werke* (6 vols., Leipzig, 1812–25), 4/1:214. The metaphor comes from Luke 16:3.

4. See especially Johann Gottlieb Fichte, *The Vocation of Man* (1800), ed. R. M. Chisholm (Indianapolis and New York, 1956), pp. 89–90; *Sämmtliche Werke* (8 vols., Berlin, 1845–46), 2:254–55.

5. The *locus classicus* of the "old distinction" is Thomas Aquinas, *Summa contra Gentiles,* 1.3–8.

6. An echo of Horace (*Epistles,* 1.6, 31–32). The theme recurs more than once in Hegel's early manuscripts and in the *Phenomenology of Spirit.*

7. See the preceding note and Psalm 115:4–8.

8. By translating *Schauen* here as "intuition," Cerf and Harris do not bring out the linkage with *Anschauung* in the preceding sentence.

9. The text reads simply: "aber soweit als *sie* wirklich *sie* vereinzelte so würde *sie* nichts Schönes sein" (italics added by Cerf and Harris).

10. Hegel deals with this "reconciliation" at length in the *Phenomenology,* where his treatment of "Enlightenment" is relevant to his discussion of the principle of "eudaemonism" here.

11. Literally "not eternal intuition and bliss" (*night die ewige Anschauung und Seligkeit*).

12. In context "eins mit dem andern" may mean no more than "they are together."

13. The text could also mean: "either analyzing its own abstraction or leaving it intact [i.e., unanalyzed]."

14. The Cerf-Harris translation reads "in-completed," but the term used by Hegel, *verunvollständigt*, contains the double negative.

15. Cerf and Harris translate as "[proper] matter." However, in his more recent translation of the *Encyclopedia Logic*, Harris uses "ob-ject" for *Gegenstand*.

16. "Culture," "formative process," and "formative process of culture" all represent *Bildung* or *bilden* in this peroration.

17. Pascal, *Pensées*, 441. The expression "God godself is dead" is from a Lutheran passion hymn by Johannes Rist.

18. Literally, "the speculative Good Friday that once (or in other respects) was historical" (*der sonst historisch war*).

19. Compare the reference to the "Golgotha of Absolute Spirit" in the concluding sentence of the *Phenomenology of Spirit*.

The Resumption of the Whole into One

1. This phrase is used by Karl Rosenkranz (*Hegels Leben* [Berlin, 1844; r.p. Darmstadt, 1969)], p. 179) to characterize Hegel's approach to religion in his earliest system. The text that follows is Rosenkranz's summary of Hegel's argument. Our selection begins with the third sentence of the second paragraph of Harris's translation; the preceding material is of a transitional character.

2. That is, suggests Harris, the religious community does not need virtuosos of religious experience.

3. Harris translates *Gottesdienst* literally as "divine service."

4. *gerechte Notwendigkeit.* Harris comments: reconciliation involves both justice (like punishment) and necessity (like fate).

5. According to Harris (*System of Ethical Life and First Philosophy of Spirit,* ed. & trans. Harris and Knox [Albany, 1979], pp. 83–84), Hegel identified these three forms with (1) Greek religion, (2) the whole Judaeo-Roman-Christian tradition, and (3) a new philosophical religion that would incorporate the truth of the first two (a post-Christian religion of the spirit). Later, this typology was significantly modified (among other things Greek religion was distinguished from nature religion and the idea of a philosophical religion was abandoned), but the dialectic of identity, difference, and mediation was retained.

6. Harris translates *Der Phantasie ihres Pantheismus* literally as "For the imagination of its pantheism."

7. The Jewish people.

8. Harris translates *Dasein* as "finite existence."

9. According to Rudolf Haym (*Hegel und seine Zeit* [Berlin, 1857; r.p. Hildesheim, 1962], p. 509 n.13), Hegel's actual words were: "In the context of our ethical customs this new religion would have had to make the gallows, which is now what the cross was then, into its battle standard."

10. Literally "necessary" (*notwendigeres*).

11. Harris translates *der Einzelnen* as "of the single [believers]." Similarly, in the second sentence following, he translates *in dem Einzelnen* as "in a single [worshiper]." In the last paragraph of the text, he translates *Jeder Einzelne* as "Every single [person]." Since *Einzelne* often combines the meaning of singularity and individuality, it can be rendered as "single individual" without having to add something in brackets. Harris's objective is to maintain a consistent distinction between *Einzelne* and *Individuum,* but the consistency sometimes produces an awkward translation.

12. *Einzelheit;* Harris translates literally as "singularity."

13. The terms translated "patria" and "patriotically" are *Vaterland* and *vaterländisch.* For the final occurrence, Harris translates as "fatherland."

14. E.g., Friedrich Schelling.

15. Harris instead inserts "in nationalism"; but it is the prosaic, worldly character of Protestantism (the opposite side of its otherworldly yearning) that seems to be more at issue here.

16. Hegel uses this term in a technical sense employed by Schelling. Harris here lets it stand without translation, but earlier he renders it as "level," which is appropriate here as well.

17. Haym (*Hegel und seine Zeit,* p. 165) continues here: "This idealistic sphere forms an adventurous realm without rules; it has tumbled together at random from the histories and the imagination of all peoples and climates, without significance or truth for nature, which is placed in subjection to it, and equally without allowing that the spirit of the individuals of a people can maintain their right within it; it is without personalized [*eigentümliche*] imagination, as it is without personalized consecration."

18. We have slightly altered the translation of the last sentence from Harris's version to make its syntactic structure clear. Haym (p. 165) adds: Through philosophy "reason gets it vitality [*Lebendigkeit*] and nature gets its spirit back again."

3. PHENOMENOLOGY OF SPIRIT (1807)

The Absolute as Spirit

1. In this paragraph Hegel provides a summary of developments in recent philosophy. He is thinking in the first instance of Spinoza's doctrine of God as the one substance and of the vigorous critique of it by Pierre Bayle, Christian Wolff, Sebastian Kortholt, Johannes Colerus, H. E. G. Paulus, F. H. Jacobi, and others. The reference to "thinking as thinking" is traceable to C. G. Bardili and K. L. Reinhold. With the concept of "intellectual intuiting" [*intellektuelle Anschauen*], Hegel has in mind Friedrich Schelling, whose philosophy of identity conceives of intellectual intuition as the unity of thought and being (*Werke,* ed. K. F. A. Schelling, division 1 [Stuttgart and Augsburg, 1856–61], 4:361ff., esp. 368–69).

2. Hegel is probably thinking here of Spinoza's concept of the *amor dei intellectualis* (*Ethics,* part 5, props. 33, 35, 36); and he may also be alluding to a formulation of Friedrich Schiller (*Über Anmuth und Würde* [Leipzig, 1793], p. 109).

3. Hegel is thinking here of Schelling's thesis that form and essence (*Wesen*) are one in the absolute, of Fichte's establishment of an absolute principle (*Grundsatz*) of philosophy, and of Fichte's and Schelling's conception of intellectual or absolute intuition. See Friedrich Schelling, *Werke,* 4:367–68; and Johann Gottlieb Fichte, *Werke,* ed. I. H. Fichte (Berlin, 1845–46), 1:91; 2:375.

4. Critiques of an external purposiveness are found for Hegel especially in Bacon and Kant as well as Spinoza—critiques that discredit the concept of purpose in Schelling's philosophy of identity.

5. See Aristotle, *Physics,* 194a28ff., 198b10–199b33, 291b13–14; *De coelo,* 658a8–9; *De partibus animalium,* 432b21–22; *Metaphysics,* 1072b1–4.

6. The first proposition is advanced by I. Görres (*Glauben und Wissen* [Munich, 1805], p. 115) and Johann Jakob Wagner (*System der Idealphilosophie* [Leipzig, 1804], p. 28), the second and third by Fichte (see *Werke,* 5:186, 543).

7. On the doctrine of being and the one, see Xenophanes, Zeno, Melissos, and especially Parmenides. Hegel may also be thinking of the reception of Parmenides' doctrine by Plato and the Neoplatonists.

8. See Karl Leonhard Reinhold, *Beyträge zur Berichtigung bisheriger Mißverständnisse der Philosophen* (Jena, 1790), pp. 94, 109; and Fichte, *Werke,* 1:91.

9. On the understanding of God as spirit in the Christian religion, see John 4:24.

10. Philosophical analyses of representation contemporary to Hegel are found in Johann Nicolas Tetens, Karl Leonhard Reinhold, and Ernst Platner.

The Science of the Experience of Consciousness

1. Hegel is thinking here of Kant's critique of epistemology (see *Critique of Pure Reason,* trans. N. Kemp Smith [London, 1930], B xvi ff., xxii–xxiii), which Hegel characterizes in a similar way in his lectures on the history of philosophy. He may also have in mind John Locke's critique (see *An Essay Concerning Human Understanding,* 11th ed., vol. 1 [London, 1735], introduction, pp. 4–5).

Religion

1. This is the introductory section of chap. 7 of the *Phenomenology,* titled "Religion."

2. These are the topics of the preceding chapters of the *Phenomenology* (chaps. 1–6). Consciousness (chaps. 1–3), self–consciousness (chap. 4), and reason (chap. 5) correspond to the logical dialectic of identity, difference, and mediation; or of universality, particularity, and individuality; or of being in-itself, for-itself, and in-and-for-itself. Reason manifests itself as ethical, cultural, and moral spirit (chap. 6), as religion and art (chap. 7), and as absolute knowing or philosophy (chap. 8), the latter two being the shapes of absolute spirit. Religion appears in the preceding shapes of consciousness, but to identify Hegel's treatment of it there would require a detailed analysis and is not necessary for purposes of this edition. For such an analysis, see Daniel P. Jamros, *The Human Shape of God: Religion in Hegel's Phenomenology of Spirit* (New York, 1994).

3. On the translation of *Wesen, Sein,* and *Dasein,* see below, "The Revelatory Religion," n. 7.

4. We translate *Einzelheit* uniformly as "individuality," although some interpreters prefer "singularity."

5. We omit the next two sections of the chapter, which treat "Natural Religion" and the "Religion of Art." Natural religion is religion at the stage of consciousness; the religion of art is religion at the stage of self-consciousness; and revelatory religion is religion at the stage of the mediation of the first two, namely reason and spirit. Natural religion is further divided into religion at the stage of sense-certainty (the religion of light [*das Lichtwesen*], i.e. Judaism and Zoroastrianism), religion at the stage of perception (the religion of life, i.e. animism, Hinduism), and religion at the stage of the understanding (the religion of the artificer, i.e. Egyptian religion, Islam). This material is reorganized and greatly expanded in the lec-

tures on the philosophy of religion. The religion of art is Greek religion, and it receives a very lengthy discussion in the *Phenomenology.*

The Revelatory Religion

1. *Die offenbare Religion.* Both Baillie and Miller translate this as "the revealed religion," thus blurring the distinction Hegel intended between *offenbar* ("revelatory," a *process* of opening, manifesting) and *geoffenbart* ("revealed," a *content* given in past events or figures). Christianity is "revelatory" because its God is intrinsically revelatory, self-disclosing, self-communicating; but this truth about God is also "revealed" in historical, "positive" fashion. Revelatoriness is for Hegel the more fundamental quality.

2. *Das Selbst ist das absolute Wesen.* This proposition characterizes the Roman world and Roman religion, in which the ethical spirit and beauty of Greek religion have been lost, leaving only the finite self with its abstract legal status and grandiose claims. The ensuing "unhappy consciousness" of the Roman world serves as the transition from Greek to Christian religion.

3. *Rechtzustand,* i.e., the Roman state, discussed at some length in a preceding chapter (chap. 6.A.c).

4. Hegel adopts here as a philosophical concept an expression of Martin Luther, who, almost alone in the history of Christian theology, interpreted the death of Christ as the death of God. See *Kritische Gesamtausgabe,* vol. 50 (Weimar, 1914), p. 589. In his lectures on the philosophy of religion, Hegel alludes to the passion hymn "O Traurigkeit, O Herzeleid" by Johannes Rist (1641), the second stanza of which reads: "O great woe! God himself lies dead. On the cross he has died; and thus he has gained for us by love the kingdom of heaven." See *Lectures on the Philosophy of Religion,* ed. and trans. Peter C. Hodgson et al. (Berkeley and Los Angeles, 1984–87), 3:125 n. 163.

5. Hegel now turns specifically to the revelatory or Christian religion and develops, in the next few pages (down to n. 11), a speculative theory of incarnation: the first "side" is the divine becoming human, the second is the human becoming divine. Hegel's "divestment" (*Entäußerung*) corresponds to the christological doctrine of divine "emptying" (*kenosis*), which likewise reverses into an "exaltation" of the human (see Phil. 2:5–11). *Entäußerung* can also be translated as "externalization" or "alienation," but with a loss of distinction between this term and *Entfremdung.*

6. Cf. 1 John 1:1.

7. Hegel here uses the expression for God popular with rational theology (and employed as well by Schleiermacher), *das höchste Wesen.* But this "supreme being" is not (as it was for rationalism) a remote and inaccessible entity; rather for Hegel it is the *highest* or *absolute* being precisely by its

coming down into historical process, by its divestment of abstract divinity. The divine "essence" is to be in relation, to be absolving being. The word *Wesen* contains for Hegel the double meaning of "being" (Latin *ens*) and "essence" (Latin *essentia*). God is that being which is the essence of all beings, or "essential being." When it refers to God and is not preceded by an adjective such as "absolute," "divine," or "supreme," we normally translate *Wesen* as "essential being" in order to distinguish it from *Sein,* which is being in the mode of immediacy or sheer existing. In virtue of incarnation, God also takes on "determinate being," *Dasein,* which we translate as "determinate existence" or in some contexts as simply "existence." The adjective *seiende(s),* "existing," "subsisting," is a closely related form.

8. ". . . durch diese Vollendung ist das Wesen so unmittelbar *da,* als es Wesen ist."

9. "Gott ist also hier *offenbar,* wie *er ist; er ist* so *da,* wie er *an sich* ist; er ist da, als Geist."

10. The allusion here is to John 16:7: "It is to your advantage that I go away, for if I do not go away, the Advocate [the Spirit] will not come to you; but if I go, I will send him to you."

11. Hegel proceeds now to consider the content of the revelatory religion—absolute spirit—in its three constitutive moments of pure thought, representation, and self-conscious subjectivity, or of identity, differentiation, and reunification, which correspond conceptually to the representational form of the Christian Trinity (Father, Son, Holy Spirit). He offers a triadic speculative redescription of the content of this religion in a form adequate to its concept. Here all the essential elements of his interpretation of Christianity are articulated for the first time; they are refined and simplified later on in the lectures on the philosophy of religion.

12. This is the first of the trinitarian moments, that of pure thought or identity—yet not, according to Hegel, an empty essence but already absolute spirit, which contains internal differentiation within itself. Thus the first moment corresponds representationally not so much to the "Father" as a distinct hypostasis of the Trinity as it does to the immanent or intradivine Trinity as a whole.

13. An allusion to John 1:1ff.

14. Hegel is beginning to discuss here the second of the trinitarian moments, that of representation (*Vorstellung*) and difference (*Unterschied*), expressed representationally in the figure of the "Son." It includes such topics as creation of the world, the fall, sin and evil, incarnation and reconciliation. Representation for Hegel is an utterly necessary moment in the process of absolute spirit as a whole. It is not simply a way of looking at things that is superseded in conceptual thought, nor is its referent merely a

myth that does not in itself really exist—although Hegel is commonly mis-read as saying just this. Rather, spirit must enter into real, sensible, materi-al diremption, where it is re-presented in specific historical events and images. Representation remains a constitutive moment of the divine life even as it is sublated. God sets godself forth (*vor-stellt*) in and as the world. In the Preface (above, p. 94) Hegel reminds us that the life of God "sinks into the realm of what is merely edifying, and even insipid, if the serious-ness, the anguish, the patience, and the labor of the negative are lacking from it."

15. Cf. Gen. 1:1.

16. Cf. Gen. 3. On Paradise as an "animal garden" (*Tiergarten*) or zoo, i.e. a place of innocent creatures, see *Lectures on the Philosophy of Reli-gion,* 2:526 incl. n. 30.

17. Hegel apparently is referring here to Jacob Boehme's portrayal of the fall of Lucifer from God; cf. *Aurora, oder: Morgenröhte im Aufgang,* in *Theosophia Revelata,* vol. 1 (Hamburg, 1715), pp. 149, 178. Karl Rosenkranz suggests that Hegel's critique is directed not only against Boehme but also against Friedrich Schelling; cf. *Hegel's Leben* (Berlin, 1844), p. 188. Schelling based his doctrine of the fall of finite things from the absolute on Plato; cf. *Philosophie und Religion* (Tübingen, 1804), p. 35.

18. Hegel here alludes to one of Boehme's central concepts; cf. *Aurora* in *Theosophia Revelata,* pp. 98, 258. See also Rom. 1:18.

19. Hegel here begins the discussion of the third trinitarian moment, that of self-consciousness, subjectivity, and reunification, which is associated with the (Holy) Spirit and the community of faith. It is notable that the third trinitarian figure is *also* a philosophical concept, indeed the concept that encompasses all other concepts and is the only adequate name of God. The *Aufhebung* entailed in the transition from the second to the third moment is also an *Auferstehung,* and Hegel offers here a speculative theology of res-urrection and spiritual presence, which continues to the end of the chapter.

20. Something *absolutely* (or "in truth") other than absolute being would constitute a dualism in Hegel's view. All of essential being's relations are internal rather than external; that is why it is "absolute" and "spirit." But within the whole that is absolute spirit, a whole that contains all finite rela-tions, there is genuine finitude and otherness.

21. Cf. John 1:14.

22. Hegel may be alluding here to certain expressions of Schelling and Giordano Bruno. God and nature are not separated for Schelling, and he regards finite things that had fallen from the absolute as simply nothing. By contrast, an identification of good and evil is only alluded to in Schelling. (Cf. Friedrich Schelling, *Bruno oder über das göttliche und natürliche*

Princip der Dinge [Berlin, 1802], p. 179; and *Philosophie und Religion,* pp. 37, 40, 41.) Hegel was familiar with Bruno through Schelling's work as well as that of J. G. Buhle and F. H. Jacobi.

23. Hegel's point appears to be that evil is to be found at the very heart of goodness, if goodness means a simple being-with-self or self-knowing, for this being-with-self also withdraws *into* itself and becomes self-centered. Evil is like a cancer that grows on goodness.

24. Cf. Rom. 6:11.

25. "*Gott selbst gestorben* ist." See n. 4. The reflexive pronoun *selbst* is not gendered, thus our translation is not unfaithful to the German.

26. In the Preface, Hegel speaks, in alluding to Schelling's philosophy of identity, of "the night in which . . . all cows are black" (*Phänomenologie des Geistes,* ed. Johannes Hoffmeister [Hamburg, 1952], p. 16). In the present passage he seems to be speaking more generally of the Enlightenment philosophy of subjectivity, which replicates the "unhappy consciousness" of Roman religion. This night is, however, the necessary precursor to the dawn of a new day in which substance has been subjectified and spiritualized. The abstract supreme being (the "Father") must die, together with the historical mediator (the "Son"), in order for universal, world-encompassing spirit ("Holy Spirit") to be born.

27. This is Hegel's critique of juridical, punitive theories of atonement according to which divine justice is satisfied through the payment of a human penalty. Hegel's concept of atonement, by contrast, is that it is a process intrinsic to the divine life: spirit is in itself essentially reconciliatory.

28. I.e., Christ.

4. ENCYCLOPEDIA OF THE PHILOSOPHICAL SCIENCES
(1817, 1827, 1830)

Absolute Spirit: Art, Revealed Religion, Philosophy

1. Against the Nicolin-Hoffmeister edition (Hamburg, 1959), the critical edition (Hamburg, 1992) follows the reading of the 2nd (1827) rather than the 3rd (1830) edition at this point: ". . . sondern Glauben vielmehr ein Wissen ist und jener [*not* jenes] nur eine besondere Form von diesem . . .". The antecedent of *jener* ("the former") is *Glaube* ("faith"), not *Wissen* ("knowledge").

2. *Existenz* is translated as "existence," *Dasein* as "determinate existence."

3. The "religion of fine art" is Greek religion.

4. Probably a reference to Judaism, which is the "religion of sublimity"

in the philosophy of religion lectures, while Greek religion is the "religion of beauty."

5. Echoes of what Hegel says later about Buddhist and Egyptian religion may be detected here.

6. Hinduism is the "religion of fantasy."

7. This could be an allusion to the "religion of magic," or possibly to Roman religion.

8. *Die geoffenbarte Religion*. The "authentic" or "consummate" religion is both "revealed" (*geoffenbart*) and "revelatory" (*offenbar*), i.e., it is both *revealed* in a historical, empirical manner and *revelatory* of (open to) the truth that is God. God is essentially self-manifesting, self-absolving spirit, thus absolute spirit. In the *Phenomenology of Spirit* and the *Lectures on the Philosophy of Religion* Hegel names Christianity "the revelatory religion"; in the *Encyclopedia,* "the revealed religion." Both names are appropriate, but the former is more characteristic of Hegel's distinctive approach.

9. See Plato, *Phaedrus,* 247a; *Timaeus,* 29d-e; and Aristotle, *Metaphysics,* 1.2 982b32–983a5.

10. Carl Friedrich Göschel, *Aphorismen über Nichtwissen und absolutes Wissen im Verhältnisse zur christlichen Glaubenserkenntniss* (Berlin, 1829); see esp. pp. 65–66. See also Hegel's review of this work in *Jahrbücher für wissenschaftliche Kritik,* 1 (1829): 789–835, esp. 802–3. The correspondence between Göschel and Hegel shows that they did not know each other. Only after the appearance of Hegel's review did Göschel (at that time a judge on the court of higher appeals) for the first time write to Hegel, who subsequently answered by sending him the third edition of the *Encyclopedia.*

11. This and the following four paragraphs set forth the content of revealed religion in the form of a philosophical triad derived from Hegel's logic and system. The triad is composed of: (*a*) the idea of God in and for itself, the moment of universality (the immanent Trinity, the "Father"); (*b*) the idea in diremption or differentiation, the moment of particularity (creation and fall of the world); (*c*) the appearance of the idea in the form of spirit, the moment of individuality (the history of redemption, reconciliation, and restoration). This has the peculiar effect of locating both the "Son" and the "Spirit" in the third moment, while the second moment is given over to the dirempted world. A similar arrangement was found in Hegel's 1821 lecture manuscript on the philosophy of religion, but in subsequent offerings of these lectures (1824, 1827, 1831) the philosophical triad was modulated into a theological trinity such that the second moment encompasses both differentiation and reconciliation and is associated with the figure of Christ, while the third moment is that of the community of faith and

the Spirit. However, Hegel did not make a similar adjustment in the *Encyclopedia;* §§ 567–570 go back to the first edition (1817) and remain unaltered in the second and third editions (1827, 1830).

12. *Einzelheit* can also be translated as "singularity," or as "singular individuality." The human face is a prime instance of something that is *einzeln,* uniting universal and particular elements in a unique manifestation.

13. I.e., Christ.

14. I.e., Christ as an objective, historical fact or "example."

15. For the charge of atheism, Hegel is probably thinking of Jacobi's critique of Spinoza. See Friedrich Heinrich Jacobi, *Ueber die Lehre des Spinoza* (Breslau, 1789), p. 223 (*Werke* [6 vols., Leipzig, 1813–25], 4/1:216). Regarding the charge of pantheism, Hegel most likely has in mind Tholuck and von Baader. See Friedrich August Gotttreu Tholuck, *Die Lehre von der Sünde und vom Versöhner* (Hamburg, 1823), pp. 224, 231–32, 248; and Franz Ritter von Baader, *Fermenta Cognitionis: Sechstes Heft* (Leipzig, 1825), p. xiii. The charges of atheism and pantheism began to be brought specifically against Hegel's own philosophy in the mid-1820s, and Hegel used the occasion of this remark, added to the second edition of 1827, as a means of responding at length; a similar response is found in the 1827 philosophy of religion lectures.

16. Hegel proceeds here with rather lengthy quotations from Hindu and Islamic literature. He cites several of the sayings of Krishna as found in August Wilhelm Schlegel's edition of the *Bhagavad-Gita* (Bonn, 1823); and he quotes several stanzas from the poetry of Jalal al-Din Rumi as translated into German by Friedrich Rückert in 1821. The purpose is to demonstrate that a crude pantheism is found neither in Hinduism nor in Islam. Krishna does not make himself out to be "everything" but the quintessence, the essential being or universal substance, of everything. The spiritual unity described by Jalal al-Din Rumi is an exaltation above everything finite and particular. These citations and Hegel's comments on them are omitted from the present edition.

17. In § 50 of the Preliminary Conception of the *Logic.* Hegel is thinking primarily of Jacobi's critique of Spinoza. In *Ueber die Lehre des Spinoza,* Jacobi interprets Lessing's "one and all" as Spinozism and thus as pantheism (p. 23); he also accuses Spinozism of being atheism (pp. 10, 232), although in a qualified sense (see Jacobi's *Werke,* 4/2). The relevant texts by Spinoza are found in his *Ethics,* part 1.

18. Literally, "attach the itch to it in order to be able to scratch it [*ihr die Krätze anhängen um sie kratzen zu können*]."

19. For the reference to Epicurus, see Cicero, *De divinatione,* 2.17.40; and *De natura deorum,* 1.8. Hegel's allusion to "pores" is based on John

Dalton's theory of gas: see "Weitere Erörterung einer neuen Theorie über die Beschaffenheit gemischter Gasarten," in *Annalen der Physik,* ed. Ludwig Wilhelm Gilbert, vol. 13 (Halle, 1803), p. 442. In current parlance this view might be called "the God of the gaps."

20. Here and in the final two paragraphs, Hegel recapitulates the doctrine of the triple syllogism as set forth in the *Logic* of the *Encyclopedia,* §§ 181–89. The first figure of the syllogism, in which nature mediates between the logical idea and spirit, specifies the order of the philosophical system (logic, nature, spirit). In a valid syllogism, according to Hegel, each of the elements must in turn occupy the middle position. Thus in the second syllogism, spirit mediates between the logical idea and nature; and in the third, the logical idea mediates between nature and spirit. The basic assumption of Hegelian philosophy is that the logical idea functions as universal principle (*Allgemeinheit*) in the syllogisms, nature as particular quality (*Besonderheit*), and spirit as singularity or individuality (*Einzelnheit*). The result is speculative or absolute idealism, as opposed to subjective idealism (for which finite spirit or mind is universal principle) and naturalism or materialism (for which nature is universal principle). Absolute spirit, or infinite subjectivity, encompasses and unifies all three figures of the syllogism.

21. Hegel quotes the Greek text in the edition published by Isaac Casaubon (Lyons, 1590). See Aristotle, *Metaphysics,* 12.7 1072b18–30. Hegel himself translated this passage, interspersed with commentary, in his lectures on the history of philosophy (*Werke,* vol. 14 [Berlin, 1833], pp. 330–31). Nicolin and Pöggeler reproduce Hegel's version, supplementing it at points where it is incomplete; ours is a translation of this German version. Hegel renders *nous* variously as "thought" [*Gedanke*], "thinking" [*Denken*], "thinking reason" [*denkende Vernunft*].

5. FOREWORD TO HINRICHS'S *RELIGION* (1822)

The Reconciliation of Faith and Reason

1. Friedrich Schleiermacher's *Der christliche Glaube,* published in 1821–22, failed in Hegel's view to provide such an objective content; thus it could not claim to be a true *Glaubenslehre.* Much of what follows is a critique of Schleiermacher's theology of feeling.

2. The allusion here is to post-Kantian philosophers such as F. H. Jacobi, J. G. Fichte, and J. F. Fries.

3. In the 1830 edition of the *Encyclopedia,* § 62 remark, Hegel identified this astronomer as Joseph Jérôme le François de Lalande, director of the Paris Observatory from 1768 to 1807. For further information, see Eric von

der Luft, ed. and trans., *Hegel, Hinrichs, and Schleiermacher on Feeling and Reason in Religion* (Lewiston, N.Y., 1987), pp. 253–56 n. 4.

4. In his polemic against religious subjectivity, Hegel used the terms "feeling" (*Gefühl*) and "sensation" (*Empfindung*) more or less synonymously, which indicates that, in contrast to Schleiermacher, he regarded feeling as a sense-based mode of awareness. Yet Hegel himself recognized a distinction between sensation and feeling in the *Encyclopedia* (1830), §§ 402–03. For a discussion of this matter, see *Lectures on the Philosophy of Religion,* ed. and trans. Peter C. Hodgson et al. (Berkeley and Los Angeles, 1984–87), 1:268–69 n. 20.

5. Hegel quotes loosely from the Luther Bible's translation of 1 Cor. 2:14. He may also be alluding to Rousseau's idea of a "natural religion" as found in *Émile,* bk. 4, and *The Social Contract,* bk. 4, chap. 8. For further information, see von der Luft, pp. 258–60 n. 5.

6. This is clearly a reference to Schleiermacher and also a caricature of him. For Schleiermacher spoke not merely of "a feeling of dependence" but of "the feeling of *utter* [*schlechthinnig*] dependence," which is a prereflective awareness of the whence and whither of human existence in the world, and it is obvious that no animal could have such a feeling. However, Schleiermacher did not express himself as clearly in the first edition of *The Christian Faith* (1821–22), to which alone Hegel had access, as in the second (1830), where for the first time he introduced the adjective *schlechthinnig.* For further discussion of this matter, see Hegel, *Lectures on the Philosophy of Religion,* 1:279–80 n. 37. Hegel also alludes in the passage that follows to a distinction between the feeling of *liberation,* which he thinks is characteristic of the religion of free spirit (Christianity), and the feeling of *dependence* or *servitude,* which he attributes primarily to Roman religion (and with which by implication Schleiermacher is associated). See *Lectures on the Philosophy of Religion,* 2:218–19 n. 292, 443–44 n. 551.

7. *Phaedo,* 89d ff.; *Republic,* 3.411d-e.

8. These matters are discussed in the *Encyclopedia,* in the *Philosophy of Right,* and especially in Hegel's 1824 philosophy of religion lectures, in that portion of the "Concept of Religion" just preceding the selections contained in this volume (*Lectures on the Philosophy of Religion,* 1:258–310). The treatment in the 1822 "Foreword" provides a compact summary of the analysis developed in greater detail in the later lectures.

9. Probably an allusion to Schlegel's description of Kant in his *Geschichte der alten und neuen Litteratur,* published in a revised edition in Schlegel's *Sämmtliche Werke* in 1822. However, Schlegel referred to "worldly knowledge" (*Weltwissenschaft*) rather than "worldly wisdom" (*Weltweisheit*). See *Kritische Friedrich-Schlegel-Ausgabe,* ed. Ernst

Behler, vol. 6 (Munich, 1961), pp. 398–99; for fuller information, see von der Luft, pp. 262–64 n. 10.

10. See Plato, *Phaedrus,* 247a; *Timaeus,* 29d-e; and Aristotle, *Metaphysics,* 982b32–983a5.

11. Hegel's mention of Karl Daub (1765–1836) and Philipp Marheineke (1780–1846) in such a favorable light suggests that in the controversies following his death he would have sided with the thinkers comprising the Hegelian middle as opposed to the left-wing philosophical critics of religion and the right-wing theological defenders of orthodoxy.

12. Hegel concludes by quoting from a letter written to him by Hinrichs describing the purpose of his work, which we omit. He signs the foreword "Hegel" and dates it "Berlin, Easter 1822."

6. LECTURES ON THE PHILOSOPHY OF RELIGION (1824)

Introduction: On the Philosophy of Religion

1. A reference to the underworld river *Lēthē*, the personification of oblivion. The souls of the departed drank of this river and thus forgot all they had said or done in the upper world. This myth is found in many forms, from Plato to Dante.

2. In the school philosophy of the sixteenth, seventeenth, and eighteenth centuries, natural theology was considered a philosophical discipline. Hegel was familiar with it primarily in its Leibnizian-Wolffian form, according to which the third and final part of *metaphysica specialis,* following rational psychology and cosmology, was *theologia naturalis.* Wolff defined it as "the science of what is possible through God, i.e., of what is in God, and of what can be known through what is in God." See Christian Wolff, *Theologia naturalis methodo scientifica pertractata* (Frankfurt and Leipzig, 1739, 1741), Pars prior, § 1. Natural theology was a forerunner of philosophy of religion, which began to be established as an academic discipline only toward the end of the eighteenth century. Hegel was aware of the novelty of the discipline and thus he devoted considerable attention to its definition.

3. The concept of God as a "being of the understanding" (*Verstandeswesen*) is less a concept of natural theology itself than of the criticism of it, especially by Kant. Hegel intends to advance to a concept of God as *spirit* (*Geist*), and that entails grasping the relationship between God and consciousness, or objectivity and subjectivity, in religious experience and religious community. Spirit is a *relational* concept. In the *Lectures on the Philosophy of Religion, Wesen* is generally translated as "essence," but in some

contexts, such as the present one, "being" is more appropriate.

4. In natural theology God is not designated simply as *ens,* but as *ens a se* (being from, or of, itself) or as *ens perfectissimum* (most perfect being). See Christian Wolff, *Theologia naturalis,* Pars prior.

5. An allusion to Friedrich Schelling.

6. In this section Hegel develops more explicitly and consistently his controversy with the theological and philosophical views of his time, which are rooted in the Enlightenment. The so-called "rational theology" (*Vernunfttheologie*) is really based on understanding (*Verstand*) and rationalistic argumentation or exegesis (*Rasönnement*) rather than on reason (*Vernunft*). More recent forms of rational theology share with the theology based on feeling (*Gefühl*) the conviction that in the strict sense nothing can be known of God. Finally there is the purely historical approach in theology, which gives up any claim to its content, dealing only with historical data like "counting-house clerks" who handle other people's money but have no wealth of their own. All these approaches have the effect of driving a fatal wedge between religion and cognition, the former being relegated to a private realm and the latter reserved for the everyday secular world.

7. A reference to the exegesis and dogmatics of theological rationalism, as represented by H. E. G. Paulus, J. F. Röhr, and J. A. L. Wegscheider.

8. Hegel was probably familiar with this expression, which may be traced back to the twelfth century, through Lessing.

9. Hegel has in mind the views of Kant and Jacobi.

10. The neglect of the doctrine of the Trinity, which Hegel criticizes here and elsewhere in the *Lectures,* may be traced to deism and the so-called neologians, e.g., W. A. Teller and J. G. Töllner. But his criticism is directed primarily against Schleiermacher's *Glaubenslehre* since it treats the doctrine of the Trinity only in the concluding four paragraphs.

11. The designation of God as a "supreme being" is common in the deistic literature of the seventeenth and eighteenth centuries (e.g. Herbert of Cherbury) as well as in the school philosophy (e.g. Christian Wolff). But since Hegel is here referring to "modern theology," it can be surmised that his equation of the noncognizability of God with the designation of God as a supreme being contains a hidden polemic against Schleiermacher, who used this expression several times in the *Glaubenslehre.*

12. This is the third topic that Hegel promised to take up in the opening paragraph of the Introduction, but he treats it only briefly. He contends that philosophy of religion is actually closer to "positive religion," that is, historically mediated and revealed religion based on the doctrinal content of the church, than it is to rational theology. However, a division has emerged between the philosophy of religion and the teaching of the church, a divi-

sion that presupposes a doctrine of double truth—"two kinds of reason and two kinds of spirit"—and Hegel's critique of this notion is what constitutes the substance of this section. Catholic theology with its speculative proclivities avoided this split more successfully than did Protestant theology.

13. This antithesis may be traced back to the ancient church but not to the New Testament. In *Faith and Knowledge* Hegel contended that modernity has transcended this antithesis (see selection 2); but in his Foreword to Hinrichs's philosophy of religion he expressed doubts about the success of this transcendence (see selection 6).

14. The doctrine of double truth may be traced back to the thirteenth century. Somewhat later it was propounded especially by William of Ockham and Pomponazzi, but was rejected by the church at the Fifth Lateran Council (1512–1517).

15. At this point Hegel abruptly drops the discussion of the relationship of the philosophy of religion to positive religion, which has uncovered the question of double truth. Not only this but other "preliminary questions" seem to have to be disposed of before philosophy of religion can turn to its proper object, namely God and the religious knowledge of God. He enumerates several of these questions—not only that of double truth, but also the question of the limits of reason, the view that God is apprehended only in the mode of feeling and has no objectivity over against the consciousness of the believer, and the notion that philosophy of religion must first demonstrate that there *is* a God before God can be cognitively grasped. But these and all other so-called preliminary questions must be set aside, Hegel says, because they cannot be investigated and settled in advance of actually *doing* philosophy of religion. The only way to investigate the capacity of cognition is to engage in cognitive acts. There is no epistemological prolegomenon to philosophy that is not already speculative philosophy. The polemic in this section is directly principally against Kant, Jacobi, and Schleiermacher.

16. The reference here is probably to the attempt by certain philosophers to argue for the lack of relation between reason and positive religion, notably Vanini, Bayle, and Descartes, who are mentioned in this connection in Hegel's *Lectures on the History of Philosophy*.

17. While Hegel's account does not permit a positive identification of the two positions to which he refers, both could be ascribed to Kant. The notion that the attempt at comprehension degrades the infinite to something finite points to Jacobi.

18. The view that religion has its proper place in the realm of feeling was widespread in Hegel's time and took different forms. Probably Hegel had in mind the views of Jacobi, J. F. Fries, and Schleiermacher. The first edition

of the latter's *Der christliche Glaube* (1821–22) lent itself especially to Hegel's interpretation; in the second edition (1830–31) Schleiermacher expressed himself more cautiously on a number of points criticized by Hegel and others.

19. Hegel probably is referring here to the role played by the proofs of the existence of God in the natural theology of Wolff, Baumgarten, and, earlier, Spinoza. In this paragraph he clearly repudiates a position later advocated by Ludwig Feuerbach, who heard these lectures and may have found in their depiction of atheism the seeds of his own emerging atheism.

20. This anecdote is contained in a collection of witticisms written in Greek, collected by Hierocles of Alexandria and Philagrios the Grammarian in late antiquity. However, the reference is not to a Gascon but to a Scholastic, and in his 1827 philosophy of religion lectures and 1825–26 history of philosophy lectures Hegel also refers to "a Scholastic." Thus we must assume that Griesheim simply erred in his transcription at this point.

21. The German of this sentence is difficult to construe, and the meaning is not entirely clear. The basic point seems to be that acts of cognition and states of feeling are possible within religion because God, by entering into otherness as a singular "this" (*das Diesen*), and by relating to subjective feeling, makes God to be the object of such acts and states. Similarly, as the next sentence indicates, the determination that God *is* falls within the treatment of religion rather than being something that must be demonstrated in advance, abstractly.

22. The Concept of Religion in the 1824 lectures does not actually correspond to the summary of it given here until the last section, and then only partially. The summary describes the three moments of the concept of religion, which correspond to the logical moments of the concept as such, namely abstract identity or universal substance (the metaphysical concept of God), differentiation or consciousness (the theoretical religious relationship, knowledge of God), and mediation or reunification (the practical religious relationship, cultus). But Hegel adopted this logical structure of the Concept of Religion only in 1827; the 1824 Concept is still largely concerned with preliminary matters such as the establishment of the speculative standpoint vis-à-vis the empirical, and with a continuing polemic against the views of the time. Hegel clearly had arrived at his mature conception of the Concept of Religion in 1824 but appears to have been distracted from putting it into place by his preoccupation with opposing views. The debates with these views, however, produced some of his deepest insights.

23. Hegel is thinking of the cosmological, teleological, and ontological proofs. He does not discuss other, more ancient proofs (such as the proof

from consensus of the peoples) or more modern proofs (such as the moral proof in Kant). Since he regards the proofs as indicative of distinctive ways of thinking about God (as opposed to actually demonstrating God's existence), he treats them (except in the 1827 lectures) in relation to specific religions—the cosmological proof in relation to the Oriental, Jewish, and Greek religions, the teleological proof in relation to the Roman religion, and the ontological proof in relation to the Christian religion.

24. Hegel designated Christianity variously as "the consummate religion" (*die vollendete Religion*), "the revelatory religion" (*die offenbare Religion*), and "the absolute religion" (*die absolute Religion*). The first is the title used in Hegel's lecture manuscript; the second is especially characteristic of the 1824 lectures; and the third is the title adopted by the original editors of Hegel's works although it is the one he himself used least frequently.

25. See Mark 1:15; Gal. 4:4; Eph. 1:10.

26. With the term "theodicy" Hegel situates philosophy of religion in the ancient tradition of the "justification of God," which reaches back into antiquity and in particular to Stoicism. He is probably thinking above all of Leibniz's *Essays on Theodicy* (1719).

The Speculative Concept of Religion

1. The following summary draws partly on my editorial introduction to vol. 1 of the *Lectures on the Philosophy of Religion*, pp. 71–73.

2. This transitional section is actually the last section of "Empirical Observation."

3. The term Hegel uses here, *Empfindung,* functions roughly as a synonym for *Gefühl,* "feeling." It serves to underscore for him the always sensuous character of feeling.

4. This section, which actually begins "The Speculative Concept of Religion," sets forth a *definition* of the concept of religion from the speculative point of view: religion is not merely the *consciousness* of the absolute (the "affirmative" relationship of finite consciousness to the infinite), but also the *self-consciousness of absolute spirit,* mediated in and through finite consciousness. Thus on the highest plane, religion is not merely a human but a divine affair, and it is the divine process or movement that makes the religious relationship possible. However, philosophy requires that the *necessity* of this concept of religion be *demonstrated,* not merely presupposed. Hegel turns to this task in the next section (having made a premature beginning part way into this section), by means of a brief phenomenological description of the rise of nature and finite spirit to the absolute, the articulation of which is the task of the whole of philosophy after the logic and

prior to the philosophy of religion—a task Hegel first addressed in his *Phenomenology of Spirit*. Once this phenomenology has reached its goal, it discovers that its result is its real presupposition, namely, that absolute spirit "is the first and alone true," the real foundation of the rise of consciousness to it. This is the speculative insight, and phenomenology, like empirical observation, ends by passing into speculation.

5. The next five paragraphs initiate in a preliminary (or premature) way the discussion of the *necessity* of the concept of religion as thus defined. But Hegel then abruptly returns to the problem of definition and further advances it significantly (with the paragraph beginning, "If the concept of religion is to be further elucidated . . .") before going on to the matter of necessity. These five paragraphs would make better sense if transposed to the beginning of the next section.

6. Lucilius Vanini (1585–1619) was an Italian free thinker who was tried and convicted on charges of atheism, for which he was burned at the stake. In self-defense at his trial, he picked up a piece of straw from the ground and said that already this straw was proof enough for him of the existence of God. Hegel was familiar with this report from various sources, such as the histories of philosophy of Brucker and Buhle, to which reference is made in his discussion of Vanini in the *History of Philosophy*.

7. The expression *sich entschließt*, which Hegel uses in a similar way in the Heidelberg *Encyclopedia* and in the *Science of Logic,* is translated rather freely as "unlocks itself in the resolve" in order to bring out the root sense of un-locking or re-leasing (*ent-schließen*) that is contained in the act of resolving upon something. Hegel begins here a compact summary of the major transitions of his philosophical system: the self-releasing of the *logical idea* to go forth into nature, into the externality of the natural world; the concentration of *nature* into its center (the concept) so that it may pass over into spirit (finite consciousness); the rise of *spirit* from its natural origins through various determinate phases of consciousness until it attains its home in the absolute. The task of philosophy is to demonstrate the *necessity* of these transitions. It does this by means of a description of the way in which things progressively present themselves as phenomena to consciousness, and the method is therefore (in the Hegelian sense) phenomenological. In fact what is offered here is a summary of the leitmotivs of both the *Phenomenology of Spirit* and the second and third parts of the *Encyclopedia of the Philosophical Sciences* as they bear upon and found the philosophy of religion.

8. Hegel makes the same point metaphorically in the 1821 lectures by referring to a stream flowing in opposite directions (*Philosophy of Religion,* 1:227 n.115). This "counterthrust" might be described as a "speculative

reversal," in which what emerges as the *result* of philosophical demonstration, namely, absolute spirit, proves also to be its *foundation,* the speculative premise of the whole phenomenological process of the rise of consciousness out of nature and of its being drawn toward its telos. This is Hegel's version of the hermeneutical circle.

9. If the concept of religion is absolute spirit in its self-mediation, then we can expect that the concept will develop or "realize" itself in the three moments of its substantial self-unity, its self-differentiation, and its self-reaffirmation (or return to self). These moments correspond to the logic of the concept itself—namely universality, particularity, individuality; or identity, difference, mediation—and are definitive of the moments of religion: the abstract concept of God, religious consciousness or representation, and religious cultus or worship. The concept of God does not remain a purely logical concept; it becomes an actual, existent concept or "idea" by positing a real, external world with which it enters into relationship. This is intrinsic to and constitutive of the very essence of God, and likewise the religious relationship in its theoretical and practical forms is intrinsic to religion.

10. The "idea in its self-equivalent affirmation" is the logical idea as the unity of nature and spirit, that which mediates between them as the universal principle of both—the so-called "logical mediation," the first of the three mediations that make up the whole system of philosophy (*Encyclopedia* [1830], § 187). As logical idea, God is absolute, universal substance, not yet outwardly differentiated, inwardly self-related but not yet entering into real relationship with the world; God has not yet "appeared." This is the "abstract concept" of God that is present in different forms in all religions, and it constitutes the first moment of the concept of religion. But in the 1824 lectures Hegel does not consider it further because here he is focusing on the religious *relationship,* and relationship presupposes differentiation. The first two moments together—the substantial, unitary God and differentiated human consciousness—constitute the "theoretical" religious relationship; while the third moment, the affirmative overcoming of the difference, constitutes the second, "practical" relationship. In the 1827 lectures, the exposition is structured according to the three moments, not the two relationships.

Determinate Religion: Introduction

1. Goethe, in *Wilhelm Meister,* referred to the non-Christian religions as "ethnic religions" or "religions of the peoples (or nations) [*Völker*]." Christianity, by contrast (for Hegel), is a universal religion, the religion of humanity.

2. Hegel treats under "nature religion" (in the following order) the religion of magic (African and Eskimo), the religion of ancient China, the religion of being-within-self (Buddhism, Lamaism), the religion of phantasy (Hinduism), the religion of light (Persian religion), and the religion of the enigma (Egyptian religion).

3. The fourth or last stage is that of the absolute, consummate, or revelatory religion, Christianity, which does not belong among the determinate religions.

Christianity: The Consummate Religion

1. A probable reference to Schleiermacher's *Glaubenslehre,* which interprets the traditional content of religion as the expression of the feeling of utter dependence.

2. A comparison of the age of the Roman Empire with the subjectivism and secularism of the present day is developed by Hegel at the end of his 1821 lectures. See *Lectures on the Philosophy of Religion,* 3:159–62.

3. A reference to Judaism.

4. A reference to Greek religion.

5. The "abstract" or "metaphysical" concept of God designates the fundamental way in which a religion *knows* God. The so-called proofs of the existence of God are really, according to Hegel, ways of knowing and relating to God, not proofs in the strict sense. The cosmological and teleological proofs are associated with various determinate religions in Part 2 of the lectures, while the metaphysical concept of God in the Christian religion takes the form of the ontological proof.

6. With the expression "the most real of all beings" [*das allerrealste Wesen*] Hegel alludes, as does Kant in the *Critique of Pure Reason,* B 624 ff., to the concept of the *ens realissimum,* which he associates with that of the *ens perfectissimum,* as found especially in Descartes, Wolff, and Baumgarten. On the designation of the *ens realissimum* as "the conceptual sum [*Inbegriff*] of all reality," see Kant, *Critique of Pure Reason,* B 601, B 610–11.

7. Descartes argues to this effect in *Meditations,* 5.

8. See Kant's *Critique of Pure Reason,* B 631, B 626–27.

9. Hegel summarizes Anselm's argument in his own terms. Anselm defines God as "that than which nothing greater can be conceived" (*Proslogion,* 2). Equivalents to the language of "perfection" are found elsewhere in the *Proslogion,* but not as premises of the Anselmian proof.

10. Hegel's criticism of the indeterminacy of Anselm's expression is anticipated by Gaunilo's *Response* appended to the *Proslogion.*

11. Hegel alludes to the connection seen by Descartes between the *cogi-*

to ergo sum and the idea of God: Descartes, *Principles of Philosophy,* 1:13, 14; *Discourse on Method,* 4. With regard to Spinoza, see *Ethics,* I.vi, II.i, ii.

12. An exact source for this brief allusion cannot be found in Leibniz's work, but see *Monadology,* 48.

13. Hegel is most likely alluding to Descartes's *Principles of Philosophy,* 1:51, 52. Regarding Spinoza, see n. 11.

14. Hegel applied to each of the religions the analytic categories worked out in the "Concept of Religion," namely a religion's abstract concept of divinity (in the form of "proofs"), its concrete representation of God (the "theoretical relationship"), and its cultic community (the "practical relationship"). He approached the Christian religion in similar terms in the 1821 manuscript but discovered that the categorical structure did not work well at this point. The reason is that the "concrete representation" of God in Christianity takes the form of the Trinity, and the third trinitarian "person" or "element" is that of the presence of God as Spirit in (and as constitutive of) the cultic community. In other words, for Christianity concrete representation *includes* cultic community. Thus when Hegel lectured in 1824, he converted the threefold division of the manuscript's treatment of the consummate religion into a twofold division. The second part examines the "development" of the idea of God in terms of the three moments of the Trinity—in representational language, the "persons" of the Father, Son, and Spirit; in conceptual language, the moments of divine self-identity, self-differentiation, and self-return. These yield the three "elements" that constitute the substance of Hegel's speculative redescription of the Christian religion.

15. Hegel is here engaged in a wordplay based on the verb *setzen: sich setzt* ("posits itself"), *Voraussetzung* ("presupposition"), and *setzt sich voraus* ("sets itself forth [or forward]"). Spirit must not merely posit itself "in itself" (*an sich*); it must also "set itself forth" or "appear" in the world in order to arrive at its end and thus *be* spirit in the full sense. For this reason the end is at the same time the "presupposition" (*Voraus-setzung*) of spirit. This wordplay is repeated several times below.

16. With the distinction between "universality" (*Allgemeinheit*), "particularization" (*Partikularisation,* or "particularity," *Besonderheit*), and "singularity" (or "individuality," *Einzelheit*), Hegel alludes to the three determinate categories of the concept and to the three figures of the logical syllogism (see *Encyclopedia* [1830], §§ 183–87). Thus the first version of the trinitarian distinction can be considered the logical distinction, as compared with those that follow, based on subjective consciousness, space, and time.

17. A reference to the categories by means of which the determinate reli-

gions were treated in Part 2. These categories were carried over to the consummate religion in the 1821 manuscript but were dropped in 1824 and thereafter, for the reasons explained in n. 14. Hegel here uses the term *Gestalt* ("figure") instead of the more commonly employed *Vorstellung* ("representation"). He notes here that the cultus is to be included among the three forms in which the idea of God develops (as the "third element"), rather than being added on as a separate topic.

18. This is an allusion to Goethe's *Die Braut von Corinth*, vv. 120–23.

19. Aristotle, *De caelo*, 1.1 (268a10–15).

20. Plato, *Timaeus*, 34c–35b.

21. On the Trimurti, see Hegel's discussion of Hinduism in part 2 of the 1824 lectures (*Lectures on the Philosophy of Religion*, 2:326–28).

22. In the preceding materials Hegel has not depicted the Father as universal in this explicit form, but such a reference might not have been transmitted by the sources available for the 1824 lectures.

23. See above, n. 15.

24. See above, n. 15.

25. Hegel's information on the Gnostics and Neoplatonists derived largely from August Neander, *Genetische Entwicklung der vornemhsten gnostischen Systeme* (Berlin, 1818).

26. See Job 38:4-7.

27. See Jacob Boehme, *Aurora, oder Morgenröhte im Aufgang*, in *Theosophia revelata* (1715), col. 149.

28. See Satan's speech to Beelzebub in Milton's *Paradise Lost*, canto 1, lines 8–10.

29. This remark could be directed against Johann Gottfried Herder, who offers such an interpretation in *Aelteste Urkunde des Menschengeschlechts*, vol. 2 (Riga, 1776), pp. 108–9.

30. For support of this interpretation, Hegel refers in the manuscript to Johann Friedrich von Meyer, whose annotated biblical translation, *Die heilige Schrift*, was published in 1819.

31. See Leibniz, *Monadology*, 24.

32. This entire discussion reflects the Pauline theology of the divided will; see esp. Romans 7.

33. On the organization of this section, see n. 43.

34. Kant advanced this argument (in the second and third *Critiques*) in connection with his theory of the existence of God as a postulate of practical reason; and Fichte, in his essay on belief in a divine government of the universe (1798).

35. Hegel here actually introduces a *third* consideration, distinct from the second. These three paragraphs taken together summarize what might

be described as a threefold argument for the *possibility, necessity,* and *actuality* of the appearance of God in a single human individual. The final point serves as a transition to the next section, since it requires attending to concrete historical matters.

36. See Mark 1:15 and parallels.

37. Cf. Matt. 6:34: "Do not be anxious about tomorrow, for tomorrow will be anxious for itself. Let the day's own trouble be sufficient for the day."

38. Hegel seems to refer here not to the love of God but only to the love of neighbor (cf. Matt. 22:36-39).

39. Although Hegel mentions the "life" of Christ, he does not in fact discuss it further in the 1824 lectures, as he did in the 1821 manuscript, where he showed the "conformity" between the life of Christ and his teaching. In 1824 the discussion of the "life" has focused entirely on the teaching.

40. Hegel is apparently thinking especially of Gnostic teachings, with which he was familiar through Neander's descriptions (see n. 25).

41. A phrase from the second stanza of the passion hymn "O Traurigkeit, O Herzeleid" by Johannes Rist (1641).

42. Cf. John 4:48: "Unless you see signs and wonders you will not believe." The renunciation of "signs and wonders" is found at various places in the Synoptic tradition.

43. This is a summary of the three main points taken up under the theme of the history of reconciliation (n. 33): the idea of reconciliation, the historical presence of Christ, and the transition to spiritual presence, i.e., to the community.

44. Cf. John 16:7: "It is to your advantage that I go away, for if I do not go away, the Counselor will not come to you; but if I go, I will send him to you."

45. See Johannes Kepler, *Harmonice mundi,* book 5, chap. 3.

46. Hegel apparently spoke of both moving bodies (Kepler) and falling bodies (Galileo), but Griesheim has confused or conflated them in this passage.

47. A reference to the cosmological and teleological proofs discussed by Hegel in relation to the determinate religions in Part 2.

48. Hegel does not intend to deny that in the more fundamental sense spirit *is* historical (*geschichtlich*) in its process of self-distinguishing and self-relating. Especially in the 1827 and 1831 lectures, he refers to "the divine history" or "the eternal history, the eternal movement, which God godself is." But this historicity of God as spirit is not subject to the external, empirical mode of investigation suitable for past, factual data; in this sense it is no *Historie.* This point is especially emphasized in the 1824 lectures:

there is no proof of faith from history, even though faith does have a historical point of departure. There remains in Hegel's thought an unresolved tension between two senses of history (for which he does not maintain a consistent terminological distinction either)—the intrinsically historical (*geschichtlich*) and "simply present" process that spirit is, and the now-past historical (*historisch*) events in which this process "appears."

49. A variant to this passage is found in Hegel's miscellaneous papers, at the end of which occurs an image, borrowed from Schiller, that is reminiscent of the concluding lines of the *Phenomenology of Spirit:* "The subsistence of the community is its continuous, eternal becoming, which is grounded in the fact that spirit is an eternal process of self-cognition, dividing itself into the finite flashes of light of individual consciousness, and then re-collecting and gathering itself up out of this finitude—inasmuch as it is in the finite consciousness that the process of knowing spirit's essence takes place and that the divine self-consciousness thus arises. Out of the foaming ferment of finitude, spirit rises up fragrantly."

50. In his *Lectures on the History of Philosophy,* Hegel criticizes the Kantian-Fichtean view that the good on the one hand remains bound to the moral activity of the individual subject, but on the other hand can be realized only in infinite progress.

51. Hegel discusses Persian dualism in Part 2. As for Kant, he has in mind the latter's distinction (found, e.g., in *The Fundamental Principles of the Metaphysics of Ethics*) between the sensible world and the rational or intelligible world. Because the connection between these worlds is not comprehensible, it is impossible to understand how moral freedom might exercise a causality in the sensible world.

52. See Matt. 12:31; Mark 3:28.

53. The mystery cults at Eleusis, in ancient Attica.

54. "Reflection" (*Reflexion*) is Hegel's term for the philosophy of the Enlightenment, i.e., the "reflective philosophy of subjectivity," as expressed in the subtitle to *Faith and Knowledge* (selection 2.1 above). Reflective philosophy is critical philosophy because it interprets objective reality in terms of the critical categories of the mind. What is "reflected," then, is the cognitive faculty of finite consciousness, not the rational structure of objective reality or of the "concept," as is the case with truly "speculative" philosophy. Reflective philosophy represents an indispensable advance beyond the immediacy and dogmatism of everyday experience (empiricism) and precritical metaphysics and theology. Thus the clash between the church (or church dogmatics) and reflection was inevitable. But because reflection is locked into the finite categories of the "understanding" (*Verstand*), it is unable to grasp the dialectical identity that underlies its abstract and partial images. It thus remains a finite, alienated mode

of thought, oscillating between an abstract, empty unity on the one hand and a capricious, arbitrary individualism on the other.

55. Hegel here describes the ideology of Enlightenment rationalism. It accepts the reflective critique of traditional religious dogma but substitutes for it merely subjective ethical and cognitive criteria, ending with abstract and empty self-identity over against the equally empty beyond.

56. This is the only significant discussion of Islamic religion in the lectures (a few scattered references are found elsewhere). Islam lacks a place in Hegel's schema of religions. The reason appears to be that, unlike the other religions, Islam does not represent an earlier phase of religious consciousness that has been or can be sublated in the consummate religion. Rather it stands in antithesis to Christianity as a contemporary rival. Thus the proper place for its treatment is in the context of various challenges to the Christian religion in the modern world. In any event, Hegel's knowledge of Islam was quite limited.

57. In the 1827 "Concept of Religion," Hegel appeals to Plato and Aristotle for a refutation of the view that God is "jealous" of any knowledge of God.

58. A variant possibly based on Hegel's personally edited copy of Griesheim reads: "In the [branch of] philosophy that is theology, the one and only task . . . ."

59. This is no longer simply the religious community but the community of philosophy. Hegel believes that theology has abandoned its true vocation (namely to know God cognitively, to reconcile reason and religion) and now resides in the first or second estate although its spiritual home should be the third. Its vocation has been taken over by speculative philosophy. At the conclusion of the 1827 lectures Hegel remarks, "Philosophy is to this extent theology."

SELECT BIBLIOGRAPHY

COLLECTED WORKS OF HEGEL

Werke. Vollständige Ausgabe, edited by an Association of Friends. 18 vols. Berlin: Verlag von Duncker und Humblot, 1832 ff. Some volumes issued in second editions. Reprinted with minor revisions and additions as Jubiläumsausgabe, edited by Hermann Glockner (Stuttgart: Fr. Frommanns Verlag, 1927–30); and as Theorie Werkausgabe, edited by Eva Moldenhauer and Karl Markus Michel (Frankfurt am Main: Suhrkamp Verlag, 1969).

Gesammelte Werke. Edited by the Academy of Sciences of Rhineland-Westphalia in Association with the Deutsche Forschungsgemeinschaft. 40 vols. projected. Hamburg: Felix Meiner Verlag, 1968 ff. The new critical edition.

Vorlesungen: Ausgewählte Nachschriften und Manuskripte. Edited by the Staff of the Hegel Archives. 11 vols. projected. Hamburg: Felix Meiner Verlag, 1983 ff. Hegel's Berlin lectures edited in accord with the critical edition.

Hegel's major works are individually available in the Philosophische Bibliothek series, published by Felix Meiner Verlag. These volumes are being revised in accord with the critical edition and are the most accessible form for the German texts.

MAJOR WORKS BY HEGEL IN TRANSLATION

The Difference between Fichte's and Schelling's System of Philosophy. Translated by H. S. Harris and Walter Cerf. Albany: State University of New York Press, 1977.

Early Theological Writings. Translated by T. M. Knox, with an Introduction by Richard Kroner. Chicago: University of Chicago Press, 1948.

Elements of the Philosophy of Right. Edited by Allen W. Wood, translated by H. B. Nisbet. Cambridge: Cambridge University Press, 1991.

Encyclopedia of the Philosophical Sciences. Part 1: The Science of Logic. Part 2: The Philosophy of Nature. Part 3: The Philosophy of Spirit. Translated by William Wallace and A. V. Miller. 3 vols. Oxford: Clarendon Press, 1892 (revised 1975), 1970, 1971.

The Encyclopedia Logic. Translated by T. F. Geraets, W. A. Suchting, and H. S. Harris. Indianapolis: Hackett Publishing Co., 1991.

Faith and Knowledge. Translated by Walter Cerf and H. S. Harris. Albany: State University of New York Press, 1977.

The Jena System, 1804–5: Logic and Metaphysics. Translated by John W. Burbidge and George di Giovanni. Kingston and Montreal: McGill-Queen's University Press, 1986.

Lectures on Aesthetics. Translated by T. M. Knox. Oxford: Clarendon Press, 1975.

Lectures on the History of Philosophy. Translated by E. S. Haldane and Frances H. Simson. 3 vols. London: Kegan Paul, Trench, Trübner & Co., 1892, 1894, 1896.

Lectures on the History of Philosophy. Edited and translated by Robert M. Brown et al. 3 vols. Berkeley and Los Angeles: University of California Press, 1990–.

Lectures on Natural Right and Political Science: The First Philosophy of Right (Heidelberg, 1817–18). Translated by J. Michael Stewart and Peter C. Hodgson. Berkeley and Los Angeles: University of California Press, 1995.

Lectures on the Philosophy of History. Translated by John Sibree. New York: Dover Publications, 1956.

Lectures on the Philosophy of World History. Introduction: Reason in History. Translated by H. B. Nisbet, with an Introduction by Duncan Forbes. Cambridge: Cambridge University Press, 1975.

Lectures on the Philosophy of Religion. Edited and translated by Peter C. Hodgson et al. 3 vols. Berkeley and Los Angeles: University of California Press, 1984–87.

The Letters. Translated by Clark Butler and Christiane Seiler. Bloomington: Indiana University Press, 1984.

Natural Law: The Scientific Ways of Treating Natural Law, Its Place in Moral Philosophy, and Its Relation to the Positive Sciences of Law. Translated by T. M. Knox, with an introduction by H. B. Acton. Philadelphia: University of Pennsylvania Press, 1975.

Phenomenology of Mind. Translated by J. B. Baillie. Rev. ed. London: George Allen & Unwin, 1931.

Phenomenology of Spirit. Translated by A. V. Miller. Oxford: Clarendon Press, 1977.

Philosophy of Nature. Edited and translated by M. J. Petry. 3 vols. London: George Allen and Unwin, 1970. (*Encyclopedia,* Part 2.)

Philosophy of Subjective Spirit. Edited and translated by M. J. Petry. Dordrecht and Boston: D. Reidel, 1978. (*Encyclopedia,* Part 3.A.)

Political Writings. Translated by T. M. Knox, with an Introductory Essay by Z. A. Pelczynski. Oxford: Clarendon Press, 1964.
Science of Logic. Translated by A. V. Miller. London: George Allen & Unwin, 1969.
System of Ethical Life (1802–3) and First Philosophy of Spirit (1803–4). Edited and translated by H. S. Harris and T. M. Knox. Albany: State University of New York Press, 1979.
Three Essays, 1793–1795. Translated by Peter Fuss and John Dobbins. Notre Dame: University of Notre Dame Press, 1984.

WORKS ON HEGEL'S RELIGIOUS THOUGHT

Brito, Emilio. *La christologie de Hegel: Verbum Crucis.* Paris: Beauchesne, 1983.
Burbidge, John W. *Hegel on Logic and Religion: The Reasonableness of Christianity.* Albany: State University of New York Press, 1992.
Chapelle, Albert. *Hegel et la religion.* 3 vols. Paris: Éditions Universitaires, 1964–71.
Christensen, Darrell E., ed. *Hegel and the Philosophy of Religion.* The Hague: Martinus Nijhoff, 1970.
Crites, Stephen. *In the Twilight of Christendom: Hegel vs. Kierkegaard on Faith and History.* Chambersburg, Pa.: American Academy of Religion, 1972.
Dickey, Laurence. *Hegel: Religion, Economics, and the Politics of Spirit, 1770–1807.* Cambridge: Cambridge University Press, 1987.
Fackenheim, Emil L. *The Religious Dimension in Hegel's Thought.* Bloomington: Indiana University Press, 1967.
Garaudy, R. *Dieu est mort. Étude sur Hegel.* Paris: Presses Universitaires de France, 1962.
Gascoigne, Robert. *Religion, Rationality and Community: Sacred and Secular in the Thought of Hegel and His Critics.* The Hague: Martinus Nijhoff, 1985.
Harris, H. S. *Hegel's Development. Vol. 1: Toward the Sunlight, 1770–1801. Vol. 2: Night Thoughts (Jena 1801–1806).* Oxford: Clarendon Press, 1972, 1983.
Houlgate, Stephen. *Freedom, Truth and History: An Introduction to Hegel's Philosophy.* London and New York: Routledge, 1991.
Iljin, Iwan. *Die Philosophie Hegels als kontemplative Gotteslehre.* Bern: Francke, 1946.
Jaeschke, Walter. *Reason in Religion: The Foundations of Hegel's Philosophy of Religion.* Translated by J. Michael Stewart and Peter C. Hodgson. Berkeley and Los Angeles: University of California Press, 1990.

————. *Die Religionsphilosophie Hegels*. Darmstadt: Wissenschaftliche Buchgesellschaft, 1983.

Jamros, Daniel P. *The Human Shape of God: Religion in Hegel's Phenomenology of Spirit*. New York: Paragon House, 1994.

Kolb, David, ed. *New Perspectives on Hegel's Philosophy of Religon*. Albany: State University of New York Press, 1992.

Küng, Hans. *The Incarnation of God: An Introduction to Hegel's Theological Thought as a Prolegomenon to a Future Christology*. Translated by J. R. Stephenson. New York: Crossroad, 1987.

Lakeland, Paul. *The Politics of Salvation: The Hegelian Idea of the State*. Albany: State University of New York Press, 1984.

Lauer, Quentin. *Hegel's Concept of God*. Albany: State University of New York Press, 1982.

Link, Christian. *Hegels Wort "Gott ist tot."* Zürich: Theologischer Verlag, 1974.

von der Luft, Eric, ed. and trans. *Hegel, Hinrichs, and Schleiermacher on Feeling and Reason in Religion*. Lewiston, N.Y.: Edwin Mellen Press, 1987.

Marsch, Wolf-Dieter. *Gegenwart Christi in der Gesellschaft*. Munich: Christian Kaiser Verlag, 1965.

Merklinger, Philip M. *Philosophy, Theology, and Hegel's Berlin Philosophy of Religion*. Albany: State University of New York Press, 1993.

Olson, Alan M. *Hegel and the Spirit: Philosophy as Pneumatology*. Princeton: Princeton University Press, 1992.

O'Regan, Cyril. *The Heterodox Hegel*. Albany: State University of New York Press, 1994.

Reardon, Bernard M. G. *Hegel's Philosophy of Religion*. London: Macmillan, 1977.

Ringleben, Joachim. *Hegels Theorie der Sünde*. Berlin and New York: Walter de Gruyter & Co., 1977.

Schlitt, Dale M. *Divine Subjectivity: Understanding Hegel's Philosophy of Religion*. London and Toronto: Associated University Presses, 1990.

————. *Hegel's Trinitarian Claim: A Critical Reflection*. Leiden: E. J. Brill, 1984.

Schmidt, Erik. *Hegels Lehre von Gott*. Gütersloh: Gütersloher Verlagshaus Gerd Mohn, 1952.

Shanks, Andrew. *Hegel's Political Theology*. Cambridge: Cambridge University Press, 1991.

Splett, Jörg. *Die Trinitätslehre G. W. F. Hegels*. Munich: Alber, 1965.

Taylor, Mark C. *Journeys to Selfhood: Hegel and Kierkegaard*. Berkeley and Los Angeles: University of California Press, 1980.

Theunissen, Michael. *Hegels Lehre vom absoluten Geist als theologish-politischer Traktat*. Berlin: Walter de Gruyter & Co., 1970.

Wagner, Falk. *Der Gedanke der Persönlichkeit Gottes bei Fichte und Hegel*. Gütersloh: Gütersloher Verlagshaus Gerd Mohn, 1971.

Walker, John, ed. *Thought and Faith in the Philosophy of Hegel*. Dordrecht: Kluwer Academic Publishers, 1991.

Williams, Robert R. *Recognition: Fichte and Hegel on the Other*. Albany: State University of New York Press, 1992.

Williamson, Raymond Keith. *Introduction to Hegel's Philosophy of Religion*. Albany: State University of New York Press, 1984.

Yerkes, James. *The Christology of Hegel*. 2nd ed. Albany: State University of New York Press, 1983.

INDEX

The German for key concepts is given in parentheses.

INDEX

Fries, Jakob Friedrich, 277 n.2, 281 n.18

Gellert, Christian F., 47, 263 n.4
Genie of nations, 56–57, 263–64 n.15, 264 n.16
Glaubenslehre (Schleiermacher), 26, 155, 161, 277 n.1, 280 nn.10, 11; 286 n.1
Gnosticism, 34, 226–27, 288 n.25, 289 n.40, 261 n.12
God: as absolute (inter)subjectivity, 7, 17; as absolute spirit, 7, 27, 176, 179, 222–28 (*see also* Absolute Spirit); as activity (*energeia*), 154; alleged unknowability of, 74, 77, 143–44, 160, 163, 169–70, 179–80; concept of, 199–201; death of, 15, 36, 84, 89, 117, 134, 242–43, 271 n.4; development (moments) of the idea of, 30, 33–37, 200, 219–22; as dialectical process, 93–101, 198–201; as essentially rational, 28, 184; and history, 86, 289 n.48; history of, 220–21; knowledge of, 6–7, 26–27, 143–44; as life, 59–60; as love, 224–26; metaphysical (abstract) concept of, 32–33, 212–19; as mystery, 224; and natural science, 163; negation within, 94; not jealous, 143, 170, 259, 291 n.57; as object for thinking, 222–23, 227; as object of philosophy, 4–6; as object of religion, 27; objective validity of, 165; as play of love with itself, 94, 226; presence, omnipresence of, 152, 181; as presupposition and result, 176–77, 197–98, 287 n.14; as product of feeling, 183; proofs of the existence of, 32–33, 183–84, 188, 212–19, 248, 282 n.23, 286 n.5; providence of, 51–53, 182; reality status of, 4–6, 183–84, 212–19; as revelatory, 7, 9, 23, 121–22, 143–44, 170, 209–10; as self-knowing, 154; as subject, 95–96; as substance, 93–94; as

supreme being (*höchstes Wesen*), 5, 7, 76, 161, 175, 179–80, 256, 271 n.7, 280 n.11; as unconditioned, 173; as unity of natural and spiritual, 199; as the whole (*Ganze*), 94; and world, 24–25, 149–52
Goethe, Johann Wolfgang von, 1, 224, 285 n.1, 288 n.18
Good, 128–29, 131, 230–32, 290 n.50
Good Friday, speculative, 15, 72, 83–84
Göschel, Carl Friedrich, 23, 144, 275 n.10
Greek religion, 31, 39, 52–57, 87–88, 116–19, 203–4
Grief. *See* Anguish
Griesheim, Karl Gustav von, 172

Happiness (*Glück*) (eudaemonism), 14, 76–80, 117, 266 n.10
Harris, H. S., 40, 73, 85–86, 263 n.8, 264 n.1, 267 n.5
Haym, Rudolf, 86, 268 nn.9, 17, 18
Hegel, Georg Wilhelm Friedrich: in Berlin, 3, 137, 155; in Berne, 2, 39, 58; evolution of his concept of spirit, 7–11; in Frankfurt, 2, 5, 58; in Heidelberg, 3, 137; as heterodox, 6–7, 13; in Jena, 2, 5, 72, 85, 92; life and career of, 1–3; mystical images in, 8, 10–11; in Nuremberg, 2–3, 92; system outlines of, 85; as a theologian, 4–6; as a theologian of the spirit, 6–11; treatment of Judaism by, 58, 64–65, 88; in Tübingen, 1–2, 39, 58
Hegel, Marie von Tucher, 2–3
Hegelian schools, 6
Herder, Johann Gottfried, 288 n.29
Hierocles of Alexandria, 282 n.20
Hindu religion, 149, 276 n.16
Hinrichs, Hermann Friedrich Wilhelm, 155
History (*Geschichte*), 36, 220–21, 289 n.48
Hölderlin, Friedrich, 1–2, 261 n.12

Holy Spirit: blasphemy against, 68;
coming/sending of, 13, 36, 66, 68,
244, 248–49; and community of
faith, 69–71; sin against, 251; as
unifying Trinitarian figure, 10;
witness of, 35–36, 239, 242–43,
247–50. *See also* Spirit
Horace, 266 n.6
Houlgate, Stephen, 260 n.1
Human being, humanity (*Mensch,
Menschheit*): as good and evil,
34–35, 128; as image of God, 239;
inner unity with God, 65, 68–69; as
mortal and immortal, 234–35; must
be born twice, 251; natural, 166–67,
230–32; nature of, 81; raised above
animals by knowledge of God, 166,
170; spiritual, 230–36; stages of life
of, 204
Hume, David, 4

Idealism (*Idealismus*): speculative or
absolute, 277 n.20; subjective, 80,
276 n.20
Identity philosophy (*Identitätsphiloso-
phie*), 134, 148, 151, 274 n.26
Identity principle (*Identitätsprinzip*),
255–56
Imagination (*Einbildung*), 49, 53
Incarnation (*Menschwerdung*): as the
appearance of God in human form,
89, 120–21, 238–39; as the divine in
a particular shape, 58, 63, 131,
238–39; in Jesus of Nazareth, 12,
20, 35–36, 58–69, 120–24, 145,
239–41; positive, sensuous character of, 120–22, 238–39; possibility,
necessity, actuality of, 236–39, 288
n.35; as speculative midpoint of
philosophy, 58; speculative theory
of, 20, 35–36, 58–69, 119–24, 132,
145, 236–41, 271 n.5; as unity of
divine and human nature, 12–13,
35–36, 58–69, 119–24, 132, 236–39
Individuality, singularity (*Einzelheit*),
145, 220, 268 n.11, 276 n.12

Infinite (*Unendliche*): empty, spurious,
77–84, 164, 190; and finite, 14–15,
28–29, 77–84, 190–93; overreaches
the finite, 191, 199; as pure night,
83–84
Innocence, 128
Intellect. *See* Understanding
Intuition (*Anschauung*), 75–76, 137,
139–40, 143, 147
Irony, 146
Islamic religion, 37, 150, 241, 256–57,
276 n.16, 291 n.56

Jacobi, Friedrich Heinrich, 2, 14,
72–74, 78–80, 82–83, 266 n.3, 269
n.1, 276 nn.15, 17; 277 n.2, 280 n.9,
281 nn.17, 18
Jaeschke, Walter, 4–5, 38, 260 nn.3, 11;
261 n.20
Jamros, Daniel P., 270 n.2
Jena writings (Hegel), 2, 8, 13–16,
72–91
Jesus of Nazareth, 12, 35–36, 47,
58–71, 88–89, 119–24, 239–41,
243, 289 n.39
John the Baptist, 66
John the Evangelist, 60–61
Judaism (Jewish religion), 31, 60,
64–65, 88, 202–4, 256, 265 n.7
Judgment, primal division (*Urteil*),
138, 145

Kant, Immanuel, 2, 4–5, 14, 32–33, 58,
72–74, 78–80, 82–83, 161–62, 184,
215–19, 237, 251, 265 n.4, 266 n.1,
269 n.4, 270 n.1, 280 n.9, 281 n.17,
286 nn.6, 8; 288 n.34, 290 n.51
Keate, G., 265 n.13
Kepler, Johannes, 247, 289 n.45
Kierkegaard, Søren, 36
Kingdom of God, 13, 69, 240–41
Knowledge, knowing, cognition (*Wissen, Erkenntnis*): absolute, 18, 110
(*see also* Absolute Spirit); of the
absolute, 101–10; as acquaintance,
100; as appearing, 103–4; and being

Religion (*Religion*): concept of, 28–30, 186, 190–201; as consciousness of the absolute, 110–11, 195; as consciousness of God, 205–8, 211; as consciousness *of* God and as God's *self*-consciousness, 10, 18, 23, 29, 31–32, 144, 190, 193–95, 283 n.4; consummate (*see* Christianity); determinate, 30–31, 114–16, 187–89, 201–4; as elevation from finite to infinite, 208; empirical approach to, 28; as enjoyment of life, 55–56; and ethical life, 85, 111, 117–18; and feeling, 41–43, 164–67, 281 n.18 (*see also* Feeling); forms (shapes) of, 87–88, 110–16; and God, 4–6; and heart, 41, 43, 45–46, 49, 53; history of, 15–16, 19, 30–31, 87–88, 114–16, 141, 187–89; and morality, 41, 44–46, 48–50; necessity of, 29, 194, 196–99, 284 n.5; as object to itself, 205–9; objective, 43–47; its occupation with God as liberating, 173; as one of our greatest concerns in life, 40; philosophical (a new religion), 16, 85, 91, 267 n.5; and philosophy, 24, 86–87, 146–47; its place in philosophy, 85–87; positive, 180–82, 185; as product of the divine spirit, 181; public and private forms of, 11–12; and reason, 6, 47–48, 51, 259; as relationship of infinite and finite, God and consciousness, 27, 31–32, 190–95, 205–8; as resumption of the whole into one, 15, 85–91; as self-consciousness of the absolute, 110–11, 195, 199; as self-consciousness of God, 206; and sensuality, 41, 43; subjective (private) 43–47, 49; and thinking, 168; as truth for everyone, 147, 189, 222

Religion of expediency (Roman), 203–204

Religion of spiritual individuality or of finite spirit (Greek, Jewish), 202–3, 211

Religious tolerance, 46–47

Representation (*Vorstellung*): and concept, 116, 126; as a form of knowledge, 100, 144; as a moment of the concept of religion, 201; as an ontological category, 21, 126–28, 176, 185, 220; religious, 137, 144, 147–48; as second trinitarian moment, 125, 228–44, 272 n.14; thinks in terms of external relations, 124, 126, 144

Resurrection (*Auferstehung*), 21–22, 133–34, 242, 247

Revelation (*Offenbarung*): as God becoming human, 211; intrinsic to God, 9, 23, 32, 143–44, 209–10; as revealed (*geoffenbart*), 121, 143, 205, 210, 275 n.8; as revelatory (*offenbar*), 121–22, 143, 205, 209–10, 271 n.1

Rist, Johannes, 267 n.17, 271 n.4, 289 n.41

Röhr, Julius Friedrich, 280 n.7

Roman religion, 31, 32, 88, 116–19, 203–4, 271 n.2

Roman times, 209, 262 n.23, 286 n.2

Rosenkranz, Karl, 6, 85, 267 n.1, 273 n.17

Rousseau, Jean–Jacques, 1, 278 n.5

Rumi, Jalal al–Din, 276 n.16

Sacrament of the Lord's Supper, 37, 90, 252–53

Sacrifice (*Opfer*), 54–55, 252, 263 n.10

Satisfaction (theory of atonement), 135–36, 242, 274 n.27

Schelling, Friedrich Wilhelm Joseph, 1–2, 6, 72, 85, 268 nn.14, 16; 269 nn.1, 3, 4; 273 n.17, 273 n.22, 274 n.26, 280 n.5

Schiller, Friedrich, 1, 269 n.2, 290 n.49

Schlegel, August Wilhelm, 276 n.16